SHAKESPEARE
& THE POETS' WAR

SHAKESPEARE
& THE POETS' WAR

JAMES P. BEDNARZ

Columbia University Press   New York

Columbia University Press
Publishers Since 1893
New York   Chichester, West Sussex

Copyright © 2001 Columbia University Press
All rights reserved
Library of Congress Cataloging-in-Publication Data
Bednarz, James P.
    Shakespeare and the poets' war / James P. Bednarz.
        p.   cm.
    Includes bibliographical references and index.
ISBN 0-231-12242-X — ISBN 0-231-12243-8 (pbk.)
1. Shakespeare, William, 1564–1616—Contemporaries. 2. Shakespeare,
William, 1564–1616—Adversaries. 3. Shakespeare, William, 1564–1616—
Criticism and interpretation. 4. Jonson, Ben, 1573?–1637—Contemporaries.
5. Jonson, Ben, 1573?–1637—Criticism and interpretation. 6. Literary
quarrels—England—History—17th century. 7. English drama—17th
century—History and criticism. I. Title.
PR2958.J6 B44 2000
822.'309—dc21   00-043174

c 10 9 8 7 6 5 4 3 2 1
p 10 9 8 7 6 5 4 3 2 1

To Stella and Esther
. . . for what, except for you, do I feel love?

CONTENTS

ACKNOWLEDGMENTS

THIS BOOK, the result of my continuing interest in Shakespeare's involvement with the drama of his contemporaries, owes its existence to the Henry E. Huntington Library. It was there, on a series of fellowships, that I first encountered the wide range of resources that made this intertextual study feasible. I have tried, perhaps inadequately, to acknowledge in my arguments the debts of gratitude I owe to prior scholars who have worked on the Poets' War. Of these, the most significant is to David Bevington, whose close reading of my manuscript shaped its final version. His marvelous combination of insight and generosity affords a model of intellectual inquiry. Maurice Charney offered sound advice, and Peter L. Rudnytsky crucial suggestions that significantly clarified my argument.

The formative direction and encouragement that I received at Columbia long ago from Edward Tayler, Elizabeth Story Donno, and James Mirollo, as well as the late Bernard Beckerman and Paul Oskar Kristeller, still resonate in my scholarship. My evolving interest in the early modern period continues to be refreshed by their successors, James Shapiro, whose perspicacity and kindness furthered my research, and David Kastan, whose practical criticism significantly improved its earliest draft. Eric Jager, John N. King, A. R. Braunmuller, Leeds Barroll, W. David Kay, Michael Shapiro, Milton Hassol, Martin Elsky, Richard McCoy, Thomas Cartelli, Daniel Javitch, and John M. Steadman have also, in many different ways, facilitated its completion. And the annual meetings of the Shakespeare Association of America have been essential in supplying stimulating forums for the evaluation of these matters along with an ongoing inducement to continue developing and refining my analysis. I particularly want to thank Jennifer Crewe at Columbia University Press for her independent vision and support. I also am grateful to Leslie Kriesel and Linda Secondari at the press for bringing the manuscript to completion.

Throughout the writing of this book, my career teaching Shakespeare and Renaissance literature at Long Island University has sustained my involvement with this project, and the university's granting of released time and sabbatical made its completion possible. Dean Paul Sherwin, along with my colleagues, Arthur Coleman, Joan Digby, Phyllis Dircks, Margaret Hallissy, Katherine Hill-Miller, Norbert Krapf, Edmund Miller, Suzanne Nalbantian, Dennis Pahl, Martin Tucker, Jeanne Welcher, and our students have made teaching and research a personally satisfying experience.

Earlier versions of chapters 1 and 3 appeared in *Shakespeare Studies* and *The Huntington Library Quarterly*; they are reprinted here with permission.

The woodcut of the fool with crossbow on the title page is a detail from *A Fool's Bolt is Soon Shot* by T. F. (London, 1630?). By permission of the Pepys Library, Magdalene College, Cambridge.

The views of London at the beginning of each part are from Claes Jansz Visscher's *Londinum Florentissima Britanniae Urbs* (variant, ca. 1625). By permission of the Folger Shakespeare Library.

SHAKESPEARE
& THE POETS' WAR

*Certainly it would be worth examining how the author became
individualized in a culture like ours, what status he has been given,
at what moment studies of authenticity and attribution began, in what
kind of system of valorization the author was involved, at what point we
began to recount the lives of authors rather than of heroes, and how this
fundamental category of "the-man-and-his-work criticism" began.*
> —*Michel Foucault,* "What is an Author?"

*To judge of Poets is only the faculty of Poets;
and not of all Poets, but the best.*
> —*Ben Jonson,* Timber, or Discoveries

INTRODUCTION
The Elizabethan Dramatists as Literary Critics

THE LEGEND of Shakespeare and Jonson's wit-combats is unarguably the most famous case of poetic rivalry in the annals of English literature. This book presents the theory that Jonson began in 1599 explicitly to define himself as Shakespeare's opposite through his drama, and that Shakespeare, over the course of the following two years, reacted in a series of metatheatrical plays answering his challenge. The Poets' War—the most important theatrical controversy of the late Elizabethan stage—commenced when Jonson, the younger playwright, became "Jonson," the poet, by resisting Shakespeare's influence through the invention of a new critical drama that he called "comical satire." The war continued with added momentum when Shakespeare, in response, molded his comedies to accommodate Jonson's satiric perspective while eschewing its self-confident didacticism. And the battle ended only after Shakespeare, having been stung by Jonson's attack on the Lord Chamberlain's Men in *Poetaster*, "purged" his rival in the guise of Ajax in *Troilus and Cressida*. It is consequently during the Poets' War that we find the first record of these writers' mutual commentary and criticism.

To our knowledge, Shakespeare and Jonson first crossed paths when they both wrote for the Chamberlain's Men between 1598 and 1599 and Jonson, using all the psychological ploys of a strong poet, defined himself through his drama in opposition to Shakespeare. Although Shakespeare is now often viewed merely as the butt of Jonson's process of self-creation, there is abundant evidence that he shaped his own literary representation in answering

Jonson's criticism. This first occurred between 1600 and 1601 when, after an initial show of resistance, he increasingly appropriated Jonson's emphasis on satire in *As You Like It*, *Twelfth Night*, and *Troilus and Cressida*. Always ready to capitalize on literary fashions, he gradually reflected the hard edge of Jonson's new genre. But in doing so, he composed a kind of counter-trilogy to Jonson's three comical satires, *Every Man Out of His Humour*, *Cynthia's Revels*, and *Poetaster*, that combined plot parody and personal allusion to hoist the engineer on his own petard.

But any account of this first public dialogue between Shakespeare and Jonson is falsified by removing it from its historical context as part of the highly competitive culture of late Elizabethan commercial theater. At its most heated, the Poets' War converted three Bankside theaters—the Globe, Blackfriars, and Paul's—into military camps firing paper bullets at one another. Indeed, the Poets' War provides the fullest theatrical context currently available for understanding the interactive development of Shakespeare's work. Readers of Elizabethan drama have long noticed that in a series of interrelated plays written between 1599 and 1601—not only by Jonson and Shakespeare but also by John Marston and Thomas Dekker—there arose an intense and often acrimonious debate concerning the practice of dramatic representation. This controversy, to which Dekker referred in *Satiromastix* ("To the World," line 7) as the "Poetomachia" (or "Poets' War"), was a clash of opposing ideologies of drama initiated by Jonson in 1599 when he boldly attempted to reconstruct the premises upon which Renaissance popular theater was conceived. In self-proclaimed rebellion against established Elizabethan dramatic practice, Jonson, the *enfant terrible* of commercial theater, repeatedly claimed that he alone possessed a credible form of poetic authority, based on neoclassical standards that demolished his rivals' literary pretensions. Jonson's sense of election led him to mock competing plays and prominent rivals, especially Shakespeare, and to turn against his detractors in a struggle for poetic mastery from which, at the time, no decisive victor emerged. The first great dramatic criticism in England begins with this public dialogue—at once philosophical and personal—among Shakespeare, Jonson, Marston, and Dekker.

Recent studies have indicated that between 1599 and 1601 Jonson began a labor of poetic self-creation in his trilogy of comical satires. Here, in a more intense manner than he would ever attempt again, he fictionalized his own laureate status by creating a second self to assist in the management of his plays. These works, writes Richard Helgerson, "stand on the threshold of Jonson's career." He would never again write drama of this kind, "in which a character so clearly represented his own sense of himself."[1] Jonson subsequently receded into his work or hovered at its margins in prologues and prefaces. Once he abandoned comical satire, he was free from the absolutist mythology he had invented to sanction himself through this unique genre. Near the beginning of his career, however, in a supreme act of wish fulfillment, he projected himself into the roles of Asper, Criticus, and Horace in an effort to establish for himself and for his age a new paradigm of poetic authority. Jonson's autobiographical personae are interesting not only in themselves as symbolic acts of self-fashioning but also as the first examples in the history of English drama of a playwright self-consciously defending his status and explicitly defining the literary principles upon which his art is based.

There was never a consensus at the time, even among Renaissance humanists, on the status of the "author" or "poet" who wrote plays for the commercial theater. The word "poet," the early modern term for all creators of fiction, including drama, could suggest either a madman or a sage. "He is upbraidingly call'd a *Poet*," Jonson complains in *Discoveries*, "as if it were a most contemptible *Nick-name*" (8:572), even as he insists that his audience revise its meaning in response to his own unique performance. When feeling most at ease, Drummond notes, "he was wont to name himself the Poet" (1:150). Despite his best effort, however, the Poets' War staged the term's duality. The controversy can only be reconstructed, however, by examining the relation between Shakespeare's drama and a set of linked plays by Jonson, Marston, and Dekker that are almost off the map of contemporary criticism. My goal is to present the first comprehensive account of the Poets' War as a crisis of legitimation, a literary civil war during which Jonson's vanguard project clashed with the skepticism of Marston, Shakespeare, and Dekker, who literally laughed him off the stage. Disturbed by his satiric attacks, Jonson's rivals challenged the epistemological, literary, and ethical assumptions upon which he based his assertion of poetic authority. For in their most radical mood they were willing to object to what Thomas Greene calls Jonson's "centered self" and Jonathan Dollimore terms the philosophy of "humanist essentialism."[2] Yet by virtue of its insight into the insubstantial and transient condition of human consciousness, Shakespeare's modern sensibility paradoxically militated to confer a very different kind of authorship on him, making him both Jonson's most spectacular critic and his foremost beneficiary.

I

What initially attracted scholars in the nineteenth century, who first defined the Poets' War, was the fact that it consisted of a quarrel between rival playwrights embedded in a network of self-reflexive plays closely interlinked by patterns of literary allusion and personal satire. This research, best represented by Roscoe Addison Small's *The Stage-Quarrel Between Ben Jonson and the So-Called Poetasters*, demonstrated that the dramas that constituted this debate were not autonomous and self-contained. They were instead fused parts of a single historical moment of literary confrontation that pitted Jonson against Shakespeare, Marston, and Dekker, his principal rivals in the commercial theater. But while twentieth-century scholars usually gave pride of place to Small's short volume in their footnotes, they rarely examined either its merits or its mistakes.[3] Indeed, it is a scandal of contemporary criticism that on the four hundredth anniversary of the Poets' War, Small's brilliant but outdated treatise is still cited as the definitive work on this important controversy. This is particularly unfortunate since contemporary scholarship of Renaissance drama enjoys two advantages of belatedness—the accumulation of new evidence and a more sophisticated approach to topicality. In particular, the work of David Bevington, Oscar James Campbell, W. David Kay, Cyrus Hoy, E.A.J. Honigmann, and Richard Helgerson has made it possible to perceive with greater sophistication the controversy's theoretical, generic, allusive, and institutional dimensions.[4] It is, most importantly, through Bevington's study of "Satire and the State" in *Tudor Drama and Politics* that the Poetomachia has come to be viewed as a debate over substantive issues, in which

> the authors were committed to propositions far more essential than the fleeting notoriety of a name-calling contest. Nor do the purely commercial aspects of a theatrical rivalry explain away the basic dividing issue of the proper role of satire in a commonwealth shaken by religious and dynastic uncertainties.[5]

Bevington was able to demonstrate that the Poetomachia was primarily focused on the writer's responsibility to society. The task of modern criticism at its best has been both to account for the historical significance of the Poets' War and to limit its scope, turning it into a viable narrative. "Any criticism of any play bearing as a date of production one of the three years 1599 to 1601 which does not take account of this, for the time, stage-absorbing matter, must be imperfect and of small utility," Frederick Fleay, one of the first commentators, wrote at the end of the nineteenth century.[6] But the old historicists who rediscovered the Poets' War trivialized it by treating it more as a literary anecdote than as the most complex and thorough transaction of dramatic criticism in the English Renaissance. What is worse, their multiplication of unfounded biographical identifications brought their whole enterprise into disrepute. Fleay considered the Poets' War part of an ongoing "biographical chronicle of the English stage" in which literary allusions functioned primarily as vehicles for self-aggrandizement and invective. Yet even when they did interpret Renaissance drama, the old historicists were beset with crippling individual limitations. Despite rare flashes of perception, Fleay and Josiah Penniman displayed a proclivity for self-indulgent, allegorical lock picking, while Small, whose identifications were more accurate, made errors in assessing chronology.[7]

As a result of these interpretive problems, any new study of the Poets' War still risks being dismissed in one of two mutually contradictory ways: as a study of insignificant Renaissance gossip or as a naive literalization of fiction. Thus, one group of contemporary critics accepts the historical verifiability of the Poets' War but dismisses it as a "tiresome and obscure series of backbitings" that "wasted so much theatrical energy." And a second denies that the Poets' War was a Renaissance phenomenon at all, asserting that the very attempt to decipher its meaning is a symptom of pathology: a "Victorian heirloom, like a former source of innocent merriment which any amateur psychoanalyst can tell screens a neurosis or like great-grandfather's waste tract which never yielded its ore, serves chiefly as an ornate tribute to misapplied ingenuity."[8] Surely, both of these critiques cannot be correct: the Poets' War cannot be both a historically insignificant Renaissance phenomenon and a nineteenth-century critical fantasy. On the contrary, both are wrong—the Poets' War did in fact take place and merits close study as a major debate in the English Renaissance on the nature and function of drama. Only a synthesis of old and new histories can do justice to the quarrel's rich vein of personal satire while keeping in mind the issues of literary theory its topicality particularizes.

II

Alfred Harbage's mid-twentieth-century *Shakespeare and the Rival Traditions*, the next major reconceptualization of this controversy, defined it as a "War of the Theaters," a clash between rival repertory companies. Following his example, modern critics of Renaissance drama would continue to use the rubrics "Poetomachia" and "War of the Theaters" interchangeably. Yet only the first was coined at the time; the phrase "War of the Theaters" owes its existence primarily to nineteenth-century research.[9] Harbage, however, employed the latter to define the quarrel as an institutional competition, stoked by ideological interests in a struggle for economic and social power, between the public theaters and their private counterparts. According to his much disputed formulation, the revival of two private theater companies, the Children of Paul's at the end of 1599 and the Children of Queen Elizabeth's Chapel the following year, ignited a commercial "war" between them and the established adult acting companies. What was so appealing about Harbage's approach was that it seemed to provide the controversy with a sociological context—a model of commercial struggle between the adult actors, who performed in outdoor playhouses in the suburbs for audiences composed of heterogeneous classes, and the children of the private theaters in the city, who catered to an elite audience.[10] This premise, however, cannot sufficiently explain the Poets' War.

The turn of the seventeenth century was a period of intense theatrical competition, especially among three rival repertory companies: the Children of the Chapel at Blackfriars; the Children of Paul's, who performed on the grounds of the cathedral; and the Chamberlain's Men at the Globe. Yes, this rivalry was exacerbated by the Children's return; suddenly there were two more mouths to feed from the same general population of theatergoers. The Children of the Chapel and the Children of Paul's claimed to offer superior fare to a select audience and could therefore be seen as united in their challenge to the adult hegemony. The child acting companies drew their writers, however, from the public theater, recruiting Jonson, who had just composed his two Every Man plays for the Chamberlain's Men, and Marston, who had briefly toiled for Philip Henslowe and the Admiral's Men. And these writers felt as much competition with each other as they did with their peers in the public theater.

One can easily find major exceptions to Harbage's delineation of the rival repertories. Jonson's poetic manifesto *Every Man Out* was written for the public, not the private theater. The public theater sponsored his most explosive satire. He worked intermittently for both kinds of theater and satirized a portion of his audiences at the Globe *and* Blackfriars. He also criticized the dramatic offerings of the Chamberlain's Men and Paul's Boys and mocked their most successful poets, Shakespeare and Marston. Now while it is true that institutional rivalries existed between the adult and child companies, a variety of conflicts were experienced by the acting companies that performed in and around London at the end of the sixteenth century. Tension existed between the adult and child companies, between different child companies, and between rival adult companies. Robert Sharpe's stimulating but often unreliable study, *The Real War of the Theatres: Shakespeare's Fellows in Rivalry with the Admiral's Men, 1594–1603*, for example, emphasizes the ongoing commercial struggle between the two dominant public theaters. Furthermore, the Children of the Chapel and the Children of Paul's flung as many brains at each other as either tossed at the Chamberlain's Men. The major writers for these two private theaters between 1599 and 1601—Jonson and Marston—directed as much antagonism against each other as they vented against the adult companies. The public and private theaters, moreover, formed makeshift alliances against each other, as when the Children of Paul's and the Chamberlain's Men temporarily conspired against the Children of the Chapel in 1601. This, however, did not prevent Shakespeare, as I indicate in the first chapter, from pairing Jonson and Marston as slow Ajax and rank Thersites in his parody of the Poets' War in *Troilus and Cressida*. Between 1599 and 1601, Dekker worked for the Admiral's Men, the Chamberlain's Men, *and* the Children of Paul's. *Satiromastix* was produced by a private and a public company, and Dekker drew fire from Jonson for each of these affiliations. Harbage's institutional conflict is contradicted by yet another pattern of theatrical aggression. Jonson's comical satires at Blackfriars were critiqued by public and private theaters, by Shakespeare at the Globe, Marston at Paul's, and Dekker at both playhouses.

Associated with the Children of the Chapel between 1600 and 1601, Jonson heaped as much scorn on the Children of Paul's, their writers, and their managers as he hurled at members of the Chamberlain's Men. Both troupes were social, commercial, and literary rivals that, according to Jonson, merited criticism, and they responded by collaborating against him on *Satiromastix*. In 1599, Jonson attempted to create a visionary theater of social catharsis capable of fulfilling the highest expectations for drama enunciated by the leading humanist theoreticians of his day. The world that he represented to this end was peopled largely with humorist misfits who neglected the possibility of gaining their full humanity to pursue compulsively self-demeaning delusions. One would expect that Jonson's satiric drama would from the outset be plagued by official censorship. And indeed he was threatened from this quarter throughout his career, beginning with his earliest experiment in social criticism, the ill-fated *Isle of Dogs*. But what was equally devastating was the resistance his project encountered from his fellow playwrights, who, between 1599 and 1601, turned his satiric techniques against him.

Despite the personal tone of Jonson's quarrel with Shakespeare, Marston, and Dekker, the Poets' War was, on its most abstract level, a theoretical debate on the social function of drama and the standard of poetic authority that informed comical satire. This literary debate commands attention not only because it engaged the interest of Jonson, Shakespeare, Marston, and Dekker but also, more impressively, because they were willing to argue with incredible specificity about the basic issues of their art. In a passage in *Satiromastix* alluding to the conflict, Dekker comically explains that his colleagues have been attempting to dominate each other with such "*high words*" that they have appropriately written for players wearing "Chopins," their customary elevated shoes ("To the World," line 10). By 1599, the first permanent playhouses built in London were attracting a vast following, including an inner circle highly attuned to questions of theatrical politics. It was to this knowledgeable audience that the Poets' War was addressed, as the contenders ripped each other apart to bring these special spectators together.

III

Exciting new scholarship has been done on how Shakespeare and Jonson revised their work. This aspect of their activity is a vital part of this project,
which suggests that Jonson added an interpolation to *Every Man Out* mocking
Marston and Dekker and that Shakespeare inserted the "little eyases" allusion
into *Hamlet* to deride Jonson at Blackfriars. More important in this regard,
however, is the manner in which this self-revision was affected by both writers
rethinking each other's dramatic forms. The techniques they evolved for mutual self-reflexivity required modes of interpretation that went beyond the formal limits of individual plays, as their discussion of self-construction helped
create a sophisticated audience capable of attending to both the philosophical
and personal issues involved in their debate. For this audience, individual dramas produced by competing theaters had to be played off each other for their
competing meanings to arise. The Poets' War was consequently a series of literary transactions between writers of topically charged fictions who used their
plays to master each other's language and drama. Often dismissed in our own
time as a spectacle of self-advertisement calculated to generate publicity by furnishing its audience with the verbal equivalent of bear-baiting, its personal
satire was nevertheless coordinated with a discussion of drama that was as entertaining and serious as theater itself. As Nestor remarks in *Troilus and Cressida*: "Though't be a sportful combat, / Yet in the trial much opinion dwells"
(1.3.335–36). The Poets' War is, to borrow Gregory Bateson's distinction, a social game that tests the serio-ludic limits of theater, constructed "not upon the
premise 'this is play' but rather around the question 'is this play?' "[11] The controversy was a source of amusement, but it would never have occurred if Jonson had not insisted on his unique status in a salient example of what Jacob
Burckhardt identified as the Renaissance cult of the artist as hero.

In the aftermath of Fleay's wild enthusiasm for expanding the Poets' War
to almost every drama written between 1599 and 1601, one of the most imposing problems that faces contemporary analysis is the need to establish a
plausible chronology of the plays into which its metatheatrical strategies were
written. The process of establishing the sequence is, however, fraught with all
the difficulty that attends the dating of Renaissance plays, some of which were
published long after they were first staged in altered forms that reflect subsequent revisions. A few insurmountable impediments of this kind will always
exist, but we are currently in a better position than critics were a century ago
to outline its historical dialectic. And if we work a series of refinements on the
chronological models proposed by earlier scholars, the pattern becomes relatively clear.[12] We can currently retrieve enough of its development to con-

CHRONOLOGY OF THE POETS' WAR

	PHASE I		PHASE II		PHASE III
	Autumn 1599	1600	Autumn 1600	1601	Spring–Autumn 1601
	Globe opens	Paul's reopens	Blackfriars reopens		
JONSON	Every Man Out of His Humour •	Every Man Out (3.1.1–35; 3.4.6–40) •	Cynthia's Revels ◆		Poetaster ◆ ··· The Apology for Poetaster ◆
SHAKESPEARE		As You Like It • ··· Hamlet •		Twelfth Night •	Troilus and Cressida • ··· Hamlet (2.2.337–62) •
MARSTON	Histriomastix ◀	Antonio and Mellida ◀ ··· Jack Drum's Entertainment ◀	Antonio's Revenge ◀	What You Will ◀	
DEKKER					Satiromastix ◀ •

• = performed by the Lord Chamberlain's Men at the Globe

◀ = performed by the Children of Paul's at the cathedral theater

◆ = performed by the Children of the Chapel at Blackfriars

Shaded areas indicate peripheral plays.

For dating, see the Chronological Appendix.

clude that the Poets' War had three phases, each of which was initiated by one of Jonson's comical satires followed by responses to it from Shakespeare, Marston, and Dekker. The conflict's duration can be fixed with reasonable precision as the period beginning with Jonson's bold claim to philosophical independence from the suffocating conventions of Elizabethan drama in *Every Man Out of His Humour* and concluding with his apology for *Poetaster* and Shakespeare's retort in the "little eyases" passage of *Hamlet*.

Between Jonson's aggressive manifesto and defensive apology, the Poets' War rioted across London's public and private stages in three waves of contention, each phase of which was triggered by a new comical satire. The center of my enterprise is structural morphology: the process through which the form of comedy and the status of the poet were suddenly foregrounded by Jonson in 1599. The three main sections of this book explore the strategic moves these three plays initiated as symbolic acts of literary criticism and the responses they elicited from Shakespeare, Marston, and Dekker, who measured Jonson's new drama against their own in the wake of his repudiation thereof. Answering Jonson play for play, plot for plot, they layered literary and personal allusions into their works, creating an interprofessional discourse fired by competition.

PHASE I

—*Every Man Out of His Humour* first performed by the Chamberlain's Men in autumn 1599.
—*Histriomastix, or The Player Whipped*, with imitations of *Every Man Out* and *The Case Is Altered*, performed by the Children of Paul's at the end of 1599.
—*Every Man Out*, with the addition of the Clove and Orange episodes, produced after *Histriomastix* in 1599.
—*As You Like It* acted by the Chamberlain's Men between January and 25 March 1600.
—*Jack Drum's Entertainment, or the Comedy of Pasquil and Katherine* first presented by the Children of Paul's, after *As You Like It*, between 25 March and 8 September 1600.

PHASE II

—*Cynthia's Revels, or the Fountain of Self-Love* premiered by the Children of the Chapel between 29 September and 31 December 1600.

—*Twelfth Night, or What You Will* produced by the Chamberlain's Men after 6 January but before 25 September 1601.
—*What You Will* originally presented by the Children of Paul's, after *Twelfth Night* but before 25 September 1601.

PHASE III

—*Poetaster, or The Arraignment* acted by the Children of the Chapel between late spring and 25 September 1601.
—*Satiromastix, or The Untrussing of the Humorous Poet* staged by the Chamberlain's Men and the Children of Paul's, after *Poetaster* but before 24 October 1601.
—*Troilus and Cressida* produced by the Chamberlain's Men, after the staging of *Poetaster* and *Satiromastix* but before 24 October 1601.
—The "Apologetical Dialogue" of *Poetaster* recited only once on the stage of the Blackfriars theater, after *Troilus and Cressida* but before 21 December 1601, effectively ending the Poets' War.
—*Hamlet* (first staged in 1600) acted with the addition of 2.2.337–62 (the "little eyases" passage referring to *Poetaster*, *Satiromastix*, and possibly *Troilus and Cressida*) by the Chamberlain's Men, near the end of 1601.

English drama and its criticism between Sidney's *Apology for Poetry* and Dryden's *Essay of Dramatic Poesy* underwent a complicated evolution. Drama criticism was at this time an emerging genre—a set of needs seeking realization that was steadily being formalized. It is generally agreed that no other critic between the time of Sidney's inauguration of English dramatic criticism and Dryden's validation of it contributed more to its development than Jonson. A strain of neoclassical criticism reverberates from Sidney through Jonson to Johnson and Dryden. Jonson's commentaries also had a profound impact on Shakespeare, Marston, and Dekker, who from 1599 to 1601 forged a culture of dramatic criticism *within* drama itself, building into their plays semi-autonomous strata of literary criticism that placed their works in relation to the theories and practice of their rivals. Under the competitive circumstances of the commercial theater that shaped their dissension, playwrights began the project of assessing their own quality.[13]

The question of how seriously we should take what Hamlet refers to as this "throwing about of brains" (2.2.358–59) can be answered in two different ways. It *was*, on one level, a publicity stunt calculated to draw attention to itself and an audience to the theater. In his "Apologetical Dialogue," Jonson charged that the only reason he had been attacked was for money. Predicting more personal satire in future plays, Dekker's Captain Tucca in *Satiromastix* promises the audience that, "if you set your hands and Seals to this," Jonson "will write against it, and you may have more sport," since his critics "will untruss him again, and again, and again" (Epilogue, lines 20–24), repeating the war's three phases. Marston's Lampatho Doria, his most complete caricature of Jonson in *What You Will*, fully appreciates the power of invective to attract spectators:

> This is the strain that chokes the theaters;
> That makes them crack with full-stuff'd audience.
> This is your humour only in request,
> Forsooth to rail; this brings your ears to bed;
> This people gape for; for this some do stare.
> This some would hear, to crack the Author's neck;
> This admiration and applause pursues.
>
> (2:266)

Jonson, however, foiled any plan to continue the War with his Apology for *Poetaster*, late in 1601. Nevertheless, its influence lingered, and several years later George Chapman in his "Prologus" to *All Fools* complained that the recent restoration of Old Comedy had changed the nature of comedy itself:

> Who can show cause why th' ancient comic vein
> Of Eupolis and Cratinus (now revived
> Subject to personal application)
> Should be exploded by some bitter spleens?
> Yet merely comical and harmless jests
> (Though ne'er so witty) be esteemed but toys,
> If void of th' other satirism's sauce?[14]

Referentiality in comedy at the turn of the century, Chapman reveals, had made it difficult to write without engaging in an invective of "personal application." He could easily have answered his own rhetorical question: the change had occurred when the satiric spirit of Old Attic Comedy (represented here by Aristophanes' two greatest contemporaries) was revived by the Poets' War. Jonson's responsibility for creating this climate of invective ("your humour only in request") was, for his critics, the struggle's single most important issue. The Poets' War did not invent topicality. David Bevington has shown how personal allusion, a component of social satire, had effectively served as a political weapon in Renaissance drama. The stage-quarrel merely refocused this satiric technique self-reflexively on the status of poets and players. It is widely known that Jonson criticized Shakespeare for the first time, along with Marston and Dekker, in *Every Man Out*, and that he would then go on to criticize the Chamberlain's Men, with escalating vehemence, in *Cynthia's Revels* and *Poetaster*, his final contributions to the Poets' War. Shakespeare, in reaction, criticized Jonson's new emphasis on satire through his parody of the melancholy Jaques, who would purge the world in *As You Like It*; his subversion of Jonsonian satire in the festivity of *Twelfth Night*; his purge of Jonson as Ajax in *Troilus and Cressida*; and his censure of the way the child actors had been used at Blackfriars in the "little eyases" passage of *Hamlet*. It was at this time that Shakespeare, along with Marston and Dekker, engaged in what Thomas Fuller, later in the seventeenth century, would refer to as a series of "wit-combats" with Jonson. The dialogue Fuller imagined as personal repartee can be traced back to this series of theatrical responses to *Every Man Out*, *Cynthia's Revels*, and *Poetaster* in *As You Like It*, *Twelfth Night*, *Troilus and Cressida*, and *Hamlet*. One primary objective of this study is to document the origin of the Shakespeare-Jonson legend in these seven plays. But the terms of Shakespeare's critical duel with Jonson between 1599 and 1601 become clear only when their criticism of each other is read against the simultaneous involvement of Marston and Dekker, who would find no place in the ensuing legend but were an important part of its making.

Jonson never considered Shakespeare to be one of the "band" of "poetasters" mentioned in the preface to *Satiromastix*: this barb is aimed only at Marston and Dekker. And he never directly "represented" Shakespeare on the stage, as he had the others. Although critical, Jonson occasionally treated Shakespeare with a measure of deference never allowed to the "poetasters" and reserved only for a few contemporaries, including Chapman, Donne, and Bacon. He gives us, after all, our greatest elegy on his "beloved" Shakespeare in the First Folio as well as our most tender (yet not uncritical) personal recollection in *Discoveries* of this good-natured, witty man he "loved" (8:583). Yet it was in opposition to Shakespeare that he designed comical satire to displace romantic comedy. And it was Shakespeare who, in turn, criticized Jonson's new approach even as he submitted to its influence, moving from the romantic framework of *As You Like It* through the disturbing balance of romantic and satiric sentiment in *Twelfth Night* to the satiric nihilism of *Troilus and Cressida*. For as Shakespeare sought to contain Jonson's influence, he opened his work to his satire in order to contest its authority. Between 1600 and 1601, then, these comedies mark the poets' converging difference.

IV

One of the explanations given for the dearth of contemporary theater criticism in the English Renaissance is that the status of popular literature, especially drama, was too low to elicit the same intense scrutiny that we apply to it today. "No, to Jonson, as to Sidney, and to most other Elizabethans who thought seriously on the question," writes Richard Helgerson, "English drama was a bastard child of poetry, an unmistakably illegitimate offspring. Success in such a debased kind could never establish one as a true poet." "Precisely because he hasn't sufficient *authority* in the theatrical versions," Stephen Orgel similarly assumes, "the only way for Jonson to assert his authority over the text was to alter it and publish it: the authority, that is, lies in the publication." This was not, however, Jonson's attitude when he wrote *Every Man Out* for production at the Globe, even though by the time he finished *Poetaster* he had rejected his early idealism. So even if we agree with Orgel that "virtually all theatrical literature" is "basically collaborative in nature," that does not mean that poets and players were not given special credit for their specific contributions.[15] But some recent studies of authorship have suggested, following Foucault, that the concept does not apply in its ordinary sense to English Renaissance playwrights. Thus, according to Jeffrey Masten, the Elizabethan dramatists were not really authors at all but almost entirely anonymous collaborators who worked in teams to produce commercial plays that never bore the stamp of unique individuals. How could these writers even notice differences among themselves, since, as Leah Marcus would have it, they lived before the First Folio made Shakespeare an "author" in 1623?[16] Print was important for Jonson, but his drive for fame began on the stage.

Although they wrote before our own stricter sense of intellectual property, Jonson, Shakespeare, Marston, and Dekker were identified by contemporaries as possessing a kind of proprietary interest, if not ownership, over the linguistic and dramatic forms they invented to differentiate themselves, even as they absorbed and modified one another's influence. In *Poetaster*, for instance, Marston is accused of having stolen some of Jonson's poetry, and it is suggested that they should "hang him *plagiary*" (4.3.96), in what the *OED* records as the first use of this word to mean "plagiarist." Indeed, the word is applied to both Marston and Dekker (5.3.218–20). Derived from the Latin *plagiarius*, meaning "man-stealer" or "kidnapper," the word came to denote literary theft. Jonson could make this claim of plagiarism against Marston because he had at his disposal a rich humanist tradition imbued with what Harold Ogden White in *Plagiarism and Imitation During the English Renaissance* calls a "literary theory based on imitation, yet with every safeguard for originality."[17] At the beginning of the seventeenth century, long before courts of law established their rights, some vigilant poets monitored and policed one another's efforts through satire. In this culture of intense self-reflexivity, ear-catching quotations became authorial signatures. Not only vivid phrasing but also great characters like Falstaff and provocative new genres like comical satire made their inventors famous, recognized by their audiences for their skill. "Within the heavily capitalized London theater," writes Joseph Loewenstein, "jokes, plots, habits of diction attained the status of intellectual property. There, as in most emergent spheres of an economy, property relations were drastically unsettled. Where once a playtext had been a mere means to the productive labors of an acting company, it had come to have autonomous value."[18] Already in the later 1580s, the high level of commercial drama in London achieved by a group of especially talented poets, including Marlowe, Lyly, and Kyd, made them celebrities. Their surnames (shorthand for their skills) acquired a kind of cultural capital (which has considerably grown since then) that they negotiated with the players and audiences that consumed their fictions. Yet it is important to keep in mind the difference between these two circulating credit economies. For unlike cash, which poets often seemed to lack, the currency of reputation or "credit" (its early modern synonym) was seldom negotiable in the ordinary sense of the word and, alone, never brought the kind of prosperity that theatrical entrepreneurs, such as Philip Henslowe, and great actors, such as Edward Alleyn, were to secure.

Jonson would help bring this recognition into being by demanding respect for his accomplishment, which he sanctioned, by analogy, with contemporary political sovereignty and ancient poetic precedent. But for Renaissance dramatic poets, their most compelling payment remained a weighty yet airy nothing: the spontaneous applause of the most sophisticated (but alarmingly partisan) segment of their audiences who began, in the wake of Jonson and Shakespeare's dialogue, to continue through their own only partially recoverable discussions the social process that would convert these playwrights into Dryden's admired "dramatic poets." Late Elizabethan drama was, Andrew Gurr explains, one of the few occasions "that existed for the gathering of large numbers of people other than for sermons and executions."[19] Yet it was performed in a culture that lacked, in large measure, those ancillary institutions of exegesis that foster and control the reception of popular entertainment in our own day. There were no independently established media to assess its merits in books, magazines, and newspapers. The review as such did not exist. And not much commentary survives, outside of casual references of the kind made by Thomas Nashe, digressing in an essay; John Manningham, noting gossip in his diary; or Francis Meres, cataloguing his favorite writers. At times this criticism is literally marginalized, sewn to the fringes of dramatic texts in prefaces, dedications, and epilogues as formulaic solicitations of good will and patronage.

But theater was gaining social and intellectual prestige through the power of writers like Shakespeare and Jonson, and some contemporaries were happy to accept its masterpieces as equaling or even excelling those of Greek and Roman antiquity. The establishment of the first permanent theaters in London brought into being a class of critics whose expertise was the product of their involvement in the burgeoning Elizabethan entertainment industry. The core of this group was composed of professional writers, but their debate was supported by an informed segment among the approximately 15,000 spectators visiting the London theaters weekly, who began to know the names and foster the reputations of the writers whose plays they attended and evaluated.[20] The plays of the Poets' War are an eloquent testimony to the critical sophistication of the late Elizabethan audience they both created and addressed. Robert Weimann, Annabel Patterson, and Michael Bristol have examined Shakespeare's connection to the popular tradition in the theater, and it is this *popular* rhetoric that he calls on during the Poets' War to rebuff Jonson's neoclassicism in a spectacle of poetic competition aimed at the most *elite* segment of his audience: a core of highly literate auditors upon whose opinion his reputation depended.[21] It is this select group that the First Quarto of *Hamlet* designates collectively as the "principal public audience."[22] It was for the purpose of entertaining this most privileged and educated segment of their audience (that had acquired such a keen sense of theatrical politics, frequenting the first permanent playhouses in England) that Shakespeare and Jonson defined themselves and each other through drama. "Both within and without the playhouse walk," Steven Mullaney writes, "the new theaters were redefining the place and powers of their audiences." Elizabethan theater performed the same function for its poets and players, offering them a glimpse at "the fragile condition of its own possibility."[23]

V

This book argues for a shift in the contemporary meaning of "Shakespeare," not through attribution but interpretation, away from the myth of the anonymous and remote creator, synonymous with theater itself, to the engaged, partisan inventor of witty, deconstructive paradoxes that still attest in our eyes to his superiority over Jonson. Part of my interest in the poets' debate comes from my perception that we share with them a set of basic questions concerning whether or not human beings possess a core identity, subjectivity and judgment are autonomous or contingent, and meaning is made or discovered. Jonson's reaction to the late Elizabethan crisis of self-reflection was to construct his drama as a self-justifying social and moral homeopathy that would resolve the crisis of legitimation in the theater. He was resisted so vehemently, however, because London's commercial theater had become a place where social contradictions could be acted out at the very moment when he demanded that it discover in itself a univocal meaning. Suddenly, the idea of the play had become the theater's central concern as it was forced to confront the conditions of its performance, authenticity, and accountability. Jonson's program was political insofar as he sought to formulate a notion of poetic authority that would ground his social status along with that of the class of writers he represented. Studying him in this manner involves a consideration of what Robert Evans designates as the "micropolitical" dimension of his work and career, his struggle to establish a social identity through writing, to assert his personal power in a social setting he often found inimical to his interests.[24] But it also more generally involves a consideration of "theatrical politics": the series of negotiations among poets, players, and their audiences to influence the way their authority was represented.

Franco Moretti has argued that the historical task accomplished by Elizabethan tragedy was "the deconsecration of sovereignty," since this dramatic form "disentitled the absolute monarch to all ethical and rational legitimation." "Having deconsecrated the king," he quips, "tragedy made it possible to decapitate him."[25] Comedy would perform an analogous function in dethroning the self-crowned poet and his authoritarian poetics. Jonson's intervention was fundamentally political insofar as he offered the public a social program to reform the institution of Renaissance theater according to principles of art generated by an ideal poet. During the 1590s Elizabethans began to sense with a new urgency the disintegration of an inherited sociocultural, economic, and political order. In a climate of intellectual turbulence, the grounding of legitimacy became a prime subject for debate. "How to be 'justified'— authorized—was the most 'politicizing' question of the time," Weimann writes, and for some "the question was now, more than ever, an open one." At issue was the authority of representations that "met an existential need for self-orientation and control" in answer to bewildering social change. Weimann makes a case for narrative fiction as "the most experimental, least prescribed space for unfolding (and retracting) self-sustained images and meaningful imaginings of a *subiectum* in a new mode of representation."[26] But it was during the Poets' War that drama became the definitive site for the struggle to articulate a new mode of unauthorized representation that examined the very process of legitimation with a new skepticism that would permanently alter the canon of Western literature.

Jonson knew that he could not have faced a more formidable opponent, especially since Shakespeare had just completed his English history plays on the War of the Roses, culminating in the Henriad's exploration of the ambiguities of political sovereignty. If Shakespeare had been daring enough to examine providential beliefs about political sovereignty in light of a Machiavellian alternative, as Phyllis Rackin has demonstrated, what hope had Jonson to construct a poetic sovereignty in its image?[27] Shakespeare's turn from the Henriad to his Poets' War trilogy provided an analogous setting in which to question the idea of authority as it applied to contemporary poets and players. Here he would be even more radical in undermining Jonson's search for a new poetic legitimacy as he created a modernist poetics in which representation became the site of contradiction. While Jonson's comedy during this period tended to be authoritarian and self-promoting, Shakespeare's was indeterminate, self-effacing, and skeptical.

Comedy became the preferred dramatic form in which to deconstruct the concept of poetic authority and to insert in its place a play of wit that resisted dogma and didacticism. And if, as Moretti contends, tragedy reemerged in the late sixteenth century in reaction to "the figure of the new prince" having "entered the stage of history," the invention of comical satire was enabled by a parallel process. It came into being with the appearance onstage of the absolute poet whose word was moral law. It was made possible by the same idealizing mythology. But just as the poet demanded to be crowned, the very mode of legitimation on which his recognition depended was being radically undermined in tragedy. So that like the ideology of the absolute monarch, in a period of intense epistemological crisis, Jonson's conception of the ideal poet originated at the very moment when it was most vulnerable.

Yet unlike the monarch who was native to tragedy, the absolute poet had to invade, destroy, and reconstruct comedy to possess it, and his only power was the strength of his art. Having set out to conquer comedy, Jonson found himself embroiled in a literary civil war against his usurpation. In contrast to the tragedy of regicide, however, festive comedy, obeying the law of its kind, limited itself to Jonson's public humiliation, not his execution, with a spirit of carnival rebellion against the constraints of law. Through its probative breach in authorization, festive comedy functioned to undo the dictatorial poet who would attempt to constrain its liberty. Yet it would destroy itself in the process of self-preservation. For in his effort to contain comical satire, Shakespeare assimilated attitudes and techniques that would unravel festive comedy in his passage from *As You Like It* to *Troilus and Cressida*. He would undermine the genre in the act of defending it, in order to respond to the greater sense of social anxiety that Jonson's drama had mirrored and aroused.

1 SHAKESPEARE'S PURGE OF JONSON
The Theatrical Context of *Troilus and Cressida*

IN HIS *History of the Worthies of England* (1662), Thomas Fuller concluded a series of biographical notes on Shakespeare with a now famous passage contrasting the dramatist with Ben Jonson. Fuller's rendition of their rivalry is elaborated in terms of a vivid literary daydream that has become a cornerstone in the legend of the playwrights' association:

> Many were the *wit-combats* betwixt him and *Ben Jonson*, which two I behold like a *Spanish great Galleon* and an *English man of War*; Master *Jonson* (like the former) was built far higher in Learning; *Solid*, but *Slow*, in his performances. *Shakespeare* with the *English man of War*, lesser in *bulk*, but lighter in *sailing*, could turn with all tides, tack about and take advantage of all winds, by the quickness of his Wit and Invention.[1]

Fuller cleverly evokes their conflict as an epic struggle that reenacted the sea battle of the Armada—with predictable results. It remained for William Gifford, writing about a century and a half later, to provide Fuller's fantasy with a local habitation and a name. Turning the daydream into an anecdote in his biographical introduction to *The Works of Ben Jonson* (1816), Gifford asserts that Sir Walter Ralegh "had instituted a meeting of *beaux espirits*," including Shakespeare, Donne, and Jonson, "at the Mermaid," a celebrated London tavern. It was there, he continues, that "in the full flow and confidence of friendship, the lively and interesting 'wit-combats' took place."[2] This unsubstantiated biographical context, showing Shakespeare and Jonson as witty tavern companions, was generally accepted as historical fact until I. A. Shapiro's rigorous study of "The Mermaid Club" revealed that Gifford had fictionalized Fuller's account in order to celebrate a utopian moment in English literary history—a gathering that "combined more talent and genius, perhaps, than ever met together before or since."[3]

Once we have honed away Gifford's elaborations, however, we are still left with the question of the extent to which Fuller's characterization of Shakespeare and Jonson as mighty opposites was merely the visualization of a Restoration commonplace: the balance of Jonson's rich neoclassical learning against Shakespeare's superior inventiveness. There is at present a general consensus, reflected in the work of S. Schoenbaum, that Fuller's characterization of Shakespeare was based solely on "lines laid down by Jonson," upon which Restoration historians wildly elaborated. The very idea of their wit-combats, Schoenbaum writes, illustrates "the imagination of the biographer operating upon tradition"; it is a myth that lives on, among the legion of "old ghosts" that "haunt biography and criticism." Shakespeare's wit-combats with Jonson were, in other words, a Foucauldian "author formation" peculiar to the Restoration, a period that reinvented the greatest dramatists of the Renaissance as conflicting paradigms of "Nature" and "Art," or, as Fuller puts it, "Wit" and "Learning." This misleading determination is reinforced by Gary Taylor's engaging survey, *Reinventing Shakespeare: A Cultural History from the Restoration to the Present*, which implies that nothing shaped Shakespeare's reputation between the time that he "reinvented himself almost every day" as a writer and actor "who juggled selves" and the period when John Dryden and Thomas Rymer retrieved it for posterity.[4] I am convinced, however, that the dichotomy between a learned, slow "Jonson" and an inspired, quick "Shakespeare" was a Renaissance construction invented and reinvented by the authors themselves before contemporary London audiences took up the process of author formation that the Restoration then inherited. This only becomes apparent, however, through a thorough examination of Shakespeare's role in the Poets' War, which reveals the late Elizabethan origin of Fuller's martial fantasy.

I

Just after the Poets' War had ended, a student production at Cambridge recalled its climax and prompted its audience to decide for themselves who had won. In a scene written for the second part of *The Return from Parnas-*

sus, produced at St. John's College for the Christmas season of 1601–2, the anonymous author has the students impersonating Richard Burbage and William Kemp not only reveal that Shakespeare participated in the struggle but also affirm that by the strength of his wit he managed to overcome all other combatants in the process. "Kemp" especially exults in Shakespeare's victory over Jonson:

> Why here's our fellow *Shakespeare* puts them all down, ay and *Ben Jonson* too. O that *Ben Jonson* is a pestilent fellow. He brought up *Horace* giving the Poets a pill, but our fellow *Shakespeare* hath given him a purge that made him beray his credit.[5]

The possibility that the student author of this passage might have disagreed with the *stultus* Kemp about the outcome of the Poets' War suggests the lack of a consensus. But although his tone is hard to determine, there is no question about the nature of the controversy to which he refers. The contest between Shakespeare and Jonson to establish their poetic reputations at each other's cost refers to a theatrical controversy Dekker first called the "Poetomachia." To understand how Shakespeare "purged" Jonson in *Troilus and Cressida*, we must first come to terms with its antecedent: Jonson's purge of Marston in *Poetaster* for questioning his status as a poet. For just as Jonson had begun to target Shakespeare in *Every Man Out*, Marston drew his fire by writing *Histriomastix*, and this in turn led to a contest between Jonson and Marston—far more brutal than the former's simultaneous involvement with Shakespeare—during which they contributed three plays in succession, lampooning each other with varying degrees of sarcasm. With pointed allusions, Marston caricatured Jonson in *Histriomastix, Jack Drum's Entertainment*, and *What You Will*. Jonson countered with parodies of his rivals in *Every Man Out of His Humour, Cynthia's Revels*, and *Poetaster*, through which he vented the full power of his acerbic wit. When the anonymous author of *2 Return from Parnassus* informs us that Jonson "brought up *Horace* giving the Poets a pill," he is recalling Jonson's longest and most explicit denunciation of Marston and Dekker in act 5, scene 3 of *Poetaster*, in which Crispinus and Demetrius, the playwrights' thinly veiled caricatures, are arraigned for slandering Jonson's persona of poetic authority. At the climax of this play, Horace feeds emetic "pills" to Crispinus, who vomits tidbits of Marston's peculiar diction.

Although critics have unanimously agreed that the pill mentioned in *2 Return from Parnassus* was that administered by Jonson in *Poetaster*, they have been at odds over the meaning of the purge that Shakespeare is said to have given Jonson. One influential interpretation, accepted by Josiah Penniman and popularized by J. B. Leishman in his edition of *The Three Parnassus Plays*, claims that the purge is actually *Satiromastix*, which had been associated with Shakespeare simply because he was a member of the Chamberlain's Men, one of the two companies that produced it. But this interpretation is undercut by the fact that Horace is never literally purged in *Satiromastix*. He is "untrussed" (or stripped bare), threatened with whipping, and crowned with nettles after being convicted of arrogance and self-love. "It may well be," Leishman writes, "that for the majority of Elizabethan playgoers and play-readers, the Globe and the Chamberlain's Men were as much 'Shakespeare's theatre' and 'Shakespeare's Company' as for us of to-day." Penniman, however, had admitted with unusual candor that his was a "possible, but rather unsatisfactory solution of the difficulty."[6]

Penniman and Leishman's theory that Shakespeare purged Jonson in *Satiromastix* remains unconvincing for three reasons. First, it overlooks that the passage spoken by Kemp twice cites Shakespeare as being directly involved in the Poets' War. The players are in fact specifically celebrating their "fellow" Shakespeare's revenge on their most consistent detractor. Second, since there is no record of any Elizabethan speaking of the Globe and "the Lord Chamberlain's Servants" as "Shakespeare's," this notion is anachronistic. And third, Leishman doesn't do justice to the deliberate wordplay upon which the wit of the passage in *2 Return from Parnassus* depends. Before accepting *Satiromastix* as the purge of Jonson, we should first explore the plays that Shakespeare wrote during this period to see if a credible antecedent can be found. In particular, scholars have not examined the full network of external and internal evidence that links the patterns of topical allusion in *Troilus and Cressida* to this theatrical context. But Shakespeare's reason for purging Jonson only becomes intelligible when it is viewed as a commentary on the shocking quarrel between Jonson and Marston—the topical prototypes of Ajax and Thersites—in the three plays each wrote against the other between 1599 and 1601.

II

Jonson abruptly terminated the Poets' War late in 1601, when he penned an "Apologetical Dialogue" for *Poetaster* stating that he had done no more than reluctantly defend himself. Here a character called simply the "Author" (who might have been "acted" by Jonson) admits to his audience that for

> three years,
> They did provoke me with their petulant styles
> On every stage: And I at last, unwilling,

But weary, I confess, of so much trouble,
Thought, I would try if shame could win upon 'hem.
(LL. 96–100)

In 1619, Jonson was explicit about the prime source of his irritation when he confided to Drummond that his satire of Marston in *Poetaster* was retaliatory: that he "beat" Marston and took his pistol after being "represented" by him on the stage (1:140). Small, more than a century ago, was the first modern critic to discover that the source of Jonson's anger was a *roman à clef* in *Histriomastix*. And in order to understand how Shakespeare critiqued Jonson, we have first to determine how he incorporated the latter's violent quarrel with Marston both on- and offstage. For the issues of poetic authority involved in Shakespeare's parody of Jonson and Marston only become evident once we have examined their constructions of "the author and his rival" in their competing comedies.

During the first phase of the Poets' War, Marston began particularizing his response to Jonson's assertion of poetic authority by representing him under the name Chrisoganus in *Histriomastix*. This name, as I document in chapter 3, recalls a satiric epigram in *Skialetheia* (1598), written by Marston's cousin.[7] Marston applies it to a poet who praises his own "rich invention" with "its sweet smooth lines" and insists on the preeminence of his "art," only to be rebuffed by the actors for his insolence. What is most disturbing about Marston's treatment of Jonson, however, is that when Chrisoganus denounces the barbarous "multitude" for betraying him, Mavortius, who had been begging him to compromise, denounces him as a "translating scholar" who only wants "To lash the patient" (3:257–58). What Marston finds amusing is Jonson's heroic attempt to bring neoclassical values to the popular theater, and he particularizes his criticism by mentioning the genres Jonson currently employed (drama, satire, and epigram), his characteristic mode of self-aggrandizement, his work's chronic dependence on scholarship, and his poverty. Marston's charge that Jonson was not an *originator* (as *he* insisted) but a translator who merely paraphrased the classics would forever follow him. Jonson had recently written *Every Man Out* (1599) for the Chamberlain's Men, and Marston, working for the Children of Paul's, travestied his relationship with the public theater. The very title of Marston's play, *Histriomastix, or The Player Whipped*, indicates that personal parody was to be viewed within the broader context of his theatrical milieu.

In the "Apologetical Dialogue," which was cut "by Authority" (4:317) from the 1602 Quarto and first printed in the 1616 Folio, Jonson claims that he was drawn into the controversy in only that one play, after tolerating caustic allusions from 1599 to 1601. This statement is accurate to the extent that *Poetaster* shows a fury not evident in earlier works, but it is somewhat disingenuous, since, as I will further explain in chapter 5, he first parodied Marston and Dekker as Clove and Orange in two short passages he added to *Every Man Out* (3.1.1–35 and 3.4.6–40). Having come to St. Paul's to socialize and having spied an approaching company of courtiers, Clove launches into a pompous speech featuring samples of Marston's strained diction, including the title of his new play, *Histriomastix*. Jonson resented having been made to mouth Chrisoganus's stilted jargon and turned Marston's rhetoric against him, exposing him as a fraudulent scholar.

Harbage stereotyped the War of the Theaters as a combat between coterie and popular acting companies. But Jonson's mockery of his colleagues contradicts this distinction: *Every Man Out* spoofs both Shakespeare at the Globe and Marston at Paul's. Indeed, Jonson's first recorded criticism of Shakespeare appears in *Every Man Out*, the play in which he created the mythic dichotomy he embellished for the rest of his life. Yet his most significant assault on Shakespeare's credit, I argue in the next chapter, is not discovered in its amusing surface allusions but in its symbolic act of generic transgression: its substitution of comical satire for festive comedy. It was in this new comic medium that Jonson lodged his first public criticism of Shakespeare by texturing into its dialogue a combination of personal and professional mockery, linking his rival's outlandish aspiration to gentility with his absurd diction and ridiculous plotting. Thus, perhaps only in the First Quarto Jonson applied personal topicality to a play whose structure was from the start anti-Shakespearean, as he added to formal innovation a parody of the man and his work. It is through this set of allusions (in what became the defining style of the Poets' War) that he conjoined in anecdotal form the body of the poet with the body of his work.

Jonson's most famous slight of Shakespeare in *Every Man Out* is his sly allusion to the poet's newly acquired coat of arms bearing the word *Non sanz droict* (Not without right): the clown Sogliardo is advised to adopt the heraldic motto, "*Not without mustard*" (3.4.86).[8] This personal parody, to which I will have reason to return in chapter 4, is moreover supplemented by other playfully aggressive comments, including criticism of two recent plays, *Julius Caesar* and *Henry V*, alongside allusions to *1 Henry IV* and *Two Gentlemen of Verona*. Jonson's attack on *Julius Caesar* and *Henry V* is conditioned by a neoclassical perspective that stigmatizes Shakespeare's artlessness through his purported failure of diction in the former and his unity-violating chorus in the latter. A passage from *Julius Caesar* that Jonson found to be absurd, "O judgment! thou art fled to brutish beasts, / And men have lost their reason"

(3.2.104–5) is quoted by the indiscriminate Clove: "*Reason long since is fled to animals*, you know" (3.4.33). In the same spirit of mockery, Carlo Buffone disappears from the drama with a facetious lament, "*Et tu Brute!*" (5.6.79), a phrase for which Shakespeare had no classical authority. The Chorus of *Henry V* that asks the audience's acquiescence in violating the unities of time and place, allowing Henry to travel from Calais to London between scenes, is yet another target. Shakespeare had "humbly" asked his auditors, in the king's name, to "let him land, / And solemnly see him set on to London" in their minds' eye, since "So swift a pace hath thought that even now / You may imagine him upon Blackheath" (5.Chorus.13–16). Jonson restages this request when his commentator asks the audience to

> let your imagination be swifter than a pair of oars: and by this, suppose PUNTARVOLO, BRISK, FUNGOSO, and the dog arriv'd at the court gate, and going up to the great chamber. MACILENTE and SOGLIARDO, we'll leave them on the water, till possibility and natural means may land 'hem.   (4.8.175–81)

This critique is underscored by the Induction, where Mitis asks Cordatus, "how comes it then, that in some one Play we see so many seas, countries, and kingdoms passed over with such admirable dexterity?" and he ironically responds, "O, that but shows how well the Authors can travail in their vocation, and outrun the apprehension of their auditory" (lines 281–86). *Henry V* is Shakespeare's only play that follows the classical tradition of having choruses between all acts, and Jonson indicates that when his rival uses ancient forms, he botches the job, violating a prime classical premise—the unity of place—in attempting to be "classical." Part of the humor of Jonson's joke comes from the fact that his mock excuse for Shakespeare's violation of the unity of place paraphrases Falstaff's self-defense in *1 Henry IV*—"'Tis no sin for a man to labor in his vocation" (1.2.104–5). That Jonson is here measuring his own poetic powers against those of Shakespeare is revealed in the final words of *Every Man Out*, where Asper solicits the audience for applause with the reminder that if they accept this new play, they "may (in time) make lean MACILENTE as fat as Sir JOHN FALSTAFF" (5.11.85–87). The gleeful aggression that Jonson brings to this deconstruction of Shakespearean *topoi* is perfectly represented by the treatment of Puntarvolo and his dog. "It seems doubtful," writes Anne Barton, "that Puntarvolo . . . would have been accompanied by so palpably engaging and omnipresent a dog had Jonson not been remembering Launce and his friend Crab in *Two Gentlemen of Verona*."[9] The dog's seemingly gratuitous poisoning by Macilente is a provocative joke, another symbolic act of iconoclasm that violently subordinates romantic comedy to comical satire.

Jonson's reservations about *Julius Caesar* and *Henry V*, two recent plays probably still performed at the Globe, are part of the first recorded instance of his dissatisfaction with Shakespeare's work, an obsessive theme to which he returns throughout his career in his comedies, the conversations with Drummond, and the notes of *Discoveries*. The Prologue added to the 1616 folio edition of *Every Man In* repeats his disparagement of the Chorus that "wafts you o'er the seas" (line 15), again distinguishing his own superior conception of drama. Asked to contribute commendatory verse to the First Folio of 1623, Jonson praised Shakespeare as the culminating genius of literary history, but still had to mention, for the sake of honesty, his "small Latin and less Greek." And when Heminges and Condell in their epistle "To the Great Variety of Readers," prefacing the First Folio, expressed wonder at Shakespeare's fluency, the "easiness" with which he uttered his thoughts, remembering that they "scarce received from him a blot in his papers" (sig. A3ʳ), Jonson objected. Although the actors praised their fellow for having "never blotted out line," Jonson replied, "would he had blotted a thousand," not in malice, he protested, but because Shakespeare's wit "flowed with that facility, that sometime it was necessary he should be stopp'd" (8:583–84). The consistency of this judgment is revealed when he again cites a line from *Julius Caesar* in *Discoveries* to illustrate the absurd diction produced by Shakespeare's copiousness: "His wit was in his own power;" Jonson writes, "would the rule of it had been so too. Many times he fell into those things, could not escape laughter: As when he said in the person of *Caesar*, one speaking to him; *Caesar, thou dost me wrong.* He replied: *Caesar did never wrong, but with just cause*: and such like; which were ridiculous" (8:584). Jonson recalled this line again a decade after Shakespeare's death, still relishing its humour in the Induction to *The Staple of News* (1626) (lines 36–37). Since the passage in *Julius Caesar*, addressed to Metellus Cimber, now reads, "Know, Caesar doth not wrong, nor without cause / Will he be satisfied" (3.1.47–48), it is likely that the original line was altered in deference to Jonson's barb by either Shakespeare or a subsequent editor, who left a half line indicating the revision.[10] The basic literary distinction between learned Jonson, the scholar, and imaginative Shakespeare, fancy's child, fundamental to Fuller's history and to Restoration and Romantic criticism generally, thus finds its origin in the topical allusions of *Every Man Out*. Jonson felt that to be honest was to be critical, and although he lavishly praised Shakespeare's dramaturgy on other occasions, admitting that there "was ever more in him to be praised than to be pardoned," he nevertheless maintained that single but multifaceted critique he summed up in three short words: "Shakespeare wanted Art" (1:133).

III

Despite Jonson's polemics against Shakespeare, however, it was Marston who remained Jonson's most vicious antagonist and who earned his parody as Thersites by beginning to hammer away at his arrogance in *Jack Drum's Entertainment*. Here, Brabant Senior, his second Jonson surrogate, is "made as foolish as his dupes," as "Marston takes their side against him, making him fall into the pit he digged for others."[11] In this new parody Brabant/Jonson is crowned with a "Coronet of Cuckolds" and numbered among the fools (3:240). Jonson subsequently retaliated against Marston in *Cynthia's Revels*—beginning the second phase of the Poets' War—by staging the triumph of Criticus, favored by Arete, Mercury, and Cynthia, over his detractors Hedon/Marston and Anaides/Dekker.

Marston's strategy for dealing with Jonson was to classify his dedication to scholarship as a humour. Through Lampatho Doria in *What You Will*, he answered *Cynthia's Revels* by having his final authorial scapegoat re-create the pedantic arrogance of Chrisoganus and Brabant Senior. Lampatho/Jonson is "a fusty cask / Devote to mouldy customs of hoary eld," who recites his poetry, spits, and says, "faith, 'tis good" (2:246), recalling the closing boast of *Cynthia's Revels*, "By God, 'tis good, and if you like't, you may" (Epilogue, line 20). Lampatho, like Jonson, delights in the "ridiculous humour" of others (2:247) and ludicrously threatens those who cross him: "So *Phoebus* warm my brain, I'll rhyme thee dead, / Look for the Satire" (2:248). Yet Jonson's stand-in is finally convinced by Quadratus that nothing is "more vile, accursed, reprobate to bliss, / Than man, and 'mong men a scholar most" (2:257). Jonson's project of self-creation is scorned by his own persona, the transformed Lampatho, who looks back on his past in horror. Marston's Jonson now confesses that he has "wasted lamp-oil" and "baited" his "flesh" for nothing. Announcing his conversion to the doctrine of Socratic ignorance, he admits that "I fell a-railing, but now . . . I know I know naught but I naught do know" (2:258). Marston again submits his Jonsonian impersonation to the indignities of Jonson's conventional plotting. Cracking under the pressure of Marston's arguments, Lampatho embraces the "fantastical" existence (2:250) that the erring courtiers of *Cynthia's Revels* had renounced in bidding farewell to their "fantastic humours" (Palinode, line 5).

This pattern of topical allusion seems restrained by comparison with the third phase of the Poets' War, during which Jonson launched a frontal assault on Marston and Dekker in *Poetaster*. This was, in the phrasing of *2 Return from Parnassus*, the play in which he "brought up *Horace* giving the Poets a pill" and in the process provoked Shakespeare's purge. Setting his play in Augustan Rome, Jonson returned to the drama of self-justification with a vengeance by identifying himself with the ideal poet Horace under attack by Rufus Laberius Crispinus and Demetrius Fannius, his spiteful rivals. Jonson explains that Demetrius/Dekker, with Crispinus/Marston's assistance, has been hired by Histrio, a member of an unscrupulous acting company, "to abuse HORACE . . . in a play" (3.4.323). Jonson had discovered that the Chamberlain's Men had commissioned Dekker to rebuke him in what later became *Satiromastix*, and he raced to complete *Poetaster* before its attack. The result includes an arraignment of Marston and Dekker before a literary tribunal that convicts them of slander. Found guilty, Crispinus is singled out for his infamous purge, as Horace feeds him emetic pills that force him to vomit Marston's exotic vocabulary. "How now, Crispinus?" Tibullus asks, sensing his distress:

> CRISPINUS   O, I am sick—
> HORACE   A basin, a basin quickly; our physic works. Faint
>   not, man.
> CRISPINUS   O—*retrograde—reciprocal—incubus.*
> CAESAR   What's that, HORACE?
> HORACE   *Retrograde, reciprocal* and *Incubus* are come up.
> GALLUS   Thanks be to JUPITER.
> CRISPINUS   Oh—*glibbery—lubrical—defunct*—o—
>
> (5.3.464–72)

This protracted scene, which continues for another fifty-three lines, contains fourteen examples of Marston's vocabulary from *The Metamorphosis of Pygmalion's Image, Certain Satires, The Scourge of Villainy, Jack Drum's Entertainment, Antonio and Mellida, Antonio's Revenge,* and *What You Will.*[12] In *Shakespearean Negotiations,* Stephen Greenblatt insists that literature is a "collective production," since "language itself, which is at the heart of literary power, is the supreme instance of a collective creation."[13] But what is striking about Jonson's indictment of Marston's language is that he offers it only because he knows it will remain Marston's. Insisting that individuals are best identified through speech, Jonson writes in *Discoveries* that "*Language* most shows the man; speak that I may see thee" (8:625). We derive our most personal thoughts from public language, but inflections of style identify poets as the creators of the words they use. Hearing Marston's vocabulary travestied at Blackfriars, Jonson's audience was evidently capable of localizing his criticism of Paul's.

Dekker immediately answered Jonson in *Satiromastix*, in which he again brings Horace on stage, this time to be humiliated by Crispinus and Demetrius. Although Dekker seems to have written only this one play for the Poets' War, he accounts for its entire history when he fuses Jonson's three satiric aliases:

> you must have three or four suits of names, when like a lousy Pedicu-
> lous vermin th'ast but one suit to thy back: you must be call'd *Asper*, and
> *Criticus*, and *Horace*, thy title's longer a reading than the Style a the big
> Turk's: *Asper, Criticus, Quintus, Horatius, Flaccus*.   (1.2.309–14)

Dekker recapitulates the history of Jonsonian self-representation from Asper in *Every Man Out* through Criticus (changed in the Folio to Crites) of *Cynthia's Revels* to Horace (using his full name) in *Poetaster*. The grand metapersona they create is Sultan Jonson, the poet so at one with his works that he regally walks through their frames. Dekker never purges Jonson, but he does ponder feeding him his own medicine when Crispinus wonders:

> should we minister strong pills to thee:
> What lumps of hard and indigested stuff,
> Of bitter *Satirism*, of *Arrogance*,
> Of *Self-love*, of *Detraction*, of a black
> And stinking *Insolence* should we fetch up?
>   (5.2.218–22)

Convicted of slander, Horace is then crowned with nettles (instead of the coveted bays), "untrussed," and threatened with whipping. From statements in *Poetaster* and *Satiromastix* it appears that Dekker's self-vindication was sponsored by the Chamberlain's Men as a form of class-action suit against their erstwhile colleague, who, having written his two Every Man plays in their employ, was now allied with their competition, the Children of Queen Elizabeth's Chapel, who produced *Cynthia's Revels* and *Poetaster* against them. In the concluding Palinode to *Cynthia's Revels*, the reformed courtiers vow to abandon "play houses . . . and all such public places" (lines 25–26). Although the players seek the distinction of heraldry, Jonson remarks in *Poetaster*, they are already "blazoned" in the "*Statute*" (1.2.53–54)—the thirty-ninth of Elizabeth (1597/98)—by which actors were numbered with rogues, vagabonds, and beggars, unless in the service of a nobleman. In a final irony, writing for Blackfriars, Jonson associated Marston and Dekker with the adult actors, just as Marston had linked Jonson to them in *Histriomastix*. In

Poetaster, the Poets' War came full circle when Chrisoganus's unfortunate affiliation with Sir Oliver Owlet's Men was revived in Histrio's sordid employment of Crispinus and Demetrius.

IV

That Shakespeare was acutely aware of the final and most inflammatory stage of the Poets' War is revealed in the First Folio version of *Hamlet*, where Rosencrantz anachronistically reports that the city tragedians are not faring well because they have to compete with an "innovation": satirical plays performed by children that parody them (2.2.337–62). This passage alludes to an issue I specifically deal with in chapter 9, the conflict that erupted between Blackfriars and the Globe when the latter answered *Poetaster* with *Satiromastix* and *Troilus and Cressida*, which Shakespeare composed partly to compensate for the theoretical weakness of Dekker's satire. Jonson refers to the Children of the Chapel as "so many *wrens*" in *Cynthia's Revels* (Induction, line 122). Shakespeare, however, saw them as "little eyases" or young hawks, whose predatory instincts had been nurtured by a malicious falconer. Jonson in *Cynthia's Revels* had twice employed the phrase Rosencrantz uses—"common stages"—to stigmatize the adult actors (Induction, line 182; 4.3.118–19). In *Hamlet*, Shakespeare voices his distress over the vituperative tenor of the Poets' War that had obliterated the boundary between art and life.

In this cultural moment of intense self-reflexivity, audiences as well as poets and players were subjected to a unique dramatization of theater, so that even though Jonson's Tucca is a soldier in *Poetaster* he is afraid of going to the theater because he fears being parodied. Dekker's Tucca in *Satiromastix*, an imitation of an imitation, voices the same concern:

> A Gentleman, or an honest Citizen, shall not Sit in your penny-bench Theatres . . . but he shall be Satir'd and Epigram'd upon, and his humour must run upo'th Stage: you'll ha' *Every Gentleman in's humour*, and *Every Gentleman out on's humour*.   (4.2.52–57)

The effect of Jonson's criticism on the Globe, Shakespeare remarks in *Hamlet*, is that "many wearing rapiers are afraid of goose-quills and dare scarce come thither" (2.2.343–44), for fear of being satirized for patronizing an unfashionable theater. Jonson's single intention, Tucca explains, is to make "fashion-mongers quake" at his "paper Bullets" (5.2.201). Indeed, Shakespeare himself concedes that those who had rallied under the Globe's banner have been vanquished by Blackfriars. For Shakespeare, however, the most upsetting aspect of *Poetaster* was its disturbing parodies of several of the Chamberlain's Men under aliases. And in the "little eyases" passage he emphasizes only one dimension of the struggle: Jonson's attack on his company.

This topical commentary—a metacritical discourse on recent theatrical history—illustrates Shakespeare's familiarity with the Poets' War, but there are two pieces of contemporary evidence that suggest that he directly answered Jonson on behalf of his company. The first of these, as we have seen, is the allusion to Shakespeare's "putting down" of Jonson and everyone else in *2 Return from Parnassus*. The second is found in the "Apologetical Dialogue" of *Poetaster*, where Jonson admits that he satirized specific members of the Chamberlain's Men and regrets that some of their more enlightened number have retaliated with unexpected severity:

> Now, for the Players, it is true, I taxed 'hem,
> And yet, but some; and those so sparingly,
> As all the rest might have sat still, unquestion'd,
> Had they but had the wit, or conscience,
> To think well of themselves. But, impotent they
> Thought each man's vice belong'd to their whole tribe:
> And much good do't 'hem. What th' have done 'gainst me,
> I am not mov'd with. If it gave 'hem meat,
> Or got 'hem clothes. 'Tis well. That was their end.
> Only amongst them, I am sorry for
> Some better natures, by the rest so drawn,
> To run in that vile line.
>
> (LL. 141–52)

The only candidate ever proposed for Jonson's allusion to "some better natures" is Shakespeare; his plural number belies a singular identification. The person to whom Jonson was referring was both player and poet for the Chamberlain's Men, someone who took offense as an actor but responded as a dramatist. "To run in that vile line" means to write satirical plays against Jonson. Even Leishman, who excludes Shakespeare from the purge mentioned in *2 Return from Parnassus*, admits: "It is almost certain that among these 'better natures', he [Jonson] had Shakespeare in mind: for what other member of the Chamberlain's company did he ever publicly express admiration or friendship." Jonson's phrase "some better natures" anticipates his later praise of Shakespeare in *Discoveries*: "He was (indeed) honest, and of an open, and free nature" (8:584). And in *Troilus and Cressida* we find the purge in the dialogue that provides the historical foundation for Fuller's account of a wit-combat between Shakespeare and Jonson.

V

The claim that *Troilus and Cressida* contains Shakespeare's answer to Jonson depends on three kinds of evidence. First, the play's text is intelligible in terms of the reference in *2 Return from Parnassus*. Second, *Troilus and Cressida* functions as an extension of the Poets' War, sharing in the same themes and techniques that appear in the plays of Jonson, Marston, and Dekker. And third, the purge can be explained as a thematic component of its drama. The contention originates in Frederick Fleay's often erratic insights. Frequently relying on little more than a hunch, in *A Chronicle History of the Life of William Shakespeare*, Fleay surmises that Jonson was Ajax, Dekker was Thersites, Chapman was Achilles, and Shakespeare was Hector. Of these couplings, however, only the allusion to Jonson as Ajax is credible. It was accepted by Small, who wrote that it "is certain that, as Fleay has suggested, the description applies exactly to Jonson and that the character of Ajax is at least in part a personal hit." Herford and Simpson, as well as William Elton, have concurred with this assessment, and their suggestions enable us to discuss the full meaning of Shakespeare's purge of Jonson.[14]

As Elton observes, the language of *2 Return from Parnassus* is more precise in its connotations than readers had heretofore recognized. Kemp's line, "our fellow *Shakespeare* hath given him a purge that made him beray his credit," uses the word "beray" as a synonym in Elizabethan parlance for "befoul" or "beshit." Elton concludes that "Shakespeare 'purged' Jonson by satirizing him as a witless braggart soldier compounded of humours, and berayed his credit—befouled his reputation—by naming him Ajax, signifying a privy."[15] Shakespeare needed Ajax for the depiction of Trojan history, but he built into the role a reference to Jonson in

THOMAS NASHE, *Have with You to Saffron-Walden* (1596), SIG. F4ʳ
The Folger Shakespeare Library

order to expose him by proxy to his own comic plotting. Ever since John Harington in *The Metamorphosis of Ajax* (1596) encouraged his readers to pronounce the hero's name with a stress on the second syllable ("a jakes"), it had had a latent comic association. Harington incited a reply from an anonymous rival who took him to task in *Ulysses Upon Ajax*, or in other words, "Ulysses on the privy." In the same year as Harington's treatise, Thomas Nashe had boasted that his pamphlet *Have with You to Saffron-Walden* (1596) would so infuriate Gabriel Harvey that he would have to "beray" himself upon reading it. In order to emphasize his point, Nashe includes a woodcut caricature (see illustration), entitled "*Gabriel Harvey, as he is ready to let fly upon* Ajax."[16] Shakespeare works this pun into the dialogue of *Troilus and Cressida* in the jest behind Thersites' remark that "Ajax goes up and down the field, asking for himself" (3.3.245)—that is, the hero, frightened on the battlefield, seeks a place to relieve himself. Shakespeare had featured the same pun in the name of the melancholy Jaques of *As You Like It*, and uses it in *Troilus and Cressida* to stigmatize the new breed of formal satirists as unwholesomely noxious "anal" characters.

"In his first two plays for Shakespeare's company," writes Clifford Leech, Jonson "had labelled himself the 'humours' dramatist, and the label stuck."[17] Between 1599 and 1601, however, a witty allusion to Jonson as Ajax possessed an added degree of particularity since Jonson, in all three comical satires, insisted that the poet was a moral physician who purged the humours of his sick contemporaries. On the most obvious level, then, Shakespeare brands Jonson with a scatalogical reference that typifies his work, but more profoundly, he uses the same word to challenge the basis of the cathartic theory of comical satire. Jonson had already employed the language of ancient Greek moral and physical purgation at the end of *Every Man in His Humour*, where the learned Doctor Clement laments that "election is now governed altogether by the influence of humour" and that contemporary society "must have store of *Ellebore* given her to purge these gross obstructions" (5.3.344–50). Horace likewise administers hellebore, an extremely potent purgative used to remedy mental illness, to Crispinus/Marston at the climax of *Poetaster*. If the title of *Every Man in His Humour* suggests that a "humourous" disposition is endemic, in *Every Man Out* Jonson seeks to put the audience "out" of its humour, not in the modern negative sense of being beside oneself but rather in the sense of being emancipated from absurdity. Jonson sought to achieve this psychic reformation by pressing upon his audience a series of dramatic epiphanies in which the play's formerly deluded characters experience the clarification of self-knowledge. Witnessing this spectacle of conversion, he hoped, would force spectators to undergo a cathartic purge of their corresponding humours. The metaphor that literature was a moral medicine was a commonplace of

Renaissance humanism, but Jonson's three spokesmen—Asper, Criticus, and Horace—give it a special prominence in comical satire.[18] Asper speaks with derision of spectators plagued with misconceptions about themselves and Jonson's plays: "And therefore I would give them pills to purge, / And make 'hem fit for fair societies" ("After the Second Sounding," lines 175–76). Even though some of these diseased spectators might resist his cure, he resolves to "Squeeze out the humour of such spongy natures, / As lick up every idle vanity" (lines 145–46). In *Cynthia's Revels*, Criticus uses the language of purgation to characterize the difference between himself and his sick detractors Anaides and Hedon, who "Do nothing out of judgement, but disease" (3.3.30), and about whom the poet-doctor professes only concern:

> What wise physician have we ever seen
> Mov'd with a frantic man? The same affects
> That he doth bear to his sick patient,
> Should a right mind carry to such as these.
>
> (3.3.33–36)

At the play's conclusion, the narcissistic courtiers who have drunk of the fountain of self-love are directed instead to the fountain of self-knowledge, where they are "*purged*" of their "*maladies*" (Palinode, line 37). In *Poetaster*, Horace reinvigorates this *topos* when he volunteers to cure Crispinus:

> HORACE   Please it great CAESAR, I have pills about me
> (Mixed with the whitest kind of *ellebore*)
> Would give him a light vomit; that should purge
> His brain and stomach of those tumorous heats. . . .
> CAESAR   O! be his AESCULAPIUS, gentle HORACE;
> You shall have leave, and he shall be your patient.
>
> (5.3.391–97)

By 1601, having completed his third and final comical satire, Jonson had established for himself a new poetic identity, in the words of *Satiromastix*, as "he, that pens and purges Humours and diseases" (5.2.307). Indeed, the subtitle of Dekker's comedy calls him "*the Humourous Poet.*" Shortly before *Satiromastix* was written, a pamphlet by W. I. (probably John Weever) entitled *The Whipping of the Satyr* was being hawked by the booksellers, and Dekker consulted it in parodying Jonson. In his preface, Weever censures Jonson directly as "*Monsieur Humourist*," arguing that the humours he wants to purge are projections of his own moral failings and that he is not a physician but a murderer:

But, had you been . . . so mean a Philosopher as have known that *mores sequuntur humores*, you would questionless have made better humours, if it had been but to better our manners, and not instead of a moral medicine to have given them a mortal poison: . . . and therefore . . . you made sale of your Humours to the Theater, and there played . . . with the people in your humour, then out of your humour.[19]

Jonson the poisoner, according to Weever, had played hide-and-go-seek with his audience, both veiling and exposing himself in his fictions. When Shakespeare wove his topical references into *Troilus and Cressida*, therefore, he did so to serve the same purpose that had motivated Marston, Dekker, and Weever. Each had decided to purge the purger, to debunk the physician who could not cure himself, using the same bitter medicine he had dispensed. When in *2 Return from Parnassus* Kemp states that Shakespeare purged Jonson, he condenses the way in which the name and character of Ajax in *Troilus and Cressida* possessed a metatheatrical dimension that culminated a broad-based reaction against the "humourous" poet.

Shakespeare's references to Jonson in *Troilus and Cressida* are communicated primarily through the medium of poetic parody. In the servant Alexander's long description of Ajax to the curious Cressida, Shakespeare seems to mimic the exorbitant praise Jonson lavished on himself as Criticus in *Cynthia's Revels*. Viewing a parade of courtiers in Jonson's play, Cupid singles out Criticus and asks his father Mercury his name. The god of poets replies with a long encomium of Criticus that Jonson's rivals interpreted as an extreme act of poetic self-reference:

Criticus. A creature of a most perfect and divine temper. One, in whom the humours and elements are peaceably met without emulation of precedency: he is neither too fantasticly melancholy, too slowly phlegmatic, too lightly sanguine, or too rashly choleric, but in all, so composed and order'd, as it is clear, *Nature* went about some full work, she did more than make a man, when she made him. His discourse is like his behaviour, uncommon, but not unpleasing; he is prodigal of neither. He strives rather to be that which men call judicious than to be thought so: and is so truly learned that he affects not to show it. He will think, and speak his thought, both freely: but as distant from depraving another man's merit as proclaiming his own. For his valour, 'tis such that he dares as little to offer an injury as receive one. In sum, he hath a most ingenuous and sweet spirit, a sharp and season'd wit, a straight judgment, and a strong mind. *Fortune* could never break him, nor make him

less. He counts it his pleasure to despise pleasures, and is more delighted with good deeds than goods. It is a competency to him that he can
be virtuous. He doth neither covet, nor fear: he hath too much reason
to do either: and that commends all things to him.   (2.3.123–45)

Here Jonson constructs the model of an ideal centered self, the best poet academic humanism could imagine. But this elegant yet slow character sketch
of the absolute poet, with its labored Ciceronian clauses, traced without startling turns of wit in the service of self-praise, provided a target for Shakespeare, who employs it as a frame for his criticism of Jonson. Accordingly,
when Cressida remarks that Ajax "is a very man *per se*," Shakespeare uses her
servant Alexander to deconstruct Jonson's ideal:

This man, lady, hath robb'd many beasts of their particular additions:
he is as valiant as the lion, churlish as the bear, slow as the elephant; a
man into whom nature hath so crowded humours that his valor is
crush'd into folly, his folly sauc'd with discretion. There is no man hath
a virtue that he hath not a glimpse of, nor any man an attaint but he
carries some stain of it. He is melancholy without cause, and merry
against the hair; he hath the joints of every thing, but everything so out
of joint that he is a gouty Briareus, many hands and no use, or purblind
Argus, all eyes and no sight.   (1.2.19–30)

Shakespeare's passage counters Jonson's evocation of Criticus through a series
of comic deflations. Whereas Jonson associates Criticus with the divine,
Shakespeare derives Ajax from the bestial. And whereas "the humours . . . are
peaceably met" to form a paragon of virtue "composed and order'd" by Nature in Criticus, Ajax is a man into whom Nature has "crowded humours" in
a wholly discordant blend. Instead of the parallel syntax of *Cynthia's Revels*,
Troilus and Cressida depends on counterpoint and antithesis for its wit, as the
auspicious beginning of each phrase is canceled by its conclusion. Ajax is
"valiant as the lion" but "churlish as the bear" and "slow as the elephant." He
may have "valor," as Jonson claims for Criticus, but it is tainted by "folly." He
has the vices as well as the virtues of all men. His natural abilities are rendered
completely useless: he is like a multi-armed giant with gout or a blind hun-
dred-eyed monster.

Jonson is the unintentional sponsor of the satire generated against him in
Troilus and Cressida, since not only the content of this passage but also its literary form bears the stamp of his influence. One of the revolutionary sub-
genres that Jonson developed in comical satire was the character sketch, a

form he introduced to English literature in the first edition of *Every Man Out*, where he prefaced the play with characterizations of its protagonists.[20] He first incorporated such portraits within the action of a play in *Cynthia's Revels*, as we have just seen in the case of Criticus, and he repeated this procedure in *Poetaster*. Not confining himself entirely to a Theophrastan model, he felt free to create both idealized and satiric sketches, as he systematically contrasted the virtues of one good man (Asper, Criticus, or Horace) with the vices of his humorous antagonists. Shakespeare, however, returned the character sketch to its Theophrastan roots by negating Jonson's distinction, rewriting Criticus as Ajax in the generically formalized criticism of Jonson in *Troilus and Cressida*. In doing so, he created a specific literary form—the anti-Jonsonian character sketch—that was to have a long lifespan. When Jonson's contemporaries focused on the immense gulf that divided his self-glorification as Criticus on the one hand and his condemnation of Marston and Dekker as Hedon and Anaides on the other, they could not help but seek to negate his poetics. Even Jonson's Scottish host, William Drummond, included a character sketch at the end of his *Conversations* that sounds as if it had been lifted from *Every Man Out*. Only in concluding does he offer a qualified compliment:

> He is a great lover and praiser of himself, a contemner and Scorner of others, given rather to lose a friend, than a Jest, jealous of every word and action of those about him (especially after drink) which is one of the Elements in which he liveth, a dissembler of ill parts which reign in him, a bragger of some good that he wanteth, thinketh nothing well but what either he himself, or some of his friends and Countrymen hath said or done. He is passionately kind and angry, careless either to gain or keep, Vindictive, but if he be well answered, at himself.   (1:151)

Jonson had taught those with whom he associated to regard criticism as an indication of honesty, and all too often his harsh judgments returned to plague him, dressed in the same literary formulae he had devised to censure others.

Why, however, did Shakespeare in *Troilus and Cressida* ignore the figure of Horace from Jonson's most recent comical satire and base his sketch of Ajax instead on Criticus, a character in a work that was almost a year old? The answer is that not only was this Jonson's most blatant exercise in self-creation, but in praising himself through the figure of Criticus, he had borrowed phrasing from the conclusion of *Julius Caesar*, the very play whose diction he had ridiculed in *Every Man Out*. Jonson's evocation of Criticus as "A creature of a most perfect and divine temper. . . . in whom . . . the . . . elements are peaceably met . . . as it is clear, Nature . . . did more than make a man, when she made him," echoes Antony's praise of the dead Brutus: "His life was gentle, and the elements / So mix'd in him that Nature might stand up / And say to all the world, 'This was a man!' " (5.5.73–75).[21] But in converting Antony's elegy into the stuff of self-praise, Jonson adds a further touch of hyperbole. While Nature might say of Brutus, "This was a man," she is said to have created "more than . . . a man" in Criticus. Shakespeare's parody of Criticus as Ajax, the "very man, *per se*," thus springs from a desire to deflate Jonson's attitude toward himself as well as to administer retribution for Jonson's readiness to emulate language from the same play whose diction he had previously mocked. By appropriating Jonson's medium of comical satire in *Troilus and Cressida*, Shakespeare at once reclaimed his own language and turned Jonson's self-flattering rhetoric against him, just as Jonson had earlier exposed Shakespeare's purported deficiencies in *Every Man Out*.

Readers who fail to recognize the strategic pattern of imitation that underlies Shakespeare's parody of Criticus/Jonson are compelled to agree with E. K. Chambers that the description of Ajax is both "unnecessarily elaborate for its place" and "has not much relation to the character of Ajax as depicted in the play." Kenneth Muir, for instance, repeats this observation in the introduction to his Oxford edition of *Troilus and Cressida*, where he writes that "the portrait bears little or no resemblance to the character when he appears later" and conjectures that "the discrepancies" we notice "may have been due to a change of plan during the composition of the play."[22]

Rather than positing a revision for which there is no textual evidence, however, a far more convincing contextual explanation for the linguistic peculiarities of this passage is that Shakespeare's parody of Criticus/Jonson creates a disjunction in *Troilus and Cressida* between two sets of meanings, one self-contained within the opaque plot and another superimposed on it as a semi-autonomous node of literary allusion. A similar kind of disjunction is found in the discussion of *Poetaster* and *Satiromastix* between Hamlet and his former friends in medieval Denmark. Both passages are explicable only in terms of their theatrical context and were originally devised for an audience that had intimate knowledge of the Poets' War for which the commentaries were generated.

In parodying the description of Criticus, Shakespeare was faulting Jonson for the excesses of arrogance and vindictiveness for which he had been lampooned on the stage since 1599. This can be illustrated by the animal analogies that Shakespeare applies to Ajax/Jonson, who is compared in turn to the valiant lion, the churlish bear, and the slow elephant. The lion is mentioned in a positive light, even though the beast was proverbially a symbol of arrogance. So Ajax describes Achilles when he pronounces him "lion-sick, sick of proud heart" (2.3.86). That Jonson possessed the aggressive, brutal surliness of a bear had been pointed out by Captain Tucca in *Satiromastix*, who calls him "that Bear-whelp" (5.2.185) and names him the "great Hunks" (1.2.319), after the famous animal baited at Paris Garden, where Jonson had formerly acted. The comparison was probably furthered by Jonson's broad shoulders and large head, as well as by the fact that the playwrights involved in the Poets' War viewed their verbal combat against the ursine Jonson as the literary equivalent of bear-baiting.

The third animal analogy that Shakespeare devises in reference to Jonson—the claim that Ajax is as "slow as the elephant"—is even more telling. Of all the qualities attributed to Ajax, this charge of slothfulness is the one that causes Muir the most difficulty, since, he writes, it is in "apparent conflict with one's impression of Ajax's character" (in his note to 2.1.30). Muir is correct that Ajax always seems eager to come to blows. He is more than ready to beat Thersites and seeks out the challenge to single combat with Hector as a special privilege. Yet Thersites calls him "the elephant Ajax" (2.3.2) and reminds him that "when thou art forth in the incursions, thou strikest as slow as another" (2.1.29–30). Nestor similarly bids "the snail-pac'd Ajax arm for shame" (5.5.18). I propose that Shakespeare describes Ajax as slow in order to link the Greek hero to his parody of Jonson's poetics.

Contrary to what the modern reader might expect, however, when Shakespeare writes that Ajax is "slow as the elephant," he is not alluding to his rival's physical size. Jonson had not yet acquired the "mountain belly" that adorned him much later when he wrote "My Picture Left in Scotland." In fact, he was thin enough to be contrasted with the original Horace in *Satiromastix*. "Horace," explains Tucca, "was a goodly Corpulent Gentleman, and not so lean a hollow-cheeked Scrag as thou art" (5.2.261–63). Elsewhere in *Troilus and Cressida* the elephant, which was thought to have inflexible front legs, is regarded as a creature of pride by Ulysses, who remarks that it "hath joints, but none for courtesy" (2.3.105–6). But Shakespeare's allusion is primarily literary, referring simultaneously to Jonson's slow or labored style, his relatively slow pace of dramatic production from 1599 to 1601, and the slow-wittedness indicated by his dull style and retarded output. Following the cultural transmission of this epithet permits us to see how Shakespeare's involvement in the Poetomachia marks the origin of the legendary wit-combats waged by the "quick" English warship and the "slow" Spanish galleon.

Marston in *What You Will* had depicted his Jonsonian alazon, Lampatho Doria, as a waster of "lamp-oil" who slaved over his work while more sensible writers slept. But by the time Jonson came to write *Poetaster*, he was eager to

ward off this accusation of laboriousness and consequently named his Marstonian surrogate Crispinus, after the idiot who had challenged Horace to a
literary race to determine which of them could write faster. Jonson also boasted in the same play that he had composed it in only fifteen weeks, well ahead
of his antagonists, whose attack-in-progress had not yet reached the stage
("After the Second Sounding," line 14). Jonson, as a result, had it both ways:
he followed a precedent established by Horace that art should consist of extended concentration and effort, even as he beat his competition to the punch
in completing his masterpiece early. Nevertheless, in *Satiromastix* Jonson's obsessive work habits are explicitly attributed for the first time to a fundamental lack of inspiration that led to cumbersome straining for poetic effect. This
imputation must have seemed quite appropriate coming from Dekker, whose
literary output was phenomenal, especially since he had been described by
Jonson as a hack who wrote as a trade instead of a sacred vocation. From the
opening of *Satiromastix*, we encounter the figure of Horace/Jonson suffering
from perpetual writer's block, hard at work on a poem that includes phrases
from "An Ode to James, Earl of Desmond," later published in *The Underwood*, and seeking inspiration from a reluctant Muse:

> O me thy Priest inspire.
> For I to thee and thine immortal name,
> In—in—in golden tunes,
> For I to thee and thine immortal name—
> In—sacred raptures flowing, flowing, swimming, swimming:
> In sacred raptures swimming,
> Immortal name, game, dame, tame, lame, lame, lame.
> Pux, ha it, shame, proclaim, oh—
> In Sacred raptures flowing, will proclaim, not—
> O me thy Priest inspire!
> For I to thee and thine immortal name,
> In flowing numbers filled with spright and flame,
> Good, good, in flowing numbers filled with spright and flame.
>   (1.2.8–20)[23]

Horace, in his study, with a candle burning and books scattered around him,
is shown agonizing over his verse and exulting in his "rich and labour'd conceits" (1.2.85–86). "Oh the end shall be admirable," he predicts. When Crispinus and Demetrius visit his chamber they are met by the poet's lackey Asinius
Bubo, who explains with adulation that "Horace is always in labour when / I
come, the nine Muses be his midwives" (1.2.21–22). With customary arro-

gance, the poet greets his guests by commending his own verse. "Damn me if it be not the best that ever came from me," he boasts, as he hastens to explain that "my brains have given assault to it but this morning" in order to produce "the best and most ingenious piece that ever I swet for" (1.2.36–38, 101). Unaware of the scatalogical implications of his own name and language, Asinius concurs: " 'tis the best stuff that ever dropt from thee" (1.2.88–89). "I weigh / Each syllable I write or speak," Horace concludes, "because / Mine enemies with sharp and searching eyes / Look through and through me, carving my poor labours / Like an Anatomy" (1.2.194–98). Captain Tucca, assigned the role of hounding "Horace," is astounded by Jonson's paucity of wit, especially his boast that *Poetaster* was written in record time:

> What, will he be fifteen weeks about this Cockatrice's egg too? has he not cackeled yet? not laid yet? . . . His wits are somewhat hard bound: the Punk his Muse has sore labour ere the whore be delivered.
>
> (1.2.363–67)

The images of Jonson incubating the egg of a fabulous serpent famous for its deadly glance and of his prostitute muse in "sore labour" underscore the complaint that he was slow, dim-witted, and malicious. He is, Tucca later explains, a "Nasty Tortoise" whose dramas appear, like Christmas, "but once a year" (5.2.201–3).

Although Jonson had already been taken to task in *What You Will* and *Satiromastix* for his laborious method of composition, it is in *Troilus and Cressida* that the specific epithet "slow" is first applied to him as a term of derision. Marston and Dekker had implied it, but they had never used this particular multifaceted word, which was to haunt Jonson's reputation. That Jonson was cognizant of this negative characterization by Shakespeare is apparent in the same "Apologetical Dialogue" to *Poetaster*, where he regrets that "some better natures" have maligned him. Listing the "particular imputations" voiced against the Author, his friend Polyposus confides, "they say you are slow, / And scarce bring forth a play a year" (lines 193–94), to which the poet replies with contempt:

> 'Tis true.
> I would, they could not say that I did that,
> There's all the joy I take i' their trade,
> Unless such Scribes as they might be proscrib'd
> Th' abused theaters.
>
> (LL. 194–98)

Only stoic self-sufficiency saves him from despair when the ignorant multitude condemn his strenuous endeavors:

> O, this would make a learn'd and liberal soul,
> To rive his stained quill, up to the back,
> And damn his long-watch'd labours to the fire;
> Things, that were born, when none but the still night,
> And his dumb candle saw his pinching throes:
> Were not his own free merit a more crown
> Unto his travails than their reeling claps.
>
> (LL. 209–15)

But Jonson was unable to suppress the use of "slow" to stigmatize his poetic
project. Just as he had impugned Shakespeare's artlessness, Shakespeare had in
turn diagnosed his inverse literary failing—a tediousness devoid of inspiration. The myth of Shakespeare and Jonson as paradigms of nature and art, as
I will further illustrate in chapters 2 and 4, arises out of their personal exchange during the Poets' War. Shakespeare's quip that Jonson was as "slow as
the elephant" took root at once in contemporary criticism, and the author of
2 Return from Parnassus was the first to play on it in Ingenioso's criticism of
Jonson for being "so slow an Inventor, that he were better betake himself to
his old trade of Bricklaying."[24] The word soon found wide dissemination in
both defenses of and attacks on Jonson. John Davies of Hereford, for instance, in "*To my learnedly witty friend*, Mr. Benjamin Jonson" (1617), claims
that his mind's fecundity made it difficult for him to compose quickly:

> that Plenty makes thee scarce,
> Which makes thee slow, as sure in *Prose* or *Verse*,
> As say thy worst detractors; then if thou,
> For all eternity, writ'st *Sure* and *Slow*,
> Thy *Wits*, as they come thronging out of door,
> Do stick awhile, to spread their praise the more.[25]

For Davies the perceived liability of Jonson's slowness turns out, upon reflection, to be an asset, a guarantee that his thoughts will endure. What makes
his use of this word particularly significant, however, is that it reinforces our
understanding of a previously unrecorded allusion that Davies makes to
Shakespeare's parody of Jonson as Ajax in *Troilus and Cressida*. Indeed, after
the anonymous author of *2 Return from Parnassus*, Davies provides the most
important outside reaction to the Poets' War. A poet himself, he was also a

consumer of fictions, a theatergoer and reader extremely conversant with contemporary theatrical politics.

About two years after *Troilus and Cressida* (1609) was published, Davies in a poem called "Paper's Complaint" in *The Scourge of Folly* recalled the controversy by scolding the otherwise exemplary Jonson for demeaning himself as "Ajax" when his "wit was then with Will annoyed." What is more, the speaker of Davies' poem—the virginal Paper—alludes to Shakespeare's purge of Jonson as Ajax in *Troilus and Cressida* using terms that recall the recently published commentary on it in *2 Return from Parnassus* (1606). Early in the poem, Paper complains of how she has been soiled by a writer she calls Ajax, who has turned his pen into an enema and holds himself "supreme" above the "witless Multitude." What makes her plight particularly troubling, Paper reveals, is that she has been defecated on by the same man who can dress her in the finest rhetoric:

> Another comes with Wit, too costive then,
> Making a Glister-pipe of his rare Pen:
> And through the same he all my Breast becakes,
> And turns me so, to nothing but *Ajax*.
> Yet Ajax (I confess) was too supreme
> For Subject of my-his wit-royalled *Ream*,
> Exposed to the rancor of the rude,
> And wasted by the witless Multitude.
> He so adorned me that I shall nere
> More right, for kind, than in his Robes appear,
> Whose Lines shall circumscribe uncompassed *Times*:
> And past the wheeling of the Spheres, his Rhymes
> Shall run (as right) to immortality,
> And praised (as proper) of Posterity.
> Yet sith his wit was then with Will annoyed,
> And I enforced to bear what Wit did void,
> I cannot choose but say as I have said,
> His wit (made loose) defiled me his Maid.[26]

The "costive" (or constipated) Jonson, known for being slow (rare Ben's "rare Pen"), turns paper into "a jakes" that he "becakes" (or as the *Parnassus* poet would say, "berays") with excrement pumped through the "Glister-pipe" of wit. In apologizing for *Poetaster*, Jonson had denounced Marston and Dekker as monstrous "unclean birds, / that made their mouths their clysters, and still purge / From their hot entrails" (lines 219–21). In *2 Return from Parnassus*, Shakespeare was said to have purged him. Here, however, in a twist on that passage's interpretation of *Troilus and Cressida*, Ajax/Jonson is so annoyed "with Will" that he evacuates (or "voids") himself on Paper. Jonson, Paper explains, deserved his reputation as Ajax in his futile bid to be held "supreme" in a highly antagonistic print culture that Paper wittily calls "my-his wit-roy-alled *Ream*." The contentious realm or ream of print (the world of my-his) that the royal pretender shares with his rivals (and print itself) provides no sanctuary from the "witless Multitude" that "exposes" and "wastes" him. Yet Paper genuinely appreciates Jonson's achievement, except for the "soiled Glass" of his Poets' War plays, published between 1600 and 1602, that served only to "oppress the Stage" in drama,

> Where each man *in*, and out *of's humor* pries
> Upon him self; and laughs until he cries,
> *Untrussing humorous Poets*, and such *Stuff*. . . .
> O wondrous *Age*! when *Phoebus' Imps* do turn
> Their *Arms* of Wit against themselves in scorn. . . .

The likelihood that Davies is referring to Will Shakespeare as one of Ajax/Jonson's opponents in the Poets' War is corroborated in two ways. First, Paper immediately balances her censure of Jonsonian satire (lines 29–46) by reluctantly denouncing Shakespeare's "Art of Love" expressed in the "eternal lines" of *Venus and Adonis*, his "lewd" Ovidian narrative poem (lines 47–58). This pairing of Jonson and Shakespeare as rivals is appropriately followed by a discussion of the Nashe-Harvey flyting (lines 63–84). Second, in Epigram 159 in the same volume (in a cluster of poems on Jonson and his later rivals Samuel Daniel and Inigo Jones), Davies grants to Shakespeare alone, under the same nickname, the monarchy of wit:

> Some say (good *Will*) which I, in sport, do sing,
> Hadst thou not played some Kingly parts in sport,
> Thou hadst been a companion for a *King*;
> And, been a King among the meaner sort.
> Some others rail; but, rail as they think fit,
> Thou hast no railing, but a reigning Wit.[27]

Despite his participation in the Poets' War, Shakespeare remained unscathed, and Jonson could never rival him, Davies states in this first poetic celebration of the poet-player's literary accession. Davies respected Jonson's sometimes captious poetry, but having seen Shakespeare onstage as a king, he imagined him alone, offstage, as the theater's undisputed sovereign poet.

In subsequent criticism, then, Jonson's slowness would become as identifiable a target as his railing or envy in works that contrasted him with witty "good Will" Shakespeare. John Milton's first published English poem, "On Shakespeare," in the Second Folio (1630) thus contrasts the "shame" of Jonson's "slow endeavouring art" with the effortless "flow" of Shakespeare's "easy numbers."[28] By the time Fuller had selected the epithet "slow" to stigmatize Jonson in contrast to "quick" Shakespeare, it had long been a literary cliché. A commonplace book of the period contains the following anecdote reflecting this legacy:

> Mr. Ben. Jonson and Mr. Wm. Shakespeare Being Merry at a Tavern
> Mr. Jonson having begun this for his Epitaph:
>> Here lies Ben Jonson that once was one
> he gives it to Mr. Shakespeare to make up, who presently writes:
>> Who while he liv'd was a slow thing
>> and now being dead is Nothing.[29]

The double portrait of a slow, learned Jonson and a quick-witted Shakespeare that Fuller and Dryden popularized and passed on to Coleridge for further Romantic elaboration was thus ultimately derived from their own criticism of each other during the Poets' War, not invented during the Restoration.

VI

Shakespeare's literary criticism of Jonson's poetics in *Troilus and Cressida* is embedded within the play's dramatic structure as a secondary semiotic system of contextual reference. Long before Ajax is introduced, Shakespeare alerts his audience to the polemical relation his play bears to Jonson's didactic dramaturgy. Jonson begins *Poetaster* by bringing an "armed *Prologue*" before the audience to slay the allegorical monster Envy and to justify his own militancy:

> If any muse why I salute the stage,
> An armed *Prologue*; know, 'tis a dangerous age:
> Wherein, who writes, had need present his *Scenes*
> Forty-fold proof against the conjuring means
> Of base detractors and illiterate apes,
> That fill up rooms in fair and formal shapes.
>> (PROLOGUE, LL. 5–10)

Jonson's beleaguered spokesman is particularly vigilant about "that common spawn of ignorance, / Our fry of writers," who are eager to "beslime" his fame (lines 18–19). Once his Prologue slays Envy, Jonson explains the meaning of this dramatic tableau and states that he will fearlessly confront his rivals in a similar manner:

> the *allegory* and hid sense
> Is, that a well-erected confidence
> Can fright their pride, and laugh their folly hence.
>
> (LL. 12–14)

In *Troilus and Cressida*, Shakespeare evokes these lines when his Prologue similarly enters "in armour." But, lacking Jonson's "well-erected confidence," this new spokesman-warrior is a figure of tentativeness and indeterminacy:

> and hither am I come,
> A prologue arm'd, but not in confidence
> Of author's pen or actor's voice, but suited
> In like conditions as our argument.
>
> (LL. 22–25)[30]

The Prologue of *Troilus and Cressida* is eminently "suited" to the play he introduces. Where Jonson's Prologue predicts the triumph of reason over malice, Shakespeare's heralds a world where such "confidence" is entirely misplaced. Shakespeare's Prologue expects no standard of reason from spectators and thus invokes them to "Like or find fault, do as your pleasures are, / Now good or bad, 'tis but the chance of war" (lines 30–31). This assertion, linking judgment to pleasure or appetite rather than to certainty, epitomizes the play's pervasive skepticism, which counters the intellectual arrogance of the comical satires where Jonson projects a purportedly unassailable set of fixed moral and literary values. In inserting his most caustic commentary on the Poets' War into *Troilus and Cressida*, Shakespeare portrays this literary agon not as a legal proceeding in the style of *Poetaster* and *Satiromastix* but as part of the archetypal war of Western culture.

Shakespeare's imitations of *Poetaster* in the Prologue and of *Cynthia's Revels* in his portrait of Ajax in *Troilus and Cresssida* bear an important structural relation to each other. In asking his auditors to recognize the Jonsonian source for the Prologue's language, Shakespeare was preparing them for the purge that he delivers to Ajax. Trapped within a dramatic context, Ajax/Jonson is subjected to the same minute scrutiny he had directed at his literary victims. Although Shakespeare inherited much of the love story of his play from Chaucer, the Ajax material he elaborates within it exhibits a more immediate theatrical concern. Shakespeare's wide-ranging critique of Jonson has three main plot coordinates: (1) the abusive quarrel of Ajax with Thersites, which comes to represent the meaningless wrangling of the Poets' War; (2) the gulling of Ajax by the Greek generals, which undermines the principle of self-confidence championed in the comical satires; and (3) Ulysses' discussion with Achilles about the impossibility of achieving any knowledge of the self that is not socially mediated, during which Ajax is cited as an example of a man who mistakes his own value.

The pairing of Ajax with Thersites as combatants locked in mutual antagonism features the most personal parody of Jonson in *Troilus and Cressida*, as these two characters' scathing rebukes suggest Jonson's struggle with Marston. In his taunting language of sexual perversion, disease, and the bestial—all enlisted for the sake of railing—Thersites reflects Marston's satiric assault on Jonson. Like Marston's satiric persona Theriomastix (The Scourge of the Beast) in *The Scourge of Villainy*, "rank Thersites opes his mastic jaws" (1.3.73) (with sticky, scathing speech) to tongue-lash Ajax for the arrogant sluggishness he shares with previous Jonsonian personae, such as Lampatho Doria:

> Why, 'a stalks up and down like a peacock—a stride and a stand; ruminates like a hostess that hath no arithmetic but her brain to set down her reckoning; bites his lip with a politic regard, as who should say there were wit in this head and 'twould out—and so there is; but it lies coldly in him as fire in a flint, which will not show without knocking.
>
> (3.3.251–57)

The often virulent *ad hominem* abuse that Jonson and Marston exchanged from 1599 to 1601 is restaged at the beginning of the second act, where Ajax, having failed to gain Thersites' attention, resorts to a mixture of invective and violence:

AJAX   Thou bitch-wolf's son, canst thou not hear?
            Feel then.   *Strikes him.*
THERSITES   The plague of Greece upon thee, thou mongrel
            beef-witted lord!
AJAX   Speak then, thou whinid'st leaven, speak; I will
            beat thee into handsomeness!
THERSITES   I shall sooner rail thee into wit and holiness, but I think
            thy horse will sooner con an oration without book than
            thou learn a prayer without book. Thou canst strike,
            canst thou? A red murrion a' thy jade's tricks.

                                                    (2.1.10–20)

On the basis of style alone, Harbage, who usually rejects any hint of a connection between Shakespeare's characters and his contemporaries, was nevertheless prepared to acknowledge that the audience of *Troilus and Cressida* would have viewed Thersites as Marston:

> of all the hypothetical identification of characters in Shakespeare's plays, that of Thersites with Marston has the most to recommend it. . . . The voice of Thersites is remarkably like the voice of John Marston. He is at once enraged and exhilarated by the sexuality and other abuses against which he inveighs: his railing is uncouth and filled with the imagery of disease. A kind of gleeful morbidity links the pair, and would have made the association inevitable in the minds of contemporaries.[31]

But this analogue is not only sustained in the play's language; it is woven into a series of reinforcing topical allusions. When Thersites scoffs at Ajax that "thy horse will sooner con an oration . . . than thou learn a prayer without book," Shakespeare appears to be referring to an embarrassing event in Jonson's life. Jonson prided himself on his physical prowess, viewing himself as a soldier as well as a scholar, and projected this attitude in his dramatic personae as well as his private conversations. He boasted to Drummond of having killed two men, the first during his service in the Low Countries and the second in 1598, when in a duel he murdered Gabriel Spencer, one of Henslowe's actors. Jonson was convicted of this second murder but was not executed because he proved in court that he could read a Bible verse in Latin, thus taking advantage of the laws allowing literate individuals to plead "benefit of clergy" by reciting their "neck-verse." Jonson only had his goods confiscated and was branded on the thumb.[32] It is this incident that lurks behind Thersites' rebuke. Jonson himself had previously, in *Cynthia's Revels*, recalled his own experience when the child actor of the Induction announces the name of this work, which was probably posted on a sign near the stage: "the title of his play is 'CYNTHIA's Revels,' as any man (that hath hope to be saved by his book) can witness" (lines 40–42). In *Satiromastix*, Tucca had similarly taunted Horace: "Art not famous enough . . . for killing a Player, but thou must eat men alive?" (4.2.61–62), adding later that his "best verse . . . was his white neck-verse" (4.3.105–6). Earlier in the same play Bubo tells Horace that "for thy wit thou mayst answer any Justice of peace in *England* I warrant; thou . . . readst as legibly as some that have been sav'd by their neck-verse" (1.2.114–17).

Ajax's trouncing of Thersites during this same scene re-creates the physical violence into which the Poets' War escalated when Jonson (in his own words to Drummond) "beat Marston and took his Pistol." Indeed, Drummond mentions this incident twice in separate contexts (1:136, 140), and Jonson even commemorated his triumph in Epigram LXVIII, "ON PLAYWRIGHT," savoring Marston's overthrow:

> Playwright convict of public wrongs to men,
> Takes private beatings, and begins again.
> Two kinds of valour he doth show, at once;
> Active in's brains, and passive in his bones.
>
> (8:49)

The plot of *Troilus and Cressida* fictionalizes Jonson's assault in modern stage directions concerning Thersites, as Ajax "*Strikes him,*" "*Beats him*" again, and then "*offers to strike him*" through seventy-eight lines of dialogue. Thersites is left with only one consolation: "I have bobbed his brain more than he has beat my bones" (2.1.69–70). The antagonistic symbiosis of Ajax and Thersites locks them in a combat of invective from which neither can emerge victorious. This, Shakespeare implies, is the outcome of the Poets' War, a skirmish of wits in which Jonson and Marston only managed to expose each other's flaws.

Jonson's shortcomings detailed by Shakespeare in *Troilus and Cressida* are not completely literary, however, since they reflect a problem grounded in the man himself. What makes Ajax intolerable is his overweening pride, his unshakable certainty in his own merit, despite his patent folly. In order to emphasize this quality, Shakespeare imitates one of the central plot characteristics of Jonsonian comedy in his depiction of Ulysses' plan to undermine Achilles' reputation by gulling Ajax into thinking himself superior to even the greatest of the Greek warriors. One of the key features of Jonson's satiric method was the exposure plot. Shakespeare applies the same device when the Greek generals, under the influence of Ulysses, act as a band of gull-gropers in exposing Ajax, inflating his conceit for the audience's derision. Agamemnon's caveat can be read as the prime theme of Shakespeare's parody, warning against the pitfalls of self-vindication:

> He that is proud eats up himself. Pride is his own glass, his own trumpet, his own chronicle, and whatever praises itself but in the deed, devours the deed in the praise.   (2.3.154–57)

After Ajax has been stoked with false praise, coupled with a denigration of his rival Achilles, he earnestly tells Nestor, "I do hate a proud man as I do hate the engend'ring of toads," to which the elderly statesman offers an amused aside, "And yet he loves himself. Is't not strange?" (2.3.158–60). The ensuing dialogue draws Ajax out to the very limits of arrrogance and jealousy when, in attacking Achilles, he actually defines his own defects.

AJAX	A paltry, insolent fellow!
NESTOR	[Aside] How he describes himself!
AJAX	Can he not be sociable?
ULYSSES	[Aside] The raven chides blackness.
AJAX	I'll let his humour's blood.
AGAMEMNON	[Aside] He will be the physician that should be the patient.

(2.3.208–14)

In the surface plot of *Troilus and Cressida*, Ulysses' strategy fails to achieve the desired effect, and his objective, like so much of the play's action, never reaches fruition. Achilles is not prodded into combat by the temporary inflation of Ajax's honor. But as part of the covert plot, the theatrical inside story, the episode succeeds in "letting" Jonson's "humour's blood." Ulysses's final encomium in this scene flatters Ajax for his learning: "Fam'd be thy tutor, and thy parts of nature. / Thrice fam'd beyond, beyond all erudition" (2.3.242–43). These words, as Honigmann observes, "have little to do with Ajax's pretensions, but connect with Jonson's."[33] Jonson's tutor had been William Camden, to whom he dedicated the first quarto of *Cynthia's Revels* (1601) as an "*Alumnus.*" In *Twelfth Night*, Shakespeare had used the exposure plot to ridicule the upstart Malvolio, and in *Troilus and Cressida* he gave it another self-reflexive twist to stigmatize Jonson, who had staked much of his dramatic reputation on this plot strategy.

The most important contribution that *Troilus and Cressida* makes to the Poets' War is its delineation of how the satiric impulse had turned against itself in a self-subverting struggle for poetic mastery. By contesting the logic of self-justification central to Jonson's humanist program, Shakespeare highlighted a crisis of legitimation in late Elizabethan drama. Although Jonson had claimed for himself a pivotal role as the arbiter of cultural judgment, Shakespeare negated the first principles on which he had grounded his perspective—the conviction that he was capable of obtaining a knowledge of truth. The confutation of Jonson's dogmatism is most forcefully broached when Ulysses, discussing Ajax's fame with Achilles, agrees with the unnamed author whose book he reads that

no man is the lord of any thing,
    Though in and of him there be much consisting,

Till he communicate his parts to others;
Nor doth he of himself know them for aught,
Till he behold them formed in th' applause
Where th' are extended; who like an arch, reverb'rate
The voice again, or like a gate of steel,
Fronting the sun, receives and renders back
His figure and his heat. I was much rapt in this,
And apprehended here immediately
Th' unknown Ajax.
Heavens, what a man is there! A very horse,
That has he knows not what.

(3.3.115–27)

Rather than positing an inner voice of conscience as the arbiter of identity, Ulysses states that man is capable of knowing himself only by understanding what others think of him. Where Jonson had taken upon himself the mantle of poetic authority through Asper, Criticus, and Horace, affirming his right to judge himself and others, Shakespeare stresses the dependence of the individual on the "applause" of spectators who determine his significance. Shakespeare uses this theatrical metaphor to distinguish between the poet/actor and the source of dramatic validation, the audience's reaction. The consequence of this theory of the social determination of worth is an effective invalidation of the aggressive self-assertiveness that gave rise to the Poets' War, since each antagonist would judge his success according to this radically decentered perspective, not by what he thought of himself but by what his critics conceived him to be. It was consequently Shakespeare's paradoxical destiny both to participate in the Poets' War and to confute the fundamental assumptions that brought it into existence.

VII

The unflattering references to Jonson in his fictional cognate Ajax and the critique of comical satire that are textured into the plot of *Troilus and Cressida* have both a personal and a literary component. The Poets' War was a witty game of covert allusions that combined a strange mixture of playfulness and aggression. The quarrel generated considerable tension, especially between Jonson on the one hand and Marston and Dekker on the other. But this did not prevent Jonson from subsequently collaborating with Dekker on an entertainment for James I in 1604, nor did it hinder Marston from dedicating *The Malcontent* to his "friend" Ben Jonson in the same year.[34] At the end of

1601, when Shakespeare wrote *Troilus and Cressida*, he had two personal reasons for attacking Jonson. Jonson had not only parodied Shakespeare's coat of arms and several of his plays in *Every Man Out*, but he had also travestied the Chamberlain's Men in a far more vicious manner in *Poetaster*. That *Satiromastix*, the play originally commissioned to refute *Poetaster*, was unsuccessful is apparent from Rosencrantz's statement in *Hamlet* that the Chapel Children were able to carry it away. Shakespeare, by that time, had however attempted to purge Jonson in a more sophisticated manner. Unlike Dekker in *Satiromastix*, Shakespeare in *Troilus and Cressida* refused to sanction the authority of reason upon which Jonson had grounded his poetics and sought instead to undercut the most critical element of his rival's defense. This multifaceted encounter between Shakespeare and Jonson at the climax of the Poets' War in turn became the basis for Fuller's commentary.

Fuller's account thus preserves an element of historical truth that during the nineteenth century was transformed into an unalloyed literary myth, once Gifford had severed the events of the Poetomachia from their theatrical origins and transposed them into the pseudobiographical context of the Mermaid Tavern. Fuller's concept of "*wit-combats*" between Shakespeare and Jonson is a transitional stage in this process of fictionalization, inasmuch as it contains vestigal recollections of the Poets' War. His evocation of a "*Slow*" Jonson reiterates Shakespeare's first application of the word in the topical allusions of *Troilus and Cressida*. But by the time that Fuller repeated this epithet, it had become part of the myth of "Shakespeare and Jonson." Fuller had lost contact with the Poets' War that had rattled the London stages more than sixty years earlier, but he preserved the language of the original debate. Having reviewed the evidence that Shakespeare purged Jonson, let us now examine in detail the escalating critical engagement that constituted the three phases of the Poets' War, beginning with the production of *Every Man Out* at the Globe.

PART ONE

S. Paules Church

the water house

THAMESIS

The Bear Gardue   The Globe

"I will not do as PLAUTUS, *. . . beg a Plaudite, for god's sake; but if you (out of the bounty of your good liking) will bestow it; why you may (in time) make lean* MACILENTE *as fat as Sir* JOHN FALSTAFF.*"*

—Every Man Out of His Humour

2 JONSON ON SHAKESPEARE
Criticism as Self-Creation

IN 1599 Ben Jonson invented comical satire—a new kind of drama that he conceived as an assault on existing theatrical conventions. In doing so, he not only precipitated a profound change in the structure of late Elizabethan drama but also instigated the Poets' War, a debate on the nature of poetic authority that arose in the subsequent attacks on and defenses of his bold dramatic experiment. In Jonson's First Folio, only three plays are designated (in early modern spelling) "comicall satyres": *Every Man Out of His Humour*, *Cynthia's Revels*, and *Poetaster*. Through this innovative trilogy he rejected the work of his competitors, especially Shakespeare, as inadequate for inducing the social catharsis that he then conceived as being the principal rationale for literary representation. Motivated by the humanist ideal of a theater of social transformation, Jonson originated a satiric form that embodied what G. K. Hunter has described as "an insistence on judgment, which is completely new in Elizabethan comedy."[1]

One major incentive Jonson had for inventing comical satire was that it provided him with an alternative mode of writing comedy in a late Elizabethan theatrical culture dominated by Shakespeare. It was at this early point in his career, writes Anne Barton, that the "young Jonson of the 1590's forged a comical style for himself by dissenting from the Elizabethan popular tradition which achieved its finest realization in the comedies of Shakespeare."[2] The motto *"Non aliena meo pressi pede"* (I don't walk in other people's steps) that he emblazoned on the title page of *Every Man Out* epitomizes what

Harold Bloom has eloquently termed "the creative mind's desperate insistence upon priority."[3] Still, Jonson never conceived of the poet as an autonomous creator. Instead, he held a dialectical view of representation that involved the simultaneous discovery and creation of meaning. He regarded imitation, the ability to "convert the substance or Riches of an other *Poet* to his own use," as a prerequisite for poetic achievement, and he urged writers "to make choice of one excellent man above the rest, and so to follow him, till he grow very He" (8:638). Yet he was aware of the danger of unreflective mimicry "wherein every man, forgetful of himself, is in travail with expression of another" and "we so insist in imitating others, as we cannot . . . return to our selves" (8:597). A further complexity in Jonson's situation, however, is that in rejecting Shakespearean comic precedent in *Every Man Out* he purged *Every Man In* as well, or at least the part—its open-ended subjectivity—that most resembled Shakespeare.

I

Scholars once thought that Jonson had revolutionized Elizabethan theater by inventing the "comedy of humours" and that *Every Man in His Humour* was *the* pivotal play through which the younger dramatist established a new comic paradigm. And it was widely believed that its dark sequel, *Every Man Out of His Humour*, was an artistic dead end and theatrical failure. Yet, due to the pioneering work of W. David Kay, critics now generally agree that *Every Man Out*, not its predecessor, "marks a watershed in Jonson's work" and was recognized as such by his contemporaries. Prior to the composition of *Every Man Out*, Kay observes, Jonson had been "content to write superior plays of a popular nature, occasionally introducing new type characters to the stage but essentially following, not leading, the current dramatic fashion."[4] "*Every Man Out* represents a major change in psychic weather," concurs John Gordon Sweeney. Its innovation, he suggests, "is not just a new choice of subject or genre but a radical shift in Jonson's relation to his audience," toward "an amazing vision of theater as a real social force" that "transforms its spectators by calling on them to enact their own best selves."[5]

The most frequently cited explanation for this shift in Jonson's comedy in 1599 was formulated by Oscar James Campbell in the only comprehensive study of comical satire.[6] Campbell believes the Bishops' ban on the publication of verse satire in June of that year channeled its subversive energies into drama. Jonson's new form represented the return of the repressed; its distinguishing characteristic was its importation into drama of elements already present in formal verse satire, especially the controlling voice of the poet. But while parallels between these literary kinds do exist, Campbell reduces the genre of comical satire to the persona of the satirist, overestimates the influence of the ban on Jonson's work, and disregards the evolution of his dramaturgy from 1598 to 1599. Since Jonson was not involved in publishing verse at this time, he was unaffected by its censorship. Besides, the ban on satire seems to have been ineffective. When Jonson published *Every Man Out* in 1600, the fact that its title page designated it a comical *satire* did not prohibit it from being printed in at least two, if not three, editions that year, generating a minimum of 1,400 available copies. On the contrary, the quarto of *Every Man Out* met with less interference than its script had at the Globe, where Jonson was forced to change the ending by eliminating his depiction of Queen Elizabeth.[7]

In tracing the origin of comical satire to formal verse, Campbell neglects a more important factor: the process of generic revision that led Jonson from *The Case Is Altered* through *Every Man In* to *Every Man Out*. Anne Barton points out that these three early comedies involve a two-stage rebellion against Elizabethan comic conventions through which he increasingly estranged himself from the Plautine norm of *The Case Is Altered* that aligned his work with Shakespeare's. She endorses Kay's reformulation of Jonson's career when she explains that in *Every Man Out*, "he fought his way out of the brilliant but restricting manner of the early humour plays" with "the help of Aristophanes." Barton acknowledges that *Every Man In* was probably only "moderately successful" and that it did not bring "the kind of attention and acclaim that he received in the following year when . . . he pushed his new method to a conscious, and very literary, extreme." But she also regards it as a transitional play that "mediates in certain important respects between *The Case Is Altered* and the three more rigorous and unbending comical satires which succeeded it."[8] *Every Man Out* established Jonson's reputation as an innovator, but it did so as the result of a revolution that began, however tentatively, with *Every Man In*.

Every Man In and *Every Man Out* are what Herford and Simpson call "humour comedies" to the extent that they postulate that character is determined by powerful psychological fixations to which Jonson, influenced by Galenic medical terminology, refers by analogy as "humours." Since "in every human body / The choler, melancholy, phlegm, and blood, / . . . Receive the name Humours," Jonson explains in *Every Man Out*,

> thus far
> It may, by *Metaphor*, apply itself
> Unto the general disposition:
> As when some one peculiar quality

Doth so possess a man, that it doth draw
All his affects, his spirits, and his powers,
In their confluctions, all to run one way.
("AFTER THE SECOND SOUNDING," LL. 98–108)

But applying the rubric "humour comedy" to both Every Man plays elides their major difference. The phrase "every man in his humour" suggests that consciousness is comprised of ineradicable compulsions. It furthermore implies a benign and self-deprecating acceptance of "humour" as a universal condition of subjectivity. Yet such a condition must always be psychologically imbalanced, limited by its partial perspective, and slightly absurd in its manifestations. It is bound to be appetitive and irrational. The phrase "every man out of his humour," however, implies that "humour" induces a false consciousness that must be purged for a potentially ideal human condition to emerge. Since the term "humour comedy" flattens out this distinction, it is helpful to identify *Every Man In* as a humour comedy but distinguish it from the genre of comical satire created to supplant it. The linked titles of Jonson's Every Man plays suggest that the latter is a sequel, yet not a single character or plot strand from *Every Man In* is continued in *Every Man Out*. Like Jonson's original spectators, instead of finding *Every Man In, Part II*, we encounter a new fiction with new characters in a new genre that purged the theory of subjectivity implicit in his earlier poetics.

Humours seem ineradicable in *Every Man In* because they are produced by the four basic domestic relations that defined an Elizabethan middle-class household: descent (the father-son pairing of Lorenzo Senior and Junior); affinity (the husband and wife, Thorello and Biancha, echoed in Cob and Tib); consanguinity (the brothers Giuliano and Prospero); and service (the master-servant relation of the Lorenzos and Musco, Thorello and Pizo, and Doctor Clement and Formal). Each of these symbiotic social couplings engenders a characteristic set of interlocking psychological fixations. Lorenzo Senior is a humourist to the extent that his role as a father prompts him to worry excessively about his son's well-being, just as Lorenzo Junior's humour is shaped by a need to evade supervision. Thorello and his wife Biancha are spurred by the very condition of their union to suspect each other of being unfaithful. Prospero, the younger brother, is witty and carefree in the face of his disenfranchisement, while his older half-brother Giuliano has the peremptory temper of a privileged man. And just as Lorenzo Senior and Thorello seek to control their servants, Musco and Pizo assert their independence. The social bonds that conjoin these characters also divide them psychologically from one another.

This social *discordia concors* is presided over by the madcap magistrate Doctor Clement, who, at the play's conclusion, fosters festive tolerance by clearing up the misconceptions that have aggravated relations between the characters' stereotypical temperaments. A walking oxymoron, he amalgamates eccentricity and law, imagination and reason, symbolizing a benign acceptance of "humour" as the subjective container of perception. It is through Clement's intercession that Lorenzo Junior is pardoned for exhibiting the humour of youth, the overprotective father Lorenzo Senior is resigned to his son's pursuit of pleasure and forgives the impertinence of his servant Musco, the jealous husbands Thorello and Cob resolve to trust their wives, and the elder brother Giuliano is encouraged to show less aggression toward Prospero, his younger sibling. Clement condones the humours of Lorenzo Junior and Musco—the rebellious son and servant—because he accepts the "wit" and "imagination" of high-spirited humour as expressions of a necessary *élan vital*. Elizabeth Woodbridge has observed that *Every Man In* lacks a coherent ethical perspective because the "line of division" that separates its characters is "drawn, not on a basis of honesty, but on a basis of wit." Such a play, she writes, "can scarcely be called moral, though no one would call it immoral either, unless it were a zealot. . . . If it teaches anything it teaches that it is convenient to have a quick brain, a ready tongue, and an elastic conscience."[9] In other words, the high-spirited *Every Man In* tempers judgment with tolerance.

Jonson, however, sets limits on his generosity by his punitive treatment of Bobadilla, a cowardly soldier, and Matheo, a plagiarizing poet, who are punished for counterfeiting the gentleman's arts of arms and letters. Their crime is that (along with their naive imitator Stephano) they aspire to be members of the social class that Jonson celebrates at the center of his fiction through his sympathetic portrayal of Lorenzo Junior and Prospero. "Humour," Pizo explains, is "a monster bred in a man by self-love and affectation, and fed by folly" (3.1.157–58). Yet in *Every Man In* only these two charlatans are sentenced to be jailed and pilloried for pretending to be what they are not. Humour comedy, with its peculiar blend of saturnalian release and social conditioning, conforms to the norm of Elizabethan festive comedy. It liberates human desire from the restraint of unnecessary inhibition, even as it implies a necessary measure of self-constraint. It functions, moreover, as a vehicle for social reconciliation by balancing the divergent claims of its heterogeneous audience, predicating unity on the basis of tolerance and compromise. "The point of view, if not the subject matter, of *Every Man In His Humour* is almost Shakespearian," comments Robert Ornstein. "Here, near the start of his career, was a tolerant amused acceptance of humours that blunts the edge of corrective satire."[10] It is impossible to be out of one's humour in *Every Man In*, since "humour" is an inherent condition of subjectivity: social relations are dialectical, as are the perspectives they engender, so the best that characters can do is be accommodating. This sociability entitles most of them to a place at the promised wedding feast of festive comedy. But such a gathering must, to some extent, resemble a feast of fools.

Yet for all this movement toward social adjustment, what makes humour comedy problematic is its lack of psychological epiphanies. Although the humourists agree to be tempered, they never undergo a rigorous moral transformation. Though the characters partake in the shared experience of subjectivity, their idiosyncrasies isolate them from each other. This is why Gabriele Bernhard Jackson calls *Every Man In* a "comedy of non-interaction" in which "a group of personages in a state of chronic introspection is brought together by a central action which loosely unites them, or rather, brings them into proximity." This is different, she observes, from Shakespeare's "comedy of interaction," where minds transfigured together "grow to something of great constancy." In *Every Man In*, she concludes, there can be "no *together*, since each mind is transfigured separately," and "no mutual element can be deduced from the interweaving of confusions."[11] Brought together at last, the humourists of *Every Man In* still seem self-deluded and alone, and even to speak of their transfiguration, as Jackson does, is to overestimate the change in its denouement. What sets not only Shakespeare but also Chapman apart from Jonson at this time, Barton notes, is that "they freely embraced the idea that characters might change fundamentally, and for the better, as the result of one day's mirth."[12] But this distinction, I would caution, is only true for *Every Man In* and should remind us of the difficulty of making generalizations about Shakespeare's and Jonson's approaches to comedy. For Jonson based *Every Man Out* on the idea that consciousness could indeed be radically changed for the better by great theater. The kind of transformation he envisioned, however, was certainly not Shakespearean.

II

Arguing for the possibility of unassailable standards of judgment, Jonson's first comical satire pushes its characters and audience toward the perception of an empirical reality that purges the life-lies of appetitive humour. Humour comedy and comical satire are similar to the extent that the deep structure of both genres involves a series of converging plot lines in which mobile bands of characters display their obsessions. But they are antithetical insofar as *Every Man Out*—beginning with its startling opening scene—reevaluates *Every Man In*'s collective subjectivities.

Three trumpet blasts introduced plays in the Elizabethan public theater. These "soundings" formalized the playgoing experience and imparted an air of martial authority. They summoned spectators to attention, furnishing a formal transition between the world outside the theater and the events represented onstage. After the third sounding the Prologue spoke. All three comical satires, however, (and only these plays in the Jonson canon) are launched "after the *second* sounding," with scenes that invade the theater. When Asper, the presenter of *Every Man Out*, marches out on the stage of the new Globe— after the second sounding—he seems to voice real anger at a society in crisis as he outlines the need for Jonson's new genre:

> Who is so patient of this impious world,
> That he can check his spirit, or rein his tongue?
> Or who hath such a dead unfeeling sense,
> That heaven's horrid thunders cannot wake?
> To see the earth, cracked with the weight of sin,
> Hell gaping under us, and o'er our heads
> Black rav'nous ruin, with her sail-stretched wings,
> Ready to sink us down and cover us.
> Who can behold such prodigies as these,
> And have his lips seal'd up? not I: my language
> Was never ground into such oily colours,
> To flatter vice and daub iniquity:
> But (with an armed, and resolved hand)
> I'll strip the ragged follies of the time,
> Naked, as at their birth.
> ("AFTER THE SECOND SOUNDING," LL. 4–18)

In the character sketches added to the First Quarto of 1600, Asper is one of only two characters (the other being "*the Author's friend*," Cordatus) immune from criticism. "*He is of an ingenious and free spirit*," Jonson writes, "*eager and constant in reproof, without fear controlling the world's abuses. One, whom no servile hope of gain, or frosty apprehension of danger, can make to be a Parasite, either to time, place, or opinion*" (lines 1–6). And although Jonson's prefatory material describes him as the play's spokesman, Asper implies he is its author:

> Well I will scourge those apes;
> And to these courteous eyes oppose a mirror,
> As large as is the stage, whereon we act:
> Where they shall see the time's deformity

> Anatomiz'd in every nerve and sinew,
> With constant courage and contempt of fear.
> ("AFTER THE SECOND SOUNDING," LL. 117–22)

After the induction, Asper returns as an "actor, and a Humourist" (line 214), taking on the role of his opposite, Macilente: a "*Scholar . . . who (wanting that place in the world's account, which he thinks his merit capable of) falls into such an envious apoplexy, with which his judgement is so dazzled, and distasted, that he grows violently impatient of any opposite happiness in another*" (characters, lines 8–13). Asper acts this role until the play's climax, at which point he becomes himself again.

Saturated with metatheatrical allusions, comical satire announces the significance of its revisionism. In the play's superior moral community we invariably encounter two pivotal characters—the author's surrogate who invents "devices" to purge humourists and the monarch who sanctions him. Through this coupling of poet and sovereign—Asper and Queen Elizabeth in *Every Man Out*, Criticus and Cynthia in *Cynthia's Revels*, and Horace and Augustus Caesar in *Poetaster*—Jonson asserted that literary and political power were equal sources of moral authority. And since Asper, Criticus, and Horace are in various ways ideal self-projections, comical satire becomes the medium through which Jonson first postulates his own ideal status.

Despite Jonson's defense of his new genre's neoclassical poetics, its multiple plots are entirely unclassical. No matter how much he was influenced by ancient literary theory and practice, his rich plotting remained indebted to native dramatic traditions. *Every Man Out* takes shape from a different kind of old comedy: the estates satire of the morality tradition. Within its web of interconnected episodes, characters drawn from representative classes of English society are purged of their illusions in the third and fifth acts. The first of these purges occurs when Sordido, the grain hoarder saved from suicide by those he has starved, announces his conversion: "Out on my wretched humour, it is that / Makes me thus monstrous. . . . / I am by wonder chang'd" (3.8.40–41, 55). The remainder are reserved for the fifth act, where a sequence of such climaxes ends the play.[13] To ensure that the audience recognizes their significance, Jonson's commentators, Mitis and Cordatus, analyze and predict them between scenes. In the chorus following Sordido's conversion, Mitis wonders "what engine" Jonson "will use to bring the rest out of their humours!" (3.8.95–96), and Cordatus advises him to expect "a general drought of humour among all our actors" (3.9.149). By the end of the fourth act, however, the impatient Mitis again queries how Jonson "should properly call it, *Every man out of his Humour*, when I saw all his actors so strongly pursue, and continue their humours?" Cordatus replies that Mitis will have to wait for the conclusion when, at the "height of their humours, they are laid flat" (4.8.163–68).

In Jonson's purge of festive comedy, the promise of the wedding feast that concludes *Every Man In* degenerates into a violent tavern scene in *Every Man Out*. Where *Every Man In* ends with the coupling of Lorenzo Junior and Hesperida, *Every Man Out* focuses on the disintegration of Delirio's marriage to Fallace. Unlike a festive comedy such as *A Midsummer Night's Dream*, which depicts the irrational attraction of unmarried lovers complicated by misalliances that end happily, *Every Man Out* traces the erosion of marriage through a husband's discovery of his wife's infidelity. Henceforth Jonson's treatment of sexual desire would be wholly subsumed by the "device" or "trick" of the exposure plot, which became the mark of his comedy in *Epicoene*, *Volpone*, and *The Alchemist*. By revising this pivotal motif, he challenged Shakespeare's concession to desire at the expense of judgment.

In Shakespearean comedy, marriage or its promise sanctions desire in a communal spectacle before the actors and the audience disband. His most radical closural variation before 1599 was to delay, not deny, the alliances of *Love's Labor's Lost* (which might have been realized in *Love's Labor's Won*). At the end of *Every Man Out*, however, romance is subjected to satire: Macilente leads the doting merchant Delirio to the debtor's prison where his pampered wife Fallace has come to seduce the dissolute courtier Fastidious Brisk. "Ay? is't thus," Delirio asks Macilente, who replies that he must either believe this ocular proof or cling to a delusion.

> MACILENTE Why, look you, sir, I told you, you might have suspected this long afore, had you pleas'd; and ha' sav'd this labour of admiration now, and passion, and such extremities as this frail lump of flesh is subject unto. Nay, why do you not dote now, signior? Methinks you should say it were some enchantment, *deceptio visus*, or so, ha? If you could persuade yourself it were a dream now, 'twere excellent: faith, try what you can do, signior; it may be your imagination will be brought to it in time, there's nothing impossible.
>
> FALLACE Sweet husband:
>
> DELIRIO Out lascivious strumpet.
>
> (5.11.6–17)

Expressed in terms of a visual epistemology in which seeing is knowing, Delirio, the delirium of desire, recognizes his fallacy or Fallace. Against desire's tendency to falsify experience, Jonson brings to bear the pressure of a new empiricism. In Shakespeare's comedies, social conflict is routinely resolved by conceding error, subjectivity, and the contingency of perspective.[14] Macilente dares Delirio to assume the role of a Shakespearean lover by claiming that what he sees was caused by "some enchantment," "*deceptio visus*," "a dream," or "imagination," since "there's nothing impossible." Indeed, from *The Comedy of Errors* to *Twelfth Night*, Shakespeare's comedies are regularly resolved by granting the lie Delirio rejects. In *A Midsummer Night's Dream*, Delirio might have replied that he had "but slumb'red here / While these visions did appear. / And this weak and idle theme, / No more yielding but a dream" (5.1.425–28). He might have concurred with the similarly betrayed Hermia: "Methinks I see these things with parted eye, / When every thing seems double" (4.1.189–90). The jealous husband Ford, falsely suspecting his wife to be cuckolding him in *The Merry Wives of Windsor*, asks, "Is this a vision? Is this a dream? Do I sleep?" (3.5.139–40). The play answers yes in affirming his wife's unassailability, as from *The Comedy of Errors* to *As You Like It* Shakespeare predicates feminine constancy as an absolute against which to measure masculine betrayal.

Every Man Out ends with the masquelike epiphany of Queen Elizabeth, whose presence on stage cures Macilente: the envy (Macilente) that exposed desire (Delirio) is purged by judgment (Elizabeth). Asper becomes Macilente only to be transformed back into a pacified Asper when the queen's cathartic power "*strikes him to the earth dumb and astonished*," thus "*putting him clean Out of his Humour*" (3:602–603). As he explains, in Jonson's conclusion for performance before the Queen:

> . . . in her graces,
> All my malicious powers have lost their stings.
> Envy has fled my soul, at sight of her, . . .
> My stream of humour is run out of me. . . .
> And I have now a spirit as sweet, and clear,
> As the most rarifi'd and subtle air.
>
> (LL. 2–15)

Gone is the crowded scene of social reconciliation that concludes festive comedy. Now only the poet-scholar-actor Asper and the impersonated queen share center stage as icons of moral authority. Comical satire is not a primarily negative or parodic genre, since it furnishes a counter-ideal for what it condemns. Delirio is disenchanted by Fallace, after which Macilente and, by implication, the audience are enchanted by Elizabeth. Comical satire recapitulates the happy ending of the comedy of humours. But *Every Man Out* shows a professional bias in narrowing the community that partakes in that moment to Asper and Elizabeth. The play that opens with defiance for the real ends with an ideal reverence.

Yet the original conclusion of *Every Man Out*—in which an actor impersonated Queen Elizabeth—proved to be so controversial that Jonson was forced to alter it, replacing the queen's appearance with an account of her effect. "It had another *Catastrophe* or Conclusion, at the first Playing," Jonson recalls in the First Quarto, which "many seem'd not to relish . . . and therefore 'twas since alter'd" (3:602). Still, he defended his original choice as integral to his poetics, since he could not have discovered a more *"worthy* Figure, *than that of her Majesty's: which his* Election *(though boldly, yet respectively) us'd to a* Moral *and* Mysterious *end"* (3:602). As in the later masques that evolve from this experiment, the sovereign's "Figure" helps to stabilize the new genre. Why did it prove so inflammatory? Stephen Orgel plausibly explains that "when Ben Jonson mimed the queen openly, in *Every Man Out of His Humour,* the theater was considered to have overstepped its bounds, making the monarch subject to the whim of the playwright. Only Jonson would have presumed so far, using the power of royalty to establish the authority of his fiction." When actors are allowed to impersonate the monarch, David Kastan relates, representation tends to undermine rather than confirm political authority. What was dangerous about Jonson's representation of royalty in *Every Man Out* was that despite its encomiastic mood, it threatened, in Orgel's words, an "erasure of the distinction between sovereign and subject."[15] The form of political power collided with the power of literary form. When at the end of 1599 the play was produced at court, however, Elizabeth was content to have her actual presence create the necessary balance between poet and monarch, as Macilente addressed her directly in the play's third conclusion.

Modern readers of comical satire rarely focus on this important element of resolution. John Enck, for instance, writes that the "comic tempo" of *Every Man Out* features a single technique of "discontinuity" that "emphasizes ineffectuality through ardent schemes which, worthless from the start, come a cropper or dribble away." Through this technique, he concludes, Jonson established an "unprecedented" and "puzzling change" in theatrical representation that significantly "altered drama" at the turn of the century.[16] Yet comical satire is meant to leave its audience restored. Each play concludes with an idealized moment of concord: a pageant of the true poet and monarch. Whatever discontinuity may fragment society at large is transcended in this final moment of social rapport. Witnessing this spectacle of conversion, Jonson reasoned, would encourage spectators to undergo a cathartic purge of their own corresponding humours. The effect would be a purely moral comic equivalent of Aristotelian *anagnorisis*. The sight of Elizabeth, the antitype of Fallace, transforms Macilente back into Asper. Each of the three comical satires ends with a scene of social harmony that unites the Jonsonian poet and his responsive monarch.

Much late sixteenth-century satiric comedy, Walter Cohen observes, "structurally excludes a positive moral perspective from the action," since its "vigor derives from the disjunction between the social assumptions and resolution of the plot, on the one hand, and the implicit moral judgment by the author, on the other."[17] Comical satire breaks this pattern. L. C. Knights suggests that Jonson's plays "do not merely attack abuses in the light of an accepted norm, they bring in question the ability of the society depicted to formulate and make effective any kind of norm that a decent man would find acceptable." In his view, it was only in the poems and masques, prepared for an elite audience, that Jonson's "acceptance of shared codes in a given social order" encouraged him "to formulate and proselytize for an ideal."[18] But this is true only for Jonson's great Jacobean comedies. It was not the case in 1599.

III

A new sense of purpose led Jonson in *Every Man Out* to idealize both the nature of the theatrical medium he employed and his own role as a dramatist. Through comical satire he distinguished himself from his competitors by insisting that the putatively disgraced medium of commercial drama could serve as the basis for a specifically literary career. At the Globe, Jonson defined his new form of Aristophanic comical satire in opposition to Shakespeare's Plautine festive comedy and made this contrast an explicit theoretical concern of his drama. In one of the most suggestive exchanges between Mitis and Cordatus, the former worries that Jonson's new play might disappoint the Globe's audience, whose expectations of comedy are Shakespearean. In response to this criticism, Jonson's "friend" Cordatus defines the theoretical superiority of comical satire to the genre it was constructed to supplant.

MITIS   I travel with another objection, signior, which I fear will
                 be enforc'd against the author, ere I can be deliver'd of it.
CORDATUS What's that, sir?
MITIS   That the argument of his *Comoedie* might have been
                 of some other nature, as of a duke to be in love with a
                 countess, and that countess to be in love with the duke's
                 son, and the son to love the lady's waiting maid: some

such cross-wooing, with a clown to their servingman,
better than to be thus near, and familiarly allied to
the time.

CORDATUS You say well, but I would fain hear one of these
autumn-judgements define once, *Quid sit Comoedia*?
If he cannot, let him content himself with CICERO'S
definition (till he have strength to propose to himself a
better) who would have *Comoedie* to be *Imitatio vitae,
Speculum consuetudinis, Imago veritatis*; a thing throughout pleasant, and ridiculous, and accommodated to the
correction of manners: if the maker have fail'd in any
particle of this, they may worthily tax him, but if not,
why—be you (that are for them) silent, as I will be
for him.

(3.6.191–211)

The influence of Jonson's dichotomy cannot be overestimated. For four centuries critics have repeated its myth of a native, unlearned, romantic Shakespeare and a classical, scholarly, satiric Jonson. There has been a tendency in
criticism to blame literary history for initiating, in Russ McDonald's words,
"the process which has dissociated Shakespeare and Jonson from each other,
or, rather, joined them, in a familiar and invariable relation," as "two distinct
personae," employing antithetical philosophies and dramatic styles. It was
through the efforts of late seventeenth- and eighteenth-century critics, Jonas
Barish has maintained, that "the luckless Jonson was yoked to Shakespeare in
an odious tandem from which two centuries of subsequent comment would
scarcely extricate him."[19] Granted, literary history reified their differences,
but Jonson was *primarily* responsible for stereotyping their opposition in
Every Man Out. Barish and McDonald are right to insist that the rigid myth
of Shakespeare and Jonson as mighty opposites conceals significant similari-
ties. But while it is helpful and liberating to explore the common sources of
Elizabethan comedy that they shared, it is equally important to acknowledge
their profound difference between 1599 and 1601. For their strategic intertextuality can best be understood within specific historical horizons. There is
hardly one "Shakespeare" or "Jonson," so universal claims about their differences can only be misleading. Selecting the Shakespeare of *As You Like It* instead of *Troilus and Cressida* for comparison with the Jonson of either *The Alchemist* or *Bartholomew Fair* produces conflicting conclusions. Choosing
either *Every Man In* or *Every Man Out* to represent Jonson's relation to Shakespeare similarly biases the results.

When Cordatus divides dramatists at the Globe between Jonson and the rest, he does not, of course, explicitly name Shakespeare. Still, modern critics have frequently understood his target, based on the remarkable similarity between the romantic tale of cross-wooing Mitis proposes and the plot of *Twelfth Night*.[20] Barton writes that Jonson's plot parody is "alarmingly prescient." But when John Manningham saw *Twelfth Night* in 1602, he described it as being "much like . . . *Menaechmi* in Plautus," and, as I argue in chapter 7, it is consequently possible to read the play as a vindication of Shakespeare's Plautine dramaturgy in the wake of Jonson's criticism.[21]

The main deficiency of Shakespeare's poetry, according to Jonson, is its failure to establish a controlling moral perspective. He was the first, but by no means the last, of Shakespeare's critics to have expressed this opinion. In the eighteenth century, Samuel Johnson agreed that Shakespeare "sacrifices virtue to convenience, and is so much more careful to please than to instruct, that he seems to write without any moral purpose." Jonson's criticism is valid, Enck argues, since if comedy "continues telling the unvarnished truth," it "can do little with romantic love" because it "insists on vitality and human freedom, both antithetical to romantic moods."[22] Determined to accept greater responsibility for his comedies, Jonson saw little choice but to reject Shakespeare's universe of transgressive desire.

Jonson was able to contest Shakespearean paradigms through the flexible doctrine of neoclassical humanism, based on the new popularity of Aristotle's *Poetics*. According to classical and Renaissance literary theory from Aristotle to Minturno, comedy was solely a vehicle for corrective ridicule. "Comedy," Sidney writes in the *Apology*, is "an imitation of the common errors of our life," which the poet "representeth in the most ridiculous and scornful sort that may be, so as it is impossible that any beholder can be content to be such a one." Jonson's definition of comedy as an imitation of life, mirror of manners, and image of truth is attributed to Cicero by the fourth-century grammarian Aelius Donatus in his *Commentum Terenti*, but the exact phrasing of this passage in *Every Man Out* is copied from Antonio Sebastiano Minturno's *De Poeta* (1559). One of the most famous literary treatises of the Cinquecento, *De Poeta*, remarks Bernard Weinberg, stands as "a colossus among 'artes poeticae,' " and upon its shoulders Jonson stood.[23] There is a striking rhetorical ploy in Jonson's contrast between the naive and irrational formula of Shakespearean comedy, derived from Plautine farce modified by the Italian novella, and his own dedication to theory: Shakespeare's poetics is represented by a ludicrous plot paradigm in English, while his own theoretical approach cites Cicero in Latin. Jonson was an imposing scholar, and for the first time in his career he deliberately projected this sense of himself in an effort to distinguish his writing from Shakespeare's.

It is impossible to overestimate the importance of literary theory for Jonson. The rhetoric of neoclassicism provided him with a discourse that advertised itself as the standard of authority on questions of literary analysis. By layering literary criticism onto the plotting of *Every Man Out* and by defining it by what it was not as well as by what it was, Jonson positioned comical satire in relation to current praxis. Fusing his writing with a classical base, he allowed ancient authority to speak through him, as he imagined an audience in both the public and private theaters whose interests were not only literary but also philological and historiographic.[24] By pointing out the defects of the current scene and showing that he possessed the power necessary to reform drama, he constructed a commanding place for himself on the London stage. In neoclassical criticism he had discovered an approach that stressed the necessity of verisimilitude and didacticism, and with these two standards he confronted the mimetic absurdity and moral malaise of contemporary drama.

It is very difficult for contemporary readers of Renaissance drama, attuned to the intellectual faultlines of postmodern literary theory, to recover the intellectual excitement generated by the humanist reformulations of ancient critical thought, some aspects of which, like the doctrine of unities, seem to place arbitrary restrictions on imagination. Renaissance neoclassicism has moreover been seen as a negative philosophy of history, since whatever transformative power it possessed was surrendered to a static view of experience. Even though it was "unquestionably a force for change in relation to a mainly feudal-clerical society," Walter Cohen observes, he agrees with Erich Auerbach that classicism was easily adapted by "the absolute monarchies of western Europe." Nevertheless, Don Wayne is correct in objecting to this perception as being too reductive. "Before we dismiss classicism as dogmatic or unhistorical," he suggests, "we ought also to recognize that for the poet, as for the philosopher and the scientist of the early seventeenth century, the appeal to a universal and objective 'order of things' was an assertion of the right to think and to speak with relative freedom." It was vital to Jonson because "it constituted a legitimation of the ontological status of the writer as an independent subject in spite of his subjection to others within the prevailing social order."[25] It was by vigorously asserting this independence of judgment in *Every Man Out* that Jonson invented the very means of calling all social norms into question.

Neoclassical theory, established in England by Sidney's *Apology for Poetry*, had such a strong appeal for Jonson because it espoused a philosophical con-

ception of theater wholly different from the burgeoning Elizabethan entertainment industry with which he was uncomfortably involved. He too perceived a disparity between comedy's potential and its debased practice, which,
in Sidney's words, "play-makers and play-keepers have justly made odious."
Neoclassical criticism was an avant-garde form of Renaissance thought that
insisted that individuals partake of a collective wisdom for which classicism
provided the basis. Sidney and Jonson both expressed confidence in poetry's
transformative power. The principal function of literature, Sidney states, is
not only to draw us as far as we can go toward perfection, but, more important, to move us to action. "For as Aristotle saith, it is not *gnosis* but *praxis*
must be the fruit."[26] Sidney's attitude toward the commercial theater might
well have remained the same, even if he had lived to see the flowering of English drama in the last decade of the sixteenth century. His perspective has
more to do with his theoretical commitment than with the quality of the
plays he attended. Jonson made the same charges against the drama in his
First Folio of 1616 that Sidney made in 1581. They were, of course, not alone
in the struggle to establish a new mimetic base for Renaissance literature.
Throughout Europe a rising satiric culture defined itself in terms of a neoclassical ideal that belittled the irrational assumptions of popular art.

Yet Jonson understood the threat that the classical past posed to originality. He chafed at the thought of being known as a translating scholar-poet,
slavishly devoted to the ancients. In avoiding the influence of Shakespeare, he
was not about to be absorbed by Aristophanes. That is why Cordatus is so circumspect in stating that comical satire is both new and akin to Old Comedy
("After the Second Sounding," lines 231–32). Although comical satire initiated a renaissance of Old Comedy, it was still *sui generis*. When Mitis asks if
Every Man Out has been constructed to "observe all the laws of *Comedy* . . .
according to the Terentian manner," which is the only "authentic" style (lines
235–44), Cordatus replies that tradition is innovation. Jonson saw himself as
reviving not the letter but the spirit of Old Comedy, and he conceived of his
work embedded in an evolving tradition in which Aristophanic comedy was
only a constituent part, a series of innovations extending in antiquity from an
origin in anonymous song to the New Comedy of Menander and Plautus.[27]
Improvisation resides as a contradiction at the heart of his classicism. Although the Old Comedy of Aristophanes was "absolute" and had "fully perfected" the comic "Poem," Jonson comments, it was part of a tradition in
which poetic "license" and the "free power" of invention triumphed over formalism. Yet he reserved this freedom for himself alone: while he counte-
nanced his own deviations from theory, he could be merciless to others.
Shakespeare's transgressions against the "laws" of writ—such as his violation

of the unity of place in the Choruses in *Henry V*, which call on the audience to use its "imagination" to rectify the faults of drama—were particularly inexcusable because they were so willful.

Although Jonson argues that comical satire is sanctioned by neoclassical theory, this does not mean that he follows any of the classical writers he cites. Indeed, the multiple plot structure of *Every Man Out* has rightly been called "unclassical."[28] In practice, his sources were often nearer at hand. One important parodic component of Jonson's new drama was contemporary; he rewrote Shakespearean romantic reconciliation as satiric exposure. Another of its subterranean strengths was the crowded estates satire of the medieval morality plays. The first character to be purged in *Every Man Out*—the grain hoarder Sordido—undergoes a religious conversion. Jonson's own conversion to Catholicism in 1598 might have served as a catalyst for his new drama of moral transformation. Yet it is also possible to see in the range of humourists who parade through *Every Man Out* versions of the generalized "type" characters of New Comedy that Sidney applauds in the *Apology*. Viewing Terentian comedy, Sidney argues, allows us to experience "what is to be looked for of a niggardly Demea, of a crafty Davus, of a flattering Gnatho, of a vainglorious Thraso," since each is defined by a "signifying badge"—a name, dress, and manner—that reveals its vice. While Old Comedy dealt with the satire of particular individuals under their own names, New Comedy, like the medieval moralities, specialized in the caricature of general types. Thus, it might be said that in *Every Man Out* both kinds of old comedy, the native and classical, merged with New Comedy in a complex blend of traditions.[29]

Neoclassical theory provided Jonson with a justification, not a blueprint, for his self-creation as a poet through the medium of comical satire. On a practical level, he would have accepted the premise that "new genres are formed from realignments of existing genres."[30] He depicted himself as revolting against the conventions of his own day in order to recover convention on a deeper level. His claim to originality has to be read against the background of the Elizabethan entertainment industry that he simultaneously sought to participate in and reject. The past was an ally in the war against the present; even the words he uses to claim originality on the title page of the First Quarto are from Horace, who had similarly distinguished himself from his competitors. Yet Jonson insisted in *Discoveries* that the ancients were guides, not commanders.

IV

When Jonson considered the question of which of his early works were valuable enough to be preserved in the First Folio, he began with the two

Every Man plays. He would repeat this dual chronology in the induction to *The Magnetic Lady, or Humours Reconciled* (1640), where he announces that "the *Author*" who had begun "his studies in this kind with *Every Man in His Humour*, and after *Every Man Out of His Humour*," was here "shutting up" the "Circle" of his career (Induction, lines 99–105). Hence, by beginning the First Folio with *Every Man In* followed by *Every Man Out*, Jonson commemorated a crucial shift in his early career from "humour comedy" to "comical satire." The effect of this juxtaposition was to create a selective literary auto-biography in the first two folio texts.[31]

Through his two Every Man plays, Jonson had come into his own within Shakespeare's orbit, and the pair might have appeared in retrospect to constitute a single accelerating act of repudiation. It was through their evolution that he first enunciated the principles behind his vision of a theater of judgment. In *Every Man In* he foreshadowed his new program in Lorenzo Junior's eloquent defense of the "Blessed, eternal, and most divine" state of poetry against detractors of the art (5.3.314–43), while *Every Man Out* converted theory to practice. *Every Man In* pays homage to the genre in which Shakespeare was the acknowledged master, but it increases the ratio of satire to romance, beginning the process of morphological revision that ends with *Every Man Out*. Placed at the opening of the First Folio, the Every Man plays document a movement away from Shakespeare; to underscore their oppositional trajectory Jonson introduced the revised *Every Man In* with a famous Prologue contrasting its merits with his rival's defects. Yet in doing so, he expanded the critique of Shakespeare that he had first published in *Every Man Out* sixteen years earlier:

> Though need make many *Poets*, and some such
> As art and nature have not bettered much;
> Yet ours, for want, hath not so lov'd the stage,
> As he dare serve th'ill customs of the age:
> Or purchase your delight at such a rate,
> As, for it, he himself must justly hate.
> To make a child, now swaddled, to proceed
> Man, and then shoot up, in one beard, and weed,
> Past threescore years: or, with three rusty swords,
> And help of some few foot-and-half-foot words,
> Fight over *York* and *Lancaster's* long jars,
> And in the tiring-house bring wounds to scars.
> He rather prays, you will be pleas'd to see
> One such, today, as other plays should be.

Where neither *Chorus* wafts you o'er the seas;
Nor creaking throne comes down, the boys to please;
Nor nimble squib is seen, to make afear'd
The gentlewomen; nor roll'd bullet heard
To say, it thunders; nor tempestuous drum
Rumbles, to tell you when the storm doth come;
But deeds, and language, such as men do use:
And persons, such as *Comoedie* would choose,
When she would show an Image of the times,
And sport with human follies, not with crimes.
Except, we make 'hem such by loving still
Our popular errors, when we know th'are ill.
I mean such errors, as you'll all confess
By laughing at them, they deserve no less:
Which when you heartily do, there's hope left, then,
You, that have so grac'd monsters, may like men.

(LL. 1–30)

Jonson points his critique at the "many *Poets*," driven by "need," who can be improved by neither "art" nor "nature," but only Shakespeare can be associated with all the absurdities he names. Jonson thus dilates the attack he had begun in *Every Man Out*, at the turn of the century, when he summarizes Shakespeare's success as a series of ludicrous concessions to popular taste. Now that Shakespeare's career was either ending or over, Jonson multiplied examples and accused him of violating standards not only of art but also of nature. Having been subjected to his rival's dialectical play on these terms in 1600, Jonson now gave him no options. His Prologue was written between 1612 and 1616, and its placement at the beginning of the First Folio gives it the appearance of a general introduction through which he again definitively asserts his superiority to Shakespeare.[32] As in *Every Man Out*, before stating his poetic credo, Jonson rejects Shakespearean practice as a popular flawed alternative. Shakespeare was unable to control his work adequately, Jonson reiterates, because he sought to please rather than instruct, preferring imagination to judgment. What is particularly revealing is that Jonson evokes the same Ciceronian definition of comedy he had called upon in *Every Man Out* when he renders Cicero's phrase "imitation of life, mirror of manners, image of truth" as "an Image of the times."

In commending *Volpone* (1607), Francis Beaumont praises Jonson for being the first playwright to bring "Art" to English drama by insisting on the "*rules*" of "Time" and "Place."[33] The Prologue to *Every Man In* accuses Shakespeare of violating both precepts, although the mockery begins obliquely, with not a parody but a parallel. Jonson's first target is comedy, and just as none of Shakespeare's festive comedies literally furnishes the cross-wooing depicted in *Every Man Out*, so none of his late romances literally shows an infant becoming a bearded sexagenarian. Indeed, Jackson has shown that in lines 7 and 8 Jonson paraphrases Thomas Shelton's translation of *Don Quixote* (1612): "What greater absurdity can be . . . than to see a child come out in the first scene of the first act in swaddling clouts, and issue in the second already grown a man, yea, a bearded man?"[34] But is it possible that Jonson was not thinking of the growth spurt of Marina in "mouldly *Pericles*" or the rapid maturation of Perdita and Florizel in *The Winter's Tale*, since Shelton's phrasing ends with a reference to Shakespeare's English history plays, which also stretch time, transforming wounds into scars? The Chorus of *Henry V* laments that the battle of Agincourt can only be disgraced by the players' "four or five most vile and ragged foils" (4.Chorus, line 50). Jonson shrinks the players' means even further by reducing their enactment to "three rusty swords" and a "few" bombastic words (lines 9–10). In *Every Man Out*, Jonson had first expressed his displeasure with the absurd demands on the imagination that Shakespeare made in his comedies and histories. He had used his own Chorus not only to comment on Shakespeare's scenes of cross-wooing but also to parody the Chorus of *Henry V* that "wafts you o'er the seas," shuttling between England and France.

Shakespeare had used the Chorus of *Henry V* in a conspicuously classical manner even as he employed it to the provocatively anticlassical end of challenging the arbitrary limitations imposed on dramatists by the rules of time and place that distinguish what Polonius calls "the scene individable" from "the poem unlimited" (2.2.399–400). A little imagination is all that is required, Shakespeare suggests, for the "unlimited" play's success. The Chorus consequently encourages us to assist it in "jumping o'er times, / Turning th' accomplishment of many years / Into an hour-glass" (Prologue, lines 29–31), and it even waits to "digest / Th' abuse of distance" (2.Chorus, lines 31–32) as Henry travels from London to Southampton. Shakespeare challenged the unity of time in his romances as well. *The Winter's Tale* is a "poem unlimited" in which "Time, the Chorus," is brought forward to abolish the classical rule of time: "Impute it not a crime / To me, or my swift passage, that I slide / O'er sixteen years," he argues, "since it is in my pow'r / To o'erthrow law, and in one self-born hour / To plant and o'erwhelm custom" (4.1.4–9). And Time cancels the rule of place by asking the audience to "imagine" themselves leaving Leontes' problems in Sicilia to focus on Florizel in "fair Bohemia" (4.1.19–21). In his notebook, Jonson would, of course, find another element in this geographical transposition ridiculous: Shakespeare's error in giving Bohemia a seacoast (1:138). Jonson evidently understood that Shakespeare was trying to be witty by challenging classical precepts, but he treated the defiance of these two principles as a sign of willful ignorance.

The "Shakespeare" of Jonson's Prologue to *Every Man In* relies on bad props and bombast to pander to his audience's "popular errors." He sends down the "creaking throne" (line 16), when Jupiter "*descends in thunder and lightning*" (throwing a thunderbolt) in *Cymbeline* (after 5.4.92) and when Juno "*descends slowly in her car*" in *The Tempest* (after 4.1.74). The "roll'd bullet" (line 18) is part of the larger cluster of allusions to *The Tempest*, including the eponymous "tempestuous drum" used for its "storm" scenes (lines 19–20). For in a particularly inspired use of quotation in his concluding line, Jonson asks those who have formerly applauded unnatural representations of mankind— like the "servant-monster" Caliban (3.2.3), who would go on to become a symbol of Shakespeare's matchless imagination—to appreciate his own greater verisimilitude. Upon discovering Caliban, Trinculo conceives a scheme for exhibiting him at a fair in England, making himself rich, since "not a holiday fool there but would give a piece of silver to view him": "There," he tells Stephano, "would this monster make a man" (2.2.30). Patrons of *The Tempest*, Jonson implies, were gulls who enjoyed Shakespeare's display of this odd, seemingly unnatural creation on the stage. Caliban, like Falstaff before him, presented a peculiar challenge to Jonson's conception of comedy. All that Jonson could do to diminish his rival's unruly success was to cite Martial's boast in Epigram X.iv that, "You will not find here Centaurs, nor Gorgons and Harpies: our page is concerned with comprehending men" (lines 9–10). "If there be never a *Servant-monster*" in *Bartholomew Fair*, Jonson writes in his Induction to that play, it was only because he was "loath to make Nature afraid in his *Plays*, like those that beget *Tales, Tempests*, and such like *Drolleries*" (6:16).

Jonson chose four Elizabethan plays for the opening of his First Folio in order to suggest the shape of his early career. The Every Man plays at the beginning of the volume commemorate the subtle two-part transition from humour comedy to comical satire. In looking back over more than a decade, Jonson, who changed his characters' names, rewrote part of the text, and gave *Every Man In* a London rather than a Florentine setting, might then with some justification have viewed it, not *Every Man Out*, as the beginning of his rejection of Shakespearean norms.

One sign of Jonson's growing prominence in 1598 was that he was commissioned to write for the Lord Chamberlain's Men, the most important players in England. This placed him, perhaps for the first time, in a working relationship with Shakespeare. He was now required, as Russ McDonald states, "to write not only for Shakespeare's audience but also for Shakespeare's company and, in a practical sense, for Shakespeare himself."[35] This encounter produced an early masterpiece that Jonson both praised and excused in its First Folio dedication to William Camden as "of the fruits, the first" (3:301).

Every Man Out initiates a period during which Jonson reiterated and, under attack, modified his literary and philosophical premises in *Cynthia's Revels* and *Poetaster*. And he ended the Poets' War, late in 1601, by announcing another change of genres. "Since the *Comic* MUSE / Hath prov'd so ominous to me," he explained, "I will try / If *Tragedy* have a more kind aspect" ("Apologetical Dialogue," lines 222–24). Wounded by criticism, he abandoned comical satire and eschewed writing comedy. *Sejanus*, however, proved to be even more ominous when in the third phase of his career, from 1601 to 1603, he came full circle as a dramatist, dropping his antagonism toward popular theater and collaborating on the same traditional genres he had disdained. He even swallowed his pride enough to dress up *The Spanish Tragedy* and cook up *Richard Crookback* for Henslowe as he moved back to the cultural mainstream. Following the social optimism of the comical satires, however, Jonson's new pessimism invalidated his commitment to social change as the golden age of Augustus in *Poetaster* gave way to the iron age of Tiberius in *Sejanus*. Jonson's idealism was now split off from the drama and channeled into the court masque, which developed out of his experiment.

Jonson wrote his Every Man plays in sequence from 1598 to 1599; their coordinated titles, unique in the canon, and circumstance of production underscore their connection. His affiliation with the Chamberlain's Men encouraged him to distinguish himself from his own earlier, more conventional work and simultaneously from Shakespeare, who was his employer, his competitior, and an actor in *Every Man In*. For the first time, with *Every Man Out*, he gave his rival a "typological significance" as he began to write the history of his artistic development as a parable of his rejection of Shakespeare.[36] It would have been hard for Shakespeare to have missed its point. *Every Man Out*, the first play Jonson published, attracted so much attention that the quarto went through three editions before interest in its polemic was exhausted. Printed in the grand style (with more material than was publicly acted, a dedication, character sketches, and afterthoughts), it became not only the most theoretical but also the longest play printed in the English Renaissance.

Jonson's purge of Shakespearean comedy was an extremely ambitious undertaking because he believed that his rival excelled as a comedian. When the buskined Shakespeare wrote tragedies, Jonson observes in his famous elegy, he equaled the ancients, but "when [his] Socks were on, / Leave [him] alone, for the comparison / Of all, that insolent Greece, or haughty Rome / Sent forth, or since did from their ashes come" (lines 37–40). This opinion would have been particularly true of Shakespeare in 1599, before he had entered his great tragic period from *Hamlet* to *Coriolanus*. Yet it was still credited in the eighteenth century by Thomas Rymer and Samuel Johnson, who notes that Shakespeare's "tragedy seems to be skill, his comedy to be instinct."[37]

Like Shakespeare, Jonson served his poetic apprenticeship re-creating Roman farce as festive comedy. Indeed, both dramatists began their careers as Plautine imitators. Renaissance comedy was regularly vindicated in reference to Plautus, whose works were a cultural marker of dramatic excellence. Polonius commends the players in *Hamlet* by noting their facility in performing works by the two most revered classical Latin dramatists: "Seneca cannot be too heavy, nor Plautus too light" (2.2.400–401). Shakespeare imitated Plautus as a rite of passage: *The Comedy of Errors* exhibits its pedigree by combining *Menaechmi* and *Amphitryon*. The phrase "comedy of errors" echoes the technical vocabulary of Plautine comedy, and when the play was produced at the Inns of Court in 1594/5, the author of the *Gesta Grayorum* duly noted its resemblance to *Menaechmi*.[38] Shakespeare would modify, broaden, and enrich his Plautine mimetic base, especially with amorous intrigue garnered from popular literature of the medieval tradition in English, French, and Italian novellas. But, as we have already seen, the underlying classical prototype was still apparent to John Manningham in 1602.

Shakespeare was approximately eight years older than Jonson and had already established his reputation in comedy when the latter was listed by Meres as among "our best for tragedy."[39] Shakespeare's doubling of Plautine plots served as a precedent for Jonson's *The Case Is Altered*, which fused *Captivi* and *Aulularia*. The strategy proved successful for both playwrights, who were soon similarly commended. "The Muses would speak with Plautus's tongue, if they would speak Latin," and they "would speak with Shakespeare's fine filed phrases, if they would speak English," Meres ventured, and Charles Fitzgeffrey even suggested that Plautus could call *The Case Is Altered* his own.[40] Jonson's early forte, then, was also Shakespeare's, and Robert Ornstein has perceptively suggested that he sacrificed part of his genius in turning to comical satire:

> Jonson's determination to strike out on a new path of satiric realistic comedy was, no doubt, inevitable and right. But in deliberately rejecting the earlier romantic mode of comedy, Jonson, I suspect, denied something of his own genius, for there is in his earliest masterpiece, *Every Man In His Humour*, a sweetness and amiableness of temper not to be found again in his art.[41]

By substituting Aristophanes for Plautus, Jonson symbolically reversed his chronological relation to Shakespeare, turning a position of belatedness into one of priority. He thus came to terms with Shakespeare in two stages that reverse the pattern of rebellion and submission that E. Pearlman has diagnosed as the psychological dynamic shaping Jonson's career.[42] Pressed to define the new genre, Cordatus replies: "only this I can say of it, 'tis strange, and of a particular kind by itself, somewhat like *Vetus Comoedia*: a work that hath bounteously pleased me" ("After the Second Sounding," lines 230–33). "If all the salt in the old *comedy* / Should be so censur'd," Jonson writes in defense of *Poetaster*, "What should be said of ARISTOPHANES?" Wasn't he among the ancient poets whose "names we now / So glorify in schools," or "at least pretend it?" (lines 186–92). There is no evidence that the debate between Aeschylus and Euripides on their competing forms of drama in *Frogs* contributed to the conception of the Poets' War. Jonson had only to be familiar with the typology of ancient theatrical history to use Aristophanes' authority to counter Plautus's popularity.

In the part of Donatus's *Commentum Terenti* now attributed to Evanthius, that critic defines Old Comedy as direct social satire. Its "arguments," he writes, "were not wholly invented by the ancient poets," since "things that happened to the citizens were often sung in the presence of those to whom they happened, and with mention of their names." But personal criticism, he continues, met with censorship that led first to the development of the more indirect *satyra* (which influenced Lucilius and Horace) and then to its suppression by New Comedy, "whose argument is most common . . . and brings less bitterness to the spectators."[43] Through the invention of comical satire, however, Jonson made Old Comedy to succeed its successor. Thus, Asper insists that he "will not do as PLAUTUS, . . . beg a Plaudite," and, in rejecting New Comedy's concluding gesture of submission, demands the "bounty" of applause.[44] Only judicious approbation would allow his own starved satirist Maciente to swell to the size of Shakespeare's famous *miles gloriosus*, fat Jack Falstaff. Yet not everyone applauded his new program. And the anonymous author of *Lingua*, a student play written after the Poets' War, upbraids a character who probably suggests Jonson with the caveat: "that fellow in the bays . . . *Comedus* . . . has become nowadays something humorous, and too, too Satirical, . . . like his great grandfather *Aristophanes*."[45] At first, Jonson complemented Shakespearean comedy by offering a significantly more satiric alternative. But since George Chapman's *An Humourous Day's Mirth* popularized humour comedy as a subgenre of festive comedy in 1597, Jonson's reputation as an innovator was not due to his first Every Man play. And no matter how provocative that play might have been, it would have seemed timid a year later when its sequel mocked Shakespeare and contested his work by substituting comical satire for festive comedy.

In *Some Account of the Life . . . of Mr. William Shakespeare* (1709), Nicholas Rowe, his first biographer, states that Shakespeare made Jonson famous by convincing the Chamberlain's Men to produce one of his early plays that they had decided to reject. The script of what appears to be *Every Man In* was being returned, Rowe writes:

> with an ill-natur'd Answer, that it would be of no service to their Company, when *Shakespeare* luckily cast his Eye upon it, and found something so well in it as . . . to recommend Mr. *Jonson* and his Writings to the Public. After this they were profess'd Friends; tho' I don't know whether the other ever made him an equal return of Gentleness and Sincerity. *Ben* was naturally Proud and Insolent, and in the Days of his Reputation did so far take upon him the Supremacy in Wit, that he could not but look with an evil Eye upon any one that seem'd to stand in Competition with him.[46]

Rowe might have come across this scenario as part of a still vibrant oral biography, or he might have imagined it, based on the appearance of Shakespeare's name among the principal actors who premiered in *Every Man In* and Jonson's disparaging remarks about him in *Every Man Out* and *Discoveries*. Dryden had taught Rowe to consider envy as a factor in Jonson's opinion of Shakespeare. Jonson was not introduced to the public by Shakespeare in 1598. But the tale Rowe tells of his bid for poetic "Supremacy" captures his growing intellectual dissatisfaction with Shakespearean norms as he translated humour comedy into comical satire and defined himself in relation to a new poetic ideal. Jonson's "evil Eye" did indeed glance at his benefactor, rival, and friend in the criticism of *Every Man Out*.

V

Recognizing the significance of *Every Man Out* as the most important dramatic experiment of Jonson's early career compels us to reconsider two widely held misinterpretations of late Elizabethan theatrical history. First, it contradicts the theory that Jonson found neither drama nor satire to be an adequate vehicle for sanctioning his laureate aspirations. He did not have to base his claim to poetic authority on his own character instead of a choice of genres— comical satire was proof of his status. Even though he subscribed to the premise that only a good man can write a good poem, he knew that a poet's worth can best be judged by his work. His confidence in *Every Man Out* as a vehicle for self-vindication even allowed him latitude to parody himself when the "scurrilous and prophane Jester" Carlo Buffone mocks him as a starved poet who socializes with players in taverns:

> This is that our *Poet* calls *Castalian* liquor, when he comes abroad (now and then) once in a fortnight, and makes a good meal among Players, where he has *Caninum appetitum*: marry, at home he keeps a good philosophical diet, beans and buttermilk: an honest pure Rogue, he will take you off three, four, five of these, one after another, and look villainously when he has done, like a one-headed CERBERUS (he do' not hear me I hope) and then (when his belly is well ballac'd, and his brain rigg'd a little) he sails away withal, as though he would work wonders when he comes home. He has made a Play here, and he calls it, *Every Man out of his humour*.
>
> (PROLOGUE, LL. 334–46)

Jonson could include this ironic self-portrait because it was countered by the play itself. These words, in a marvelous example of contained subversion, are put in the mouth of a man whom Cordatus vilifies as "an impudent . . . railer," one who "will sooner lose his soul than a jest, and prophane even the most holy things, to excite laughter." "No honorable or reverend personage whatsoever can come within the reach of his eye," Cordatus adds with a backward glance at Jonson, "but is turn'd into all manner of variety" (lines 357–63). Buffone fills the gap left by Asper's departure with a carnival spirit of festive abuse that heralds the parade of humourists. His excess ends, however, when Puntarvolo seals his mouth with candle wax. Once Marston represented Jonson as Chrisoganus in *Histriomastix* later in 1599, however, he became more guarded.

Second, a new appreciation of the place of *Every Man Out* in theatrical history calls into question the commonly held opinion that satiric comedy was a creation of the private theater. Literary historians have been too eager to assume that there were fixed ideologies separating the public and private theaters, and that "satiric comedy" was "the private theater's fundamental contribution to the public stage, a crucial impetus behind the expanding range of representation available to audiences at the Globe and elsewhere in the early seventeenth century."[47] It now appears that the opposite was true: comical satire premiered at a public theater, the Globe, where rival traditions coexisted.

The performance of *Every Man Out* by the Chamberlain's Men at the newly erected Globe in 1599 marks the first point at which Jonson publicly distinguished himself from Shakespeare. We will probably never know how much of *Every Man Out* was acted or added for publication, as Jonson began his four-year hiatus from writing for the company. Yet even if all the local allusions to Shakespeare were interpolations, the emergence of comical satire would still constitute the most serious challenge to the comedy he wrote. That Shakespeare first reflected on the invention of comical satire in *As You Like It* is the main argument of the fourth chapter of this book. But before he reacted, Marston, who had recently become affiliated with the Children of Paul's, quickly issued his own answer to *Every Man Out* and became Jonson's most outrageous opponent. So it is to *Histriomastix* at Paul's that we now move, before returning to the Globe several months later for Shakespeare's first response to Jonson's innovation in the artificial forest of Arden.

"He had many quarrels with Marston, beat him, and took his Pistol from him, wrote his Poetaster *on him; the beginning of them were that Marston represented him in the stage."*

—Conversations with William Drummond

3 REPRESENTING JONSON
Histriomastix and the Origin of the Poets' War

Histriomastix was published in 1610 in a version that requires so many characters that it is impossible to know exactly how the play was produced in 1599.[1] It seems clear, nevertheless, that Marston altered an outdated six-act morality play to serve as a vehicle for representing Jonson, a powerful precursor who had already established his reputation as a satirist in the Elizabethan commercial theater. In evaluating Jonson, Marston was announcing his own arrival. As one might expect, Marston's attitude toward his successful competitor, whose literary project was uncomfortably similar to his own, was fraught with ambivalence: a mixture of admiration and derision, respect and independence. But until recently, most literary historians of Elizabethan drama had accepted Fleay's mistaken suggestion that Marston's depiction of Jonson as Chrisoganus is wholly positive.[2] Marston, we are told, set out to flatter Jonson in *Histriomastix*, but Jonson misinterpreted the play either because he mistook Marston's panegyric for satire or because he felt that Marston had invaded his privacy, since any biographical representation by a poetaster, no matter how flattering, merited contempt. It was Jonson, not Marston (according to Herford and Simpson), who initiated the Poets' War by stridently attacking the author of *Histriomastix* as Clove in *Every Man Out*, showing his displeasure with what was an act of homage (1:25). There is no doubt that Jonson parodied Marston in *Every Man Out*. Clove is an intellectual charlatan who briefly enters the play for the sole purpose of rattling off examples of eccentric diction, culled in part from

Histriomastix and the verse satire of *The Scourge of Villainy* (1598/99). "Yond'
gallants observe us; . . . let's talk fustian a little, and gull 'hem: make 'hem believe we are great scholars" (3.4.6–8), Clove whispers to his confidant Orange,
before ending his absurd monologue with the assurance that all he has said is
verified by "Plato's *Histriomastix*" (3.4.29). But was Jonson legitimately "provoked" in *Histriomastix*, as he would later imply in apologizing for *Poetaster*?
Or was he indeed, contrary to his own statement to Drummond, the instigator of the Poets' War?

I

Alvin Kernan, the first major critic to reject the prevailing interpretation of
Chrisoganus as a positive character, describes him as "a mere pedant" whose
learning is "so bookish, so contrary to common sense, and so obviously
loaded with Latin tags that it seems a parody on arguments of this type."[3]
Using scholastic language "as ridiculous as the alchemical gibberish in *The Alchemist*," Chrisoganus, according to Kernan, neglects his proper function,
wastes his intellect, and instead of "instructing nobles in their moral duties,"
tries to "lead them into the bogs of speculative thought." And even though
"he is right in his evaluation of others," Chrisoganus lacks "humility and understanding of his own culpability." *Histriomastix* is accordingly "a study in
social breakdown, and the ranting satirist is pictured as one form of abnor-
mality, little better than the other debased characters among whom he lives
and on whom he feeds." Kernan's reading directly contradicts David Riggs's
assessment that "Marston seems to have intended *Histriomastix*, the play that
lurks at the origin of the *poetomachia*, as an expression of solidarity between
himself and Jonson."[4] Kernan's argument, however, depends primarily on an
interpretation of the tone of *Histriomastix*, which, as in much of Marston's
writing, is notoriously difficult to ascertain. While Kernan suggests that the
tenor of Chrisoganus's dialogue reflects nothing but "impractical, scholastic
hair-splitting," George Geckle argues instead that his language embodies the
wisdom of "the first of Marston's educated social critics and political leaders."[5]
Did Kernan and Jonson misread encomium for irony in their similar interpretations of *Histriomastix*?

To answer this question, one does not have to look farther than Marston's
choice of "Chrisoganus" as a pseudonym for Jonson. The word literally means
"golden born" and appears at first glance to suggest Jonson's unique status as
an inspired philosopher-poet. But Marston borrowed the name from a recently published satiric epigram on Jonson by his friend Everard Guilpin, in
Skialetheia, or A Shadow of Truth (1598). In the first and only other applica-

tion of this name to Jonson, Guilpin censures the poet for straining to achieve the effect of *terribilitá*. Why does Jonson make such ferocious grimaces at the world, Guilpin wonders, when all this posturing is superfluous? His face is already naturally offensive:

> Of Chrysogonus. 30
> *Chrysoganus* each morning by his glass,
> Teacheth a wrinkled action to his face,
> And with the same he runs into the street,
> Each one to put in fear that he doth meet:
> I prithee tell me (gentle *Chrysogone*)
> What needs a borrowed bad face to thine own?[6]

The wit of this epigram depends on our knowing that Jonson was generally considered by his contemporaries to be ugly and given to exaggerated facial expressions. Guilpin's epigram is the first published parody of Jonson. It employs a satiric technique that Mikhail Bakhtin has called "the grotesque image of the body," a strategy through which the satirist emphasizes the grossness of physical reality, especially the face, in order to undermine any sense of connection to an ideal order.[7] This approach was soon to become a standard *topos* of Jonson criticism, which he later countered (when he had become obese) in such poems as "My Picture Left in Scotland" by stressing the difference between appearance and reality. According to Guilpin, Jonson as a satirist is both physically and psychologically deformed, a grotesque of nature who further distorts himself through his belligerent posturing in a berserk example of Renaissance self-fashioning. Here we find him sculpting his fearful persona in his mirror before taking it "into the street," a joke that implies that there is little difference between the private and public man, the naturally ugly face and its projection as a social mask. When a painted portrait of Jonson is brought out on the stage in *Satiromastix*, Captain Tucca sarcastically remarks: "by this will I learn to make a number of villainous faces more, and to look scurvily upon th' world as thou dost" (5.2.263–65).[8] Jonson's swarthy, pock-marked face afforded his critics an easy and constant opportunity for satire. Even though the name Chrisoganus seems at first to be complimentary, indicating that Jonson is fortunate to have been "golden born," Guilpin casts an ironic glance at Jonson's dark complexion, just as Dekker describes Horace/Jonson in *Satiromastix* as a "copper-faced rascal" (1.2.285) and a "saffron-cheek Sun-burnt Gypsie" (1.2.367–68) with a face "like a rotten russet Apple, / When 'tis bruis'd" (4.3.93–94). When the personal abuse of the Poets' War reached a climax in 1601, Dekker specialized in the satire of "our un-

SKIALETHEIA.
OR,
A ſhadowe of Truth, in cer-
taine Epigrams and
Satyres.

At London,
Printed by I. R. for Nicholas Ling, and are
to bee ſolde at the little Weſt doore of
Poules. *1598.*

handsome-faced Poet" (5.2.153). Although Jonson began his career as a strolling player, Dekker writes, he was not able to "set a good face upon't" (4.1.129). Not even Jonson's acne is overlooked; Dekker refers to his "perboiled face" (5.2.253), "full of pocky holes and pimples," "punched full of . . . holes, like the cover of a warming pan" (5.2.237; 258–59). Like Guilpin, Dekker records his amazement at Jonson's animated features: "It's Cake and pudding to me," he writes, "to see his face make faces, when he reads his Songs and Sonnets" (4.3.98–99).[9]

Marston's name Chrisoganus carries a double meaning, apparently praising Jonson as the "golden-born" poet even as it advertises its source in Guilpin's recent satire. That Marston (along with members of the play's audience, including his friends and acquaintances who had read *Skialetheia*) knew the import of Guilpin's epigram is indisputable. He and Guilpin were second cousins whose lives and works are intertwined. The "striking impression one receives from Guilpin's satires," writes D. Allen Carroll, "is the close affinity they have with Marston's."[10] If my proposal concerning Marston's struggle to establish his own poetic identity is correct, he added "Satyra Nova," his attack on Joseph Hall, to the enlarged edition of *The Scourge* (1599) in a verse epistle addressed to "his very friend, master E. G." shortly before he featured Guilpin's name for Jonson in *Histriomastix*.[11] Guilpin consequently served as both a source and a sounding board for Marston's two principal acts of literary aggression at the commencement of his career, as he turned from verse to drama. The evidence strongly suggests that Marston changed the focus of his adversarial criticism from Hall to Jonson late in 1599. From that time forward Jonson alone served as his significant opponent in an ongoing critique that extends from *Histriomastix* through *Jack Drum* to *What You Will*. This supposition in turn strengthens two related assumptions: first, that *Histriomastix* was produced in the final weeks of that year by the Children of Paul's, after *Every Man Out* had already been staged by the Chamberlain's Men; and second, that Jonson added his parody of Clove to the previously completed acting script of that play directly to counter Marston's recent criticism.[12]

II

In translating Chrisoganus from epigram to drama, Marston expands on Guilpin's prototype. As we would expect, he amplifies the range of Jonsonian attributes and associations in a comic plot, and he situates his new Jonson surrogate in a social context that re-creates the late Elizabethan literary/theatrical scene. This contemporary social milieu is suggested by Chrisoganus's interaction with two specific cultural groups—a coterie audience whom he

ineffectually seeks to educate and the common players with whom he unsuccessfully negotiates the sale of his plays. The Chrisoganus of *Histriomastix* represents Jonson's troubled relationships with his patrons and the common players. By writing Jonson into the plot, Marston speculates, through drama, on
his theoretical and personal strengths and weaknesses.

It shouldn't surprise us that Chrisoganus is introduced as a philosopher
dedicated to the pursuit of epistemological certainty or that he advocates the
acquisition of universal knowledge in an educational program that fuses the
liberal arts and the sciences. It was in 1599, Jonson tells us in "An Execration
upon Vulcan," that he began to accumulate the books and manuscripts, the
"twice-twelve years' stor'd up humanity" (line 101) that were destroyed by fire
in 1623. Especially through his study of literary criticism, Jonson was at this
time beginning to define his own relation to the ideal model of the poet-
scholar. It was during this period, Richard Helgerson has observed, that Jonson first sought to present himself as a "poet laureate"—"a virtuous, centered,
serious self, characterized by its knowledge of and fidelity to itself and the governing ethos of the age." And it was then, he notes, that Jonson first actively
sought to test the viability of his literary program by soliciting patronage from
the Elizabethan elite.[13]

Chrisoganus, in the first act of *Histriomastix*, is surrounded by a coterie of
aristocrats, merchants, and lawyers who volunteer to act as his "Patrons," even
as he insists that his goal is beyond materialism: "To make you Artists answers
my desire, / Rather than hope of mercenary hire" (3:254). Chrisoganus's second set of social relations is introduced in the third act, where he unexpectedly appears as a confident, even smug, dramatist associated with the public
theater. In this role, he arrogantly lectures Sir Oliver Owlet's Men, a band of
witless players, on the value of his "rich invention" with its "sweet smooth
lines" while denouncing the barbarous "multitude" who fail to appreciate his
art (3:273). Both of Chrisoganus's professional relationships, however, break
down during the course of *Histriomastix*. In the second act, the coterie audience rejects scholarship for pleasure, and in the third, the players reject the
learned poet in favor of his rival Posthaste, who tailors his work to fit the popular audience Chrisoganus spurns. If the behavior of Chrisoganus were exemplary in both relationships, it would be fair to say that Marston idealized
Jonson in *Histriomastix*. But although the coterie audience and the common
players are at fault for repudiating scholarship, Chrisoganus's didactic program is also called into question by his failure to command moral authority
and to cement social relationships that justify his vocation.

Chrisoganus's problems begin when the nation's new prosperity causes his
upper-class patrons to forsake scholarship and pursue more "pleasing sports"

that "fit the Plentious humour of the Time" (3:257). The scholar tries to stave off their retreat by asking, "What better recreations can you find, / Than sacred knowledge in divinest things?" but the restless aristocrats refuse to capitulate. "Your books are Adamants," Philarcus responds, "and you the Iron / That cleaves to them till you confound your self." His companion, the extrovert Mavortius, agrees:

> I cannot feed my appetite with Air,
> I must pursue my pleasures royally, . . .
> And leave this Idle contemplation
> To rugged Stoical Morosophists.
>
> (3:257)

Again, Chrisoganus cautions, "O! did you but your own true glories know, / Your judgements would not then decline so low," but the nobles' pursuit of appetite over judgment deafens them to the pleas of the man they now mock as "Master *Pedant*." "'Tis still safe," Philarcus continues, "erring with the multitude," to which Chrisoganus curtly replies, "A wretched moral; more than barbarous rude" (3:257). There is certainly an element of satire aimed at the nobles who forsake reason for instinct. They are, in this sense, analogous to the common players who err with the multitude in patronizing Posthaste, the instinctual poet-player, rather than the poet-scholar Chrisoganus. The nobles' substitution of appetite for reason leads to the civil war of the fifth act. Here too, Chrisoganus is unable to intercede and is summarily rebuffed by both factions. What is most interesting about Chrisoganus, then, is his failure to hold on to an elite constituency that perceives its interests to be at variance with his. He is incapable of resisting the ascendent "humour of the Time," which not only is beyond the control of his didactic program but dooms it to failure from the start.

Chrisoganus's program fails because he himself is unable to live up to the Stoic standard he sets for others, a standard that demands self-control as the prerequisite for social harmony. He has a particularly difficult time mastering the humours of Pride and Envy. When the allegorical figure of Envy enters in the third act, she predicts that her influence over the commonwealth will result in class warfare that includes the denigration of Chrisoganus:

> Now shall proud Noblesse, Law, and Merchandize,
> Each swell at other, as their veins would break;
> Fat Ignorance, and rammish Barbarism,
> Shall spit and drivel in sweet Learning's face,

> Whilst he half-starv'd in Envy of their power
> Shall eat his marrow, and himself devour.
>
> (3:277)

Envy does not allow even Chrisoganus to escape her control over human destiny, and instead of affirming his resistance to the passions of the moment, she catalogues his fate among her social effects. Under her spell he quarrels with the players and refuses to sell his plays at the customary price of six pounds, declaring that rather than let his "book pass, alas for pride," he will force the players to "starve" until they "fawn and crouch to Poesy" (3:273). Chrisoganus's envy surfaces later in his long soliloquy on the subject, during which he curses the "idiot world" for neglecting him and wishes himself "consum'd in air" (3:281). "The best Poets," the actor Gulch observes, have "grown so envious / They'll starve rather than we get store of money" (3:283). Thus, if Chrisoganus's didactic program, with its Stoic art of self-control, is intended to change the nation, it fails dismally. Marston suggests that Jonson's humanism, although apparently lofty in its aspiration, is incapable of even reforming its main proponent.

Even though the nobles are themselves morally compromised, one of them, Mavortius, seriously questions Chrisoganus's, and by implication Jonson's, claim to the moral authority vested in the poet's sacred office. Bored and irritated by Chrisoganus's pedantic lecturing and superior attitude, Mavortius finally cuts him short in a pointed denunciation directly applied to Jonson:

> How you translating scholar? you can make
> A stabbing *Satire*, or an *Epigram*,
> And think you carry just *Ramnusia's* whip
> To lash the patient; go, get you clothes,
> Our free-born blood such apprehension loathes.
>
> (3:257–58)

Reference to the genres that Jonson was currently employing (satire, epigram, and, elsewhere, drama) is here combined with an indictment of his belligerence and self-aggrandizement, pedantry (mocked as mere translation), and poverty. Jonson was, of course, engaged in translation and reinterpretation of ancient texts. "He was better Versed and knew more in Greek and Latin than all the Poets in England and quintessenceth their brains" (1:149), he boasted to Drummond. "His inventions are smooth and easy," Drummond admitted, "but above all he excelleth in a Translation" (1:151). Marston's description of

Jonson as a "translating scholar" calls to mind not only his skill in rendering the classics in English but also the echoes of these texts that pervade his work. In *Histriomastix*, Marston was the first critic to censure Jonson for being too dependent on scholarship.

It might be countered that the accuser Mavortius is himself flawed and does not constitute an authorial voice, so that his critique of Chrisoganus, rather than Chrisoganus himself, is being satirized. But in stating that Chrisoganus is unworthy to "carry just *Ramnusia's* whip," Marston, who had opened *The Scourge* by vaunting that he bore "the scourge of just *Ramnusia*, / Lashing the lewdness of *Britannia*" ("Proemium in Librum Primum," lines 1–2), is clearly putting Jonson in his place. This whip, entitling its bearer to act as the scourge of the underworld, functions as one of Marston's literary signatures. In *Faunus and Melliflora* (1600), for instance, John Weever writes of "the excellency, / Of the *Rhamnusian* Scourge of Villainy."[14] In *Every Man Out*, Jonson's spokesman Asper vows to "strip the ragged follies of the time" and "Print wounding lashes in their iron ribs" with "a whip of steel" ("After the Second Sounding," lines 16–20). In *Histriomastix*, Chrisoganus/Jonson is thus implicitly contrasted with Marston himself and found unfit to bear this symbol of satire wielded by the author of *The Scourge*. Mavortius's dismissal of Chrisoganus with the words "go, get you clothes," reminds us of Jonson's financial distress. His poverty must have been particularly onerous at this time, since after his conviction for murdering Gabriel Spencer in 1598, all his property would have been confiscated as part of his punishment.[15] The stigma of poverty might be mitigated by Chrisoganus's denunciation of "This idiot world" that "comforts all / Saving industrious art" (3:281), were he not so soundly answered: "Peace prating Scholar" and "A pox upon this linguist, take him hence" (3:287).

Histriomastix thus harbors an ambivalent attitude toward Jonson, whom Marston viewed simultaneously as a mentor and flawed rival. The question is not whether Jonson is satirized in *Histriomastix*, but how deep satire runs against the current of compliment. Jonson and Marston had both engaged in the writing of formal verse satire, and Marston had even published his work in this genre, long before Jonson. But by 1599 Jonson had already achieved considerable success as a playwright for both the Admiral's and the Chamberlain's Men, while Marston was still struggling through a period of apprenticeship. In what was most probably his first production for Paul's, Marston felt impelled to position his own writing in relation to Jonson's and to achieve a form of symbolic domination in drama that he had been unable to secure in life. In *Histriomastix*, Marston seeks to contain Jonson's influence by acknowledging his erudition, even as he dramatizes his arrogance.

Kernan's reading may exaggerate the denigration of Chrisoganus, but it is certainly not more exaggerated than the theory that he is "a literary ideal." Marston maintains what Schoenbaum has called a "precarious balance" between conflicting motives that makes it difficult, if not impossible, to be sure of his meaning in all instances.[16] Kernan's failure to consider the possibility that Chrisoganus represents Jonson allows him to avoid assuming that the character must be depicted in an honorific manner *because* of its personal reference.

But since Kernan believes that all representations of satirists in Elizabethan fictions, without exception, demonstrate moral flaws, he goes too far in seeing *nothing* positive in Chrisoganus. Elizabethans did not automatically isolate Stoic fortitude from the function of moral censure; nor did they believe that every act of satire was an illegitimate attack, based on critical malice. That "righteous anger" was often exempt from classification along with the other passions can be readily seen in Aristotle's *Nicomachean Ethics*, one of the most widely disseminated classical treatises in the English Renaissance. Aristotle provided a moral justification for satire that Jonson would join to an ideal of Stoic fortitude in *Cynthia's Revels*, where he trades a measure of tranquility for the rewards and frustrations of social involvement. Yet to some of his critics, both in the Renaissance and at present, he had lost his center in a hopeless bid to synthesize two competing modes, philosophical detachment and angry social engagement. But the theory that all satirists necessarily follow a "cankered muse," since anger is a vice, is a monolithic indictment of satire that not only blocks an understanding of Jonson's humanist standard but also prevents a more nuanced, albeit contradictory, reading of *Histriomastix* that does justice, at least in part, to the experience of most readers who have located elements of panegyric in Marston's ambivalent play. Why, for instance, should Chrisoganus be allowed to regain his status in the commonwealth at the end of the play instead of being sent into exile with Posthaste and his actors? One has only to examine Marston's later and far more derisive portraits of Jonson as Brabant Senior in *Jack Drum's Entertainment* or Lampatho Doria in *What You Will* to sense that he was still pulling punches in *Histriomastix*. Or better yet, one has only to consider the difference between Marston's ambivalent treatment of Jonson as Chrisoganus and his merciless parody of Anthony Munday as Posthaste *in the same play* to come to a similar conclusion. For Marston contrasted Jonson not with Shakespeare but with his former nemesis, the public hack and Catholic-hunter, Anthony Munday. *Histriomastix* was written before Jonson had even thought of parodying Marston, and Marston would turn completely against Jonson only after he had been stung by his rival's hostile response in *Every Man Out*.

III

Contrary to the impression given by its title, *Histriomastix, or The Player Whipped* is not concerned solely with theatrical affairs. Rather, it is an estates satire that offers a comprehensive critique of Elizabethan society, numbering among its targets nobles, lawyers, merchants and their wives, and tradesmen, along with players and their "poets." On its most general level, *Histriomastix* is an anti-acquisitive satire that illustrates the corrupting influence of prosperity, which undermines the commonwealth by encouraging pride, envy, and, inevitably, civil war. Why then does Marston refer only to the players in the title of his work, if he means to lash society as a whole? He evidently wants to advertise one of the unique features of his drama: its remarkably specific satire on contemporary theatrical affairs. For in the act of inserting himself into the commercial culture of Elizabethan theater, Marston re-creates that culture in a subplot of his drama as a means of symbolically asserting his control over it. In that subplot, as Marston's title suggests, the main target for satire is not Chrisoganus but his rival Posthaste and the company of incompetent actors he leads. When Shakespeare writes in *Hamlet* that "there was for a while no money bid for argument, unless the poet and the player went to cuffs in the question" (2.2.354–56), he is thinking of the vogue created by *Histriomastix*.

Marston's metatheatrical subplot contains a deceptively simple fable of poets and players. Chrisoganus is a philosopher surrounded by a coterie audience that admires his intellectual gifts, while his opposite Posthaste is a buffoon who advocates naive improvisation and organizes a group of wayward tradesmen into a company of incompetent actors, called Sir Oliver Owlet's Men. The actors solicit work from Chrisoganus, but because his price is too high they choose Posthaste's plays instead, only to have their subsequent productions mocked. In the final act, Sir Oliver's Men lose their aristocratic patronage and, since they will not work, are impressed into foreign service, while the outcast Chrisoganus, who had been forsaken by his followers, weathers adversity and eventually regains the favor of the intellectual audience that deserted him.

No player is actually whipped in *Histriomastix*; the title is metaphoric, referring in a general sense to the work's harsh criticism of the acting profession. But there is one player, the most fully developed of Marston's actors, for whom the title is particularly appropriate, and that is Posthaste, a jack-of-all-trades in the popular theatrical tradition. Posthaste is an alazon, a literary boaster, negatively characterized in a flat portrait that lacks the nuances of praise and blame afforded to Chrisoganus. But he is the only other character

in *Histriomastix* who represents a particular poet, in this case Anthony Munday, one of Jonson's ideological opponents in the public theater. Posthaste/
Munday and Chrisoganus/Jonson thus come to represent a division in late
Elizabethan drama between two diametrically opposed approaches to dramatic composition: the debased native tradition and its more sophisticated
humanist counterpart.

Marston uses the name Posthaste to characterize Munday as a literary Hot-
spur who prefers extemporaneous acting and spontaneous improvisation to
deliberate thought. The character also contains a covert reference to Munday's
role as a duplicitous government agent. Munday was a balladeer, playwright,
and business agent for the Admiral's Men, an author and translator of romances, and a writer of civic pageants. Yet he also served, between 1588 and
1596, as "Messenger to Her Majesty's Chamber," a position that he first an-
nounced on the title pages of his translations of *Palladine of England* and
Palmerin D'Oliva, both published in 1588. Although Munday was officially required by his office to carry the queen's correspondence throughout England,
his primary function was that of a pursuivant, a recusant hunter who, under
the direct supervision of Richard Topcliffe, persecuted nonconformists and
Roman Catholics. In this capacity as a Messenger of the Chamber, Munday
writes, he was compelled "by Her Majesty's appointment, . . . to *post* from
place to place on such affairs as were enjoined."[17] Among the hidden ironies
of *Histriomastix* are that Jonson had converted to Catholicism in 1598, that he
had been arrested by Topcliffe in 1597 for his part in writing *The Isle of Dogs*,
and that he had himself parodied Munday along similar lines as Antonio Balladino in a passage added to *The Case Is Altered* (1.2.1–83). Marston's contrast
between Chrisoganus and Posthaste was thus existential as well as literary.

Marston's covert references to Munday begin with Posthaste's first appearance, when he converses with Incle, a member of his new company. "We can
all sing and say," Posthaste exults, and "soon may learn to play."

> INCLE   True, could our action answer your *extempore*.
> POSTHASTE   I'll teach ye to play true *Politicians*.
> INCLE   Why those are th' falsest subtle fellows live.
>
>   (3:250)

The conjunction of extemporaneous acting and political duplicity creates
a particularly strong biographical referent. Marston was clearly familiar with
the story that Munday, early in his career, had been a failure at improvisa-
tional acting. After Munday had published his account of the capture and execution of Edmund Campion, an anonymous Catholic priest answered him

in a pamphlet, *The True Report of the Death And Martyrdom of M. Campion* (1582). The priest, out to discredit Munday any way he could, related that Munday went as a spy to Rome, where he picked up a taste for improvised acting. But when "this scholar . . . did play extempore, those gentlemen and others which were present can best give witness to his dexterity, who, being weary of his folly, hissed him from the stage."[18] Marston weaves this gossip, with its key word "extempore," into *Histriomastix* and even includes a fictional re-creation of Munday's fiasco. When the actors gather to rehearse *The Prodigal Child*, Posthaste volunteers to perform it "extempore" (3:260), only to be rebuffed. But when *The Prodigal Child* is halted by its learned audience, Posthaste breaks in: "My Lords, / of your accords, / some better pleasure for to bring, . . . I *Posthaste* the Poet, / extempore can sing" (3:265). Landulpho provides a theme for Posthaste to improvise on, but when the poet concludes, he responds: "I blush in your behalves at this base trash" (3:266).

Munday had written political pamphlets, including *A Watch-Word to England to Beware of Traitors* (1584), was a low-level government functionary, and had served in various "employments" for the City of London. For these reasons, Posthaste offers to teach the players how to *impersonate* "true *Politicians*," and the gullible Clout later asks, "Is't not pity this fellow's not employed in matters of State?" (3:260). But Incle rejects Posthaste's offer to instruct him because the word "politician," in its negative connotation, refers to a "politic" person—a schemer, plotter, or intriguer—thereby suggesting an indictment of Munday's career as a government informant. The word was also commonly used to describe an acting company's business agent, and Munday was regularly employed by the Admiral's Men in this capacity.

Munday, whom Jonson evokes as Antonio Balladino in *The Case Is Altered*, had been a ballad singer in his youth, and Marston combines this activity with Munday's theatrical interests to produce a caricature of an immoral poet wholly devoted to the creation of the lowest forms of popular entertainment. Plays and ballads are indistinguishable for Posthaste. Asked by the actors how he is proceeding with "the new plot of the prodigal child," he replies, "There's two sheets done in folio, will cost two shillings in time" (3:259). Even Munday's honorary association with the draper's guild, which he often touted on the title pages of his publications, is drawn on by Marston to indict his intellectual superficiality. Posthaste absurdly defines himself as a "Gentleman, that hath a clean shirt on, with some learning" (3:263). Lulled by prosperity at the beginning of the play, Gulch voices the actors' pleasure with Posthaste's humble style: "Well fellows, I never heard happier stuff. / Here's no new luxury or blandishment, / But plenty of old England's mother words" (3:260). Drayton had similarly praised the "true method" of Munday's "home-born style" in his commendatory poem to *The Second Book of Primaleon of Greece* (1596). But soon even the players, who formerly regarded Posthaste as "a Gentleman scholar" (3:263), come to understand that his work is a tissue of rhetorical absurdities and that his name, posted near the playhouse entrance before performances, is a bad advertisement for their company. So they consequently shout him down when he begins to recite the beginning of his new work: "Our Prologue peaceth. . . ."

> GULCH Peaceth? what peaking Pageanter penned that?
> BELCH Who but Master *Posthaste*.
> GUTT It is as dangerous to read his name at a play-door
> As a printed bill on a plague door.
>
> (3:282)

As Gulch implies, Posthaste/Munday was at the time also writing civic pageants. Marston's criticism is summarized in the Italian aristocrat Landulpho's rebuke when the players try to pass off Posthaste's drivel to an elite audience. After being subjected to an odd blend of romance and morality in a discontinuous play fusing *Troilus and Cressida* and *The Prodigal Child*, Landulpho explodes:

> Most ugly lines and base brown-paper stuff
> Thus to abuse our heavenly poesy,
> That sacred offspring from the brain of Jove,
> Thus to be mangled with prophane absurds,
> Strangled and chok'd with lawless bastard's words.
>
> (3:264)

Even though Marston makes the actors look ridiculous, he shows the quality of a theatrical performance to be primarily a function of the dramatic text upon which it is based, so that the company's selection of a poet invariably determines its artistic vision. Posthaste is both the players' choice and a player himself. He is the quintessence of the lowest common denominator of popular taste, and his fate in *Histriomastix* is inextricably tied to that of his fellows.

Despite his criticisms of Jonson, Marston shows far more respect for Chrisoganus than for Posthaste. This dichotomy between the poet-scholar and the poet-player must be factored into any consideration of Chrisoganus's status in the play. In opposition to the usual fare offered by the Elizabethan entertainment industry, Chrisoganus advocates a higher standard of "Art" than his culture is generally willing to accept. He voices the despair of those disaffected academics at the end of the sixteenth century who watched others prosper

> whilst pale *Artisans*
> Pine in the shades of gloomy *Academes*,
> Faint in pursuit of virtue, . . .
> For want of liberal food: for liberal Art,
> Give up the goal to sluggish *Ignorance*.
> (3:282)

This is a far cry from the moral and technical incompetence of Posthaste, in comparison to whom Chrisoganus *is* golden. Although Marston's representation of Jonson derives from Guilpin's in *Skialetheia*, it cannot be reduced to parody but is instead fundamentally ambivalent. Marston's attitude toward Munday, on the other hand, is *entirely* sarcastic. Critics who either equate Chrisoganus with Posthaste or distinguish them as polar opposites misread the play. What blinds most readers to Chrisoganus's intellectual and moral flaws is what appears to be his exemplary position as both a humanist scholar who argues for self-control and an accomplished playwright who denounces a popular but discredited theater culture. Indeed, when the nobles again seek his assistance at the conclusion of the play, Chrisoganus is still treated as a paragon of spiritual "concord" whom the "heavens have created" (3:296).

Histriomastix, however, is hedged with doubts about the ability of Jonson's humanist poetics to reform society. In the central action of the play, Chrisoganus is incapable of morally transforming a nation that resists his rhetoric. And according to the view of social history projected in the play's cyclical plot, it is the "humour of the time" and not the moral power of the poet-scholar that determines the nature of human consciousness. *Histriomastix* is, above all, an anti-acquisitive satire, the main purpose of which is to define the way in which social reality is controlled by a series of changes, beginning with Peace (Act 1) and Plenty (Act 2), through the disruptive phases of Pride and Envy (Act 3), leading to War (Act 4), until, with Poverty (Act 5), Peace (Act 6) miraculously returns, and with it the goddess Astrea, who initiates a golden age. Before each of the acts, the time's "humour" is handed on from one reigning deity to another in an allegorical tableau that attributes historical causation to the collective spirit of the age. Thus, in an effort to contain Jonson's satiric humanism, Marston creates a deterministic universe modeled on the common medieval notion of a Wheel of Fortune. Marston's treatment of this theme can be summarized by a poem translated by George Puttenham in

The Art of English Poesy (1589) from the coauthor of the *Romance of the Rose*, Jean de Meun.

> Peace makes plenty, plenty makes pride;
> Pride brings quarrel, and quarrel brings war;
> War brings spoil, and spoil poverty,
> Poverty patience, and patience peace:
> So peace brings war, and war brings peace.[19]

The one difference between de Meun's version of history and Marston's, however, is that Marston superimposes a golden age inaugurated by the accession in act 6 of Queen Elizabeth, who is invoked as the goddess Astrea. "I resign," Peace submits. "What I am is by Thee, my self am thine." It is Astrea who now brings in tow the "*Arts*" that will "flourish" under the true "Queen of *Peace*" (3:301). Peace's commendation of Elizabeth/Astrea voices the hope that time will now stand still for the new political order occasioned by her masque-like presence:

> Mount Empress, whose praise for *Peace* shall mount,
> Whose glory, which thy solid virtues won,
> Shall honor *Europe* whilst there shines a Sun.
> . . . live as long
> As Time hath life, and *Fame* a worthy tongue. . . .
> All sing *Paeans* to her sacred worth,
> Which none but Angels' tongues can warble forth:
> Yet sing, for though we cannot light the Sun,
> Yet utmost might hath kind acceptance won.
>
> (3:301)

Jonson attempts to depict the analogous power of poet and sovereign in the original conclusion of *Every Man Out*, when he represents Asper and Elizabeth together on stage. Marston, however, sees the same relationship quite differently in *Histriomastix*. Rather than strengthening the status of the poet, Marston's political mysticism, associated with the rise of Astrea/Elizabeth, makes the poet-scholar wholly subject to and dependent on an external source of power. At best, the poet can only hope to be bathed in the influence of the "Sun" he "cannot light." If the nobles return to his instruction it will be as a result of Astrea's rule, not anything Chrisoganus has personally done. The sage will benefit from an age of peace that turns its eyes toward scholarship, but he cannot fix its vision. Marston undermines the concept of poetic authority, since the didactic program Chrisoganus advocates does nothing to bring about the reign of Astrea with which *Histriomastix* triumphantly ends.

IV

The generation of satirists that emerged in the late 1590s—writers such as Marston, Jonson, Hall, Donne, Guilpin, Weever, and Davies—is so homogeneous in its social and educational background that modern critics often treat it as a group that shares a common intellectual orientation. Whether analyzed with Harold Bloom's theory of the anxiety of influence or René Girard's concept of "mimetic rivalry," these satirists are generally depicted as having quarreled with each other *only* because they were so similar. Availing himself of Girard's notion of a crisis of "No Difference," Riggs concludes of Jonson and Marston that: "A contemporary [Elizabethan] observer would . . . have surmised that two men who resembled one another so closely were bound to quarrel. The Elizabethan theory of social order rested on the assumption that two individuals will behave peacefully if—and only if—they can assign each other to a graduated social hierarchy."[20] This assessment explains how the obsessive ranking of poets in *The Scourge* and *Histriomastix* is meant to leave the impression that only the author John Marston and, perhaps, his friend Everard Guilpin are worthy of the audience's attention. Both on the page and on the stage, Marston sought to increase his and Guilpin's credit at the expense of the satirists Hall and Jonson. Marston had gained considerable notoriety for his literary flyting with Hall between 1598 and 1599. Indeed, for their efforts at personal satire Marston and Hall together received one very good and another devastating review. The always enthusiastic Francis Meres saw a healthy exchange of views in the invective they launched against each other since, he argues in *Palladis Tamia* (1598), it served as a vehicle for verifying and correcting otherwise uncontested philosophical assumptions. It was through this war of truths, Meres maintains, that dogma submits to dialogue:

> As that ship is endangered, where all lean to one side, but is in safety, one leaning one way, and another another way; so the dissension of Poets among themselves, doth make them, that they less infect their readers. And for this purpose our Satirists, Hall, [and] *the Author of . . . Certain Satires* . . . are very profitable.[21]

Some Elizabethans, however, were terrified by the excessive contention for status that threatened to undermine the very concept of social hierarchy. This indeed was the way in which John Whitgift, Archbishop of Canterbury, and Richard Bancroft, Bishop of London, viewed the controversy between Marston and Hall when, on 1 June 1599, they ordered a general ban on the publication of epigrams and satires and the confiscation of all copies of *The Scourge*, *Skialetheia*, and *Virgidemiae*. They also stipulated that, among others, the works of Marston and Guilpin, the instigators of the latest war of words, should be publicly burned, an order that was carried out three days later by the stationers. Marston was, from the start, interested in evaluating his rivals in an aggressive manner, and he transferred his involvement in "the dissension of Poets" from *Certain Satires* and *The Scourge* to *Histriomastix*, exchanging adversaries—Hall for Jonson—with genres. Although *Histriomastix* was performed without civil or ecclesiastical interference, it met with literary and personal retaliation. Marston's representation of Jonson as Chrisoganus prompted not only Jonson's parody of Marston in *Every Man Out* but also Jonson's assault and robbing of him (as he twice bragged to Drummond). Jonson commemorated the drubbing in Epigram LXVIII, on the "Playwright convict of public wrongs," who "Takes private beatings" (lines 1–2).

Yet the Girardian concept of imitation (the mimetic rivalry of "No Difference") used by Riggs to explain the literary war between Marston and Jonson unduly minimizes the philosophical disagreements that divided Marston, Hall, and Jonson at the end of the sixteenth century. The satirists of the late 1590s were not carbon copies of each other who created controversy merely to disguise their similar premises and programs. Marston's peculiar difference in philosophical outlook, as much as his need to distinguish himself from the pack, conditions his critiques. What separates him from his two rivals is their unequivocal commitment to the idea of their own moral and literary authority. Marston viewed Jonson and Hall as possessing a set of values based on right reason and Stoic self-sufficiency, out of which they commanded the authority of punitive satire. And although on occasion he assumes the same stance, he repeatedly rejected the philosophical certainty predicated by his rivals. "Hall's self-complacency, and the calm confidence with which he assumed the censor's seat," writes Arnold Stein, "were gall to Marston."[22] This self-confidence, so alien to Marston, allows Chrisoganus to turn aside the threat of philosophical skepticism posed by Mavortius, who seeks to drive a wedge between knowledge and the arts that is inimical to didactic humanism:

MAVORTIUS   But if (by Art) as all our Artists say,
             There is no real truth to be attain'd,
             Why should we labour in their loves bestow?
             The wisest said: *I know I nothing know.*

CHRISOGANUS   The wisest was a fool for saying so.

$$(3:249)$$

After Chrisoganus's attempted refutation of Socrates, the issue comes to a stalemate and Philarchus generously concedes, "Although I am not satisfied in this, / It doth me good to hear him thus discourse" (3:250). What is unique about Marston, as critics have long noticed, is the degree to which his faith in the humanist program of right reason and didactic satire is constantly erased by doubt that leads to a new and critical phase in the development of Renaissance satire in which the ideal of self-knowledge is replaced by skepticism. Whereas Jonson and Hall affirmed their sense of poetic authority on personal conviction and turned their social and literary critiques outward, Marston redirected the scourge upon his rivals *and* himself, in sado-masochistic abuse that denies the fundamental conception of a humanist poetics. Who else would write in the margin of his own satire, "*Huc usque Xylinum*" (up to this point, bombast)?[23] In his first volume, *Certain Satires*, Marston defined himself as a poet by cultivating an oppositional voice of self-incrimination as an answer to Hall's expression of poetic authority:

> But since myself am not immaculate,
> But many spots my mind doth vitiate,
> I'll leave the white robe and the biting rhymes
> Unto our modern Satyr's sharpest lines.

$$(2.11–14)$$

"Beneath the brash bluster of the satires," observes Arnold Davenport, "there lurks a dark pessimistic weariness that falls little short of complete despair."[24] This doubt about the nature of poetic authority informs not only Marston's self-presentations but also his ambivalent representation of Jonson as Chrisoganus in *Histriomastix*. And even if Marston had held Jonson in high regard, this scruple would have found its way into his critique. It is at these crucial junctures in his writing that Marston embraces the "naturalism" of the Counter-Renaissance and contradicts the didactic model of his humanist precursors.[25] In his movement away from the ideal, he created the persona of the snarling satirist whose vision reflects the dark truth of human inadequacy. Instead of the humanist standards of truth and fame, Marston identifies his work with "Opinion," the source of human error, and "Detraction," the subverter of merit. *The Scourge* ends with a prayer "To everlasting Oblivion," a phrase that anticipates the inscription that Marston would later order for his tombstone in the Middle Temple church: *Oblivioni Sacrum*.

What links Marston's critique of Hall in *Certain Satires* with his critique of Jonson in *Histriomastix* is his questioning of humanist poetics. In the satires Marston makes explicit the doubts about literary didacticism that underlie his depiction of Chrisoganus. In Satire IV of *The Scourge* (lines 99–166), for instance, the Aristotelian proposition that virtue can be acquired through "*our will or force*" is denied, a position that contradicts the basic premise of didactic satire and at the same time leads to Marston's model of historical determinism in *Histriomastix*. In "Satire VII: A Cynic Satire," the most pessimistic in the volume, Marston begins by assuming the compromised voice of Shakespeare's Machiavellian Richard III: "*A Man, a man, a kingdom for a man.*" The phrasing is Shakespeare's, but the project is that of the cynic Diogenes (equally admired by Nietzsche), who "lit a lamp in broad daylight and said, as he went about, 'I am looking for a man.' "[26] Marston, however, proves no more successful than Diogenes, since "*Circe's* charm / Hath turn'd them all to Swine" (lines 4–5). The human condition might be so hopeless, Marston ventures, that neither the educated "will" nor the supernatural order of grace can rectify its distress. If Seneca's *Epistles* are right, he speculates, that the "souls of men, from that great soul ensue":

> Then sure the slime that from our souls do flow
> Have stopp'd those pipes by which it was convey'd.
>
> (LL. 197–200)

Jonathan Dollimore, who fully appreciates Marston's struggle with Stoicism, captures the Augustinian or Calvinist tenor of this passage when he writes that "Marston uses a Protestant estimate of man to deny the stoic belief in man's rational estimate of man." Dollimore, however, takes this argument too far when he adds that Marston is here "suggesting also that man is so degenerate that he has *no* relation to God," and that thus he "violates the central premise of Calvinism (or at least jars its most sensitive nerve)."[27] For Marston ends the next satire by praying for inspiration:

> Return, return, sacred *Synderesis*,
> Inspire our trunks, let not such mud as this
> Pollute us still. Awake our lethargy,
> Raise us from out our brain-sick foolery.
>
> (8.211–14)

That Jonson associated this concept of "*Synderesis*," the infusion of inspiration or grace, with Marston's theological perspective is indicated by his selection of this wonderfully abstruse word for ridicule in *Every Man Out* (3.4.22).[28] Marston is not as radical as Dollimore would have us believe; he comes closer to being an anti-Pelagian theologian than a materialist. Although Marston's satire makes an essential contribution to the emergence of subjectivity in late Renaissance culture, he never challenges the notion that there is a supernatural order, the domain of a *deus absconditus*, controlling human experience. Jonson knew this full well, since he slyly comments to Drummond that "Marston wrote his Father-in-Law's preachings and his Father-in-Law his Comedies" (1:138). The epiphany of Astrea/Elizabeth at the conclusion of *Histriomastix* is symbolically equivalent to the "sacred *Synderesis*" that Marston prays for in *The Scourge*. Marston's thought leads from skepticism about the value of corrective satire in his poetry and drama to his ordination as an Anglican priest in 1609, at the end of his literary career.

Modern criticism has trivialized the Poets' War by characterizing it as either a series of personal vendettas or a publicity stunt designed to generate a profit. It would be wrong, of course, to exclude either of these motives as a contributing factor. Mercenary self-advertisement might be said to be at the root of all careerist activity. Nevertheless, the Poets' War involved much more serious issues. Even if the plays constitute a literary social game, this game involved the reputations of several of the most important writers of the late Elizabethan period. The controversy it generated spilled over into physical violence when Jonson not only parodied but also assaulted and robbed Marston for subjecting him to public ridicule. But, more important, the Poets' War involved a debate on the theory of literature. No matter how *ad hominem* the criticism became, it continued to be defined in relation to a philosophy of literature Jonson literally represented. As a struggle to establish literary reputations, the Poets' War was consequently both as playful and as serious as literature itself. The stage-quarrel thus afforded Marston and Jonson a means of aggressively expressing differences that inhered in their divergent approaches to literary theory.

In *Histriomastix*, Chrisoganus displays not only Marston's divided attitude toward Jonson but also his ambivalence about the satiric movement of which he was a member and his skepticism about the didactic value of literature itself. The character of Chrisoganus supplied him with a vehicle for reflecting on the problems facing any self-appointed professor of poetic authority. But it should not surprise us that Jonson resisted being used in this manner. The paradox of Marston's participation in the Poets' War is that he sought to obtain the rewards of glory—intellectual mastery and cultural predominance over Jonson—by philosophically questioning the redemptive value of poetry. As Jonson began to advocate the notion of a literary career based on the elevated status of the poet, Marston retaliated by scaling back Jonson's claims. In the "Apologetical Dialogue" to *Poetaster*, Jonson complained that he had been "provoked" (lines 96–98) by Marston, and it now appears that he was justified in rejecting Marston's ambivalent representation of him in *Histriomastix*.

"I do now remember a saying, 'The fool doth think he is wise, but the wise man knows himself to be a fool.'"

—As You Like It

4 SHAKESPEARE IN LOVE
The Containment of Comical Satire in *As You Like It*

THE ANONYMOUS author of *2 Return from Parnassus* implies that Shakespeare purged Jonson in reaction to *Poetaster*, and the preponderance of evidence corroborates the theory that he did so in *Troilus and Cressida*, a play that assimilated and negated the poetics of comical satire. Support for this view is found not only in *Troilus and Cressida* but also in the metatheatrical commentaries of *As You Like It* and *Twelfth Night* that precede it. In these three comedies written between 1600 and 1601, Shakespeare responded with increasing forcefulness to *Every Man Out*, *Cynthia's Revels*, and *Poetaster*. The first pairing of dramaturgical statement and response, *Every Man Out* and *As You Like It*, premiered at the newly opened Globe theater during its first year of operation. During this crucial first year at the Globe, the Chamberlain's Men appealed to their audience's heterogeneous tastes by offering them Jonson's comical satire, invented to abolish festive comedy, and Shakespeare's festive comedy, designed to deflate comical satire. Rather than simply defending Shakespeare's popular genre against Jonson's elitist critique, they sponsored alternative versions of comedy. The result was a dynamic repertoire that balanced Shakespeare's proven form against Jonson's provocative experiment. With *Every Man Out* the company met the growing demand for satire (whetted by the success of *Every Man In*) with a sequel that intensified Jonson's new emphasis on invective. Then, with *As You Like It*, the company's "ordinary poet" defended his embattled genre in a play whose title advertised its continuity with his prior successful comedies at the

Theater and Curtain.[1] While Aristophanic Jonson advocated revolutionary standards of art, reason, and satire, Plautine Shakespeare tested them against the opposing standards of nature, instinct, and imagination.

Every Man Out would not have been performed without Shakespeare's consent. As both a sharer in the company and its principal poet, he would have been among those charged with selecting its repertoire. He allowed or even encouraged the players to stage Jonson's comedy because he found it intellectually challenging, even though its principles repudiated his own. He would have understood that he was—in Jonson's schema—closer to Antonio Balladino than to Asper. But the fact that he did not serve as one of the play's principal comedians, as he had in *Every Man In*, symbolizes his alienation from its argument. His absence from the cast of *Every Man Out*, combined with evidence that he appeared in *As You Like It*, shows a pattern of oppositional self-definition through which he first explored the terms of the playwrights' growing estrangement.

That the Chamberlain's Men produced both the neoclassically inspired *Every Man Out* and the popular *As You Like It* is symptomatic of the company's historical position. The opening of the Globe in 1599 marks a midpoint in the troupe's evolution from its organization in 1594 to control of both the Globe and Blackfriars theaters in 1608. At this time Jonson began to aim his work at the "gentlemen," while Shakespeare split his attention between the general audience Jonson dismissed and the elite segment he courted. The Chamberlain's Men didn't have to choose between *As You Like It* and *Every Man Out*. Both were deployed as part of a strategy to consolidate the company's hold on a heterogeneous audience while seeking new ways to increase its attraction for that audience's most sophisticated and profitable members. Jonson's challenge was unmistakable: in *Every Man Out* he posited—for the first time—a distinction between his own self-conscious artistry and Shakespeare's instinctive artlessness. Asper informs the Globe's audience that *Every Man Out* is such an objectively good drama that "if we fail, / We must impute it to this only chance, / 'Art hath an enemy call'd *Ignorance*' " ("After the Second Sounding," lines 217–19). Marston succinctly defined Jonson's credo as: "Art above Nature, Judgement above Art."[2]

In *As You Like It* Shakespeare answered Jonson's objections to festive comedy in two interconnected ways. First, he tested the standards of "art" and "judgment" against the imperatives of "nature" and "folly" in a metatheatrical subplot involving Jaques (the satirist), Touchstone (the fool), and William (the clown). Through this new topical material he personalized the superiority of festive comedy over comical satire. His purge of Jonson as Ajax in the subplot of *Troilus and Cressida* recapitulates the literary joke he first made in bestowing the name "Jaques"—which in Elizabethan pronunciation is a homonym for "Ajax"—on the melancholy satirist who rejects festive solutions. In his response to *Every Man Out*, Shakespeare began "to run in that vile line" from Jaques of *As You Like It* to Ajax of *Troilus and Cressida*.

Second, Shakespeare used the pastoral element of festive comedy, with its bias toward nature, to counter Jonson's conception of art. By writing a festive comedy that included the "cross-wooing" and "clown" Jonson had censured and a plot based on Thomas Lodge's recent novella, Shakespeare acknowledged affiliations that would have struck Jonson as artless. Since *Much Ado About Nothing* had been urban, Shakespeare's return to pastoral seems strategic. He chose a genre, as Frank Kermode and Edward Tayler have indicated, that was constructed on the all-embracing categories of nature and art.[3] These dialectically opposed yet mutually dependent divisions of experience would become in future criticism synonymous with "Shakespeare" and "Jonson." Yet *As You Like It* is complex; though it seems to justify a natural teleology, it also suggests the inextricable entanglement of nature and art in Rosalind's counterfeit courtship and her concluding masque of Hymen. Shakespeare's drama is remarkable for its tendency to challenge its own premises: the play's benign naturalism mocks its own grinning. Orlando saved Oliver's life because he was motivated by "kindness, nobler ever than revenge, / And nature, stronger than his just occasion" (4.3.128–29). But by being "natural" in *As You Like It* one becomes a "fool": "Nature's natural, the cutter off of nature's wit" (1.2.49–50). The "natural philosopher" Corin strikes a perfect balance when he explains that "he that hath learn'd no wit by nature, nor art, may complain of good breeding, or comes of a very dull kindred" (3.2.29–31). Wit springs from either art or nature, so the witless can cite the absence of either as the cause of their deficiency. Yet one of the most striking paradoxes of *As You Like It* is that the most seemingly natural literary kind is also the most artificial.

Shakespeare discovered in pastoral's dialectic the terms for defusing comical satire, as he countered Jonson's heuristic program with a skeptical humanism underwritten by Socratic ignorance and Erasmian folly. Here Jonson's mockery of the "ridiculous" surrenders to the irony of the "ludicrous," as Asper's assertion of unequivocal truth gives way to Touchstone's determination that "the truest poetry is the most feigning" (3.3.19–20).[4]

I

Shakespeare's main source for *As You Like It* was Thomas Lodge's popular novella *Rosalind: Euphues' Golden Legacy* (1590).[5] And even when we take into consideration Shakespeare's proclivity for finding instead of inventing plots,

his comedy is unique in its fidelity to this single antecedent. *As You Like It* follows *Rosalind* so closely that their main plots can be conflated into a single
narrative.[6] Onto this stock, however, Shakespeare grafts three new characters—Jaques, Touchstone, and William—designed to offer a metatheatrical
commentary on the issues Jonson had raised.

Ever since Campbell popularized the theory that Jaques "serves as an amusing representative of the English satirists" and their "doctrines," critics have
agreed that Shakespeare intended the character to reflect the rise of satire at
the end of the 1590s.[7] We first hear of Jaques when Duke Senior's retainers recall his railing, as "most invectively he pierceth through / The body of the
country, city, court" (2.1.58–59). Shakespeare created him, Peter Phialas stresses, "not only to introduce into the scheme of the play allusions to the less attractive features of human life but also to satirize a particular type as well as
the general attitude of the new satiric school at the turn of the century."[8]
David Bevington suggests that he represents Shakespeare's assimilation of
contemporary influences and that his "satirical voice in the forest of Arden offers a valuable if limited contribution" to the play's "many-sided view of humanity."[9] His speech on the seven ages of man is one of the play's most memorable passages, and Shakespeare would increasingly give credence to this
perspective as he moved from *As You Like It* through *Twelfth Night* to *Troilus
and Cressida*. Yet here he exhibits his strongest resistance to its allure as Jaques,
"the agent and the object" of satire, reduces its motivating spirit to an arbitrary and extreme humour.[10]

"My often rumination," Jaques explains, "wraps me in a most humorous
sadness" (4.1.18–20). His satire is a symptom of melancholy, not a cure. "Monsieur Melancholy" is a satirist like Asper and a humourist like Macilente, who
can only "rail against . . . the world, and all our misery" (3.2.278–79). When
Duke Senior states, "I love to cope him in these sullen fits, / For then he's full
of matter" (2.1.67–68), he puns on the source of Jaques' "matter" of invention:
the diseased bodily fluids that produce satire. Jaques' melancholy reveals a partial truth about experience, but in *As You Like It* joy is privileged over grief. "I
had rather have a fool to make me merry," Rosalind explains, "than experience
to make me sad" (4.1.27–29). *Every Man Out* isolates the satirist from the humourist, while *As You Like It* negates this distinction.

Thus, while "few critics accept that Jaques himself represents Jonson,"
writes Russ McDonald, "his satiric credo may fairly be called Jonsonian." In
particular, he notes, Jaques' colloquy on satire with Duke Senior in 2.7 "is
Jonsonian in spirit and diction," although "complicated by dramatic circumstances."[11] It is here that the satirist allegorizes his name when he asks the
Duke for authority to *purge* his sick auditors:

> give me leave
> To speak my mind, and I will through and through
> Cleanse the foul body of th'infected world,
> If they will patiently receive my medicine.
>
> (2.7.58–61)

Jaques' phrasing evokes the purge metaphor of comical satire in a passage that reveals the source of his name, which we should not be misled into pronouncing with a French accent. Anglicized in the early modern period, the name was regularly punned with the word "jakes," which in the first quarto of *King Lear* (1608) is spelled "iaques" (sig. E1ᵛ; 2.2.67). This pronunciation is the basis for Harington's anecdote in *The Metamorphosis of Ajax* about a flustered lady-in-waiting who introduces one Mr. Jaques Wingfield as "*M. Privy Wingfield*."[12] That is why Touchstone slyly refers to him as "Master What-ye-call't" (3.3.73). The satirist who vows to "Cleanse the foul body of th'infected world"—to purge it through satire—is the conduit and receptacle of filth. As Helen Gardner observes, he is "discredited before he opens his mouth by the unpleasantness of his name."[13] According to Renaissance medical theory, melancholy caused constipation, making Jaques a "jakes." When in *Every Man In* Stephano, who feigns a fashionable melancholy, is offered the use of Matheo's study, he responds: "I thank you sir, . . . have you a close stool there?" (3.1.87–88). Since "Jaques" and "Ajax" are homonyms, Shakespeare uses *the same pun* to score the same topical point—"running in that vile line" from Jaques in *As You Like It* to Ajax in *Troilus and Cressida*—in parodies that bracket his involvement in the Poets' War.

In *As You Like It* Duke Senior rejects the would-be purger because he lacks moral authority and only contributes to the current malaise. And when Jaques presses his case—"What, for a counter, would I do but good?"—the duke responds that he would only further sicken society by committing "Most mischevious foul sin, in chiding sin":

> For thou thyself hast been a libertine,
> As sensual as the brutish sting itself,
> And all th' embossed sores, and headed evils,
> That thou with license of free foot hast caught,
> Wouldst thou disgorge into the general world.
>
> (2.7.64–69)

Jaques' corrective satire is diseased vomit; he can only verbally disgorge the "embossed sores, and headed evils" he has acquired through sexual license.

Such criticism at the Globe can only infect "the general world." "I will chide no breather in the world but myself," Orlando informs him, "against whom I know most faults" (3.2.280–81). But instead of directly addressing the Duke's charge, Jaques defends satire as an impersonal indictment of vice. When he attacks the citizen's wife or poor gallant for vanity, he objects, his critique is general and hence legitimate:

> Why, who cries out on pride
> That can therein tax any private party?
> Doth it not flow as hugely as the sea,
> Till that the weary very means do ebb?
> What woman in the city do I name,
> When that I say the city-woman bears
> The cost of princes on unworthy shoulders?
> Who can come in and say that I mean her,
> When such a one as she, such is her neighbor?
> Or what is he of basest function,
> That says his bravery is not on my cost,
> Thinking that I mean him, but therein suits
> His folly to the mettle of my speech?
> There then! how then? what then? Let me see wherein
> My tongue hath wrong'd him; if it do him right,
> Then he hath wrong'd himself. If he be free,
> Why then my taxing like a wild goose flies,
> Unclaim'd of any man.
>
> (2.7.70–87)

This condemnation of fashion mongers—middle-class women and lower-class men who dress above their station—would likely have reminded listeners of Fallace, the spendthrift merchant's wife, and her lover Fastidious Brisk, the bankrupt but ostentatiously dressed pseudocourtier in *Every Man Out*. Cordatus had similarly claimed that Jonson's characters did not represent his contemporaries:

> For that were to affirm, that a man, writing of NERO, should mean all Emperors: or speaking of MACHIAVEL, comprehend all Statesmen; or in our SORDIDO, all Farmers; and so of the rest; than which, nothing can be utter'd more malicious, or absurd. Indeed, there are . . . narrow-ey'd decipherers . . . that will extort strange . . . meanings out of any subject, be it never so conspicuous and innocently deliver'd. But to such (where

ere they sit conceal'd) let them know, the author defies them, and their
writing-tables. . . .

(2.6.166–75)

To name one is not to attack all. But elsewhere Jonson concedes that he does
at times obliquely refer to living individuals in some of his characters. He acknowledges having "tax'd" some of the players in *Poetaster*, a drama he admitted to having written "on" Marston. In defending *Volpone* he would boast that
his personation was almost too subtle to be detected: "Where have I been particular? where personal? except to a mimic, cheat, bawd, or buffoon, creatures
(for their insolencies) worthy to be tax'd? Yet, to which of these so pointing-
ly, as he might . . . have . . . dissembled his disease?" (5:18).

"Possibly enough Jonson may be glanced at," Herford and Simpson concur, since Jaques' "vindication of satire" is "substantially Jonson's."[14] But the
question of whether Jonson was the model for Jaques hardly does justice to
the sophisticated manner in which Shakespeare implies that this is the case
while deploying the character in a symbolic narrative. "That Jonson, and Jonson only, is 'translated' in the person of Jaques is, I think, beyond doubt,"
writes Arthur Gray. Although "Shakespeare's criticism of Jonson is general,"
he continues, his "identity is proclaimed in the date of *As You Like It*, in personal incidents, in character, in dramatic motive."[15] But though Jaques' language of purgation and denial of personal reference are Jonsonian, both are
also mainstays of the new satiric movement. While Marston builds personal
details into his Jonson caricature, Shakespeare's subtler innuendo verges on
being "Unclaim'd of any man." Jaques represents an attitude shared by a new
generation of writers, including Donne, Guilpin, Rankins, Weever, Hall,
Harington, Jonson, and Marston. Those who saw themselves in its mirror deserved to be so viewed. Still, in the Elizabethan commercial theater this kind
of satirist appears only in *Every Man Out* and *Histriomastix* before stepping
forward in *As You Like It*.[16]

II

Though he invokes Jonsonian satire, however, Jaques is part of a dramatic
fiction more symbolic than mimetic. A third of his lines praise the clown
Touchstone, an estimation Jonson would have detested. None of the modern
commentators who identify Jaques' attitude with Jonson's account for the fact
that when he lauds Touchstone's wit and asks to serve as the duke's retainer in
motley—his "only suit"—his reverence is counter-referential, an ironic inver-
sion of a Jonsonian paradigm. In *Ben Jonson's Parodic Strategy*, Robert Watson

observes that his characters often serve as literary markers—"strategic reductions" of his rivals' work—that encode literary theory in a "hierarchy of texts." "Jonson's comedies," he writes, "are acts of theatrical imperialism" in "a proud campaign for sovereignty in drama" through which he transforms his competitors into "self-dramatizing characters" acting out "unhealthy literary forms."[17] *As You Like It* turns this strategy against Jonson.

Shakespeare insists that the fool not only subsumes the satirist but is superior to him, insofar as he admits that folly rather than wisdom is the universal condition of human experience. Touchstone, like Rosalind, exemplifies C. L. Barber's notion of "a mocking reveller," a character who yields to festivity by accepting the natural as irrational.[18] At the turn of the seventeenth century a renewed interest in the fool led to such plays as George Chapman's *All Fools* and a flurry of publications, such as *Fool upon Fool* (1600), *Pasquil's Foolscap* (1600), and *The Hospital of Incurable Fools* (1600). By adapting an Erasmian defense with roots in Socratic ignorance and Christian folly, Shakespeare aligns himself with the most skeptical manifestation of Renaissance humanism to bolster his case against Jonson. In contrast to Jonson's attempt to distinguish the judicious from the humoured, Shakespeare emphasizes their common fallibility. Whereas Jonson's satirist makes absolute moral judgments and resists desire, Shakespeare's fool derides a natural condition he embraces.

Once the Poets' War had become more aggressive in its second phase, Shakespeare imagined this same subordination of critic to fool with greater vehemence in the punitive fantasy of *Twelfth Night*. Jaques' respect for Touchstone's wit and Malvolio's disdain for Feste's folly are variations on a single theme. The only difference is that *Twelfth Night* shows greater irritation in reiterating the same hierarchy, as the critic resists identifying with the fool until he is forced to acknowledge their resemblance.

Touchstone embodies festive comedy in all its contradictions. Robert Armin, the actor for whom the role was created, wrote a book, *Fool upon Fool*, that distinguished between "natural" and "artificial" varieties, between idiots who stumbled on wit and professional jesters. In practice, however, they were often difficult to differentiate, as in the case of Touchstone, who is both "the cutter off of Nature's wit" (1.2.49–50) and a "deep contemplative" (2.7.31). It is necessary, then, not to draw too firm a line between clown and fool—rustic buffoon and court jester—since Shakespeare blurs this distinction. "Touchstone" is generically labeled "Clown" in the First Folio's speech-prefixes, while in the dialogue he is also called a "motley" or "clownish fool." Like Lear's fool, he never has a name: he only takes on the *alias* "Touchstone" when entering the forest of Arden. If the clown is associated with nature and the fool with art, Touchstone fuses both. The scope of his satire, moreover, is remarkably comprehensive; if he criticizes the tenets of comical satire, exposing the flaws of art, he ridicules festive comedy as well, even as he submits to its imperatives.

Jaques' long endorsement of Touchstone and his recognition of the satiric potential of clowning (2.7.12–34) constitute Shakespeare's first explicit praise of folly. Earlier clowns, beginning with the Dromios of *The Comedy of Errors*, show wit on occasion, but none exhibits his talents as ostentatiously as Touchstone and none receives such glowing reviews within the play. "The wise man's folly," Jaques explains, "is anatomized / Even by the squand'ring glances of the fool" (2.7.56–57). "He uses his folly like a stalking horse," Duke Senior agrees, behind which he "shoots his wit" (5.4.106–7). And when Celia threatens to have him "whipt for taxation" for mocking her father, the usurping Duke Frederick, Touchstone's retort summarizes his special status: "The more pity that fools may not speak wisely what wise men do foolishly" (1.2.86–87).

In Renaissance neoclassicism from Sidney through Jonson, the clown is a vilified personification of commercial theater. Tallying the "gross absurdities" of popular dramatists in the *Apology*, Sidney had famously complained that "mongrel tragi-comedies" had begun "mingling kings and clowns not because the matter so carrieth it, but thrust in clowns by head and shoulders, to play a part in majestical matters, with neither decency nor discretion."[19] Jonson went so far as to urge the character's elimination from his native genre, which he achieved in his last two comical satires. In *Every Man Out*, however, he only debased the clown's function and diminished his wit. After Musco (later called Brainworm) of *Every Man In*, Jonson's last sympathetic Plautine clown, the fools of *Every Man Out*, such as Carlo Buffone and Sogliardo, became one-dimensional humourists.[20]

Jonson personalizes his argument through analogy by comparing Shakespeare to the social-climbing country clown Sogliardo, whom he describes as "*An essential Clown . . . so enamour'd of the name of a Gentleman, that he will have it, though he buys it*" (characters, lines 78–80). Returning from the Heralds, he brags, "I can write myself a gentleman now; here's my patent, it cost me thirty pounds" (3.4.52–53). Sogliardo is not a caricature of Shakespeare, but when Puntarvolo suggests that the "word" of his new coat of arms should be "*Not without mustard*" (3.4.86), parodying Shakespeare's "*Non sanz droict*," the hit is palpable. Indeed, this quip might have sparked Touchstone's jest about the knight who did not lie when he swore that "the pancakes" were "good" and "the mustard was naught," although the pancakes were bad and the mustard good, because he swore "*by his honor*," and "if you swear by that that is not, you are not forsworn" (1.2.63–77). Shakespeare's joke about honor and mustard turns Jonson's critique on its head and mocks the social pretension Shakespeare had been accused of exhibiting.

Having acquired a coat of arms in 1596 in his father's name, with a motto probably of his own devising, Shakespeare could call himself a "gentleman." But in 1599, the issue of his gentility had become potentially embarrassing when he attempted to upgrade his shield by placing the Arden pattern of his mother's more prestigious side of the family on its sinister side and moving the Shakespeare crest to its dexter half. Jonson could have known of these affairs at the College of Arms through his friendship with William Camden, the Clarenceux King-of-Arms, who assisted Sir William Dethick, Garter King-of-Arms, in drawing up the grant for the impalement, which was not issued. The problem was that the heralds found it difficult to know from which branch of this ancient family the Ardens of Wilmcote had descended and had used the pattern of the Ardens of Park Hall before scratching it out and adding that of the Ardens of Cheshire. In 1602, the original bid for gentrification by "Shakespeare the Player" was included in the charges Ralph Brooke, the York Herald, planned to bring against Camden and Dethick for certifying "mean" persons.[21] Sogliardo's suggested coat of arms differs from Shakespeare's, being organized around "A swine without a head, without brain, wit, any thing indeed, ramping to gentility" (3.4.64–66). But it is hard to miss Jonson's imputation that Shakespeare was clownish in his bid to purchase honor.[22]

Shakespeare answered Jonson's attack on clowning by identifying poetry with Ovidian desire instead of Horatian reason. "I am here with thee and thy goats," Touchstone tells the shepherdess Audrey, "as the most capricious [variable and goatlike] poet, honest Ovid, was among the Goths [pronounced 'goats']." Ovid, whose seducer's manual *The Art of Love* and alleged affair with Augustus's granddaughter were thought to have caused his exile to bleak and barbaric Tomis, embodied a defiance of humanist ideals.[23] And when Audrey asks if "poetry" is "a true thing," Touchstone replies:

No, truly; for the truest poetry is the most feigning, and lovers are given to poetry; and what they swear in poetry may be said as lovers they do feign.

(3.3.19–22)

To counter Plato's accusation in the *Republic* that poets are liars, a charge repeated in Stephen Gosson's *School of Abuse*, Sidney had described poetry as an art in which "feigning may be tuned to the highest key of passion" to move its audience to virtuous action. Indeed, the "feigning" of "notable images," he argued, was a "right describing note to know a poet by."[24] Touchstone agrees that for poets fiction is as good as fact, but he reverses Sidney's polemic by insisting that poets "feign" or "pretend" because they "fain" or "desire" and are willing to lie to achieve their amorous ends. Sidney had begun *Astrophil and Stella* with the line, "Loving in truth and fain in verse my love to show," and Touchstone recovers this sense of the word to reject the didactic aims of English neoclassicism. Poetry, then, to reverse Sidney's critical dictum, was the expression not of "erected wit" but of "infected will."

Rather than being the play's spokesman, however, Touchstone's ironic voice is destabilized by Shakespeare, and his affair with Audrey is as far from the festive norm epitomized by Orlando and Rosalind as Silvius's Petrarchan love for Phebe. He enters the forest without enthusiasm: "Ay, now am I in Arden, the more fool I" (2.4.16), and, lacking commitment, he serves as a parody of desire on its lowest level. He wants Sir Oliver Martext to wed him to Audrey, he tells Jaques, so that "not being well married, it will be a good excuse for me hereafter to leave my wife" (3.3.92–94). As an unreliable spokesman, he incorporates in his folly a debased naturalism that balances Silvius's bloodless devotion. Between the extremes of Silvius and Touchstone, Rosalind balances attachment and detachment, synthesizing their polarity.

Shakespeare's conception of his ironic fool as a response to Jonson's self-righteous satirist was stimulated by Robert Armin's replacement of William Kemp in the Chamberlain's Men in 1600. In *2 Return from Parnassus*, when Kemp laughs with Burbage about how Shakespeare has purged Jonson, he shares in his revenge as an actor and a clown. But though Kemp still served as the personification of all that Jonson detested, by the time this scene was written he had already left the company. A court deposition by John Heminges and Henry Condell in 1619 states that although Kemp had been among the original members of the Chamberlain's Men who held a moiety of the Globe's lease, he had surrendered his share "about the time of the building of the said Playhouse . . . or shortly after." The Globe's construction began after the company signed a contract with the builder Peter Street on 26 February 1599. By 16 May, it had, as Park Honan notes, at least "a partial existence," and by September, Thomas Platter ventured "over the water" to see *Julius Caesar*.[25] Bernard Beckerman has suggested that "before the stage of the Globe was painted and the spectators admitted," Kemp "severed his connection with the Lord Chamberlain's Men."[26] But it is possible that he stayed on until the beginning of the following year. His only allusion to this event appears in his dedication to *Nine Days' Wonder*, which describes his dance marathon from London to Norwich, between 11 February and 11 March 1600, as a consequence of his departure from the Globe: "Some swear . . . I have trod a good way to win the world: others that guess righter, affirm, I have without good help danced my self out of the world."[27] "It was odd," notes Gerald Bentley, "for an actor as famous as Kempe to leave the leading company of the time."[28] It seems likely that Kemp either experienced friction with the other members of the company or was drawn to other opportunities, such as being a solo performer, or both.[29]

Kemp was notorious for his jigs and stage antics and his success as a comic numbskull in the roles of Bottom and Dogberry. Shakespeare, however, included no important clowns in either *Henry V* or *Julius Caesar*, both written in 1599. And he even shares a measure of Jonson's anxiety when he has Hamlet urge the traveling actors to "let those that play your clowns speak no more than is set down for them," since unscripted improvisation prompts "barren spectators" to laugh when "some necessary question of the play" should be considered. It has long been suspected that Kemp is here being reprimanded for a proclivity to that "villainous" disruption that "shows a most pitiful ambition in the fool that uses it" (3.2.38–45). Although it is difficult to pinpoint when Armin replaced him, through the recent examination of the problem by Evelyn Joseph Mattern it seems likely that Armin premiered as Touchstone early in 1600.[30]

This would account for the lavish praise and topicality that Shakespeare writes into the role. As Leslie Hotson first noticed, the clown's alias, "Touchstone," alludes to two of Armin's professional affiliations. A touchstone was used by goldsmiths to test the quality of metals rubbed against it, and he had served his apprenticeship in the Goldsmiths' Company (the heraldic crest of which shows a "woman clothed, holding in one hand a touchstone"). He might even have later returned to the trade or at least enjoyed the guild's privileges.[31] But the pseudonym Touchstone evoked his comic persona as well, since Armin had probably already created for himself the role of the clown Tutch in *The Two Maids of More-Clacke*. Playing on his name, Tutch confesses his double nature as truth teller and liar: "now am I tried on my own touch, / I am true metal one way, but counterfeit another." Thus, with a single stroke, Shakespeare not only named Touchstone in homage to Armin but sanctioned his status as the character who, despite his flaws, cleverly assessed the value of others.[32] The Chamberlain's Men was a repertory company, and Shakespeare shaped his plays to his fellows' skills. A versatile performer, Armin reprised Kemp's russet roles, including the broad humor of Dogberry, while fleshing out the new motley jesters Shakespeare created for him. The new poet-player was able to master Shakespeare's comic patter with a fluency that John Davies of Hereford attributed to his ability to "*wisely play the fool.*"[33] Through him, Shakespeare explored a range of new possibilities—especially his mastery of mock academic discourse—in a collaboration that climaxed in *King Lear*. In 1600, then, Armin was a new actor who could make explicit the philosophical acceptance of folly upon which festive comedy was based.

III

Shakespeare is, for the most part, what George Steiner calls an "altruistic" dramatist who submerges his voice in that of his characters, gaining immortality at the price of anonymity. Yet an amusing exception occurs in *As You Like It* when, in the last of his three topical overlays, Shakespeare represents himself as a Jonsonian caricature to seal his acceptance of the wisdom of folly. The main purpose of this short episode is to admit his own folly—that is, his own wisdom—by subjecting himself to Touchstone's censure. In the first scene of the fifth act, without the slightest forewarning, a country clown named William emerges from the forest of Arden, briefly converses with Audrey and Touchstone, and is flouted off the stage. It is likely that William, who shares both the author's first name and his birthplace, was an assay in the personally allusive style of the Poets' War, enabled by the pastoral convention of self-reference.

From the classical period to the Renaissance, pastoral poets regularly included themselves among their shepherds, from Virgil's Tityrus through Sannazaro's Ergasto, Sidney's Philisides, and Spenser's Colin Clout. The standard technique of self-portraiture in the Renaissance was to follow Sannazaro's example in *Arcadia* by depicting oneself as a mournful lover, often the victim of cross-wooing. Indeed, the attraction of pastoral self-reference was so strong that even Anthony Munday became "shepherd Tonie" in *England's Helicon* (1600). What is more, the great English examples—Philisides in the *Arcadia* and Colin Clout in *The Shepherd's Calendar* and Book Six of *The Fairy Queen*—involved cameo appearances hidden in tangled plots. These characters were planted in self-reflexive episodes for readers in the know who were meant to be surprised by the sudden emergence of truth in feigning. Having satirized a proto-Jonsonian satirist in "Jaques," Shakespeare felt obligated to generate laughter at his own expense, and he did so by re-creating himself as "William."[34] There is, furthermore, circumstantial evidence that Shakespeare acted this role alongside Armin during the play's initial run in order to implicate himself in the inescapable folly that determines the plot of *As You Like It* and the shape of human experience.

Enter William

TOUCHSTONE   It is meat and drink to me to see a clown. By my troth, we that have good wits have much to answer for; we shall be flouting; we cannot hold.

WILLIAM   Good ev'n, Audrey.

AUDREY   God ye good ev'n, William.

WILLIAM   And good ev'n to you, sir.

TOUCHSTONE   Good ev'n, gentle friend. Cover thy head, cover thy
              head; nay, prithee be cover'd. How old are you, friend?
WILLIAM   Five and twenty, sir.
TOUCHSTONE   A ripe age. Is thy name William?
WILLIAM   William, sir.
TOUCHSTONE   A fair name. Wast born i' the forest here?
WILLIAM   Ay, sir, I thank God.
TOUCHSTONE   "Thank God"—a good answer. Art rich?
WILLIAM   Faith sir, so, so.
TOUCHSTONE.   "So, so" is good, very good, very excellent good; and
              yet it is not, it is but so, so. Art thou wise?
WILLIAM   Ay, sir, I have a pretty wit.
TOUCHSTONE   Why, thou say'st well. I do now remember a saying,
              "The fool doth think he is wise, but the wise man
              knows himself to be a fool." The heathen philoso-
              pher, when he had a desire to eat a grape, would
              open his lips when he put it into his mouth, meaning
              thereby that grapes were made to eat and lips to
              open. You do love this maid?
WILLIAM   I do, sir.
TOUCHSTONE   Give me your hand. Art thou learned?
WILLIAM   No, sir.
TOUCHSTONE   Then learn this of me: to have is to have. For it is a
              figure in rhetoric that drink, being pour'd out of a
              cup into a glass, by filling the one doth empty the
              other. For all your writers do consent that *ipse* is he:
              now, you are not *ipse*, for I am he.
WILLIAM   Which he, sir?
TOUCHSTONE   He, sir, that must marry this woman. Therefore, you
              clown, abandon—which is in the vulgar leave—the
              society—which in the boorish is company—of this
              female—which in the common is woman; which
              together is, abandon the society of this female, or
              clown, thou perishest; or to thy better understanding,
              diest; or (to wit) I kill thee, make thee away, translate
              thy life into death, thy liberty into bondage. I will
              deal in poison with thee, or in bastinado, or in steel;
              I will bandy with thee in faction; I will o'errun thee
              with policy; I will kill thee a hundred and fifty ways:
              therefore tremble and depart.

| AUDREY | Do, good William. |
| WILLIAM | God rest you merry, sir. *Exit.* |

(5.1.10–59)

This one-sided *moromachia* between the learned fool and the country clown—between art and nature—becomes wittier when it is read in terms of an original performance that capitalized on Armin and Shakespeare's presence on-stage as theatrical celebrities. The caricature that Shakepeare draws of himself entering the forest of his fiction constitutes a comic etiology through which the established London poet recounts his provincial background and identifies him-self as a dim-witted country bumpkin—like Jonson's Sogliardo—baffled by the mock "wisdom" of a learned fool. Shakespeare completed his play when he was thirty-five; William, who is twenty-five, functions as a retrospective glance at his rural past that distanced him from his current married status and London resi-dence. Spenser, at twenty-five, had presented himself in *The Shepherd's Calen-dar* as Colin Clout, a "shepherd's boy"; Shakespeare, ten years older, casts him-self as a baffled but good-natured "youth" of the forest.

The Touchstone-Audrey-William triangle has roots not only in *The Shep-herd's Calendar* (1579) but also in Book Six of *The Fairy Queen* (1596), which suggested the narrative outline for Touchstone's adventure in Arden. Shake-speare comically reconfigures Sir Calidore's pastoral interlude in Book Six in Touchstone's violation of the knight's exemplary performance. Spenser's Sir Calidore, the knight of Courtesy, voluntarily becomes a shepherd and praises country life to old Meliboe (6.9.19), after having fallen in love with Pastorella, a shepherdess later discovered to be an aristocratic foundling. In courting her, Calidore is contrasted with the clownish Coridon, a country rival to whom he is always considerate, even while proving his own natural superiority, especially his courage. Furthermore, in the same episode, in a surprising moment of self-reference, Calidore inadvertently disrupts Colin Clout's vision of the Graces and causes the poet's beloved (who appears at its center) to vanish. Distraught by her disappearance and deprived of his harmonic rapture, Spenser's hapless persona smashes his bagpipe and moans (6.10.18). Shakespeare's rewriting of Spenser's pastoral episode on the lowest mimetic level is one of the play's better literary jokes. Touchstone, in place of Calidore, exchanges court life for a bucolic exis-tence, but he does so only reluctantly and details his ambivalent feelings about it to old Corin, whom he ridicules for lacking courtly manners and pandering to the rams of his flock. Once in the country, he romances an ignorant shep-herdess, Audrey (without royal connections), and menaces her ex-beau, his rus-tic competitor, William, whom he threatens to murder. Instead of accidentally upsetting the author's persona—as Calidore had done to Colin Clout—Touchstone deliberately abuses William, whom he viciously replaces in Audrey's favor. Using the pastoral convention of self-reference, Spenser and Shakespeare thus make brief appearances near the ends of their works, in scenes specifically created to show them being deprived of the pastoral happiness their fictions celebrate. Unlike Spenser, however, Shakespeare fashioned this episode of dramatic self-effacement to demonstrate the Socratic paradox that the admission of ignorance is the securest form of knowledge. And it is through this encounter that the "gentle" poet's "pretty wit" upsets "learned" distinctions in the Ur-text of all defenses of Shakespeare's natural genius. When, at the end of the seventeenth century, John Ward wrote in his diary that "Mr. Shakespeare was a natural wit, without any art at all," he unknowingly repeated a version of the poet's self-created myth, stripped of its *sprezzatura*.[35]

In the dialogue between Touchstone and Audrey that precedes William's entry, the court clown confronts her with the suspicion that "there is a youth . . . in the forest lays claim to you." "Ay, I know who 'tis;" Audrey responds, while insisting that "he hath no interest in me in the world" (5.1.6–9). Since, William Jones points out, the Globe was sometimes called "the world" (by Kemp, among others) Audrey is ironically made, on a metatheatrical level, to deny that Shakespeare had any proprietary interest in a character in a play he had written for a playhouse he partially owned.[36]

The joke that the tongue-tied country clown William represented Shakespeare as Shakespeare represented *him* is developed through the sequence of questions Touchstone asks. These not only reveal the youth's name and birthplace but also describe him as having "a pretty wit," although he is not "learned." The self-portrait that emerges fleshes out Jonson's critique but reverses its implications. At the play's opening, Celia identifies "Nature" as the source of "wit" (1.2.45), and it is in this sense—as inspiration—that Shakespeare employs it. During the Renaissance, "wit" acquired a double meaning. In Old English, the word originally referred to "the power of thinking and reasoning," but during the sixteenth century it came to mean "the ability to speak facetiously." This second meaning distinguishes Shakespeare's artful self-portrait, which exhibits what Fuller later calls "the quickness of his Wit." What "William" lacked was William's specialty, as the play's first audience was coaxed to look through the character to the poet-player who impersonated him. The punning begins when Armin/Touchstone, hearing his rival call himself William, concurs that it is a "fair" name, meaning both "attractive" and "appropriate." William, after all, plays "William playing 'William.'" Touchstone's otherwise bland response would have been amusing only if the audience recognized that the name of the nonce character he addressed was that of the actor playing "a poet playing a clown." What is most daring about this self-

representation is that it breaks the Renaissance taboo requiring pastoral pseudonyms. Here Shakespeare returns to the norm of Old Comedy, which specifically named its targets. And just as Socrates in a famous anecdote about
Aristophanes' *Clouds* acknowledged his resemblance to the distorted comic
mask of the actor who parodied him, Shakespeare admitted his nearness to the
doltish clown he played.

In *Shakespeare's Clown: Actor and Text in the Elizabethan Playhouse*, David
Wiles detects the personal dimensions of this exchange but explains it with
only partial success. He correctly assumes that the audience was "encouraged
to decipher the name 'Touchstone' as an alias for the real clown, Robert
Armin," but misidentifies his straight man as Kemp. "The other clown's
name—'William'—is repeated three times," he notes, "so that the audience
will not miss the contrast between the departing company clown, William
Kemp, and the new fool/clown," as the "traditional simple-minded rustic" was
"symbolically dismissed from the new Globe stage."[37] But it is improbable that
Kemp would have allowed himself to be humiliated in this manner, especially
since he had already been replaced by Armin. Wiles misses an important clue:
Armin's question "Wast born i' the forest here?" would have prompted a laugh
only if Shakespeare replied, "Ay, sir, I thank God." Still, anyone who was alert
enough to have expected William Kemp to appear would have been doubly
amused to find another William in his place. If Phyllis Rackin is right, William
of *As You Like It* is but one of a series of instances in which "Shakespeare associates a character who shares his own name with inarticulate, humble life obliterated by the elite textualized world of his betters."[38]

Arden is a theatrical construct populated by pastoral types. "For the learned
and literary," Helen Gardner writes, "this is one of Shakespeare's most allusive
plays."[39] That Arden is posited as a natural world that dramatizes its artificiality is apparent when the shepherdess Phebe displays her knowledge of current
poetry and literary biography in a couplet that eulogizes Christopher Marlowe
by naming him after his famous lyric, "The Passionate Shepherd," and quoting
a line (I.176) from *Hero and Leander* (1598):

> Dead shepherd, now I find thy saw of might,
> "Who ever lov'd that lov'd not at first sight?"
> (3.5.81–82)

This concise pastoral elegy is yet another example of the play's compendium
of generic motifs; Arden becomes a forest of the literary imagination even as
it takes on a more familiar geographical contour. "Ardennes" is a fictional forest lifted from Lodge's *Rosalind*, which was based on the actual territory, lo-

cated in present-day France, Belgium, and Luxembourg. But when re-creating it as the "Arden" of *As You Like It*, Shakespeare gave it a native English inflection, suggested by the rustic greetings "Good ev'n, Audrey," and "God ye good ev'n, William." This layer of referentiality superimposed over Lodge's exotic setting the Forest of Arden in Warwickshire, which surrounded the town of Stratford where he was born. "To William Shakespeare this was native ground," writes Stuart Daley, who explains how a London audience would have responded to the mention of its name:

> To many Elizabethans . . . the Forest of Arden . . . was anything but a *terra incognita* in a remote corner of the Kingdom. A dominant geographical feature of the central Midlands since the Middle Ages, by the sixteenth century the Forest or Woodland of Arden had become a famous and storied region covering over two hundred square miles in the heart of England.[40]

Shakespeare, who shares Kemp's first name, seems to have revived his part as the country clown in mock deference to Armin. But he also appears to have created the role of William of Arden—reflecting the maternal lineage he had hoped to add to his coat of arms—in answer to Jonson's charge that his artlessness had caused him to lapse into absurdity in his comedies of cross-wooing. This self-caricature is the only instance during the Poets' War in which Shakespeare is impersonated, and its deftness probably discouraged further *ad hominem* criticism.

The probability that Shakespeare played William when *As You Like It* premiered is strengthened by a late oral tradition indicating that he acted the part of old Adam, Orlando's servant. In the middle of the eighteenth century, William Oldys noted that "one of Shakespeare's younger brothers," who had been "a spectator of him as an actor in some of his plays," had identified him as wearing "a long beard" and seeming "so weak . . . that he was . . . carried . . . to a table, at which he was feasted." The story is too late to have come from Shakespeare's brother, and when Edward Capell repeated it, he attributed it instead to a relative and explained why he found it credible:

> A traditional story was current some years ago about Stratford—that a very old man of that place,—of weak intellects, but yet related to Shakespeare,—being ask'd by some of his neighbors, what he remember'd about him; answer'd—that he saw him once brought on the stage upon another man's back; which answer was apply'd by the hearers, to his having seen him perform in this scene the part of Adam: That he should have done so, is made not unlikely by another constant tradition,—that

he was no extraordinary actor, and therefore took no parts upon him but such as this.[41]

If we accept the plausibility of Shakespeare's having acted the role of old Adam, it is likely that once Orlando had "set down" his "venerable burthen" (2.7.167–68) and Adam vanished at the end of the scene, the actor who played him could also double as young William. "For the professional players," Gerald Bentley explains, "doubling" was "a normal feature of casting."[42] Like Armin, who, due to his skill as a singer, must have doubled as Amiens, Shakespeare probably played both Adam and William. By taking on these roles in 1600 he would have informed the play's original meaning with a unique metatheatricality: a middle-aged man of thirty-five would have personified an entire cycle of life in the three (if not seven) ages of man. And since he probably knew, as Camden notes in *Remains* (1605), that "Adam" in Hebrew meant "man," he would have fused in the same performance generic and specific versions of his identity.[43]

Touchstone's triumph over William in the fifth act is achieved through belligerent pseudophilosophical rhetoric aimed at Arden's natural man. The comic manipulation of academic jargon—a prime feature of Renaissance wit in the style of Erasmus and Rabelais—was one of Armin's specialties. Here its pseudoauthentication is backed by the threat of violence. Touchstone begins by citing "the heathen philosopher," perhaps Aristotle, who maintains that a thing is defined by its use. Hence, he implies, deploying a pastoral metaphor, Audrey is a grape ripe for eating. Arden presents a banquet for the omnivorous Touchstone, who feeds on William as well: it is, he admits, "meat and drink to me to see a clown." But how does he prove that he is "the man" to replace William? Mastery of rhetoric—the art of persuasion based on classical models—includes an understanding of the laws of identity, possession, and cause and effect. Since pouring water from a cup into a glass empties the former into the latter, rhetoric determines that only one rival can win. Which "he"? In Latin, *ipse* means "he himself," and Touchstone usurps the word's privileged cultural authority to insist on his superior status. But the phrase "*ipse*, he" had a specific literary connotation that Touchstone evokes to clinch his case: in Lyly's *Euphues* it denotes the successful suitor Curio, who causes Lucilla to reject the work's titular hero.[44] Jonson, who would later comment on Shakespeare's "small Latin and less Greek," quotes Cicero in Latin to justify comical satire. "Learned" Touchstone uses this same tactic to claim Audrey before translating his threat into "the boorish" to beat William. Learning for Touchstone is a weapon to bully a bumpkin; all he offers to support his assumption of privilege is the tautology "to have is to have." Unfortunately for William (the empty cup), the opposite is also true. And at this point the one-sided war between sly and dry clowns comes to a halt as William, encouraged by Audrey to leave, hospitably bids Touchstone farewell, exhibiting what Jonson would later call Shakespeare's "open and free nature."

As You Like It, Chambers writes, "does for the Elizabethan drama what the long string of pastoral poets, Spenser and Sidney, Lodge and Greene, . . . and the rest, had already done." And when "it goes beyond *Rosalind*," Edwin Greenlaw adds, it does so "in conformity to the typical pastoral plot lines of Sidney and Spenser."[45] The William episode combines two prominent love triangles in Renaissance pastoral, the self-reflexive episode and a kind of pastourelle, in which an amorous courtier seduces a country girl away from an ignorant country bumpkin. At first glance, the William-Audrey-Touchstone love triangle seems merely to repeat the Costard-Jaquenetta-Armado cross-wooing in *Love's Labor's Lost*. *As You Like It*, however, invests this mock triumph of art over nature with self-reflexive irony. Those familiar with the formula for self-representation in Renaissance pastoral had to have been surprised at Shakespeare's radical subversion of its typical expression. In the most famous use of a pastoral persona in the English Renaissance, Spenser had originally represented himself in *The Shepherd's Calendar* as the victimized Colin Clout, who loved Rosalind until his rival Menalcus "by treachery" destroyed her "faultless faith" and "the truest shepherd's heart made bleed" ("June," lines 43–48; 102–11).[46] Less original authors, faced with Shakespeare's choices, might have written themselves into the mournful Silvius yearning for Phebe or the melancholy Jaques abandoning love. But here, in a wholly parodic register, we find a nasty scene of infidelity centering on Audrey (not Rosalind), whose name suggests her worthlessness since "in the sixteenth century, the word tawdry was coined from Audrey, a name favored by the poorer classes, to suggest any cheap or garish goods."[47]

In representing himself in this manner, moreover, Shakespeare aligned himself with the native medieval tradition of poetic self-effacement. Two hundred years earlier, William Langland in *Piers Plowman* had ironically depicted himself as "Long Will," a man too weak and tall for field labor.[48] And Chaucer had poked fun at himself in *The Canterbury Tales* as a fat "elvyssh" loner whose "drasty rymyng is nat worth a toord!"[49] Both Chaucer and Shakespeare contrive to have their personae ostracized by other characters. Among a company of raconteurs, Geoffrey is censured for his artless tale of Sir Thopas, and in a play that unites four couples (a record number for festive comedy), "William's unharvested ripeness represents an opportunity not taken, and he is banished from the possibility of love."[50]

Part of the joke of Touchstone's abuse of William is the way in which he leads him through the first stages of a mock marriage ceremony—"You do love this maid?" "I do, sir." "Give me your hand"—only to dash his hopes. As the odd man out in his own work, like Bottom in *A Midsummer Night's Dream*, Shakespeare excludes himself (as Jaques does) from the scene of social bonding that gives closure to festive comedy. The title of Shakespeare's play—*As You Like It*—admits its commitment to its audience as the arbiter of theatrical value. Bequeathed to Shakespeare as the paradoxical mark of a superior poet, Chaucer's legacy is the definitive example of an author willing to depend on his audience's favor to redress his self-imputed weakness. Shakespeare repeats that paradigm, consolidating it not only with pastoral self-reference but also with the semi-autobiographical narrative he had previously devised to represent his amorous betrayal.

Although the *Sonnets* would not be published until 1609, by the time *As You Like It* was staged Shakespeare had already represented himself in them as a frustrated lover caught in a triangle involving a dark lady and a young man. In *Palladis Tamia* (1598), Francis Meres shows familiarity with Shakespeare's drama as well as "his sugared Sonnets among his private friends," which were then circulating in manuscript.[51] In 1599 two of these sonnets—"When my love swears that she is made of truth" and "Two loves I have of comfort and despair" (138 and 144)—were anthologized at the opening of *The Passionate Pilgrim*, a collection wrongfully attributed by William Jaggard wholly to "W. Shakespeare." What readers discovered in the two poems was a brief version of the *Sonnets*: a love triangle that moved from mutual self-deception to betrayal. Evidence that this erotic tale had originated several years earlier—around the time that *Venus and Adonis* (1593) and *The Rape of Lucrece* (1594) were dedicated to Henry Wriothesley, earl of Southampton—is found in a cryptic text entitled *Willobie His Avisa* (1594). What makes Henry Willobie's work so intriguing is that it contains an early biographical myth about Shakespeare—"W.S."—written by a contemporary who had read some sonnets. Willobie seeks to recruit Shakespeare's persona to strengthen the praise he offers his own idealized mistress, "Avisa" or "A." He consequently uses Shakespeare's triangle as the basis for his own fantasia. H.W. tells W.S., who "not long before had tried the courtesy of the like passion," that he loves A., and W.S., knowing better, encourages him to pursue her as a kind of theatrical audition:

> because he would see whether another could play his part better than himself, and in viewing a far off the course of his loving Comedy, he determined to see whether it would sort to a happier end for this new actor than it did for the old player. But at length this Comedy was like to have grown to a Tragedy, by the weak and feeble estate that H. W. was brought unto . . . till Time and Necessity . . . brought him a plas-

ter. . . . In all which discourse is lively represented the unruly rage of unbridled fancy . . . which Will, set loose from Reason, can devise. . . .[52]

Shakespeare's initials reveal his identity, which is hinted at again in the play
on his nickname in Willobie's allusion to the "sundry changes of affections"
that "Will, set loose from Reason, can devise." In the *Sonnets*, the poet had
similarly used his name to signify desire, telling his mistress, "Whoever hath
her wish, thou hast thy Will" (135). H.W. are the initials of Henry Wriothesley, a likely candidate for the young man of the *Sonnets*. Willobie, who probably knew the poet, fuses allusions to Shakespeare's theatrical career with details of his sonnet persona. Shakespeare refers to himself as an actor in the
public theater (sonnets 110 and 111) and as older than his male friend (sonnet
73). In *Willobie*, W.S. uses H.W. to see if "another could play his part better
than . . . the old player." Willobie's W.S., however, like Shakespeare, is a dramatist as well as an actor, who encourages H.W. to pursue A. until the "loving Comedy" he scripted "was like to have grown a Tragedy."[53]

   In the 1590s, through a process of biographical mythmaking, the poet had
become Shakespeare in love, identified with Ovid as well as Plautus. For Meres,
"the sweet witty soul of Ovid" lived in the "mellifluous and honey-tongued
Shakespeare" of *Venus and Adonis*, *The Rape of Lucrece*, and the *Sonnets*.[54] By the
turn of the century, the foppish Gullio of *1 The Return from Parnassus* mixes paraphrases of lines from *Romeo and Juliet* (2.4.39–43) and *Venus and Adonis* (1–2;
5–6), then sighs, "O sweet Mr. Shakespeare, I'll have his picture in my study at
the court." In Gullio's religion of love, Shakespeare's portrait is a devotional
relic. "Let this duncified world esteem of Spenser and Chaucer," he rhapsodizes,
"I'll worship sweet Mr. Shakespeare, and to honour him will lay his Venus and
Adonis under my pillow," imitating Alexander the Great, who "slept with
Homer under his bed's head." In the play's sequel, even Judicio admits that
Shakespeare's "sweeter verse" contains "heart-robbing lines."[55]

   In the *Sonnets* and *As You Like It*, Shakespeare's personae—"Will" and
"William"—are betrayed and displaced. But in the tales that start to be told
about him at this time, he is both the transgressor and the victor. In his *Diary*
on 13 March 1602, John Manningham records a dirty joke about Shakespeare
that imagines him in a fabliau as a deceptive seducer who outwits the charismatic Burbage:

   Upon a time when Burbage played Richard III there was a citizen grew
   so far in liking with him, that before she went from the play she appointed him to come that night unto her by the name of Richard III.
   Shakespeare overhearing their conclusion went before, was entertained,

and at his game ere Burbage came. Then message being brought that Richard III was at the door, Shakespeare caused return to be made that William the Conqueror was before Richard III.

Manningham's variation on the bed-trick concludes with a note that explains its jest: "Shakespeare's name William."[56] This tale reflects the stereotype of actors as unscrupulous libertines, but it also makes Shakespeare win for a change—through the exercise of wit. William the Conqueror would succeed as well in rumor dating from the late seventeenth century about the poet's affair with Mrs. Davenant, yet another of the triangulated stories about Shakespeare, the maker of such fictions.

IV

At its most general level, the debate between Jonson and Shakespeare in *Every Man Out* and *As You Like It* centers on the philosophical distinction between art and nature. Since Shakespeare chose pastoral for his response, one would expect him to summon an ideal Arcadian nature to contest Jonson's reformative art. From this standpoint, the play becomes, in Rosalie Colie's words, "a celebration, in varying degrees of devotion, of what is 'natural' and sustaining in human life and human environment."[57] *Every Man Out* begins in the country and ends at court; *As You Like It* reverses that movement. Here nature is "More free from peril than the envious court" (2.1.4), and Rosalind and Celia follow Duke Senior "To liberty, and not to banishment" (1.3.138). A sense of natural teleology is inscribed in the play's comic formula. Its progression from unnatural conflicts to a natural community wrought by love— for all except William and Jaques—recapitulates the movement from conflict through release to reconciliation that C. L. Barber described as the underlying structure of "Shakespeare's festive comedy."

In the main plot, flight to the green world of Arden is an escape from a society controlled by "unnatural" siblings (4.3.124). In symmetrical acts of transgression, Duke Frederick, a younger brother, deposes his older brother Duke Senior, while Oliver, an older brother, plans his younger brother Orlando's murder. Both acts are reversed when Duke Frederick senses his connection with the divine and Oliver acknowledges his bond to nature. Having met an "old religious man" in the forest, "After some question with him," Frederick is "converted / Both from his enterprise and from the world" (5.4.161–62). Rescued from death by his mistreated brother, Oliver too is instantly changed when he recognizes his capacity for love. "'Twas I; but 'tis not I," he informs Rosalind. "I do not shame / To tell you what I was, since my conversion / So sweetly tastes, being the thing I am" (4.3.135–37). In each case a self-alienating complex of narcissism, anger, and envy is voluntarily abandoned as the generators of public and private dissension submit freely to the moral norm of Shakespearean comedy. Both *Every Man Out* and *As You Like It* are cathartic fictions of moral transformation. The conversions of Oliver and Duke Frederick, like those of their analogues in *Every Man Out*, argue for the possibility of social renewal. But despite this similarity, it would be difficult to find two comedies in the English Renaissance that rest on such contradictory premises. In *Every Man Out*, catharsis culminates in a necessary alienation from society. In *As You Like It*, the main characters surrender to others and learn to live according to nature, whose aim is to make odds even.

Still, in a characteristically dialectical maneuver, Shakespeare acknowledges that nature is neither rational nor wholly benign. Part of the difficulty of understanding *As You Like It* is that the play systematically undermines the normative standard it advocates. Just as Touchstone balances the virtues and vices of pastoral in his clever parody of the *beatus ille* tradition (3.2.13–22), *As You Like It* espouses the benefits of living according to nature even as it suggests both the difficulty of knowing exactly what that would mean and the danger such a life would involve.

The presence of the virgin queen at the conclusion of *Every Man Out* sanctions Jonson's art by establishing a parallel between the sovereign and the poet, both of whom restrain desire through judgment. The epiphany that concludes *As You Like It* validates the play's natural teleology by evoking the concept of a supernatural art coincident with nature. "I have, since I was three year old," Rosalind reveals, "convers'd with a magician, most profound in his art" (5.2.59–61). Shakespeare links the natural to the artistic and the artistic to the marvelous. "I bar confusion," announces the god Hymen, whom Rosalind's art has secured to officiate over the play's masquelike ending; "'Tis I must make conclusion / Of these most strange events" (5.4.125–27). No precedent for this scene can be found in *Rosalind*, and Shakespeare uses it to sanctify experience through mythology, which binds together the natural, the human, and the divine as coordinated elements in a single all-inclusive order. Affirming a poetics of correspondence, Hymen imparts a divine sanction to natural events: "Then is there mirth in heaven, / When earthly things made even / Atone together" (5.4.108–10).

Yet Shakespeare does not assert desire to be either rational or amenable to reason. "Love," explains Rosalind, "is merely a madness, and I tell you, deserves as well a dark house and a whip as madmen do; and the reason why they are not so punish'd and cur'd is, that the lunacy is so ordinary that the whippers are in love too" (3.2.400–4). "We that are true lovers," Touchstone admits, "run into strange capers; but as all is mortal in nature, so is all nature in love mortal in folly," to which Rosalind replies, "Thou speak'st wiser than thou art ware of" (2.4.54–57). Furthermore, Jonson's plan to purge desire is implicitly mocked by Rosalind, disguised as Ganymede, who tells Orlando that she can cure him through the "physic" of "counsel," if he is prepared to be driven "from his mad humor of love, to his living humor of madness" (3.2.418–19). But Orlando curtly rejects this offer: "I would not be cur'd" (3.2.425). From the perspective of festive comedy, acceding to this madness is the closest we can come to wisdom. It is necessary to submit to a mysterious power beyond rational comprehension, symbolized by Hymen's epiphany. *Every Man Out* upholds the moral power of an art that Shakespeare supposedly lacked, while *As You Like It* meditates on the primal opposition between the intellectual categories of nature and art that Jonson's comical satire presupposes. The play is an encomium to nature that questions its own entanglement in the artistic and the artificial. The bathetic figure of William—the prototype of Shakespeare in love—epitomizes this dialectical engagement.

V

The myth of an artful Jonson and a natural Shakespeare that evolved over the ensuing four centuries into the controlling paradigm for understanding their relationship began as a collaborative effort at self-definition. Indeed, the playwrights confronted each other over the theory of comedy in two coordinated periods during which they explored their differences through the dialectic of nature and art. These periods of symbiotic self-reference commemorate the beginning and end of their interconnected lives as poets in the public theater. Their first exchange took place during the Poets' War. Their second began a decade later, near the end of Shakespeare's career, when in *The Winter's Tale* (1610) and *The Tempest* (1611) he nostalgically returned to pastoral comedy and was criticized again by Jonson in the new address "To the Reader," added to the first quarto of *The Alchemist* (1612); the Induction to *Bartholomew Fair* (1614); and the new Prologue (composed between 1612 and 1616) for the First Folio's revised *Every Man In*. In this case, however, Shakespeare seems to have deliberately provoked Jonson, as E.A.J. Honigmann and Harry Levin have argued, by using his final comedies in an elegiac manner to insist on the writers' difference as comedians. In these late plays we find a continuation of the debate begun a decade earlier. Levin notes that the "conjunction of Jonson and Shakespeare was never closer . . . than in the successive seasons of 1610 and 1611, when His Majesty's Servants introduced *The Alchemist* and *The Tempest* respectively." It was this proximity, he concludes, that prompted Shakespeare to use his comedy to comment on Jonson's, giving him a final "opportunity to reflect and reply, as he is said to have done in the so-called War of the Theaters."[58]

The myth that arose from their argument consequently made Shakespeare nature's paragon. By 1615, Francis Beaumont, in a jocular epistle to his friend Jonson, vows to write in a style that will let "slip (If I had any in me) scholarship, and from all Learning keep these lines as clear / as Shakespeare's best are." Preachers will henceforth cite this poet, he contends, as an example of just "how far sometimes a mortal man may go / by the dim light of Nature."[59] Beaumont's Shakespeare is Jonson's artless but witty opposite who prospers by his natural faculties. This is the Shakespeare whose flashes of genius were offset by ridiculous errors (such as a Bohemia that lies by the sea). This is the Shakespeare Dryden would prefer to Jonson, despite or even because of his imputed flaws. "Those who accuse him to have wanted learning," Dryden says, "give him the greater commendation. He was naturally learned; he needed not the spectacles of books to read nature. He looked inwards and found her there."[60]

One of the most vehement defenses of Shakespeare by a contemporary is Leonard Digges's opening elegy in John Benson's collection of Shakespeare's *Poems* (1640), in which he rejects Jonson's scholarship and plagiarism in favor of the untutored genius, "born not made," whose plays are "Art without Art unparalleled as yet."[61] The embodiment of an extreme Renaissance romanticism, Digges's Shakespeare never imitates, since to do so would be a sign of weakness. His poems are not burdened, as Jonson's are, with Greek and Latin phrases translated "Plagiary-like" (line 15) into leaden English. In his study of Digges's tribute to Shakespeare, John Freehafer cogently notes how the poem "joins forcefully in the continuing argument over the relative places of Nature and Art in the production of great poetry—an argument in which Shakespeare and Jonson came to be . . . the paradigms of the opposing principles, so that the success or failure of one of these men could be virtually equated with the success or failure of a whole philosophy of artistic creation." But Freehafer mistakenly assumes that only "men like Digges and Jonson were prepared to quarrel" over literary theory, while "Shakespeare himself seemingly was not."[62] Despite the efforts that have been made to contextualize Shakespeare's plays, contemporary criticism is still dominated by the belief that he was above the fray, that he did not respond to Jonson's censure, preferring to leave controversy to others. Shakespeare, however, was an active participant in shaping his own myth, and in *As You Like It* the quick master of dialectic first confounded the categories that Jonson used to describe him.

Among those who viewed *As You Like It* at the Globe, none made better use of its metatheatrical critique of Jonson than Marston, who reprised the play's combination of pastoral comedy and antisatirical satire in *Jack Drum's Entertainment* to create his first malicious treatment of the humour poet. How Marston used what he had learned from Shakespeare to amplify his attack on Jonson is the focus of the next chapter.

Brabant, thou art like a pair of Balance,
Thou weighest all saving thy self.
　　　　　—Jack Drum's Entertainment

5　MARSTON'S FESTIVE COMEDY
Punishing Jonson in *Jack Drum's Entertainment*

THE FIRST phase of the Poets' War ended with *Jack Drum's Entertainment, or The Comedy of Pasquil and Katherine*, which features Marston's second, more trenchant caricature of Jonson as a critic whose self-love, arrogance, and malice contaminate his theory of literature and invalidate his authority as a poet. The primary cause of Marston's reevaluation was Jonson's stinging response to *Histriomastix* in criticism he added to *Every Man Out*. Marston's reaction was to embed a shocking punitive fiction directed at his rival in an otherwise ebullient pastoral comedy inspired by *As You Like It*. In tracing the rise of this hostility, however, it is helpful first to consider *Jack Drum*'s position in the sequence of plays Marston wrote as the principal dramatist for the newly reorganized Children of Paul's.

Within two years of working for the first child acting company to be revived at the turn of the century, Marston completed five plays: a trilogy of satirical comedies that were sallies in the Poets' War and a two-part experimental tragicomedy that he called *The History of Antonio and Mellida* when it was published with additions in 1602. Along with Dekker's *Satiromastix*, these five dramas constitute the core not only of what remains but also of what we currently know about the new drama at Paul's:

Histriomastix (1599) with Chrisoganus/Jonson
Antonio and Mellida (1600)

Jack Drum's Entertainment (1600) with Brabant Senior/Jonson
Antonio's Revenge (1600/01)
What You Will (1601) with Lampatho Doria/Jonson[1]

Although modern critics continue to debate the plays' order of composition, attention to their intermittent topicality reveals the evolution of Marston's career. The timing of his two projects was dictated by practicality. In the intervals between the works in his Poets' War trilogy—perhaps waiting for Jonson's response—he wrote *Antonio and Mellida* and *Antonio's Revenge*. Within this alternating pattern Marston's three Jonson surrogates—Chrisoganus, Brabant Senior, and Lampatho Doria—reflect changing attitudes that move from the ambivalence of *Histriomastix* through the contempt of *Jack Drum's Entertainment* to the mock reconciliation of *What You Will*. These surrogates, moreover, appear in an evolving dramatic framework that features changing ratios of comical satire and festive comedy tied to Marston's shifting philosophical positions. Seldom credited with flexibility, Marston's satirical comedy at Paul's was a genre in transit between Jonsonian and Shakespearean emphases. After the assimilation of comical satire in *Histriomastix*, Marston unpredictably turned to the pastoral emphasis of Shakespearean festive comedy as a generic precedent for *Jack Drum's Entertainment*.[2] But in order to extend Shakespeare's containment of comical satire and exposure of the self-alienated satirist, he intensified his play's topicality and malice. These innovations would decisively alter the politics of late Elizabethan theater.

The title *Jack Drum's Entertainment* cleverly combines the play's benign and punitive aspects. The eponymous Jack Drum is the comedy's principal fool, who along with Timothy Tweedle embodies its carnival orchestration. Together they comprise the fife and drum of holiday abandon. The play's opening scene literally stages "Jack Drum's entertainment" as these two characters provide music for morris dancing on the Highgate village green in celebration of the feast of Whitsun. But the title also announces the punitive subplot, since the same phrase was Elizabethan slang for "rough treatment" or "showing an unwanted guest the door." "A drum," according to a contemporary joke, "should be *beaten out of doors*"; subjecting someone to "Jack Drum's entertainment" involved his public humiliation. In this sense, the phrase applies to only one character in the drama: Brabant Senior, a parody of Jonson, whom Planet denounces and crowns with the horns of a satirist and cuckold. To explore the terms of Marston's most vicious assault on Jonson's reputation, it is necessary first to consider in greater detail the criticism that provoked this festive abuse.

I

Jack Drum's satiric brutality responds to two passages Jonson inserted into *Every Man Out* in reaction to *Histriomastix*. Just as he had censured Anthony Munday as Antonio Balladino in his addition to *The Case Is Altered*, he expanded *Every Man Out* in the final weeks of 1599 to parody Marston as Clove, a character who probably first appeared on the stage of the new Globe theater before finding his way into print.[3]

In each of the two brief scenes in which Clove appears (3.1.1–35 and 3.4.6–40), Jonson attacks his scholarship. In the first, he is introduced conversing with Orange and Shift, after which the chorus comments that "he will sit you a whole afternoon sometimes, in a bookseller's shop, reading the *Greek*, *Italian*, and *Spanish*; when he understands not a word; . . . if he had the tongues, of his suits, he were an excellent linguist" (3.1.29–33). And in the second, with Orange at Paul's, Clove coaxes his friend to "talk fustian" so that gallants will "believe we are great scholars" (3.4.7–8) and begins to rant in gibberish featuring scattered words that can still be found in Marston's writing, including the title of his play:

CLOVE   Now, sir, whereas the *Ingenuity* of the time and the soul's
            Synderisis are but *Embrions* in nature, added to the paunch
            of *Esquiline*, and the *Inter-vallum* of the *Zodiac*, besides the
            Ecliptic line being *optic*, and not *mental*, but by the
            contemplative and *theoric* part thereof, doth demonstrate
            to us the *vegetable circumference*, and the *ventosity* of the
            Tropics, and whereas our *intellectual*, or *mincing capreal*
            (according to the *Metaphysics*) as you may read in
            PLATO'S *Histriomastix*—You conceive me, sir?
ORANGE   O lord, sir.
CLOVE   Then coming to the pretty *Animal*, as *Reason long since is fled
            to animals*, you know, or indeed, for the more *modelizing*, or
            enameling, or rather *diamondizing* of your *subject*, you shall
            perceive the *Hypothesis*, or *Galaxia* (whereof the *Meteors* long
            since had their *initial inceptions* and *notions*) to be merely
            Pythagorical, *Mathematical*, and *Aristocratical*—For look you,
            sir, there is ever a kind of *concinnity* and *species*. . . .

                                                            (3.4.21–39)

Since *Histriomastix* is cited, it is not surprising to find a series of quotations from that drama. Its title (The Scourge of the Player) was a pseudonym for

Marston, who had previously styled himself Theriomastix (The Scourge of the Beast) in *The Scourge of Villainy*. What is more, three of Jonson's verbal echoes—"*Zodiac*," "*Ecliptic line*," and "*Tropics*" (singular in Marston)—are clustered around Chrisoganus's statement in the first act that the sun "consummates his circled course / In the Ecliptic line, which parts the Zodiac, / Being borne from Tropic to Tropic" (3:253). "*Mathematical*" (3:252) and "Paunch of *Esquiline*" (3:273), a scatalogical reference, also appear in the play. The latter is close to "port Esquiline" from *The Scourge of Villainy* (7.185), which uses the word "circumference" (10.78) and evokes the theological concept of "*Synderisis*" (8.211). "*Pythagorical*" similarly recalls "Pythagoran" in *The Scourge* (3.125), just as the idiosyncratic use of "*intellectual*" as a noun, followed by the phrase "*mincing capreal*," echoes "His very soul, his intellectual / Is *nothing* but a mincing capreal" (11.23–24). Even a phrase mocking *Julius Caesar* (also written in 1599)—recalling "O judgment! thou art fled to brutish beasts, / And men have lost their reason"—slights Marston's repetition of Shakespearean absurdities.

In *Histriomastix*, Jonson had been represented as a "pedant" and "linguist" who repudiates Posthaste's "lawless bastard's words" (3:264). But he apparently resented being associated with Chrisoganus's stilted jargon, and through Clove he returned it to its source. In *The Scourge* Marston had derided the "affectation / To speak beyond men's apprehension, / . . . when all in fustian suit / Is cloth'd a huge nothing, all for repute / Of profoundest knowledge" (9.66–70).[4] And in *Histriomastix* he implicitly positioned himself between Munday and Jonson, only to find himself characterized by Jonson as Munday's pretentious opposite. The Balladino and Clove interpolations in *The Case Is Altered* and *Every Man Out* are coordinated acts of literary criticism. Balladino was created to defend *Every Man In* against Munday by reducing Jonson's rival to a caricature of a poet who caters to "the common sort" and despises those who "write . . . nothing but humours" to please "the Gentlemen" (1.2.61–63). Clove vindicated *Every Man Out* against Marston by highlighting his intellectual dishonesty. Each genre generated a caricature: Jonson's assault on Munday defended the comedy of humours and his parody of Marston defended comical satire. Both portraits were complementary parts of a literary strategy Jonson employed to define his work in terms of an Aristotelian mean between debased forms of popular and coterie theater. These linked parodies represent the Scylla and Charybdis of stylistic, ethical, and institutional defects he sought to avoid by creating a style of writing that was neither naive nor solipsistic but embued with a linguistic integrity he later called "language such as men do use."

What is more, Jonson further elaborates his attack on Marston's supposedly elite poetics by linking the pungent Clove with sour Orange as "an inseparable pair of Coxcombs" in what Richard Simpson first identified as a parody of Marston's association with Dekker.[5] In each of Jonson's three representations of Marston between 1599 and 1601, the caricatures are coupled: Clove and Orange become Hedon and Anaides in *Cynthia's Revels* and Crispinus and Demetrius in *Poetaster*. They are the only characters introduced together in the First Quarto's character sketches, where an elaborate description (almost as long as their appearance in the play) draws attention to the parody. Their aliases underscore their symbiosis. A pomander made from a sour orange stuck with cloves could be deployed for a variety of purposes, but Jonson was probably thinking of such oranges that were placed in glasses of ale for flavoring. "Orange," he writes, "*is the more humorous of the two (whose small portion of juice being squeez'd out)* Clove *serves to stick him, with commendations*" (characters, lines 107–9). Yet no matter how obscure Clove's diction, his connection to Orange signifies that he is a poseur, as Jonson pairs Marston with Dekker to retaliate for being linked with Munday in *Histriomastix*. They are the "Gemini or *Twins of foppery*," he writes, whose single greatest "glory is to invite Players, and make suppers" (lines 100–4).

Clove and Orange appear in a satirical cameo reserved for personal application, and that is why, Jonson slyly hints, they are alien to his work, having been superimposed on an already completed plot.

MITIS   What be these two, signior?

CORDATUS   Marry, a couple sir, that are mere strangers to the whole
            scope of our play; only come to walk a turn or two, i'
            this *Scene* of *Paul's*, by chance.

                                                    (3.1.16–19)

Jonson's parody was an afterthought composed to meet the unforeseen production of *Histriomastix* at Paul's.[6] And where else should he have added his commentary than in this "*Scene* of *Paul's*"? Marston and Dekker, he jokes, simply walked into it. The cathedral's middle aisle, where Clove and Orange converse, was a popular place for gallants to loiter, sell and buy books, find servants, and conduct business. In *Certain Satires* Marston had cited its "peopled press" among whom the parasite Ruscus makes "nods and legs and odd superfluous talk" (1.12–14), and Dekker would mock its social rituals in *The Gull's Hornbook*. Clove and Orange are there because of its nominal and geographical connection with the theater for which Marston had written *Histriomastix*. Marston might have been irritated by the parody, but if *Every Man Out* mocked *Histriomastix*, Jonson's bad review was still a good advertisement. He accepted derision as the price of engagement. Those who wanted to judge

Jonson's charges—argued on the stage of the Globe and amplified in the printed copies of *Every Man Out*—would have to see *Histriomastix* and *Jack Drum* for themselves. Jonson's annoyance was, at any rate, a stimulant. It proved to Marston that his work was challenging enough to refute, and it furnished a personal incentive to probe his rival's poetry and life with an even keener eye.

II

Modern commentaries on *Jack Drum* agree that Brabant Senior is Marston's first wholly caustic parody of Jonson. Small, Chambers, Herford and Simpson, Allen, Campbell, and Barton unanimously conclude that this parody made Marston Jonson's principal antagonist in the Poets' War. "The consensus of the best scholarly opinion," Campbell summarizes, is that Marston "expected at least part of his audience to detect in this stage-figure certain of Jonson's shortcomings."[7] Yet Marston's technique is complex, since it depends on the creation of a character who is and is not Jonson, a caricature both apparent and disguised. In early modern English, to "brabble" meant to "dispute captiously or obstinately." It was probably as a variation on this word that Marston coined his alias for Jonson, who is doubled with his fictitious brother, Brabant Junior, as symbolic extremes of satire and romance.

Brabant Senior first evokes Jonson in two short dialogues in acts 4 and 5 in which he ridicules Paul's poets and repertoire. In the first—written as a complete scene—he sneers at three of the company's playwrights applauded by his brother and Planet.

BRABANT JUNIOR	Brother, how like you of our modern wits?
	How like you the new Poet *Mellidus*?
BRABANT SENIOR	A slight bubbling spirit, a Cork, a Husk.
PLANET	How like you *Musus*'s fashion in his carriage?
BRABANT SENIOR	O filthily; he is as blunt as *Paul's*.
BRABANT JUNIOR	What think you of the lines of *Decius*?
	Writes he not good cordial sappy style?
BRABANT SENIOR	A surreined Jaded wit, but 'a rubs on.
PLANET	Brabant, thou art like a pair of Balance,
	Thou weighest all saving thy self.
BRABANT SENIOR	Good faith, troth is, they are all Apes and gulls,
	Vile imitating spirits, dry heathy Turfs.
BRABANT JUNIOR	Nay brother, now I think your judgement errs.

PLANET   Err, he cannot err man, for children and fools
                        Speak truth always.

                                                          (3:221)

Mellidus, Musus, and Decius allude to Marston, perhaps Middleton, and
Dekker—three "modern wits" associated with "*Paul's*." The first and last are
easy to decipher. "The new Poet *Mellidus*" designates Marston through his previous play *Antonio and Mellida*, and "*Decius*" is an abbreviation of "Dekker"
with a Latinized masculine ending that links it to the other two pseudonyms.

Dekker worked for the Admiral's Men from 1598 onward, but, as George
Price observes, he disappears from *Henslowe's Diary* between 6 September 1600
and 12 January 1602, "with the single exception of a record of payment to
Dekker and Chettle for *King Sebastian of Portugal* in April and May, 1601. In
1602, however, Henslowe records his astonishing productivity." Since "we cannot fill the interval of about sixteen months—the autumn of 1600 and all of
1601—with three plays, *Sebastian of Portugal*, *Blurt, Master Constable*, and
Satiromastix," Price continues, he had time to write for Paul's. Dekker worked
on fifteen plays for Henslowe in 1598, and he "could not have lived on the pro-
ceeds from these three. . . . It seems a reasonable guess that during these
months he was supplying a part, perhaps a major part, of the repertory of the
Paul's Boys."[8] All that we have left of this association, however, is *Satiromastix*
and a trail of innuendo hinting that he and Marston had collaborated on an
early version of *Lust's Dominion*. Marston received two pounds from Henslowe
in 1599 for his work on a play completed early the following year by Dekker,
Haughton, and Day, originally called *The Spanish Moor's Tragedy*. It is likely
that Marston and Dekker took a version of it to Paul's, since they are accused
in *Satiromastix* of having "cut an Innocent Moor i' the middle, to serve him
in twice; and . . . made Paul's work of it" (2.2.41–42).[9] "Paul's work" not only
indicates the play's place of production but also characterizes its poor quality,
since the phrase was an Elizabethan colloquialism for a messy or botched job.

There is not enough evidence to prove Chambers's guess that "Musus"
refers to Thomas Middleton, the only other playwright known to have written for Paul's around this time.[10] Whoever this was had a "blunt" style that
conformed to the cathedral's then prominent architectural anomaly, its un-
capped spire. But since we do not know much about Middleton's early career,
conjecture about his working at Paul's before becoming its principal poet
from 1603 to 1606 is in vain.[11] If we set aside Musus, however, we are left with
a scene in which Mellidus and Decius are dismissed with the same conde-
scension expressed toward Clove and Orange. Jonson had at that time com-
mented on only *The Scourge* and *Histriomastix*, so Marston now updates his

critique by having Brabant attack *Antonio and Mellida* as well. According to Marston, Jonson views him as insignificant, inconsistent, and vacuous: a "bubbling spirit," a bobbing "cork," and an empty "husk." When Brabant Junior then praises Decius's "good cordial sappy style," he evokes the high-spirited, sentimental quality of plays like *The Shoemakers' Holiday*. The word "cordial" suggests heartfelt sincerity and comforting affection, as well as an alcoholic drink stimulating health and comraderie. A "sappy" style was vital and juicy; the adjective had not yet acquired the sense of being "too sugary." Jonson's surrogate, however, insists on calling him a "surreined" (overworked), "Jaded" (worn-out) "wit." A "jade" was a horse of an inferior breed, a cart horse, not a riding horse, typically exhausted, vicious, and worthless. Jonson's Decius is a tired, surly hack who somehow "rubs on." For some critics this is still a cruel but accurate assessment of Dekker's prolific career. Between 1598 and 1600 alone he wrote or contributed to at least thirty-one plays for the Admiral's Men with teams of writers that included Drayton, Wilson, Chettle, Day, Haughton, Hathway, Munday, *and* Jonson.[12] As a group, Jonson concludes, the modern wits at Paul's shared two flaws: they were "vile imitating spirits" and "dry heathy Turfs," as witless and worthless as dirt.

Jonson's criticism of Paul's is reiterated in act 5 during a short conversation initiated by Sir Edward Fortune, who regrets that he did not commission a play for his Whitsuntide celebration. This time, however, Brabant responds by condemning the company's repertoire for being old-fashioned and unsophisticated, in response to Sir Edward's delight with their work:

	I saw the Children of *Paul's* last night,
	And troth they pleased me pretty, pretty well.
	The Apes in time will do it handsomely.
PLANET	I' faith I like the Audience that frequenteth there
	With much applause: A man shall not be choked
	With the stench of Garlic, nor be pasted
	To the barmy Jacket of a Beer-brewer.
BRABANT JUNIOR	'Tis a good gentle Audience, and I hope the Boys
	Will come one day into the Court of requests.
BRABANT SENIOR	Ay and they had good Plays, but they produce
	Such musty fopperies of antiquity,
	And do not suit the humorous age's backs
	With clothes in fashion.
PLANET	Well *Brabant* well, you will be censuring still,
	There lies a Jest in steep will whip you for't.

(3:234)

Planet and Brabant Junior agree with Sir Edward that Paul's is an exciting venue not only for the constantly improving child actors but also for its exclusivity. Brabant, however, who enjoys being contrary, carps about the out-of-date repertoire, which he finds, using a Jonsonian catchphrase, unfit to clothe the "humorous age's backs." Jonson's true purpose, Marston insinuates, is not to cure his audience but to cater to its fashion. Asper had threatened to lash the world, and Marston had warned Chrisoganus against brandishing "just *Ramnusia*'s whip," so Planet's threat to beat Brabant with "a Jest in steep" (a rod cured in brine to increase its bite) is a symptom of how hostile Marston's censure had become.

Jonson's sneer at Paul's repertoire covers both its reprised plays and revised scripts. The company, which was probably undercapitalized, might have drawn on work written as early as the 1580s to pad its schedule. As *Histriomastix* demonstrates, topicality could give old drama new life. Later in 1600, when he wrote *Cynthia's Revels* for the Children of the Chapel, Jonson hinted that Blackfriars was also in danger of being haunted by the ghosts of departed scripts (Induction, lines 194–97). The private theaters enjoyed a reputation for being exclusive and modern, and these theatrical specters exposed their deficiencies. Marston was so sensitive to this charge that he anticipated it by vowing in his Induction not to "torment" his audience "With mouldy fopperies of stale Poetry, / Unpossible dry musty Fictions" (3:179). When he calls himself "the new Poet *Mellidus*," he not only attests to his new fame but identifies *Antonio and Mellida* (unlike *Histriomastix*) as being entirely his own. But how exclusive were his plays at Paul's? Marston's implicit admission that his plays for Paul's Boys had not been performed at court broached an embarrassing issue. The only record of their appearance at court during this period is a payment to Edward Pearce, the Master of the Children of Paul's, noted in the Treasurer of the Chamber's Accounts, for a performance on 1 January 1601.[13] Although a private company, the troupe was never as popular there as the Chamberlain's Men.

When he is not criticizing Paul's, Brabant Senior engages in Jonson's defining enterprise. A "gull groper," he revels in exposing the weaknesses of three humourists who combine psychological and linguistic defects: Puff, the moron of formal compliment; John Ellis, the idiot Euphuist; and John fo de King, the lecherous Frenchman of broken English. Like Jonson, he blends contempt for others with self-congratulation when he introduces Planet to John Ellis: "He shall be your Fool, Planet, and you shall be his Coxcomb. Ha, ha, I have a simple wit, ha, ha" (3:192). Unable to praise others without venting a pathological disdain, he pretends to commend Puff to Planet and Brabant Junior, only to explode with derisive laughter:

BRABANT SENIOR   You shall see his humour. I pray you be familiar
with this Gentleman master *Puff,* he is a man of
a well grown spirit, richly worth your—I assure
you, ha, ha, ha.

(3:191)

What is particularly irritating about Brabant/Jonson is that he is a hypocrite
who indulges in the very bombast he mocks. In response to Jonson's criticism
in *Every Man Out,* Marston now accuses *him* of being overblown and insin-
cere as Brabant matches Puff's rhetoric with his own. "Gentlemen," Brabant
addresses his audience, "as ere you lov'd wench, observe M. Puff and me. . . .
I' faith, mark with what grace I encounter him."

PUFF   Most accomplished wit, exquisitely accoutred,
(*Puff*) Judgment, I could wish my ability worthy
your service, and my service worthy your ability. . . .
BRABANT SENIOR   I protest your abilities are infinite, your perfec-
tions matchless, your matchless perfection infinite
in ability, and your infinite ability, matchless. . . .

(3:209)

While Jonson must have been irritated by this parody of his language of formal compliment, it has long been assumed that what angered him even more
was Marston's indiscreet allusion to his sexual impropriety—the promised "Jest
in steep" with which the play concludes. Immediately after he recorded in his
Conversations that Jonson had first quarrelled with Marston after the latter had
"represented him in the stage," presumably in *Histriomastix,* Drummond completed his sentence with a personal observation: "in his youth given to Venery."
Then, continuing to document what he had been told, Drummond wrote that
Jonson "thought the use of a maid nothing in comparison to the wantoness of
a wife and would never have any other Mistress." This led him into a strange
love triangle, in which a husband arranged to have the poet cuckold him:

that a man made his own wife to Court him, whom he enjoyed two
years ere he knew of it, and one day finding them by chance was pass-
ingly delighted with it.

(1:140)

Jonson, the hero of his own fabliau, evidently enjoyed the double pleasure of
taking the wife and degrading her husband.[14] That Drummond connected

Jonson's comments on Marston representing him on the stage with a recollection of his transgressive sexuality was not accidental. In *As You Like It* Jaques had been disqualified from exercising satiric authority for being a "libertine" pricked with a "brutish sting." In *Jack Drum* Marston gave the same imputation a personal inflection. As Chambers recognizes, the main difference between the story narrated by Jonson to Drummond and the cuckolding of Brabant Senior that Marston based on it was that in the former Jonson "played the active, not the passive part."[15]

Critics from Chambers to Barton have stressed the connection between this anecdote and the jest at Jonson's expense in Marston's comedy. Obsessed with exposing the humours of the play's three gulls, Brabant Senior encourages John fo de King (whose surname suggests an obscene pun) to attempt to seduce his own wife, whom he does not identify as such, in order to amuse himself with John's failure. "I am sure she hath so cudgeled him with quick sharp Jests," Brabant scoffs, "and so battered him with a volley of her wit . . . that in conscience he'll never dare to court women more" (3:239). When Sir Edward consequently asks for one last "tickling Jest . . . ere we go in," Brabant volunteers: "Faith Gentlemen, I ha' brewed such a strong headed Jest / Will make you drunk, and reel with laughter." But his plot backfires when John returns, bragging in mispronounced English of his encounter with Brabant's wife: "she hath de finest little vart you know veare: . . . me nere touch such a vench" (3:240). And all that John can do when he realizes that Brabant has cuckolded himself is apologize and offer free language lessons. "By gor me no know, you tell a me 'twas a Courtesan," he protests, before promising to teach him "French to t'end of de vorld" (3:240). Voicing Marston's most strident anti-Jonsonian rhetoric, Planet then forcibly crowns Brabant with horns, indicts him for Jonson's faults, and numbers him among the fools:

> Come, here's thy Cap of Maintenance, the Coronet
> Of Cuckolds. Nay you shall wear it, or wear
> My Rapier in your guts by heaven.
> Why dost thou not well deserve to be thus used?
> Why should'st thou take felicity to gull
> Good honest souls, and in thy arrogance
> And glorious ostentation of thy wit,
> Think God infused all perfection
> Into thy soul alone, and made the rest
> For thee to laugh at? Now you Censurer
> Be the ridiculous subject of our mirth.
> Why Fool, the power of Creation

Is still Omnipotent, and there's no man that breathes
So valiant, learned, witty, or so wise,
But it can equal him out of the same mould
Wherein the first was formed. Then leave proud scorn
And, honest self-made Cuckold, wear the horn.

(3:240)

The incongruity between Planet's heated tirade against Jonson and the plot
of *Jack Drum's Entertainment* results from a disjunction in Brabant's dual role
as fictional character and biographical allegory.[16] Planet's rebuke, however,
has a negligible effect on the defiant Brabant. "Wear the horn?" he bellows.
"Ay, spite of all your teeth / I'll wear this Crown, and triumph in this horn."
Queen Elizabeth had purged Macilente in *Every Man Out*, but no such
transformation is available for Brabant Senior, as Sir Edward concludes the
play by requesting music to solemnize Jonson's mock coronation with "royal
pomp," as "free light Jocund mirth shall be enthroned / With sumptuous
state" (3:240).

Petrarch's public coronation in 1341 as a poet laureate on the steps of the
Capitoline in Rome symbolized a humanist ideal, and his celebrity in Western Europe made it possible for Renaissance poets, influenced by his program,
to conceive of their activity as equally significant. Although Jonson aspired to
be crowned with bays, Marston suggests, wearing horns was the closest he
would come. No matter what claims he made for *Every Man Out*—that it was
"the strongest eternal Jest / That ere was builded by Invention" (3:222)—that
play was, for Marston, only a series of practical jokes for which the author deserved to be ostracized. Jonson had brought the merchant Delirio to the point
of being cuckolded by Fallace and Fastidious Brisk at the end of *Every Man
Out*. Marston takes this comic formula a step further by concluding his play
with Brabant's self-cuckolding. A year later, when Dekker, at the climax of
Satiromastix, restaged this scene of Jonson's chastisement at Paul's and the
Globe, the already horned satyr would be recrowned with nettles.

III

Although modern critics of *Jack Drum* have largely agreed about its assault
on Jonsonian satire, they have only gradually come to recognize its commitment to a countervailing romanticism that aligns Marston's work with Shakespeare's. The main difficulty they faced was Harbage's assessment that all private drama encouraged ironic detachment. Since the "little apes" mimicked
rather than acted, all Marston's plays were uniformly read as send-ups of pub-

lic drama. Even though he "devotes a substantial part of his piece to the complications of a romantic tale," Campbell writes, he intended to approximate comical satire.[17] Marston is for this reason categorized by Caputi as a Stoic who derided the libidinal and aggressive instincts espoused by romantic comedy and revenge tragedy. Caputi consequently maintains that Marston's plotting was wholly a burlesque of popular drama, with both *Antonio and Mellida* and *Jack Drum* mocking what he calls traditional "lovers-in-distress plays." In each instance, he explains, Marston emphasizes his play's "nakedly conventional action with the clear purpose of magnifying and thus rendering more ludicrous its naive romanticism."[18] Reginald Foakes shares this position in stating that Marston's early plays served "from the beginning as vehicles for child-actors consciously ranting in oversize parts," so that their audience was "not allowed to take their passions or motives seriously." The "grand speeches," he argues, are entirely "undermined by bathos or parody."[19] Caputi's and Foakes's readings proved to be so influential because they precisely illustrated Harbage's theory that the function of private drama was to mock its public counterpart.

But were the child actors incapable of sustaining a positive and romantic mode of characterization? Is it credible, for instance, that because the children acted Chapman's *Bussy D'Ambois* it had to have been staged as farce? Madeleine Doran was one of the earliest critics to resist this tendency to reduce *Antonio and Mellida*, *Jack Drum*, and *Antonio's Revenge* to burlesque when she observed that although we habitually think of Marston as a satirist, he was capable of subordinating satire to romance. Marston's satire, she explains, is found in both "secondary actions" subsidiary to the core fiction and biting commentary that sometimes "overlaps" the "romanticially designed" main plot without negating its seriousness.[20] The same insight leads Richard Levin to challenge Foakes's premise that "parody" is "predominant" in the Antonio plays, an interpretation Levin blames on the proclivity of modern scholars to generate ironic misreadings of Renaissance drama.[21]

The most convincing refutation of the view of Marston's early drama as entirely parodic, however, has been offered by G. K. Hunter, who begins his analysis of *Antonio and Mellida* by praising Foakes and Caputi for recognizing that "the disparity between the child-actor and the adult role" was "a powerful means of presenting the meaningful artificiality of the play-world, and insisting on a dramatic vision of life." Yet the "greatest disadvantage" of their interpretation, he insists, is "that it operates within an intolerably coarse-grained view of 'parody,'" by reducing it to a single effect. They have not realized that "the clash between the child-actors and the language they spoke"—their theatrical artificiality—fostered a far wider range of responses than a parasitic travesty of public drama. Satire *was* one of the children's strengths, but to limit their effect solely to burlesque was to underestimate the varied effects of their rhetoric and the flexibility of Marston's poetics. What might at first appear to be parodied language, he suggests, could actually constitute "a love-strain more remote from everyday conversation" in which the "stilted Petrarchisms of the opera-like dialogue . . . counterpoint the base vernacular confusions" of the play's humourists.[22] Hunter locates in Marston's drama a strain of high romantic rhetoric in which "serious personal expression" is presented as being "beyond the ordinary business of living." Recent scholars, such as W. Reavley Gair, usually agree that Foakes "overstated" his case in assuming that "the grand passions" of Marston's early plays were "false." What Foakes underestimates is the deftness with which Marston manipulated his language "to create a musical rhetorical score" as he sought "to use the speeches of his characters as a pattern of rising and falling emotional tension, ranging from the grandiloquent to the humiliating."[23] T. F. Wharton, who tenders the most thorough overview of this debate on how to read Marston's drama, consequently concludes that "the balance of the argument seems to rest against the parody theorists."[24] One of the benefits of this critical reevaluation is that it allows us to coordinate *Jack Drum*'s personal and generic critiques of Jonson in a coherent explanation of its place in the Poets' War. For as long as the play is interpreted as a derivative version of comical satire spiked with *ad hominem* abuse, as Campbell contends, its intellectual focus remains obscured.[25]

IV

When it is not read as totalizing satire, Marston's pastoral experiment discloses its anti-Jonsonian bias. *Jack Drum's Entertainment* is a festive comedy that adopts the metatheatrical strategy Shakespeare had used in *As You Like It* to contain comical satire at the Globe. Set in the English countryside of Highgate, near the estate of Sir Edward Fortune, *Jack Drum* opens with a scene of carnival revelry on the feast of Whitsun. Celebrated fifty days after Easter, Whitsun (or Pentecost), "the religious answer to May Day," afforded rural revelers an occasion to rejoice in the new growth of spring.[26] Written to coincide with this Elizabethan holiday, *Jack Drum* appropriates for the private stage the spirit of those popular entertainments that Perdita in *The Winter's Tale* refers to as "Whitsun pastorals" (4.4.134). The play's joyful opening scene of bucolic festivity, filled with music, harmonizes social classes under the paternal gaze of Sir Edward Fortune, a wealthy landowner, who liberally feasts the revelers. "'Tis Whitsuntide," he shouts, "and we must frolic it" (3:182), un-

locking his cellar's supplies of drink to the morris dancers from nearby Hol-
loway, including an unnamed fool, who jest, caper, and sing before erecting a
maypole on the village green.

An intoxicated sponsor of festive sociability, Sir Edward has a pedigree be-
longing to the public theater of Jonson's Doctor Clement in *Every Man In* and
Dekker's Simon Eyre of *The Shoemakers' Holiday*. He embodies an ideal of pastoral *otium* opposed to the encroachments of *negotias* represented by the mer-
chant-usurer Mammon, with whom he debates his philosophy of life. For Sir
Edward, the world of Highgate, "My private sweet of life" (3:184), as he calls
it, is, like the enchanted precinct of Arden, a domain of pastoral release—song,
social communion, and sexuality—superior to the rival spaces of city and
court, which are dominated by contention for money and status. And when
Mammon complains that the "dry throated" revelers will devour his stocks, Sir
Edward allegorizes his own name to defend his feudal munificence:

> Tush, tush, your life hath lost his taste.
> Oh madness still to sweat in hard pursuit
> Of cold abhorred sluttish niggardise,
> To exile one's fortunes from their native use,
> To entertain a present poverty,
> A willing want, for Infidel mistrust
> Of gracious providence.
>
> (3:183–84)

"Fortune," rather than intellect or ambition, determines fate, and since fortune flows from fortune, Sir Edward explains, it is blasphemous to entertain
a "mistrust" of "gracious providence." Such an attitude—self-motivated and
self-serving—is opposed to both the confident patience of religious faith commemorated on the feast of Whitsun and the spirit of festivity the holiday engenders. Aspiring courtiers might speak of secrets of state, he adds, but "I had
rather that Kemp's Morris were their chat, / For of foolish actions, maybe
they'll talk wisely, but of / Wise intendments, most part talk like fools." Instead, he cautions, politics should be left to the "Council chamber," that
"Phoenix nest, / Who wastes itself, to give us peace and rest" (3:182). "I adore
the Sun," he continues,

> Yet love to live within a temperate zone.
> Let who will climb ambitious glibbery rounds,
> And lean upon the vulgar's rotten love.
> I'll not corrival him: The Sun will give

As great a shadow to my trunk as his:
And after death like Chessmen having stood
In play for Bishops, some for Knights, and Pawns,
We all together shall be tumbled up, into one bag.

(3:185)

Political, social, and literary aspirations are futile, he argues, since death, which invalidates status, confers legitimacy on only festive release and the intense realization of pleasure. Sir Edward is consequently a humour character in a play that prizes his sanguinity and condemns Brabant's choler as Marston, like Shakespeare, uses festive comedy to contain comical satire.

The total effect of *The Comedy of Pasquil and Katherine*—the play's alternate title—is to duplicate "the comic crosses of true love" traced in *Antonio and Mellida* through the dramatic form and language of high romanticism. It was only in *What You Will*, his next Poets' War drama, that Marston would respond to the more problematic sexuality of *Hamlet* and *Twelfth Night* by mocking his own version of romance. Here, Marston constructs a pattern of antithetical romantic possibilities in the plots involving Sir Edward's two daughters, the constant Katherine and the fickle Camelia. Sir Edward's belief in personal freedom extends to his decision never to interfere with his daughters' selection of husbands, and the liberty he bestows on them elicits their contrary humours, indicating the basic duality of human nature. Addressing the same question that Shakespeare considered in pondering the moral disparity between siblings in *As You Like It*, Pasquil asks:

Is't possible that sisters should be so thwart
In native humours? One's as kind and fair,
As constant, virtuous, and as debonaire,
As is the heart of goodness: the other, proud,
Inconstant, fantastic, and as vain in loves,
As travellers in lies: blest *Katherine*
Camelia's not thy sister, if she be,
She's bastard to the sweets that shine in thee.

(3:200)

Marston's purpose in contrasting Katherine with Camelia is to distinguish between legitimate and illegitimate forms of desire, and as long as he makes this differentiation he rejects comical satire, a genre in which romantic involvement invariably ends in moral and social disorder. Thus, while Camelia betrays her lovers, the threat to Pasquil and Katherine's union is primarily external. The spurned Mammon hires John fo de King to kill Pasquil and, when that fails, disfigures Katherine with poison. But her scars heal, and the constant lovers are reunited when Pasquil, cured of the madness brought on by their separation, responds to Katherine's restoration with poetry through which, however awkwardly, Marston strains to create a romantic sublime:

> Amazement, wonder, stiff astonishment,
> Stare and stand gazing on this miracle,
> Perfection, of what ere a human thought
> Can reach with his discoursive faculties,
> Thou whose sweet presence purifies my sence,
> And dost create a second soul in me,
> Dear *Katherine*, the life of *Pasquil's* hopes.
>
> (3:236)

If modern readers find *Jack Drum*'s plot and language ridiculous and cloying, they can take solace in the fact that Jonson agreed with them and consequently parodied Marston as Hedon in *Cynthia's Revels*. But Marston himself seems to have believed in the potential emotional impact of this story, which he based on the tale of Argalus and the disfigured Parthenia in Sidney's *Arcadia* (1593). Except for Shakespeare, Sidney was by far the most important contemporary influence on Marston's early romantic comedies *Antonio and Mellida* and *Jack Drum*. *Arcadia* was to *Jack Drum* what *Rosalind* was to *As You Like It*: a source of inspiration, not a target for ridicule.[27] Like Sidney, Marston responded to the paradoxical fate of the faithful lovers Argalus and Parthenia: "that he, by an affection sprung from excessive beauty, should delight in horrible foulness, and she of a vehement desire to have him should kindly build a resolution never to have him."[28]

In addition to following Sidney's plotting, Marston turned to the romantic dialogue of *Romeo and Juliet*'s already famous balcony scene as a rhetorical standard for the most elegant expression of erotic passion. Act 2 of *Jack Drum* begins with Puff and Mammon ludicrously serenading Katherine beneath her window at night. Once she dismisses them, however, Pasquil enters and abruptly changes the scene's linguistic register by rhapsodizing on the approaching dawn:

> The glooming morn with shining Arms
> The silver Ensign of the grim-cheeked night, hath chased
> And forc'd the sacred troupes of sparkling stars
> Into their private Tents. . . .   (3:198)

The model for this speech, as the better-informed members of Marston's audience would have known (from either its performance or the early quartos), was the description of dawn after the lovers have parted in *Romeo and Juliet*:

> The grey-ey'd morn smiles on the frowning night,
> Check'ring the eastern clouds with streaks of light,
> And fleckled darkness like a drunkard reels
> From forth day's path and Titan's fiery wheels.
>
> (2.3.1–4)

Marston was always attracted to Shakespeare's most ornate rhetoric, and Pasquil's echo of Romeo is emulative, not ironic. When Katherine tells Pasquil that she runs to him "Even with the swiftness, though not with like heart: / As the fierce Falcon stoups to rising fowl" (3:198), she paraphrases Juliet's "O, for a falc'ner's voice, / To lure this tassel-gentle back again!" (2.2.158–59). Even Katherine's excited hesitation, "Farewell, yet stay, . . . Adieu, yet hark, nay faith, adieu, adieu" (3:200), has its source in Juliet's reluctance to part from Romeo: "dear love, adieu! . . . Stay but a little, I will come again" (2.2.136–38). Marston obviously felt that the success of his comedy depended on the extent to which Pasquil and Katherine's language could approximate Shakespearean lyricism.

Rather than the heroic romanticism of *Antonio and Mellida*, a play concerned with dynastic struggle, *Jack Drum* exhibits a festive liberty unique in Marston's career. His principal reason for writing a pastoral comedy in 1600, I have suggested, was that Shakespeare had just used the genre to defend festivity against the challenge of comical satire at the Globe. Marston decided to repeat this strategy with greater specificity and harsher invective at Paul's. He offered his audience a sterner version of the genre that cultivated a complex balance of romance and satire. In doing so, Marston intricately interwove his objections to the efficacy of comical satire with both the general tenor of his play and his private vendetta against Jonson. In creating Brabant Senior, Marston eliminated the ambiguity with which he had treated Chrisoganus in *Histriomastix* in order to contest both Jonson's claim to poetic authority and the drama he created to exemplify it. Indeed, it is impossible to understand Marston's personal attack without considering its literary and philosophical dimensions.

Jonson answered Marston several months later in *Cynthia's Revels*, the first of two comical satires he wrote for the Children of the Chapel at Blackfriars. Paul's, which probably held fewer than 200 spectators, now faced the return of their ancient rivals, who were performing Jonson's latest hostile comical satire in a newly refurbished hall with a capacity of approximately 500, situated in a more affluent section of London. While trying to gain the attention of Elizabeth's court and making the most of his affiliation with the Children of the Queen's Chapel, Jonson offered new caricatures of Marston and Dekker in his core fiction to illustrate the literary and moral failings his work remedied. The next chapter details how he ignited the second phase of the Poets' War with *Cynthia's Revels* and how Marston, again inspired by Shakespeare, rebuffed this criticism in *What You Will*.

PART TWO

S.Laurens Poultney

S. Laurens Soper Hill The Exhange The Duch Churche S. Michaelis S. Peter

F L V I V S.

Winchelter Howle

South Warke.

Rivo, Saint Mark, let's talk as loose as air,
Unwind youth's colors, display our selves,
So that yon envy-starved Cur may yelp
And spend his chaps at our Fantasticness.
                                    —What You Will

6 THE WAR OF THE PRIVATE THEATERS
Cynthia's Revels or *What You Will*

A CONTROLLING principle of the sociohistorical study of Renaissance drama is the assumption that theatrical institutions constructed the ideological conflicts they staged. Yet while it is reasonable to
acknowledge that institutions shape controversy, powerful individuals also leave their stamps on the institutions they help create. This occurred
when Jonson and Marston struggled to define what coterie drama meant to
early seventeenth-century audiences.[1]

The second phase of the Poets' War involved three competing comedies—
Cynthia's Revels, *Twelfth Night*, and *What You Will*, staged at Blackfriars, the
Globe, and Paul's, respectively—in which Shakespeare and Marston again assessed comical satire and the ideal poet it presupposed. Here I will consider
how Jonson's and Marston's comedies serve as a prologue and an epilogue to
Shakespeare's; then, in the next chapter, I will examine *Twelfth Night*'s answer
to *Cynthia's Revels*. For *Twelfth Night*, which premiered between *Cynthia's Revels*, to which it reacted, and *What You Will*, which reacted to it, is positioned
fortuitously in the cross-fire of a war of the private theaters.

Harbage's *Shakespeare and the Rival Traditions* defines the "War of the
Theaters" as a conflict based on the competing interests of the public and
private companies. But the situation was both different and more complicated. The Chamberlain's Men faced renewed competition from the Children of Paul's in 1599 and the Children of the Chapel in 1600. Having been
suppressed in 1590/91 for participating in the Marprelate controversy, Paul's

Boys, with a tradition going back to the late fourteenth century, was revived by Edward Pearce, who had been appointed Master of the Choristers on 11 May 1599. That performances commenced by year's end is noted by Rowland White to Sir Robert Sidney on 13 November; he writes that William Stanley, the sixth earl of Derby, "hath put up the plays of the children of Paul's to his great pains and charge."[2] In the following year, Henry Evans, Lyly's colleague a decade earlier, rejuvenated the similarly ancient and suppressed Children of the Chapel by signing a twenty-one-year lease with Richard Burbage, effective 29 September 1600, to rent what is now called the second Blackfriars theater.

Burbage surely knew that Evans's purpose was to compete against him as a member of a syndicate including Nathaniel Giles (Master of the Children of the Chapel at Windsor), Edward Kirkham (Yeoman of the Revels), and Alexander Hawkins (Evans's son-in-law), formed to reinstate the company's regular perfomances.[3] In leasing Blackfriars—perhaps because he had no other choice than to leave the hall vacant—he increased competition for both the Globe and Paul's. What he could not have foreseen was that Jonson's affiliation with Blackfriars would lead him to attack both venues. With their "similar social cachet as a 'private' playhouse with a 'select' audience," Andrew Gurr explains, the Children of Paul's must "have seen the Blackfriars boys as more serious rivals than the adult players."[4] In choosing Jonson, who had already been caricatured twice at Paul's, Blackfriars courted controversy. That Jonson had become a private dramatist did not make him the ally of Marston, whom he detested for betraying the role's potential power. Marston countered this assault by composing variations on Shakespeare's rejoinders to Jonson at the Globe. *As You Like It* informed his critique of *Every Man Out* and *Twelfth Night* his criticism of *Cynthia's Revels*.

Their agon marks a philosophical division in coterie drama unthinkable in Harbage's account. Yet between 1600 and 1601, Jonson denounced his rivals at Paul's in *Cynthia's Revels* and *Poetaster*. Sir Vaughan therefore asks Horace/Jonson in *Satiromastix* why he stopped "laying down Bricks . . . to make nothing but . . . filthy rotten rails, such as stand on Paul's head" (4.3.158–60). The cathedral's steeple had caught fire on 4 June 1561 and burned down to its battlements. One could still pay the bellringer to visit, but it would have been wise to have followed Dekker's advice in *The Gull's Hornbook*: "when you are mounted there, take heed how you look down into the yard, for the rails are as rotten as your great-grandfather."[5] Metaphorically speaking, making "rotten rails" on "Paul's head" involved Jonson's railing against its playhouse. In *Satiromastix*, Captain Tucca thus rebukes Jonson not only for having "arraigned" his rivals "against all law and conscience" but for having "turn'd them amongst a company of horrible black Fryers" (4.3.197–99). Called "Pope Boniface" (4.3.126) in a pun linking his emaciated appearance (his "bony face") and his Catholicism, Jonson "turns" (or grills) two literary heretics, Marston and Dekker, roasting them under the gaze of the hideous Black Friars ("Fryers") at the site of their former monastery.

I

The war of the private theaters was a struggle over the reinvention of coterie drama staged for a privileged audience involved in reassessing its philosophical and theatrical allegiances. *Cynthia's Revels* offered a program of moral transformation. *What You Will* argued that the search for perfection at the expense of pleasure was self-defeating and that it was wiser to concede life's perplexities. What Marston proposed to replace comical satire was a poetry of "fantasticness" that vindicated the irrational core of experience purged by Jonsonian "art." In opposition to Jonson's neoclassically inspired Stoic idealism, he posed a rebellious Epicurean relativism. Jonson, who had just been treated to "Jack Drum's entertainment," reacted by adding two topically charged elements to *Cynthia's Revels*: an Induction punctuated with allusions to Marston's literary vices and a caricature of him as the envious narcissist Hedon. In response to this critique, Marston mocked Jonson's theory of drama in the Induction to *What You Will* and satirized him as Lampatho Doria in a parody of *Cynthia's Revels*.[6]

The Induction to *Cynthia's Revels* begins its attack "After the Second Sounding," when a rambunctious child actor impersonates two kinds of private theatergoers. He begins by mocking the "ignorant critic" (line 109) who ostentatiously sits on the stage, smoking his pipe to mask the children's body odor. Such a critic comes in his best clothes—as if he were a "piece of *perspective*" or "the decayed . . . arras, in a public theatre" (lines 148, 151–52)—only to complain that the children are ugly, their music abominable, and the poets pitiful. He then impersonates the "friend, or well-wisher to the house" (line 136), who makes one request. Since much private drama—evidently at Paul's—has been disgusting and derivative, he asks Jonson to avoid Marston's failings:

> It is in the general behalf of this fair society here, that I am to speak, at least the more judicious part of it, which seems much distasted with the immodest and obscene writing of many, in their plays. Besides, they could wish your *Poets* would leave to be promoters of other men's jests, and to waylay all the stale *apothegms*, or old books, they can hear of (in

print, or otherwise) to farce their *Scenes* withal. That they would not so penuriously glean wit, from every laundress, or hackney-man, or derive their best grace (with servile imitation) from common stages, or observation of the company they converse with; as if their invention liv'd wholly upon another man's trencher. Again, that feeding their friends with nothing of their own, but what they have twice or thrice cook'd, they should not wantonly give out, how soon they had dressed it; nor how many coaches came to carry away the broken meat, besides hobbyhorses and foot-cloth nags.

(LL. 173–89)

Cast as a generalized critique of coterie drama, Jonson's attack is aimed at Marston. Doubtless he saw the cuckolding of Brabant Senior as "immodest and obscene." He repeats the charge in Epigram XLIX, "TO PLAYWRIGHT," answering Marston's aspersion that his work has "no bawdry" with the rejoinder: "witty, in his language, is obscene" (8:42). Weever similarly reminds Marston that "foul words" can never "beget fair manners," and the *Parnassus* author describes him "lifting" his "leg and pissing against the world."[7] What is more, Jonson, whom Marston had called a "translating scholar," reviles him as a literary parasite. Whatever scraps poets leave, Marston recooks, bragging about how fast he has served these leftovers and how many "hobbyhorses" (morris dancers dressed like horses, such as those in *Jack Drum*) and "footcloth nags" (behind-the-times playgoers) have eaten it up. What makes Marston's plagiarism worse is its indiscriminateness. He steals from comical satire, old books and plays (like the Senecan tragedies whose *apothegms* he repeats or the *Histriomastix* he adapted), and the low comedy of laundresses and hackney-men, voiced by his clowns.

One of Jonson's most revealing charges is that Marston's plays "derive their best grace (with servile imitation) from common stages." Even though Marston pretends to innovate, Jonson implies, he follows Shakespeare too closely. Indeed, Marston began his career with *The Metamorphosis of Pygmalion's Image*, an Ovidian narrative in the style of *Venus and Adonis*, and in 1600 and 1601, Shakespeare continued to guide his dramatic choices. *As You Like It*, with touches of *Romeo and Juliet*, influenced *Antonio and Mellida* and *Jack Drum*; *Richard III* and *Hamlet* inspired *Antonio's Revenge*; and *What You Will* resonates with characterization, plot, and language from *Twelfth Night* and *Hamlet*. Marston had previously recognized the problem of being too enthusiastic about Shakespeare in *The Scourge* when he satirized Luscus, from whose lips "doth flow / Naught but pure Juliet and Romeo" and who could only speak in sentences "warranted by Curtain plaudities" (11.37–45) from the theater at which Shakespeare's tragedy had been performed. This was, Jonson believed, in reality Marston's problem: he was a slavish imitator of popular drama who needed to be purged by comical satire.

II

Cynthia's Revels represents Jonson's literary, philosophical, and ethical ideals in the figure of the poet-scholar Criticus, who exposes dissolute pseudocourtiers in a masque commissioned by the Queen. Here, through his alliance with the Children of Queen Elizabeth's Chapel, he assumes the role of the monarch's master of revels in a work that Barton recognizes as looking "forward to the great masques that Jonson was soon to write for James."[8] *Cynthia's Revels* redefines Jonson's relation to both the court and the commercial theater by conflating his drive for royal patronage with denigration of Marston and Dekker. Although the word "revel" usually describes either a lively entertainment or riotous festivity, in early modern English it could also signify the drawing of humours from the body. The play's main plot accordingly develops a contrast between two kinds of reveling, one that demonstrates Criticus's serene self-knowledge and another that displays the ridiculous self-love of Hedon, Anaides, Amorphus, and Asotus and their ladies, Philautia, Moria, Phantaste, and Argurion. The four courtiers represent central social problems: hedonism, impudence, lack of true conviction, and prodigality. Their mistresses serve as corresponding objects of desire: self-love, folly, fantasy, and money. Once the humourists have manifested their vices, they are reformed by the poet and monarch, whose relationship is mediated by her servant Arete (Virtue). Midway though the play, Arete leaves Cynthia's inner sanctum to assure Criticus that his rivals' fall and his rise are predestined and to commission a masque to facilitate that process:

> This knot of spiders will be soon dissolv'd,
> And all their webs swept out of CYNTHIA's court,
> When once her glorious *deity* appears . . .
> Think on some sweet and choice invention, now,
> Worthy her serious and illustrous eyes,
> That from the merit of it we may take
> Desir'd occasion to prefer your worth,
> And make your service known to CYNTHIA.
> It is the pride of ARETE to grace
> Her studious lovers; and (in scorn of time,

Envy, and ignorance) to lift their state
Above a vulgar height.

(3.4.88–103)

Criticus describes Arete as "the very power by which I am" (5.5.49), the governing principle of legitimate authority and the poet's conscience. Jonson's status as
a maker of royal entertainment is accordingly sanctioned by the sovereign he re-
creates out of his aspirations, more as an accomplice than a judge. Elizabeth had
seen his first comical satire, and he anticipated that his second would be similarly honored. He even changed his setting from the contemporary England of
Every Man Out to the Ovidian pastoral Lyly had used in *Endymion* a decade earlier to work within the Queen's preferred mode of representation. If Marston,
following Shakespeare, bent pastoral in the direction of the popular tradition in
Jack Drum, Jonson twisted it back to its classical roots in *Cynthia's Revels* by replacing the rhetoric of "nature" and "instinct" with the sterner interdictions of
"art" and "judgment." His Ovidian pastoral, however, stands that genre on its
head as an allegory of self-knowledge. Shakespeare had given his audience drama they "liked," but Jonson now tells playgoers: "Like it the more, the less it is
respected; / Though men fail, virtue is by gods protected" (5.4.651–52).

In *Every Man Out* Jonson had demonstrated the poet and monarch's power
only at the play's resolution; in *Cynthia's Revels* these partners are the plot's
prime movers. Under their command, the courtiers who have drunk from the
fountain of self-love are metamorphosed, purged of their humours, by the sip-
ping of Helicon. This is only achieved by their participation in Criticus's revels, through which, disguised as the virtues they impersonate, they are "discovered" by Cynthia, who commands their reform. From the time *Cynthia's
Revels* was produced, Criticus (softened to Crites in the Folio) was identified
as the poet's idealized persona, with Hedon/Marston and Anaides/Dekker as
foils. Jonson thus re-creates royal authority to denounce his rivals at Paul's in
a drama that charts their differences.[9]

JONSON	MARSTON	DEKKER		
Criticus	Hedon	Anaides	Amorphus	Asotus
(Judgment)	(Hedonism)	(Impudence)	(Deformity)	(Prodigality)
	DISGUISED IN THE MASQUE AS:			
	Eupathes	Eutolomos	Eucosmos	Eucolos
	(Variety)	(Courage)	(Elegance)	(Kindness)
PAIRED WITH:				
Arete	Philautia	Moria	Phantaste	Argurion
(Virtue)	(Self-Love)	(Folly)	(Fantasy)	(Money)
	DISGUISED IN THE MASQUE AS:			
	Storge	Aglaia	Euphantaste	Apheleia
	(Confidence)	(Delight)	(Wit)	(Simplicity)

"Henceforth be ours," Cynthia assures Criticus, "the more thy self to be" (5.8.35), in a play that enacts the favor it solicits. "And for this service of discovery / Performed by thee, in honour of our name," she further promises, "We vow to guerdon it with such due grace, / As shall become our bounty, and thy place" (5.11.165–68). "We have already judg'd him," Cynthia explains to Arete, before his masque begins. "Nor are we ignorant, how noble minds / Suffer too much through those indignities . . . vicious persons cast on them" (5.6.101–4).

Criticus, the embodiment of judgment, serves its abstract principle, Arete, and its political manifestation, Cynthia. Hedon and Anaides, on the other hand, are driven by hedonism and impudence disguised as variety and courage, and dedicated to self-love and folly, which masquerade as confidence and delight. Marston is called Hedon to reveal that although he once pretended to be a Stoic, he is actually an Epicurean, as evidenced by his shift from comical satire in *Histriomastix* to festive comedy in *Jack Drum*. John Weever, in *The Whipping of the Satyr* (1601), echoes Jonson's irritation with Marstonian variety:

> Take me your staff, and walk some half-score miles,
> And I'll be hang'd, if in that quantity
> You find me out but half so many stiles,
> As you have made within your Poesie. . . .[10]

Marston's many styles (as abundant as "stiles" or steps over fences and walls, often in meadows) are grounded in an unstable balance of stern censure and libertine excess, united by self-love. Dekker as Anaides epitomizes impudence and folly. Exactly how he had provoked Jonson's ire before *Satiromastix* is unclear, but his response left no doubt that he and Marston had been thus caricatured in *Cynthia's Revels*.

When Horace first appears in *Satiromastix* (still composing the verses he began in *Poetaster*), Asinius Bubo informs him that Crispinus and Demetrius intend to bring his "life and death upon th'stage like a Bricklayer" (1.2.138–39).[11] Dismissing this news, Horace reviles them as a "voluptuous Reveler" and an "arrogating puff," using the same epithets Criticus hurled at Hedon and Anaides:

HORACE   That same *Crispinus* is the silliest Dor, and *Fannius* the
                slightest cobweb-lawn piece of a Poet, oh God!
                Why should I care what every Dor doth buzz
                In credulous ears, it is a crown to me,

That the best judgments can report me wrong'd. . . .
I think but what they are, and am not mov'd.
The one a light voluptuous Reveler,
The other, a strange arrogating puff,
Both impudent, and arrogant enough.

ASINIUS   S'lid, do not *Criticus* Revel in these lines, ha Ningle ha?

HORACE   Yes, they're mine own.

(1.2.147–58)

Horace's admission, "Yes, they're mine own," makes sense only because he and Criticus, who *reveled* in the same lines, are Jonsonian personae denouncing Marston and Dekker. Through it, Dekker prompts his audience to recall Criticus's prior condemnation of the poetasters:

What should I care what every dor doth buzz
In credulous ears? It is a crown to me,
That the best judgements can report me wrong'd;
Them liars; and their slanders impudent.
        . . . when I remember,
'Tis HEDON and ANAIDES: alas, then,
I think but what they are, and am not stirr'd.
The one, a light voluptuous reveller,
The other a strange arrogating puff,
Both impudent, and ignorant enough;
That take (as they are wont) not as I merit:
Traduce by custom, as most dogs do bark,
Do nothing out of judgement, but disease,
Speak ill, because they never could speak well.

(3.3.8–31)

Dekker's Horace greets news of the conspiracy against him by remembering its inception in *Cynthia's Revels*, so according to Dekker, Criticus is Horace and Hedon and Anaides are Crispinus and Demetrius in an evolving topical network:

	JONSON	MARSTON	DEKKER
Cynthia's Revels	Criticus	Hedon	Anaides
Poetaster	Horace	Crispinus	Demetrius
Satiromastix	Horace	Crispinus	Demetrius

Yet it is important to remember that in *Cynthia's Revels* Jonson grafted attitudes and qualities that he associated with Marston and Dekker onto the stock characters of two foppish courtiers who are not intended to be identical matches, presented with journalistic realism. On the contrary, their identities are covert enough not to be instantly noticed, yet noticeable enough to be detected.

Cynthia's Revels is the first play in which Jonson depicts himself as besieged but unthreatened by Marston's and Dekker's plans to discredit him after he has exposed their folly. After Hedon's "invention" is "unluckily perverted" by Criticus, his animosity toward the "whoreson bookworm" and "candle-waster" (3.2.2–3) is shared by his friend Anaides, who is similarly unnerved by Jonson's indifference to their spite. "This afflicts me more than all the rest," Hedon sulks, "that we should so particularly direct our hate . . . against him, and he to carry it thus without wound or passion! 'tis insufferable" (3.2.19–22). Similarly smarting from Criticus's disdain, Anaides girds himself for future encounters: "Damn me, if I should adventure on his company once more, without a suit of buff, to defend my wit" (3.2.38–40). "I'll send for him to my lodging," he tells Hedon, "and have him blanketed" (3.2.7–8), a wish that Dekker would repeat in the plot of *Satiromastix*, where Horace is threatened with being spitefully tossed in the air (4.3.164–82).

The plan that Hedon and Anaides then devise is to damage Criticus's reputation by slandering him as an unsavory, pedantic plagiarist. To this end Hedon vows to "speak all the venom I can of him; and poison his reputation," adding that "if I chance to be present where any question is made of his sufficiencies, or any thing he hath done private, or public, I'll censure it . . . ridiculously" (3.2.49–51). "I'll give out," Anaides volunteers, that "all he does is dictated from other men, and . . . that I know the time and place where he stole it" (3.2.60–62). "Yet to do thee a pleasure, and him a disgrace," he confides to Hedon, "I'll damn my self" (3.2.64–65).

The name Hedon reflects Marston's flirtation with romantic Epicureanism, but the character is also—like all the flawed courtiers of the play—a study in self-love. Solely devoted to his mistress Philautia, he sneers at scholarship:

> I protest, if I had no music in me, no courtship, that I were not a reveller and could dance, or had not those excellent qualities that give a man life, and perfection, but a mere poor scholar as he is, I think I should make some desperate way with my self. . . .
>
> (4.5.54–58)

The "excellent qualities" that he sees in himself, his skill at singing and dancing, the marks of gallantry, are central components of *Jack Drum's* festive reveling. Jonson thus distinguishes between two modes of reveling in private comedy: his own, which ends in self-knowledge, and Marston's, which consists of sound and motion without sense, attuned to "the illiberal sciences, as cheating, drinking, swaggering, whoring, and such like" (2.2.92–93). He depicts Dekker's ignorance as equally self-condemning. "Death, what talk you of his learning?" Anaides asks derisively of Criticus,

> he understands no more than a schoolboy; . . . because I could not construe an Author I quoted at first sight, he . . . laughed at me. . . . I scorn him, as I do . . . his mistress ARETE: And I love my self for nothing else.
>
> (4.5.40–49)

What Jonson particularly despised was their trivialization of the concept of "courtship." Using a technique he repeats in *Poetaster*, he lampoons their poetic deficiencies in the play's courting contest, where Criticus first imitates Dekker's plain style:

> Madame, . . . I do love you in some sort, do you conceive? and though I am no *Monsieur*, nor no *Signior*, and do want (as they say) *logic* and *sophistry*, and good words, to tell you why it is so; . . . And though I be no bookworm, nor one that deals by art, to give you *rhetoric*, and causes, . . . I know it is so.
>
> (5.4.578–86)

Supplementing this linguistic impersonation, Anne Barton observes, Anaides "keeps his 'punquetto' Gelaia—Laughter, the daughter of Folly—waiting on him in male dress as a page" in a "patent travesty of the kind of romantic disguising popular in comedies written for the public theatres."[12] Marston's romanticism is then similarly derided when Criticus cuts Hedon short with "I can do you over too":

> You that tell your Mistress, Her beauty is all composed of theft; Her hair stole from APOLLO's goldy-locks; Her white and red, lillies and roses stolen out of paradise; Her eyes, two stars, plucked from the sky; Her nose, the *gnomon* of *Love's* dial, that tells you how the clock of your heart goes.
>
> (5.4.598–603)

Jonson condemns Marston's romantic hyperbole as conventional, and in place of its frivolous irrationality he offers, in the sanctuary of Blackfriars, his own superior poetics.

III

Nowhere else in Jonson's dramaturgy is his ambition more unguarded than in *Cynthia's Revels*. The disjunction between his blatant self-praise and denunciation of his rivals' self-love invited attack, and Marston at Paul's immediately attempted to invalidate comical satire by undermining its assertion of objectivity.[13] "All that exists," he insists in *What You Will*, "Takes valuation from opinion: / A giddy minion now" (2:237); as Hamlet had recently said, "there is nothing either good or bad, but thinking makes it so" (2.2.249–50). Jonson had asked his audience to cast the garland of judicious praise "Round as a crown, instead of honour'd bays, / About his *poesy*" (Prologue, lines 18–19), to which Marston answers that his own "*best's too bad, / A silly subject too, too simply clad*" (2:235). In analyzing *What You Will* as a response to *Cynthia's Revels*, I will begin with Marston's final caricature of Jonson as Lampatho Doria and conclude with his definitive statement of poetic romanticism in the play's anti-Jonsonian Induction.

The name of Marston's final Jonson surrogate—Lampatho Doria—combines two words associated with Criticus. His first name, based on the Italian *lampazo* or "bur" (as translated by John Florio in *A World of Words* [1598]), echoes Anaides' complaint that he "smells all lamp-oil, with studying by candlelight" (3.2.11–12), and his surname recalls one of Jonson's favorite words for "idiot": "the palpable *dor!*" (5.4.514–15). Prone to repeating Criticus's phrasing, Lampatho is a "tatter'd nasty taber-faced," indigent, envious, boastful, and surly poet-scholar who only values antiquity and urges freer spirits to "abandon natural propensities" (2:249). A master of sycophantic praise and satiric railing, he expects adoration from his friends and exacts revenge through poetry. Lampatho works in Jonson's favorite genres, and although he writes lyric poetry (which he reads aloud and praises), he is primarily a satirist who has just completed a kind of morality play for presentation at court.

This caricature in the subplot of *What You Will* is the centerpiece of Marston's parody, which begins in the second act when Lampatho, his admirer Simplicius Faber, and Quadratus visit the French fop Laverdure. Although Lampatho pretends to be impressed by him, he secretly encourages Quadratus to "shoot him through . . . with a jest" (2:247). Instead, Quadratus warns Laverdure that Lampatho will "prey" on him for "laughter of thy credit" (2:247). Shocked by this honesty, Lampatho answers with a threat: "So Phoebus warm my brain, I'll rhyme thee dead, / Look for the Satire. If all the sour juice / Of a tart brain can souse thy estimate, / I'll pickle thee" (2:248). Marston delivers his *coup de grâce* by taunting Jonson for assuming his own disgarded persona from *The Scourge of Villainy*.

QUADRATUS Away Idolater, why you *Don Kinsayder,*
Thou Canker-eaten rusty cur, thou snaffle
To freer spirits—
Think'st thou a libertine, an ungiv'd breast,
Scorns not the shackles of thy envious clogs?
You will traduce us unto public scorn.
LAMPATHO By this hand I will.

(2:248)

At the end of his preface to *The Scourge*, Marston assumed the aggressive pseudonym W. Kinsayder, a play on the word "kinsing," which refers to the act of castrating a dog, in an oblique allusion to his surname "mar-stone."[14] But having moved on philosophically and temperamentally, he now accuses Jonson of having revived this abandoned persona for the purpose of railing against him. Now only Jonson is interested in castrating others through satire. And when Lampatho decides to attack Quadratus's diction halfway through this harangue, Marston's new spokesman counters him and continues.

QUADRATUS A *foutra* for thy hand, thy heart, thy brain,
Thy hate, thy malice, Envy, grinning spite!
Shall a free-born that holds *Antipathy*—
LAMPATHO *Antipathy?*
QUADRATUS Ay, *Antipathy*,
A native hate unto the curse of man, bare-pated servitude,
Quake at the frowns of a ragg'd *Satirist*. . . .

(2:249)

Quadratus defends not only Marston's linguistic choices but also his freedom to quote play scraps from the public theater. Jonson had called Marston a plagiarist, and the latter's reply was to revel in citation:

Ha, he! mount *Chival* on the wings of fame!
A horse, a horse, my kingdom for a horse!
Look thee, I speak play scraps. . . .

(2:248)

Unafraid to cite Shakespeare, Quadratus runs a line from the anonymous *Mucedorus* into another from *Richard III* (5.4.7).[15] In doing so, Marston not only repeats Jonson's equestrian imagery attacking him in the Induction to *Cynthia's Revels* but—since he had prominently played on the same line from

Richard III in *The Scourge*—quotes himself quoting Shakespeare. Quadratus similarly torments Lampatho when he shouts, "Feed and be fat my fair Calipolis!" (2:285) at the emaciated Jonson surrogate. This phrase, in turn, repeats the "irregular humourist" Pistol's mangled paraphrase in *2 Henry IV* (2.4.179) of Muly Mahamet's plaintive speech to his starving mother in Peele's *Battle of Alcazar*: "Hold thee, Calipolis. . . . Feed and be fat that we may meet the foe."[16] In *Cynthia's Revels* Jonson had dismissed Marston's drama as recooked scraps; in *What You Will*, he was invited to the feast. Quoting from the public theater became a symbol of artistic freedom. It was with the same defiant spirit that Marston pilfered the subtitle of Shakespeare's latest comedy *Twelfth Night* as the name of his own play. How *Twelfth Night* fits into the second phase of the Poets' War—midway between *Cynthia's Revels* and *What You Will*—is the subject of the following chapter. What concerns us here is that *What You Will* evokes Shakespeare's latest comedy to set the stage for Marston's final denunciation of comical satire.

No parody of Jonson would be complete without a glance at his brush with the hangman, reference to his conversion to Catholicism, and a burlesque of his genres, and Marston fully obliges. In *Cynthia's Revels*, Jonson jokes about his escape from hanging in Hedon's offhanded remark about Criticus: "I wonder that the fellow does not hang himself, being so scorn'd and contemned of us that are held the most accomplished society of gallants" (4.5.50–53). "What, art melancholy Lamp?" Marston's Quadratus jests. "I'll feed thy humor; I'll give thee reason straight to hang thyself" (2:256). "And I were to be hanged," he asserts, moving from execution to salvation, "I would be choked / fantastically; he can scarce be saved / That's not Fantastical" (2:250).

The issue of Jonson's Roman Catholicism intrudes on the passage quoted above when Quadratus calls Lampatho an "Idolater" and "*Jebusite*" (2:248). The Jebusites were a tribe who were dispossessed of Jerusalem by King David, but in the seventeenth century the term was derisively used for Catholics. It is particularly witty in this instance because in Judges 1:21 the Jebusites were said to have once lived "among the children of Ben Jamin at Jerusalem."[17] Quadratus furthermore explains that though he pays Lampatho's tavern bills, sectarian differences prohibit a closer association: "but that he and I are two faiths . . . I could find in my heart to hug him" (2:277). No matter how bad his literary meals might be, his literal ones help sustain the heretical, impoverished, yet somehow endearing Jonson.

Jonson's generic preferences—lyric poetry and comical satire—are given special attention. In act 4 of *What You Will*, Lampatho reads Jonsonian verse, only to be laughed at by Quadratus, who applies his rival's favorite critical categories to a glass of claret.

LAMPATHO   Nay, hear it and relish it judiciously.
QUADRATUS   I do relish it most judicially.   [*Quad.* drinks.
LAMPATHO   *Adored excellence, delicious sweet.*
QUADRATUS   Delicious sweet, good, very good.
LAMPATHO   *If thou canst taste the purer juice of love. . . .*
             Is not the metaphor good, is't not well followed?
QUADRATUS   Passing good, very pleasing.

(2:278)

Jonson often refers to his poetry as "sweet" and "judicious," even-tempered, mellifluous, and reasonable. In *Cynthia's Revels*, he speaks of the "sweetness" of his Muse (Prologue, line 9). But when Lampatho demands, "Is't not sweet?" Quadratus soaks his poem in wine, the true "juice of Helicon," to make it even sweeter. "You wrong my Muse," Lampatho complains. "The Irish flux upon thy Muse, thy whorish Muse," Quadratus replies, using the language of purgation to counter Jonson's boast that he did not "prostitute" his Muse's "virgin strain" (Prologue, line 7). In desperation, Lampatho explodes: "I'll be revenged," to which Quadratus knowingly responds, "How prithee? in a play?" (2:278).

The Epilogue of *Cynthia's Revels* affirms the author's confidence: "I'll only speak, what I have heard him say; / *By God, 'tis good, and if you lik't, you may*" (lines 19–20). At the beginning of *What You Will*, Lampatho admires his own writing, spits, and concludes: "faith 'tis good" (2:246). But by the time he completes his play for the court, he has become more circumspect.

JACOMO   They say there's revels and a Play at Court.
LAVERDURE   A Play tonight?
QUADRATUS   Ay, 'tis this gallant's wit.
JACOMO   Is't good, is't good?
LAMPATHO   I fear 'twill hardly hit.
QUADRATUS   I like thy fear well; 'twill have better chance.

(2:283)

Lampatho's work might have a "better chance" if he showed less hubris. But not even self-effacement can forestall the court's displeasure when he offers "A Comedy, entitled *Temperance*," for the evening's entertainment. One could hardly find a better alternative name for *Cynthia's Revels*. "What sot elects that subject for the Court?" the Duke asks. "What should dame *Temperance* do here? away! / The itch on *Temperance*, your moral play!" (2:290). Comical satire is thus dismissed as a return not to Aristophanes but to the didactic drama of the Middle Ages.

What You Will stages Hedon's revenge as Marston convinces Jonson's alter ego that the goal of art is pleasure. Emboldened by this castigation, the humourist Laverdure rejects Lampatho's Stoic humanism, cheered on by Quadratus, who honors this "dear libertine" for his "most generous thought" (2:249). Criticus had maintained that if "good CHRESTUS, EUTHUS, or PHRONIMUS" had criticized him, he would have listened, but he would not heed a "voluptuous reveller" and "arrogating puff" (3.3.18–26). Quadratus replies that if "discreet *Mastigophoros*, / Or the dear spirit acute *Canaidus*," had spoken, he would have listened, but he will not tolerate an impudent railer's advice (2:249). In his catalogue of abuses, Criticus had mocked Amorphus's taste for foreign food: "to make strange sauces, to eat *anchovies, macaroni, bovoli, fagioli,* and *caviar*" (2.3.105–6). To this prohibition Quadratus responds that "A man can scarce . . . eat good meat, / *Anchovies, caviar,* but he's *Satired* / And term'd *Fantastical* by the muddy spawn / Of slimy Newts" (2:250).

By the end of act 2, Lampatho begins to see himself through Quadratus's eyes as "a fusty cask" devoted to "mouldy customs" (2:246), who now knows only that "I naught do know" (2:258). But in Marston's burlesque of comical satire the purge's effect is soon undone. Although Lampatho vows to be social, he nevertheless suffers a short relapse of Asper's imperiousness:

> Dirt upon dirt, fear is beneath my shoe,
> Dreadless of racks, strappadoes, or the sword, . . .
> I'll stand as confident as *Hercules*
> And with a frightless resolution,
> Rip up and lance our time's impieties. . . .
> Stand like an executioner to vice,
> To strike his head off with the keener edge
> Of my sharp spirit.
>
> (2:265–66)

Only the fear of being throttled subdues him. "O how despised and base a thing is a man, / If he not strive t'erect his groveling thoughts / Above the strain of flesh," Criticus had warned (1.5.33–35). But Lampatho comes to prefer embodied desire once Quadratus, pointing to Meletza, explains, "There's more Philosophy, more theorems, / More demonstrations, all invincible, / . . . drawn on her cheek" than in all the "tedious paraphrase / Of musty eld"

(2:279). "*O beauty feminine!*," Lampatho now cries, "what deep magic lies / Within the circle of thy speaking eyes" (2:279). Jonson had created comical satire to deconstruct the genre in which his surrogate was now a celebrant, as Lampatho becomes a gallant only after disowning himself. "I am a mere Scholar," he concludes, "that is, a mere sot" (2:278). He now understands that nothing matters.

At its most abstract level, the struggle between *Cynthia's Revels* and *What You Will* concerns the clash of classic and romantic ideologies of drama through the figures of the poet-scholar and the poet-gallant. The role of the gallant was modeled on an upper-class ideal that prized leisure as well as youth, but it fed the fancy of a wide range of social classes. It could fit a charismatic lower-class poet such as Jonson, a savvy lawyer at the Inns of Court, or a citizen on holiday.[18] The word might have gained popularity for its relatively relaxed class valence. To turn "gallant"—as Marston conceived it—did not require more of an investment than a sword, ink and paper to write poetry, and admission to the theater. But it did necessitate a certain carefree demeanor, an attitude toward experience that was socially accommodating or "what you will." Rather than scapegoating Jonson as forever an outsider who must remain so because of caste, Marston invites him to become a gallant, to try out the role for himself: "Apply thy spirit that it may nimbly turn, / Unto the habit, fashion of the age," he urges, "I'll turn thee gallant" (2:279).

Once he recognizes the relativity of value, Lampatho ironically becomes the proponent of Marston's theory of literature, while quoting Shakespeare, when he tells Meletza to regard him as "what you will":

MELETZA   How would it please you I should respect ye?
LAMPATHO   As anything, *What You Will*, as nothing.
MELETZA   As nothing, how will you value my love?
LAMPATHO   Why just as you respect me, as nothing. For out of
           nothing, nothing is bred, so nothing shall not beget any-
           thing, anything bring nothing, nothing bring anything.
           Anything and nothing shall be *What You Will*, my speech
           mounting to the value of my self, which is—
MELETZA   What, sweet?
LAMPATHO   Your nothing: light as your self, senseless as
           your sex, and just as you would have me, nothing.
                                                          (2:280)

Accepting the terms of Marston's universe involves granting that since the world was made from nothing, it should be valued accordingly. "Nothing" was a key topic in Renaissance discussions of ontology that weighed the notion of a creation *ex nihilo* in Genesis against Aristotle's conviction in the *Metaphysics* that "*ex nihilo nihil fit.*" Marston follows Shakespeare in assuming with Genesis that the world was made from nothing and using that perception to question social hierarchies. "The king is a thing . . . / Of nothing" (4.2.28–30), Hamlet philosophically observes, and "nothing," in this regard, served as a favorite category of existential reduction for Shakespeare throughout his career.[19] He had already made the word resonate with philosophical implications in *A Midsummer Night's Dream*, where Theseus speaks of poetry as "aery nothing" (5.1.16). Shakespeare's self-deposed Richard II had already protested that he, "With nothing will be pleas'd, till he be eas'd / With being nothing" (5.5.40–41), and his latest clown, Feste, had reminded his audience in *Twelfth Night* that "Nothing that is so is so" (4.1.8–9). And since, as in *Hamlet*, the word was slang for the vagina—"a fair thought to lie between maids' legs" (3.2.118–19)—this sexual connotation adds a degree of levity to Lampatho's description of himself as Meletza's "nothing." Being a gallant instead of a scholar, then, requires a carnival sense of nothingness that Jonson's surrogate is finally convinced to accept.

IV

With this pattern of topicality in place, the point of Marston's polemical Induction becomes clear. In response to the extratheatrical inductions of *Every Man Out* and *Cynthia's Revels*, *What You Will* has Philomuse, Doricus, and Atticus (in place of Asper, Cordatus, and Mitis) discuss the ensuing play before the candles in the private theater are lit and music begins to play. Doricus at first worries about its reception, since Jonson's partisans are in attendance: the "most fear'd Auditors" Snuff, Mew, and Blirt, a "threefold halter of contempt that chokes the breath of wit." But Philomuse assures him that Marston is unfazed by their attempts to discredit his production:

> Believe it *Doricus*, his spirit
> Is higher blooded than to quake and pant
> At the report of *Scoff's* Artillery;
> Shall he be crestfallen, if some looser brain,
> In flux of wit uncivilly befilth
> His slight composures? . . .
> Nay, say some half a dozen rancorous breasts
> Should plant themselves on purpose to discharge
> Impostum'd malice on his latest Scene,
> Shall his resolve be struck through with the blurt

> Of a goose breath? . . .
>   . . . if that some juiceless husk,
> Some boundless ignorance should on sudden shoot
> His gross knob'd burbolt, with *that's not so good,*
> *Mew, blurt, ha, ha, light Chaffy stuff?*
>
>   (2:231–32)

Jonson had criticized him as the reveler Hedon, a nasty self-serving Sybarite, and Marston's response is direct. "Hold this firm," Doricus insists:

> *Music* and *Poetry* were first approv'd
> By common sense; and that which pleased most,
> Held most allowed to pass: your rules of Art
> Were shaped to pleasure, not pleasure to your rules.
> Think you if that his scenes took stamp in mint
> Of three or four deem'd most judicious,
> It must enforce the world to current them?
>
>   (2:232)[20]

Marston based his "art" on "pleasure" long before Dryden proposed that literature could produce delight without instruction. Instead of linking poetry with rhetoric or ethics, Marston considered it autotelic. Founded on the inherent pleasure of harmonic sound, poetry owed more to feeling than to philosophy or intellect.[21] *Cynthia's Revels* is a hymn to scholarship; *What You Will* considers it a curse:

> In heaven's handiwork there's naught,
> None more vile, accursed, reprobate to bliss,
> Than man, and 'mong men a scholar most.
> Things only fleshly sensitive, an Ox or Horse,
> They live and eat, and sleep, and drink, and die
> And are not touched with recollections
> Of things o'er past or staggered infant doubts
> Of things succeeding. . . .
>
>   (2:257)

It is not reason that makes life bearable, Marston argues, but an ability to enjoy the irrational pleasures of the senses. The examined life is not worth living. Self-restraint deforms the soul more than excess ever could, and fantasy is a precondition for both salvation and the perception of beauty.

The poetics of comical satire was based on judgment, and at the conclusion of *Cynthia's Revels* Phantaste prays for strength against "*fantastic humours*" (Palinode, line 5). The Elizabethan rhetorician George Puttenham notes that in common parlance a poet was disdainfully called "a *fantastical*," while "a light headed or fantastical man (by conversion) they call a Poet."[22] But Marston celebrated this humor as the core value of his play, as Quadratus explains:

> *Fantasticness,*
> That which the natural Sophisters term
> *Phantasia incomplexa*, is a function
> Even of the bright immortal part of man.
> It is the common pass, the sacred door,
> Unto the privy chamber of the soul.
> That barr'd: nought passeth past the baser Court
> Of outward sense: by it th'inamorate
> Most lively thinks he sees the absent beauties
> Of his lov'd mistress.
> By it we shape a new creation,
> Of things as yet unborn, by it we feed
> Our ravenous memory, our intention feast:
> 'Slid, he that's not Fantastical's a beast.
>
> (2:250)

Marston derives his conception of unbridled fantasy from classical and medieval empirical traditions of physiological psychology.[23] Its theory of the faculties divided the human brain ("the privy chamber of the soul") into three ventricles, each of which was assigned a specific cognitive function: imagination, reason, and memory. Before reaching these chambers, in sequence, sensory stimulation entered through what Marston refers to as "the common pass, the sacred door." Aristotelian psychology calls this the "common sense," the faculty that changes stimuli into sensations. In Marston's model, however, the "common sense" and fantasy are identical. More important than this function of bridging the inner and outer worlds, however, is imagination's power to create, for through it "we shape a new creation, / Of things as yet unborn." In *The Mirror and The Lamp*, M. H. Abrams argues that mimetic and didactic literary theories were replaced in the eighteenth century by organic and expressive ones. But Marston's designation of fantasy as the source of creativity testifies to the rise of English romanticism as a Renaissance phenomenon. Jonson's insistence on "judgment" and Marston's emphasis on "imagination" mark the extremes of available theory. Their poetomachia was, in other words, a preliminary test of neoclassical theory, which would not be overthrown for another two centuries. How *Twelfth Night* fits intellectually and contextually into the second phase of the Poets' War as a critique of Jonson and a contested model for Marston is an issue that can now be more precisely considered.

"If this were play'd upon a stage now, I could condemn it as an improbable fiction."

—Twelfth Night

7 SHAKESPEARE AT THE FOUNTAIN OF SELF-LOVE
Twelfth Night at the Center of the Poets' War

MODERN HISTORIANS of Renaissance drama have speculated that Jonson's *Cynthia's Revels, or the Fountain of Self-Love*, Shakespeare's *Twelfth Night, or What You Will*, and Marston's *What You Will* were involved in a self-reflexive debate on the nature and function of dramatic representation. But the difficulty readers face in determining the plays' interconnections has distorted analysis. The present state of confusion is illustrated by David Riggs's account in his highly regarded biography of Ben Jonson. At the conclusion of his treatment of what he incongruously refers to (in the singular) as "the Poet's Quarrel," Riggs conveys an inchoate sense that there is a relationship among these plays when he attempts to explain how *Twelfth Night* and *What You Will* use parallel strategies to critique *Cynthia's Revels*. But an examination of his specific assertions reveals that some of his premises are erroneous:

> The Cambridge undergraduates who wrote *The Return from Parnassus, Part II* (1601–2), a burlesque of current theatrical gossip, were under the impression that Shakespeare had launched a counteroffensive against his younger rival. At one point in the play, Will Kemp, a leading actor in the Lord Chamberlain's Men, remarks that "our fellow *Shakespeare*" has given Jonson "a purge that made him beray his credit." No one has ever explained what "Kemp" was talking about, but since Shakespeare was working on *Twelfth Night; or What You Will* during the latter part

of 1601, if there was a "purge" it is presumably to be found in that play. Marston had inaugurated the Poet's Quarrel with *What You Will*, the first play to lampoon Jonson in public. Later that year, the title of *Twelfth Night; or What You Will*—apart from *Henry VIII* no other play by Shakespeare has an alternative title—invited theatergoers to associate *Twelfth Night* with *What You Will*.

The ones who registered the association would have noticed that both plays were based on a popular Italian comedy called *The Deceived*—Manningham recognized that this was the source for *Twelfth Night*—and that all three told a similar story. In the main plot, a noble suitor pursues a reluctant gentlewoman; in the subplot, a crew of courtly mischief makers play practical jokes on a graceless social climber who tries to compete with the Duke for the gentlewoman's affections. Marston assigned the latter role to Lampatho Doria, alias Ben Jonson; Shakespeare gave it to Malvolio, a surly ill-wisher, who has a number of traits in common with the twenty-nine-year-old Ben Jonson.[1]

Although Riggs concludes that "no one has ever explained" what the character Kemp meant, Herford and Simpson do exactly that. "It seems probable, on the whole," they write, "that this 'purge' was given in *Troilus and Cressida*" (1:28*n*). The evidence presented in the first chapter supports this hypothesis. The wit of Kemp's scatalogical joke about Shakespeare's having given Jonson "a purge that made him beray his credit" makes sense only as a reference to Ajax in *Troilus and Cressida*, not, as Riggs would have it, to Malvolio in *Twelfth Night*.[2] Shakespeare probably finished *Twelfth Night* early in 1601 and *Troilus and Cressida* by year's end, at which time Kemp alluded to the latter. Yet Riggs's perception that Shakespeare and Marston indicted Jonson's shortcomings in metatheatrical subplots involving Malvolio and Lampatho Doria is crucial to understanding the second phase of the Poets' War. Although *Twelfth Night* is not Shakespeare's answer to *Poetaster*, it anticipates it in significant ways.

The claim that Marston originated the Poets' War by parodying Jonson for the first time in *What You Will* also contradicts Herford and Simpson's more credible argument that Lampatho Doria (who never competes against a duke for a gentlewoman's favor, as Riggs implies) was the last of three caricatures. Shakespeare, furthermore, did not write *Twelfth Night* in response to *What You Will*; Marston named his play *What You Will* to associate it with Shakespeare's alternate title. This part of Riggs's chronology is backward. Marston imitated Shakespearean themes, characterization, plot, and diction *in every play he wrote for Paul's*. He transformed Shakespeare's strategy for containing comical satire through pastoral in *As You Like It* into the more rigorously punitive festive comedy of *Jack Drum*, and found in *Twelfth Night* a cue for his assault on *Cynthia's Revels*.

There is a consensus that all three of these plays were produced between 1600 and 1601, and that *Cynthia's Revels* appeared first, between September and December.[3] Some critics, like Riggs, maintain that *What You Will* preceded *Twelfth Night*. R. K. Turner, for instance, is cited favorably in the introduction to the New Arden edition for assuming that *Twelfth Night* is the only play in the Shakespeare canon with an alternative title (overlooking *Henry VIII, or All is True*, cited by Riggs) and concluding that *What You Will* had been Shakespeare's working title until Marston used it at Paul's.[4] But why, if Marston preempted Shakespeare's title, did the latter retain it? Why didn't he drop it entirely, conforming to his usual practice? Two main problems with this theory are that it is not corroborated by supporting evidence and it is contradicted by a pervasive pattern of imitation indicating that *Twelfth Night* influenced *What You Will* and that Marston drew attention to their connection by lifting Shakespeare's subtitle. Indeed, *What You Will* combines echoes of *Twelfth Night* and of other recent Shakespeare plays. This is not exceptional in the Marston canon; all of his plays reveal a similar influence. That is why Jonson complains in *Cynthia's Revels* that Marston's "best grace" was derived from "common stages."

During the Poets' War plays were often given alternative titles providing greater latitude for polemics. In bestowing a subtitle on *Twelfth Night* (especially one so suggestive as "What You Will," with its fusion of colloquial speech and literary allusion to Rabelais's "*Fay ce que vouldras*"), Shakespeare repeated Jonson and Marston's regular practice. What is more, *Twelfth Night, or What You Will* uses the convention in a brilliant manner. "What You Will" can be understood as either a reference to the theme of human desire or as an invitation to the audience to supply their own name for the drama. "What you will," as Olivia uses the phrase (1.5.109), was an Elizabethan colloquialism equivalent to the contemporary "whatever you want," with the implication that the speaker is resigned or indifferent to another's decision. Shakespeare's title, in this sense, describes itself and the play it represents as concepts created by its audience's imagination, beyond the author's proprietary control. "As You Like It" had promised its audience what they had already enjoyed; "What You Will" again made the play theirs but in a more problematic manner. Marston saw the implications of Shakespeare's latest work for his own continuing struggle against Jonson and appropriated the alternate title to signify his agreement with its intellectual subjectivity. Shakespeare's carte blanche became Marston's shibboleth.

Recent Marston scholarship has come to understand his debt to Shake-speare and Jonson. "Like many of Marston's plays," Finkelpearl explains, "*What You Will* has a literary, to some extent, a parasitic quality by virtue of its relationship to plays that were on the boards elsewhere," especially *Cynthia's Revels* and *Twelfth Night*. Although Marston was "artistically his own man," writes David Farley-Hills, he was "influenced by both the dominating figures of the day, the overwhelmingly successful practical man of the theater, Shakespeare, at the Globe, and the neo-classical gadfly, Ben Jonson. He made, within this powerful field of force, distinctive dramatic patterns of his own, which is considerable commendation."[5] Marston's enigma is that he seems most himself in weighing these two imposing influences against each other, triangulating the competing comic perspectives of *Cynthia's Revels* and *Twelfth Night*.

Marston adjusted his tone to match Shakespeare's. *What You Will* is more decentered than *Jack Drum*, just as *Twelfth Night* is more unstable than *As You Like It*. As Shakespeare darkened romantic comedy in *Twelfth Night*, so too did Marston in *What You Will*, but with an important difference. He became more assertive in contrasting his drama with Shakespeare's, thereby creating a form of satiric comedy equidistant between the Globe and Blackfriars, ab-sorbing the influences of both while remaining committed to neither. *Jack Drum* stretches festive comedy to its limits; *What You Will* batters the genre almost as completely as it undermines comical satire. "It is possible that Marston had more than Shakespeare's subtitle in mind," George Geckle ob-serves, noting that both comedies involve shipwrecks, gulling, Petrarchan lovers, identifying birthmarks that resolve questions of identity, and an at-mosphere of festive comedy. Still, he insists, grasping the play's paradoxical ambivalence, "when viewed overall, Marston's drama has the satiric tone of Jonsonian comedy."[6] *What You Will* appropriates the norm of comical satire to emphasize the flaws of festive comedy, even as it mocks the limitations of comical satire in light of its festive alternative. This unpredictable defiance of generic restrictions was one reason for Marston's success. Just as he yoked erotic poetry to satire in *Pygmalion's Image and Certain Satires* and comedy to tragedy in his two-part *History of Antonio and Mellida*, he superimposed ro-mantic and satiric perspectives on *What You Will*, producing a disturbing blend of satire without moral conviction and celebration without true joy.

Riggs's assertion that *The Deceived* (*Gl'Ingannati*) is the source of both *Twelfth Night* and *What You Will* is also incorrect. Yes, the transvestite disguise plot of *Twelfth Night* is ultimately based on *Gl'Ingannati*, although Shake-speare's primary source was "Of Apolonius and Silla" in *Barnabe Riche His Farewell to Military Profession* (1581). He might not have known the Italian original. But the main plot of *What You Will* was modeled on the subplot of Sforza Oddi's *I Morti Vivi* (1576).[7] In this play Marston discovered a disguise plot similar enough to *Twelfth Night* that it allowed him to comment simultaneously on Shakespeare's comedy and its critique of *Cynthia's Revels*.

I

Twelfth Night responds to comical satire in two ways. First, its main plot, involving Viola, Orsino, Olivia, and Sebastian, revitalizes the ridiculous formula of cross-wooing-with-clown that Jonson had rejected in *Every Man Out*. Second, its subplot, especially the gulling of Malvolio, echoes comical satire's exposure paradigm only to mock the standard of objectivity on which it is based. In this sense John Hollander is right in observing that "*Twelfth Night* is opposed by its very nature to the kind of comedy that Jonson was not only writing but advocating at this time."[8] Shakespeare was able to write the play that Jonson ridiculed because, in the words of Harold Jenkins, he had in effect "been composing it during most of the previous decade."[9] The main plot of *Twelfth Night*, like its title proclaiming the end of festivity, was the summation of a genre and a period that began with Shakespeare's explicit imitation of *Menaechmi* and *Amphitryon* in *The Comedy of Errors*. Its function was ironically defensive; it reveled in the comic mythos Jonson dismissed. The Malvolio subplot, as Riggs suggests, was contextually parodic, although it would not equal Shakespeare's next, more formidable attack in *Troilus and Cressida*. Standing between Jaques of *As You Like It* and Ajax of *Troilus and Cressida*, Malvolio is Shakespeare's second of three versions of the "humour" of comical satire. Again a Jonsonian technique exposes his poetics. "The plot against Malvolio," David Bevington cogently explains, "displays fully the characteristics of Jonsonian satire: an exposure plot manipulated by witty persons against a socially ambitious hypocrite who prepares his own trap, is laughed at scornfully by the audience, and is subjected to a ridiculing form of punishment befitting the nature of his offense." Bevington thus provides support for Herford's remark—which contradicts Hollander's position—that *Twelfth Night* is "the most Jonsonian comedy of Shakespeare."[10]

How is it possible for *Twelfth Night* to be both Jonsonian and anti-Jonsonian? The answer depends on our recognizing Shakespeare's active manipulation of Jonsonian elements in *As You Like It*, *Twelfth Night*, and *Troilus and Cressida*. Although he followed Jonson's example, he did so to contradict him. Nowhere is this more evident than in his coordination of the Viola and Malvolio plots in an attack on the central moral premise of *Cynthia's Revels*— justifiable self-love. Jonson's ideal poet is confident in standing by his judgment and secure in the sense of his own worth. In *Twelfth Night*, however, the most compelling virtue is Viola's selfless love for Orsino, and the most ridiculous vice is Malvolio's self-regard. Here, selflessness and selfishness admit no middle term: a loss of self rather than its secure possession is the condition of true love. This is the paradoxical moral of the play's cross-wooing.

The current assumption that "*Cynthia's Revels* is the most profound and thorough study of the psychology of narcissism in the English Renaissance" must be tested against Shakespeare's critique of Jonsonian self-assertion in *Twelfth Night*.[11] The second phase of the Poets' War was fought over the issue of self-validation, the relation of narcissism to self-reflection, the question of whether it was possible accurately to assess one's own worth. Under attack from Shakespeare and Marston, Jonson insisted in *Cynthia's Revels* on the difference between Philautia (vain self-love) and Storge (confidence), and between Moria (folly) and Aglaia (delight). Though vanity might masquerade as confidence and folly as delight, he argued, a true poet could tell them apart. At the Globe, however, Shakespeare's clown Feste finds impartiality solely in self-condemnation, acknowledging that only his enemies truly know him, since friends "praise me, and make an ass of me," while "my foes tell me plainly I am an ass; so that by my foes . . . I profit in the knowledge of myself, and by my friends I am abused" (5.1.17–20). Self-confidence, in this context, is only self-flattery.

In *Every Man Out*, it will be recalled, Jonson stereotyped Shakespeare's plot as involving "a duke . . . in love with a countess, and that countess . . . in love with the duke's son, and the son to love the lady's waiting maid . . . with a clown to their servingman." Shakespeare's improbable comedies were flawed because they were incapable of morally transforming their audiences: in place of judgment, they celebrated irrational and compulsive desire. Instead of scaling a Platonic ladder of love, Jonson's "Shakespearean" plot line traces love's descent into increasingly less noble forms, sparked by choices that violate social hierarchy and hereditary order. Not only does the duke love the inferior countess, but she prefers his son, who in turn desires her maid. Drama of this kind followed a spiral downward to the scurrilous wit of the servant clown. Jonson invented comical satire to mock the Renaissance tradition of Plautine farce with its comedy of erotic errors punctuated by wit. But the fact that his criticism might be aimed at *The Comedy of Errors*, *Two Gentlemen of Verona*, *Love's Labor's Lost*, and *As You Like It*—each with "cross-wooing" and "clown" as a "servingman"—is overshadowed by its greater resemblance to the yet unwritten *Twelfth Night*. This affinity is due not to Jonson's prescience but to Shakespeare's responsiveness to his criticism. Jonson's mock plot was intended not as allusion but as innuendo; he was not commenting on a play that

Shakespeare had written but imagining "some such" one that he might and subsequently did write. As Viola explains, in reference to Orsino and Olivia, "My master loves her dearly, / And I (poor monster) fond as much on him; / And she (mistaken) seems to dote on me" (2.2.33–35). Shakespeare usually discovered rather than invented his plots, and by building *Twelfth Night* on Jonson's mockery, he acknowledged the oblique reference to him in *Every Man Out* and used it to frame his response. His strategic revision of Jonsonian satire was thus enlisted in the creation of a play that, to its detractors, such as Samuel Johnson, "wants credibility and fails to produce the proper instruction required in drama, as it exhibits no just picture of life."[12] Surely when Shakespeare composed his comedy about a duke infatuated with a countess who prefers his servant who is in love with her master and added a servant clown, he knew he was challenging Jonson's suggestion that the worst kind of comedy he could imagine being performed at the Globe consisted of such a "cross-wooing."

Every Man Out's rebuke prompted Shakespeare to locate a cognate for the farce Jonson imagined in Barnabe Riche's popular tale "Of Apolonius and Silla" in *Riche His Farewell to Military Profession*. Whether he was familiar with the ultimate source of Riche's story, the contemporary Italian Plautine comedy *Gl'Ingannati* (1537), or its prose imitations in Matteo Bandello's *Novelle* (1554) and Pierre de Belleforest's *Histoires Tragiques* (1570) is a matter of conjecture. In any case, the Plautine pedigree of *Twelfth Night* was conspicuous to John Manningham, who found the play "much like . . . *Menaechmi* in Plautus but most like and near to that in Italian called *Inganni*."[13] Whether Manningham is referring to *Gl'Ingannati* (as is generally assumed) or either of two later comedies called *Gl'Inganni* is moot, but his concern with situating Shakespeare's play in the Plautine tradition is unmistakable. The purpose of Shakespeare's imitation of Jonson's plot parody was not to duplicate it character by character but to use its paradigm to refute Aristophanic satire from a Plautine perspective. In this way *Twelfth Night* and *Cynthia's Revels* illustrate Nancy Leonard's position that "the two great comic forms, Shakespearean romantic comedy and Jonsonian satiric comedy, are mirror images of each other," that "each kind of comedy develops in active opposition to the other," and that "in order for either form to realize itself, it must first get rid of the other."[14]

Marston saw *Twelfth Night* as a response to Jonson, and he used it in *What You Will* to signal his agreement with it. Yet he simultaneously voiced his own critique of Shakespeare's comedy. Quadratus rejects the opposing justifications of romantic infatuation and satiric disdain, represented by Jacomo and Lampatho Doria, and although *What You Will* has affinities with festive comedy (since it ends with a scene of conjugal union and social harmony), it mocks romantic love. In its main plot, the stuttering, almost cuckolded Albano and his wanton wife Celia expose the relativity, the "what you will," of desire and show none of the linguistic extravagance and libidinal sublimity of Marston's earlier couples, Antonio and Mellida and Pasquil and Katherine. Marston achieved this complex balance by finding in *I Morti Vivi* a disguise-plot love triangle approximating the main plot of *Twelfth Night*, just as he discovered the Lampatho Doria subplot in *Cynthia's Revels*.

The debate on the function of comedy in coterie drama, staged between *Cynthia's Revels* and *What You Will*, was only the most blatant dialogue in the second phase of the Poets' War. It had a subtler version as well in Shakespeare's prior response to Jonson in *Twelfth Night*. In the second phase, as in the first, the Globe provided ammunition for Paul's. For between the time that *Cynthia's Revels* and *What You Will* were produced, *Twelfth Night* articulated Shakespeare's second commentary on the genre that had originated at the Globe as a protest against his poetics.

Marston came to assess *Cynthia's Revels* in the wake of *Twelfth Night*, and he was influenced by the latter even as he tried under Jonson's gaze not to derive too much of his "best grace" from Shakespeare. Facing the pressure of trying to go beyond Shakespeare in opposing Jonson, Marston appropriated and critiqued *Twelfth Night* in a bid to situate his work between the extremes of festive comedy and comical satire. His kind of satiric comedy was at this time less festive and more satiric than Shakespeare, more festive and less satiric than Jonson. Shakespeare was thus again drawn into the quarrel through the impact that *Twelfth Night*'s criticism of *Cynthia's Revels* had on *What You Will*, as Blackfriars, the Globe, and Paul's became sites for the production of agonistic comedies.

II

One of the benefits of recognizing that *Twelfth Night* is based on "Of Apolonius and Silla" is that it allows us to see how Shakespeare uses, adapts, and expands Riche's narrative to reflect on what had become the central issue of comical satire—the connection between self-knowledge and self-love. If Riche's love story reminded Shakespeare of Jonson's critique of improbable cross-wooing, it also suggested the basis for a rejoinder to *Cynthia's Revels*. At a time when Jonson was censuring his critics by contrasting his own self-knowledge with their self-love, Riche's narrative proposed in its main character Silla a mode of irrational, selfless desire. In *Twelfth Night*, the most profound manifestation of love is shown by Viola, Silla's double, who is willing to sacrifice her own satisfaction and even work against her own self-interest in the service of another.

The *locus classicus* of Jonson's self-defense was Aristotle's discussion in the *Nicomachean Ethics* of "whether one ought to love oneself most or somebody else." Aristotle's solution, repeated in *Cynthia's Revels*, is to assert that self-love must be interpreted in antithetical ways. As a term of reproach, it describes the behavior of the majority of people who try to get "more than their share" of "money, public honours, and bodily pleasures." But, Aristotle continues, it can also serve as a term of praise. "For if anyone made it his constant endeavour to set an example in performing . . . virtuous actions, and in general always claimed the prerogative of acting honourably, such a person might be considered to have a better title to that name." Such "self-love" is praiseworthy, because a virtuous man only "assigns to himself what is most honourable and most truly good; and he gratifies the most authoritative part of himself, and obeys it in all respects." One who "loves his authoritative part and gratifies it is," Aristotle concludes, "in the truest sense a self-lover."[15] *Cynthia's Revels* ratifies this distinction by defending the justifiable self-love of Criticus against the slander of Hedon and Anaides, who accuse him of *their* vice. Since the play was registered for publication under the alternative title, *Narcissus, or The Fountain of Self-Love*, Narcissus and Cynthia (served by Criticus) symbolize the Aristotelian polarity on which the play is based.

Jonson begins *Cynthia's Revels* with the definitive example of destructive self-love: the myth of Narcissus and Echo from Ovid's *Metamorphoses* (3.339–510). In the opening masque, Mercury, at Jove's command, frees Echo from the pool at which she mourns for Narcissus, who drowned in its waters by gazing too intently at his reflection. Still infatuated with her doomed lover after 3,000 years of silence, Echo, before leaving, curses the fountain in which Narcissus lost his life and from which the self-loving pseudocourtiers soon drink:

> Henceforth, thou treacherous, and murthering spring,
> Be ever call'd the *Fountain of self-Love*:
> And with thy water let this curse remain,
> (As an inseparate plague) that who but tastes
> A drop thereof, may, with the instant touch,
> Grow dotingly enamor'd on themselves.
>
> (1.2.99–104)

Narcissus's "fountain of self-love" at the play's opening and Cynthia's "well of knowledge" (5.11.153) at its end mark the boundaries of human potential. It is only in reference to the former that Jonson writes, "Self-love never yet could look on truth" (1.2.36). Nevertheless, Jonson affirms that accurate self-reflection is possible and emphasizes this view in the first masque Criticus devises for Cynthia's revels, which features "four virgins from the palace of . . . Queen *Perfection*" (5.7.3–4) who represent the personal qualities of the ideal self. The first of these virtues and the one on which the rest depend is Storge, who is garbed in the same yellow color Shakespeare would use for Malvolio's cross-gartered stockings:

> The first, in citron colour, is *natural Affection*, which, given us to procure our good, is sometime called STORGE, and as everyone is nearest to himself, so this handmaid of reason, *allowable self-love*, as it is without harm, so are none without it. Her place in the court of *Perfection* was to quicken minds in the pursuit of honour. Her device is a *perpendicular Level*, upon a *Cube*, or *Square*. The word, SE SUO MODULO. Alluding to that true measure of one's self, which as everyone ought to make, so it is most conspicuous in thy divine example.
>
> (5.7.26–35)

Jonson, however, is careful to distinguish Philautia from Storge. How could he be faulted for arrogance when he was only being truthful? What might seem to be importunate self-assertion was the result of a special vocation. He uses classical mythology to imply that *Cynthia's Revels* originates in the transpersonal forces of intelligence and integrity that compel him to write. Mercury, the god of wit, "binds" Criticus "to his godly will" (5.1.4–5) and Cynthia commands him to perform a "service of discovery" (5.11.165).

Jonson's validation of allowable self-love contrasts with his purgation of sexual desire—the driving force of festive comedy. Indeed, much of what passes for sexuality in *Cynthia's Revels* is exposed as self-regard. Hedon, who adores his mistress Philautia as "Laura" and "Delia," worships only himself. Indeed, once the courtiers drink from the fountain of self-love, they lose all sexual drive. "Are my darts enchanted! Is their vigour gone?" (5.10.58) the angry Cupid fumes, when his arrows, aimed at the humourists, miss their mark. "Alas, poor god," Mercury muses, "that remembers not *self-Love* to be proof against the violence of his quiver!" (4.5.146–48). Criticus, however, is among the elect few, like Cynthia, "Whose souls are not enkindled by the sense" (5.5.53), and he is protected by his service to Arete from the "venom" (5.10.97) of Cupid's shafts.

By 1600 criticism of *Every Man Out* by Shakespeare in *As You Like It* and Marston in *Jack Drum* had coalesced around the issue of Jonson's narcissism.

Parodied for arrogance, he wanted to demonstrate that he understood the difference between self-delusion and self-knowledge. His acuity of perception, he argued, both proved the value of his poetry and could be inferred from it. He had been able, in his own estimation, to sidestep "the fountain of self-love" and sip from "the well of knowledge." And it is to this source of insight that Criticus directs the humourists of *Cynthia's Revels*.

An excellent account of the intertextuality of *Cynthia's Revels* and *Twelfth Night* is offered by Cristina Malcolmson, who identifies these plays as part of the "war of the theaters" and supports the opinion that their fundamental difference was the result of their obverse interpretations of "self-love."[16] After Jonson had valorized "allowable self-love" in *Cynthia's Revels*, Malcolmson contends, Shakespeare mocked it in *Twelfth Night* by contrasting Viola and Malvolio. "Malvolio's 'self-love' satirizes Jonson's version of individual value not only as self-indulgent but as socially divisive, because it privileges censuring the faults of others and praising the self over the more difficult task of preserving the harmony of social relations." Shakespeare faults Jonson, Malcolmson continues, because he "reproves those who would use . . . social fluidity for their own benefit or as an opportunity to reorder the traditional structure according to new ethical and political principles." "Such ethical and political blueprints," she concludes, "are simply fantasies of power." But Shakespeare goes beyond negatively characterizing self-love by contrasting it with Viola's selfless devotion to Orsino. The play "invites us to consider love from two angles: Viola's self-abnegating, amorous desire and Malvolio's self-deluded dream of power." And we find its "ideological bias" in its assertion that "the desire of an inferior to be matched with a superior is acceptable as long as it is motivated by love; to the extent that desire is self-interested, it is foolish and dangerous."[17] This argument is, I believe, crucial to an understanding of Shakespeare's response to *Cynthia's Revels*. Yet it must be carefully qualified.

It is important, for instance, to register just how radical Shakespeare's conception of love as irrational self-denial actually is. Viola surrenders her personal identity, gender, and class to the shaping influence of the unknown when she disguises herself as Cesario. This loss of identity is the precondition for her selfless love for Orsino. Readers who look for a realistic display of human psychology in *Twelfth Night* can only be jolted by the fact that following the shipwreck that separates Viola from her twin brother Sebastian, she makes no effort to find him for the rest of the play, even though she is convinced by the captain that he is alive. A cliché of modern criticism has her dress like her brother to preserve his memory. But when the Captain tells her that Sebastian has probably survived, since he last saw him, "Most provident in peril, bind himself . . . / To a strong mast," Viola agrees, stating that, since she herself has escaped death, his speech adds "authority" to hope (1.2.12–14, 20). Only a second accident—a chance reunion with Sebastian in act 5 (at which point Viola states that she suspected him to be dead)—brings the comedy to a close. What Shakespeare focuses on is the extent to which life is shaped by seemingly accidental events beyond human will or power. Already subjected to chance, Viola surrenders to its process. "What else may hap," she explains, "to time I will commit" (1.2.60). Victimized by experience, she now willingly accepts its unknowable agency. Confronted with Olivia's infatuation, she again signals her submission to the unpredictable disposition of events: "O time, thou must untangle this, not I, / It is too hard a knot for me t' untie" (2.2.40–41).

In Riche's "Of Apolonius and Silla," the lover's disguise is adopted to facilitate desire. Silla (Viola's predecessor) falls "so strangely in love" with Apolonius that after he leaves her father's court (to which he had been accidentally "driven by force of weather"), she follows him home, becoming his servant "in the habit of a man." Silla's devotion is finally rewarded when Apolonius discovers her true identity and accepts her as his wife "in requital of her love."[18] Unlike Silla, Viola has never previously met Orsino, although Shakespeare preserves a vestigal trace of Riche's tale in her admission, "I have heard my father name him" (1.2.28). But even after the Captain mentions Orsino, Viola first decides to serve Olivia in Illyria:

> O that I serv'd that lady,
> And might not be delivered to the world
> Till I had made mine own occasion mellow
> What my estate is!
>
> (1.2.41–44)

Orsino is a second choice offered by chance, since Olivia, sequestered in mourning, "will admit no kind of suit" (1.2.45). Modern editors tend to agree on the ostensible meaning of this dense passage, which *The Riverside Shakespeare* sensibly glosses with a paraphrase: Viola hopes that "my position in life (*estate*) might not be revealed to the world until the moment is ripe for me." Viola's cross-dressing becomes a means of concealing herself until she is ready to "be delivered to the world," and the language she uses is passive rather than active. By using the word "delivered" to intimate her own rebirth, Viola reveals the meaning of her adopted name Cesario: she, like Caesar, will experience an "unnatural" delivery.[19] Cesario will be reborn as Viola in the ripening of time. That Viola represents open-minded detachment from experience is reinforced by her request to the Captain:

> Conceal me what I am, and be my aid
> For such disguise as haply shall become
> The form of my intent.
>
> (1.2.53–55)

Her "intent" might be to sequester herself. But even if this is correct, it does not exclude a second implication. There is a sense in which the disguise is an end in itself, as acting *becomes* (or turns into) the form of Viola's detachment. Shakespeare probably wrote *Twelfth Night* immediately after *Hamlet*, so it should not be surprising that Viola shares Hamlet's sense of indeterminacy, his perception that:

> Our indiscretion sometime serves us well
> When our deep plots do pall, and that should learn us
> There's a divinity that shapes our ends,
> Rough-hew them how we will—
>
> (5.2.8–11)

Viola's decision to disguise herself as Cesario seems to offer an insuperable impediment to the love she feels for Orsino. Sent by him to woo Olivia, Viola finds herself in what seems a self-defeating situation. But in *Twelfth Night* experience is so mysterious that what seems humiliating, foolish, or threatening can prove salutary. Sebastian similarly submits to the unknown in accepting Olivia's invitation to accompany her home. "Or I am mad, or else this is a dream. / Let fancy still my sense in Lethe steep; / If it be thus to dream, still let me sleep!" (4.1.61–63). Later he explains that his "sudden accident and flood of fortune" is so miraculous that he is willing to "distrust [his] eyes" and "wrangle with reason" (4.3.11–14).

In *As You Like It*, Rosalind dresses like a male to protect herself from assault when searching for her father in the forest of Arden. Viola's construction of Cesario seems by comparison almost unmotivated, except insofar as it allows her to satisfy a desire to lose herself further in reaction to being lost. Viola's submission to time places her in the ironic position of apparently working against her own self-interest. In the ultimate proof of love, as Orsino's proxy in courting Olivia, Viola engages in behavior that would, if it were successful, invalidate her own unspoken passion. That she uncompromisingly presses Orsino's suit, although it obviates her own, is her most touching quality, especially when contrasted with Jonsonian self-love. Referring to an imaginary sister, Viola obliquely describes herself to Orsino as her "father's daughter," content to sit "like Patience on a monument, / Smiling at grief." The question she asks Orsino is Shakespeare's as well: "Was not this love indeed?" (2.4.114–15).

Comical satire is predicated on the exercise of judgment, but in *Twelfth Night* Shakespeare goes out of his way to deprive his characters of pure agency; the unseen shipwreck from which the action flows is an emblem of contingency. Viola and Sebastian find themselves directed against their will to Illyria by a power Shakespeare vaguely defines as "chance," "fortune," "providence," "time," and "nature." What you will, in this sense, is certainly not what you get.

Twelfth Night's cross-wooing contrasts Viola's psychological balance of stasis and fluidity with the nonproductive fixations of Orsino and Olivia. The world of Illyria that she and Sebastian enter by chance is governed by Orsino and Olivia's inappropriate extremes: he fixates on a woman who cannot return his love, while she refuses love entirely. Olivia's retreat from desire to honor her dead brother is both unnatural and narcissistic, according to Viola, who informs her that "you do usurp youself," since "what is yours to bestow is not yours to reserve" (1.5.187–89). Olivia can only be herself by giving herself away. These words cause her to be so overwhelmed by love for Cesario that she proves how meaningless such refusals can be. What Orsino and Olivia *will* is overruled by experience as Viola, who symbolizes the possibility of selflessness, breaks this stalemate of frustrated narcissism. Moreover, what sets *Twelfth Night* off from Shakespeare's previous festive comedies, from *The Comedy of Errors* to *As You Like It*, is the extent to which it presents mutability as a laudable component of desire. The earlier comedies concern the restoration of a broken union. In *A Midsummer Night's Dream*, for instance, Demetrius and Lysander return to Helena and Hermia and Titania is reconciled with Oberon after periods of delusion and disruption. In *Twelfth Night*, however, the comic resolution depends not on Orsino and Olivia's fidelity but on their flexibility. Yet in arguing for the need to accept change, Shakespeare simultaneously suggests a kind of stability underlying the fluidity of experience. Olivia replaces a twin with a twin, and Orsino substitutes Viola for Olivia, whose names are linked as anagrams (with the remaining letter, the "I" of identity). Nothing could be further from Jonson's celebration of an ideal, centered, rational self, resistant to change, in *Cynthia's Revels*.

If *Twelfth Night* were a comical satire, Olivia would be punished for doting on Cesario. But here, to Samuel Johnson's chagrin, her impulse is rewarded with marriage to Sebastian. Like Viola, Olivia cedes control to an unknown destiny: "Fate, show thy force," she sighs, "ourselves we do not owe [i.e., own] / What is decreed must be; and be this so" (1.5.310–11). Being mistaken about Sebastian's identity does not interfere with her happiness; on the contrary, it makes it possible. Why can't she love Orsino? She acknowledges to Cesario that it has nothing to do with his qualities, which are admirable (1.5.257–62); she does not love him simply because she does not love him. "Poor lady, she were better love a dream," the cross-dressed Viola muses when Olivia falls for her. "How easy is it for the proper-false / In women's waxen hearts to set their forms!" (2.2.29–30). Yet Olivia's dream comes true. One of the wonderful ironies of *Twelfth Night* is that Olivia marries Sebastian before the play's denouement—that is, before she discovers that Cesario is a fiction—and her blind passion prospers as extravagantly as Viola's studied self-denial.

Unrequitable desire, on the other hand, is poignantly registered in Malvolio and Sir Andrew Aguecheek, who personify the psychological extremes of hypocritical restraint and ridiculous excess. In *Cynthia's Revels*, Jonson had contrasted Criticus and Hedon as types of judgment and appetite. In *Twelfth Night*, however, the rhetoric of self-restraint only conceals sublimated desire. Duke Senior had lectured Jaques on this very point in *As You Like It*, so Malvolio in effect acts out the latter's program of world reformation, with disastrous results. Malvolio interrupts the nightly reveling of Sir Toby, Sir Andrew, and Feste only to revel in yellow cross-gartered stockings dyed in the color of self-love. He is, Maria explains, a "time-pleaser" (a self-serving flatterer), "so cramm'd (as he thinks) with excellencies, that it is his grounds of faith that all that look on him love him," and it is upon this "vice in him" that her "revenge" finds "notable cause to work" (2.3.148–53). "I know my physic will work with him" (2.3.172–73), she adds euphemistically, since her "device" is a "dish a' poison" (2.5.112), prepared "to have the . . . rascally sheep-biter come by some notable shame" (2.5.4–6). By the time Malvolio's humiliation is complete, Feste will also have enjoyed his revenge, especially in exposing the connection between ideology and power when, dressed as the curate Sir Topas, he makes an assent to Pythagorean metaphysics—a belief in the transmigration of souls (4.2.50–60)—a prime condition for "mad" Malvolio's release from confinement. Olivia's "corrupter of words" (3.1.36) undermines the very notion of intellectual authority in his improvised citations of "Quinapalus" (1.5.35) and "the old hermit of Prague, that never saw pen and ink" (4.2.12–13), and the history of "Pigrogromitus of the Vapians passing the equinoctial of Queubus" (2.3.23–24). He is indeed both a witty fool and a "foolish Greek" (4.1.18), whose final song defines the play's happy ending ("we'll strive to please you") as an illusory haven, a temporary shelter, in a world where "it raineth every day" (5.1.392). One consequence of Shakespeare's conflation of the categories of restraint and excess, learning and fatuity, is the collapse of the dichotomy between Sir Andrew and Malvolio. Malvolio (*mal voglio*) nevertheless remains the ultimate *pharmakos* in a play that rejects comical satire. By exposing his angry self-exclusion and commitment to revenge rather than reconciliation, Shakespeare confirms the wisdom of folly.

III

Jonson ridiculed the inclusion of a clown servingman in Shakespearean comedy, and Shakespeare created Feste as Touchstone's successor to enable Robert Armin again to address this criticism. The difference between *Cynthia's Revels* and *Twelfth Night* thus crystallizes in the contrasting philosophies of Criticus and Feste. While Criticus demands respect for the authority of judgment and affirms the validity of justifiable self-love, Feste illustrates the failure of reason to account for life's complexities and the danger of believing in absolutes, especially about oneself. When Olivia accuses him of being a dry fool who deserves to be whipped for being dishonest, Feste challenges the efficacy of judgment in accounting for either material or moral experience:

> Two faults, madonna, that drink and good counsel will amend; for give the dry fool drink, then is the fool not dry; bid the dishonest man mend himself: if he mend he is no longer dishonest. . . . Any thing that's mended is but patch'd; virtue that transgresses is but patch'd with sin, and sin that amends is but patch'd with virtue. If that this simple syllogism will serve, so; if it will not, what remedy? As there is no true cuckold but calamity, so beauty's a flower.
>
> (1.5.43–52)

Life is so mutable that it is impossible to provide anything but a contradictory account of its dialectical fluidity. Because it fuses opposites—from the physical dimension of "wet" and "dry" to the moral realm of "virtue" and "sin"—it can only be explained through a "patch'd" account, devised by a "patch." If you are not satisfied by this interpretation with all its contradictions, Feste laments, "what remedy?" There is "no true cuckold but calamity" because nothing bad lasts forever. Those proverbially "married to calamity"—here figured as the deceived husband—will have at least one good day, on which they will automatically betray their spouse. But, reversing this optimism, Feste also cautions that "beauty's a flower": nothing pleasurable endures. The total effect of this clowning, as Jonson had foreseen, was to destabilize rational, noncontradictory categories of thought, proving that "Foolery . . . does walk about the orb like the sun, it shines every where" (3.1.38–39).

In *As You Like It*, Shakespeare subordinates the critic to the fool by having Jaques commend Touchstone's wit, and in *Twelfth Night* he makes the same point in a more forceful manner by punishing Malvolio for not appreciating Feste. Shakespeare repeats Jonson's severe criticism of the clown's function in Malvolio's ridicule of Feste's jest: "I protest I take these wise men that crow so at these set kind of fools no better than the fools' zanies" (1.5.88–89). This is very different from Jaques' confession in *As You Like It* that, hearing Touchstone, he "began to crow like chanticleer, / That fools should be so deep contemplative" (2.7.30–31). Olivia counters Malvolio's animosity by precisely diagnosing his pathology: "O, you are sick of self-love, Malvolio, and taste with a distemper'd appetite" (1.5.90–91). It is self-love that prevents him from being of a "generous, guiltless, and . . . free disposition" and causes him to take Feste's "bird-bolts" for "cannon-bullets" (1.5.91–93). Viola supplements Olivia's *encomium moriae* with her own definition of Feste's "art":

> This fellow is wise enough to play the fool,
> And to do that well craves a kind of wit.
> He must observe their mood on whom he jests,
> The quality of persons, and the time;
> And like the haggard, check at every feather
> That comes before his eye. This is a practice
> As full of labor as a wise man's art.
>
> (3.1.60–66)

The fool, with the satirist's predatory instincts, acts like a hawk scrutinizing his prey. A significant part of his mandate is to prove the universality of his condition. He thus begins by sharing his identity with Olivia (1.5.57–72) and ends by proving his kinship with Malvolio. As Feste gloats over the steward's humiliation, the fool quotes his original criticism, "Madam, why laugh you at such a barren rascal?" (5.1.374–75), as chorus to "the whirligig of time" that "brings in his revenges" (5.1.376–77).

The experience of "what you will" is implicated in folly and madness, and because Malvolio pretends to be beyond reproach—seeking to repress the excesses of festivity—he is made the play's most notorious geek and gull. "I do not now fool myself, to let imagination jade me," he boasts at the very moment of self-delusion, "for every reason excites to this, that my lady loves me"

(2.5.164–65). "Look how imagination blows him" (2.5.42–43), Fabian observes. Maria's forged letter is crafted in the fashionable style of personal innuendo, and Malvolio's downfall is occasioned by his probing into its secret allusions—its "fustian riddle" or "simulation" (2.5.108, 139)—in an effort to locate himself "most feelingly personated" in what he reads (2.3.158–59). Sir Toby even invokes "the spirit of humors," which oversees such occasions, to "intimate reading aloud" to Malvolio (2.5.84–85), thereby facilitating his public disgrace as a "rare turkey-cock" that "jets under his advanc'd plumes" (2.5.30–32). In both *Hamlet* and *Twelfth Night*, the procedure of layering writing with an oblique topical subtext (whether in a play, such as "The Mousetrap," or Maria's letter) is a powerful mode of covert communication. Malvolio's exposure, like Claudius's before him, is brought about through the medium of personal application.

Malvolio berates the fool and opposes the spirit of festive comedy with a neoclassical respect for the decorum of person, place, and time (2.3.91–92). And when he interrupts the midnight revelers in Olivia's hall, he elicits Sir Toby's famous retort: "Dost thou think because thou art virtuous there shall be no more cakes and ale?" (2.3.114–16). His hypocritical antagonism to festivity mirrors Jonson's, and when it is coupled with the governing humour of aspiring self-love, the analogy becomes apparent. The plot to draw out Malvolio's humour so that it displays its "trick of singularity" (2.5.151–52) was long ago understood to show the influence of Jonson's fascination with social pretension.[20] The scenes in which Malvolio is observed mistaking Maria's forged note for a love letter from Olivia, presenting himself before her in yellow cross-gartered stockings, and being imprisoned as a madman could be fit into either Every Man play. Campbell thinks of this episode as Shakespeare's "comedy of humours" because it shows a character undone by his own conceit.[21] What we should keep in mind, however, is Shakespeare's special focus on creating a new character to parody a peculiar kind of humourist—one who, like Jaques before him, seeks to restrain the humour of others through ridicule, having assumed an imagined moral authority. In Shakespeare's exposure of hypocrisy, however, Malvolio learns nothing from his experience and exits promising, "I'll be reveng'd on the pack of you" (5.1.378), as if he (who had Viola's captain imprisoned for the same sport) were baited by dogs. Comical satire ends with a psychic transformation unavailable to the unregenerate Malvolio, and his vow condemns him to be a perpetual humourist. "Alas, poor fool," Olivia commiserates, using a term of endearment that makes his plight all the more bitter, "how have they baffled thee!" (5.1.369).

Throughout *Twelfth Night*, moreover, Shakespeare makes subtle linguistic and thematic references to *Cynthia's Revels*. Jonson was adept at noting

Marston's verbal tics, and in *Cynthia's Revels* he mocked the "ignorant *Poetasters* of the time, who, when they have got acquainted with a strange word, never rest till they have wrung it in, though it loosen the whole fabric of their sense" (2.4.15–18). But that Jonson himself cultivated an idiosyncratic vocabulary in *Cynthia's Revels* is glanced at in passing by Feste, who conspicuously avoids a Jonsonian locution in addressing Viola: "who you are, and what you would, are out of my welkin—I might say 'element,' but the word is overworn" (3.1.57–59). In *Cynthia's Revels*, Amorphus worries that he will say something above Asotus's comprehension or "out of his element" (1.4.85). Even though Jonson parodies Amorphus's pretentious diction, his critics accused him of using the very language he condemned. The association of the four elements with the four humours lent an added level of referentiality to this phrase. Thus, Dekker in *Satiromastix* advises Jonson that "when your Plays are misliked at Court, you shall not . . . say you are glad you write out of the Courtier's Element" (5.2.324–26). And in this same play Horace/Jonson declares that he is not offended by Tucca's railing, because "'tis out of his Element to traduce me" (1.2.134). "You are idle shallow things, I am not of your element," Malvolio peremptorily informs Sir Toby and the revelers, availing himself of the Jonsonism Feste mocks (3.4.123–24). In using the phrase "I am not of your element" after Feste has contextualized it, Malvolio strengthens Shakespeare's analogy between his own fictional self-loving hypocrite, who would censure in others his own secret vices, and his alter ego Criticus/Jonson.

The purge of comical satire, to paraphrase Hamlet, allows "the humorous man" to "end his part in peace" (2.2.322–23). But the exposure plot of *Twelfth Night* is a work of spite, indulged without pretense of reform, "For the love of mockery" (2.5.18). The fantasy inflated by the forged letter is so strong that purging it can only be devastating: "Why, thou hast put him in such a dream," Sir Toby tells Maria, "that when the image of it leaves him he must run mad" (2.5.193–94). Shakespeare accepts, with Jonson, a view of desire as a psychological drive linked to error, folly, and madness. He does not vindicate passion as rational; instead, he sees appetitive drives as beyond intellectual control, constituting at best what A. W. Schlegel calls the play's "ideal follies."[22] Olivia and Orsino are just as deluded as Malvolio through most of the play, but their indulgence is rewarded and his is not. He is a victim of self-love, but so are they: Orsino feeds on his own implacable desire, and Olivia gorges herself on her love for her dead brother. Why then should they succeed and Malvolio fail? No consistent moral can be drawn, except perhaps that one should shun as much as possible the myth of self-possession and hope for the best.

IV

Festive comedy at the Globe provided satiric comedy at Paul's with ammunition for criticizing comical satire at Blackfriars. Marston, as I have previously mentioned, borrowed the subtitle of *Twelfth Night*, a striking phrase
from Shakespeare, to use in his struggle against Jonson, and the way he flaunts
it is quite witty. In *Every Man Out*, Cordatus had described Jonson's new play
as being "strange, and of a particular kind by it self, somewhat like *Vetus Comoedia*." Marston restages this incident in his introduction to *What You Will*
to emphasize his difference. There, Doricus asks Philomuse about the new
play, "*Is't Comedy, Tragedy, Pastoral, Moral, Nocturnal* or *History?*" to which
the latter answers: "Faith perfectly neither, but even *What You Will*, a slight
toy, lightly composed, too swiftly finished, ill plotted, worse written, I fear me
worst acted, and indeed *What You Will*" (2:233). So while Jonson assimilated
comical satire to ancient genres that invested him with authority, Marston
uses Shakespeare's subtitle to disavow the significance of his work—"such un-
sanctified stuff" (2:233)—in deference to his audience.

In *Twelfth Night*, Marston found a literary model for the expression of intellectual skepticism with romantic intrigue. In Marston's principal source
(the subplot of Oddi's *I Morti Vivi*), Tersandro, presumed dead, returns to his
wife Oranta, who has decided to marry Ottavio, only to be accused of impersonating himself. This comes about because Luigi (Oranta's spurned lover)
decides to disrupt her proposed marriage by disguising Jancula as Tersandro.
His plan is overheard, though it is never executed, so that when Tersandro actually reappears he is mocked and only proves his identity with difficulty.
What is striking about Marston's adaptation of the subplot of *I Morti Vivi* is
the ease with which he uses it to create a group of characters that parallel
Shakespeare's:

Twelfth Night	*What You Will*
Olivia	Celia
Sebastian	Albano
Viola	Francisco
Orsino	Jacomo
Sir Andrew Aguecheek	Laverdure
Malvolio	Lampatho Doria
	Simplicius Faber

In the main plot of each play a woman in mourning (Olivia or Celia) is courted by a group of suitors, including a serious lover (Orsino or Jacomo) whose
plangent melancholy opens the first act. These suitors include a foolish knight

(Sir Andrew or Laverdure) who is similarly frustrated by the appearance of a character (Sebastian or Albano) who, having unexpectedly survived a shipwreck, identifies himself through a birthmark. Furthermore, each comedy ends with a revelation of identity occasioned by the appearance of this survivor, whose presence is questioned by the existence of a double (Viola or Francisco). Finally, both have subplots (not found in their principal sources) in which a harsh critic (Malvolio or Lampatho Doria) mirrors Jonson's flaws. Although Marston's treatment of Lampatho is rather benign, his admirer and follower Simplicius Faber shares Malvolio's plight: he is gulled into becoming a suitor, in a plot hatched by the servants to make him look foolish. Oddi's plot consequently provided Marston with a fiction that resembled *Twelfth Night* just enough to suggest a significant difference.

What makes Marston's approach different from Shakespeare's is its bleakness. Jacomo and Celia are Orsino and Olivia in a plot darkened by shadows of *Hamlet*. When John Manningham described *Twelfth Night* in 1602, he incorrectly remembered Olivia as being a widow (since she was apparently dressed in black to mourn her brother's death). In *What You Will*, Marston may have picked up the same visual cue in making Celia, his version of Olivia, resemble Gertrude in choosing "To match so sudden, so unworthily," with "infamous lewd haste," "scarce three months" after her husband's reported death (2:243–44). Like the late King Hamlet, Albano is eulogized as having been "absolute" in all that "was valued praiseful excellent." Hearing him so described, Jacomo responds, "Oh God! / Methinks I see him now how he would walk," (2:241), echoing Hamlet's similar visualization, "My father—methinks I see my father. . . . In my mind's eye" (1.2.184–86). Marston understood how Shakespeare's demonstrations of the inherent irrationality of human experience could be used to reject comical satire. Indeed, he deployed *Twelfth Night* against Jonson because the play had already done this so well. But he also turned much more of his sarcasm against festive comedy to secure a new, more alienated dramatic position that mapped Paul's distance from both Blackfriars and the Globe.

What makes Marston's version of *Twelfth Night* so disturbing is the absence of genuine romantic sentiment or life-affirming providentialism. Both had been key elements of *Jack Drum* and *Antonio and Mellida*. Erotic idealization is replaced by detachment, cynicism, and disillusionment. Celia is an Olivia coarsened by her resemblance to Hamlet's mother, not because Marston is parodying *Twelfth Night* or *Hamlet* but because he imagines an even more troubling vision of comedy than Shakespeare had rendered, one that includes an even greater emphasis on the arbitrary, egotistical, irrational, and cruel aspects of desire. When Albano, the stuttering shipwrecked hero, returns home and discovers that his wife is planning to wed the French fop Laverdure, it is as if Olivia had decided to marry Sir Andrew. No character in *What You Will* approximates the selfless Viola. Instead, Celia's substitution of Laverdure for Albano establishes that "the soul of man is rotten" (2:263).

Twelfth Night and *What You Will* both end with scenes of reconciliation made possible by the entrance of *i morti vivi*: the shipwrecked Sebastian and Albano. But Marston treats this recognition scene as farce. Shakespeare's ending transforms the ridiculous into the marvelous, a moment of emotional clarification and reunion induced by chance. He emphasizes, in memorable terms, the final moment of wonder before the resolution of doubt. The duke sees the doubling as an optical illusion, an epistemological problem. "One face, one voice, one habit, and two persons," Orsino muses, "A natural perspective, that is and is not!" (5.1.216–17). He combines Feste's contrary assessments, "that that is is" (4.2.14) and "nothing that is so is so" (4.1.8–9). One of Marston's narrative jokes is to trump Shakespeare by making it "impossible to reveal the identities by a simultaneous appearance of the double."[23] What complicates Albano's reconciliation is the rumor that two individuals have been hired to impersonate him. His brothers plan to disrupt Celia's intended marriage by disguising the perfumer Francisco as Albano. But Laverdure's page overhears the plot and tells his master, who contemplates dressing a fiddler as Albano to expose the ruse. Even though Laverdure's plan is never carried out, the other characters believe it has been, so that when Albano and his double enter in the fifth act everyone on stage assumes they are both impostors. "All being known," Jacomo erroneously concludes, "the French knight hath disguised / A fiddler like Albano too, to fright the perfumer, this is all" (2:292). The enraged and stuttering husband is only able to overcome Celia's doubt when he promises to reveal what she "lisped" in his ear when last he took his "leave with *Hymeneal* rights" and offers a birthmark as evidence of his identity (2:293).

The recognition scene of *What You Will* stands halfway between the purge of comical satire and the reunion of festive comedy. In comical satire, personal relations based on fraud are severed: Delirio denounces his unfaithful wife. In festive comedy, the appearance of Sebastian unties fate's knot. Marston proposes a compromise. Albano discovers that Celia is unfaithful but rejoices at their reunion. Instead of rejecting her, he accepts her behavior with only one question: "Doth not Opinion stamp the current pass / Of each man's value, virtue, quality?" (2:269). Like Falstaff in *1 Henry IV*, who reasons, "What is honour? A word. . . . Air," that one cannot "feel" or "hear," because it is "insensible" (5.1.133–37), Albano recognizes that if his "name / Were liable to sense, that I could taste or touch / Or see, or feel it, it might 'tice belief," but it is only "voice, and air" (2:269). Albano's final acceptance of Celia hovers between Jonsonian satire and Shakespearean romance. Marston's reunion is much more caustic than Shakespeare's reconciliation. His "Venice," Finkelpearl notes, "resembles Olivia's house during the 'uncivil rule' of Sir Toby Belch's drinking party."[24] Still assuming the voice of festive comedy, Albano absolves society for its failure to know him: "Duke I invite thee, love I forgive thee: Frenchman I hug thee, I'll know all, I'll pardon all, and I'll laugh at all" (2:293).

This teetering between celebration and satire is mirrored in the contrasting advice that the play's spokesman Quadratus gives to the hopeless romantic Jacomo and the bitter critic Lampatho. He tells Jacomo to hate life and convinces Lampatho to accept it. The lover of festive comedy and the satirist of comical satire are convinced to detach themselves intellectually from their pursuits—to value their experiences at nothing or "what you will." For Marston the secret is to understand that one's personal experience of others has neither meaning nor value. He encourages his audience to seek pleasure, as long as they are willing to accept, in return, the dangerous, the arbitrary, and the insignificant. Marston's ambivalence toward what he willed is found not only in his work but also in an anecdote noted by John Manningham in his famous diary on 21 November 1602. Manningham writes that Marston, who "danced with Alderman More's wife's daughter, a Spaniard born, fell into a strange commendation of her wit and beauty. When he had done, she thought to pay him home, and told him she thought he was a poet. ''Tis true,' said he, 'for poets feign, and lie, and so did I when I commended your beauty, for you are exceeding foul.' "[25] Marston's retort, with its mixture of desire and cruelty reminiscent of Touchstone's abuse of Audrey, parallels the emotional ambiguity of *What You Will*.

The terms on which Marston accepts experience are so compromised that celebration hardly seems in order. This is particularly true of his representation of the political world. His depiction of the court grows steadily more negative after his encomium to Astrea/Elizabeth in *Histriomastix*. In *Jack Drum* it is a volatile world best respected from a distance. Following the Antonio plays, however, in part through the influence of *Hamlet*, the court becomes a site of transgression. The best advice that Quadratus can give Lampatho is to "turn a *Temporist*, row with the tide, / Pursue the cut, the fashion of the age" (2:258). He will never prosper there without deception: "He that climbs a hill / Must wheel about: the ladder to account / Is sly dissemblance." Poets who seek patronage must "bear a counter-face" and can only breathe "the base dirt" of "glavering flattery" in "Princes' nostrils." The state "is young, loose, and unknit" and can "relish naught but luscious vanities" (2:259). If poets want to thrive, their fictions must be pleasing. Marston accepts festive comedy but recognizes the cost of choosing imagination over reason. Modern commentators often read his entire canon as unnuanced satire, but his early comedies for Paul's trace a kind of negative dialectic, with the thesis of comical satire and the antithesis of festive comedy converging in *What You Will.*

V

By 1601, after only two years as a professional dramatist, Marston had become, along with Shakespeare and Jonson, one of the most famous playwrights in London. In the twentieth century his reputation rests on the strength of *The Malcontent* (1604) and, to a lesser extent, on his savage verse satire and the legend of his quarrels with Jonson. What current readers still tend to underestimate, however, is his close attention to Shakespeare's work, which he imitated with varying degrees of emulation and parody throughout his career. One remarkable example of Marston's admiration is evinced in the continuation he proposed for the untitled poem we now call "The Phoenix and Turtle" when it was first published in 1601. For at about the same time that he wrote *What You Will,* using *Twelfth Night* to respond to *Cynthia's Revels,* he became Shakespeare's commentator, collaborator, and rival in print.

Shakespeare's exquisite threnody, with its seemingly simple yet profound meditation on the mystical union of true lovers, was first published in a short collection of poems appended to a book by Robert Chester, the abbreviated title of which is *Love's Martyr: or Rosaline's Complaint. Allegorically shadowing the truth of Love in the constant Fate of the Phoenix and Turtle . . . With . . . some new compositions, of several modern Writers whose names are subscribed to their several works.* At the end of Chester's volume, this selection of new lyrics is set off from what precedes it by a separate title page with the heading: "Poetical Essays on . . . the *Turtle* and *Phoenix. Done by the best and chiefest of our* modern writers . . . *never before extant."* What follows is a series of fourteen poems: two attributed collectively to "Vatum Chorus"; two by "Ignoto"; Shakespeare's untitled poem; four related lyrics by Marston; one by Chapman; and, finally, four by Jonson. Each poet had evidently been requested to respond to the myth of the magical union-in-death of the phoenix and turtledove. That these four authors were considered "the best" modern playwrights is indicated by the first chorus of poets, which specifically invokes the "*Thespian Deities*" (line 1) to "commend" their "Labours" (lines 13–14). That three of them—Shakespeare, Marston, and Jonson—were currently involved in the Poets' War does not seem to have been accidental.

Marston, whose reputation was now at its zenith, was accorded the privilege of responding to Shakespeare's lyric in print because he had already established himself in the theater as a commentator on Shakespeare's drama. The parasitic relationship that Marston had established between Paul's and the Globe is thus reflected in this volume. He had evidently been provided with a transcript of Shakespeare's poem to comment on, since his first verse— "*A narration and description of a* most exact wondrous creature, arising *out of the Phoenix and Turtle Dove's ashes*"—begins where Shakespeare's ends. Referring to his predecessor's concluding "Threnos" (or dirge) as an "Epicedium," Marston pauses to appreciate its verse before providing a supplement:

> O 'Twas a moving *Epicedium*!
> Can Fire? can Time? can blackest Fate consume
> So rare creation? No; 'tis thwart to sense,
> Corruption quakes to touch such excellence. . . .
> Then look; for see what glorious issue (brighter
> Than clearest fire, and beyond faith far whiter
> Than *Diane's* tire) now springs from yonder flame?
>
> (LL. 1–9)

Shakespeare's Threnos laments that Beauty, Truth, Rarity, and Grace lie "in cinders" (line 55) now that the Phoenix and Turtle have vanished. Yet Marston finds life in their ashes by imagining the phoenix's rebirth in the form of the glorious issue he defines in the next three poems. Viewed self-referentially, Marston's phoenix riddle allegorizes his transubstantiation of Shakespearean poetics. Was Shakespeare annoyed by this upstaging? No matter how we read "The Phoenix and Turtle," this seems to have been inevitable. If, in contrast to all other contributors to the volume, Shakespeare was suggesting that the phoenix was now extinct, Marston would have ruined his point. If, however, the bird on "the sole Arabian tree" (line 2) with which the lyric begins is the sempiternal phoenix heralding in its own funeral, Shakespeare would have been piqued if Marston's addition had distracted readers from appreciating this paradox. In *The Tempest* Sebastian expresses wonder by affirming that he now believes "that in Arabia / There is one tree, the phoenix' throne, one phoenix / At this hour reigning there" (3.3.22–24).[26] In a poem that argues "Love hath reason, Reason none" (line 47), Shakespeare might have posited the ambiguity of the phoenix's simultaneous absence and presence, death and rebirth, as an allegory of the mutable continuum of experience on the model of Spenser's Garden of Adonis. Although "Truth and Beauty" are buried, the "true" and "fair" (lines 64 and 66) are still requested to commemorate their memory. But whatever his reaction to Marston's sequel, by year's end Shake-speare would use the Trojan War to satirize Jonson and Marston through the ludicrous antagonism of Ajax and Thersites at the same time that Dekker re-placed Marston, whom Jonson had physically assaulted, as his new nemesis: "Satiromastix."

PART THREE

The Dutch Churche · S. Michaels · S. Peter · S. Mellon · S. Andrew · S. Dunston de caſt

S.

Warke.

The BRIDGE

S. Mary Queris

That Poets should be made to vomit words
(As being so raw Wit's Maw could not digest)
Hath to Wit's praise been as so many swords,
To kill it quite in earnest, and in Jest:
Then, to untruss him (before Knights and Lords)
   Whose Muse hath power, to untruss what not?
   Was a vain cast, though cast to hit a Blot.
O Imps of Phoebus, why, o why do ye
Employ the Pow'r of your Divinity
(Which should but foil vice from which we should flee!)
Upon impeaching your own Quality?
                    —*John Davies of Hereford,* Wit's Pilgrimage[1]

8 "Impeaching Your Own Quality"
Constructions of Poetic Authority in *Poetaster* and *Satiromastix*

JONSON'S LAST comical satire, *Poetaster, or The Arraignment*, performed by the Children of the Chapel, and Dekker's caustic rejoinder, *Satiromastix, or The Untrussing of the Humorous Poet*, acted by both the Chamberlain's Men and the Children of Paul's, offer competing interpretations of poetic authority crucial to the final phase of the Poets' War. Some literary historians even limit the Poetomachia to these two works, since Dekker specifically coined the term to characterize his play's conflict with *Poetaster*.[2] John Davies, quoted above, set the pattern for this reading by pairing the sensational exposure scenes: the episode in *Poetaster* (5.3.391–565) in which "Marston" is forced to vomit his obscure diction; and its counterpart in *Satiromastix* (5.2.155–346) in which "Jonson," dressed as a satyr, is untrussed and crowned with nettles.

Yet to assume that these plays constitute the entire Poets' War obscures the crucial differences among Marston's, Shakespeare's, and Dekker's responses to Jonson's literary theories. *Satiromastix* is not the summation of Shakespeare and Marston's more radical assault on academic humanism. Marston had challenged the conception of art underlying the poetics of comical satire because it imposed arbitrary restrictions on creative liberty, but Dekker accepts, with qualifications, the viability of Jonson's ideal. In *Poetaster*, Jonson anticipated an attack on him by Marston and Dekker, who seems to corroborate this suspicion by writing in *Satiromastix* that "Horace *hal'd his* Poetasters *to the Bar*," after which "*the* Poetasters *untruss'd* Horace" ("To the World," lines

12–13). But *Satiromastix* was not, strictly speaking, a collaboration. Marston might have advised Dekker, who had benefited from his three prior critiques and whose title *Histriomastix* Dekker deliberately plays on. But only Dekker is credited with its authorship in its registration *and* on the First Quarto's title page (1602), the text of which—except for the title—reflects neither Marston's diction nor his skepticism.[3] Playing his assigned role, Dekker refers to himself in the quarto's dedication as a collaborator even though he was not.

Although never assuming poetic authority himself, Dekker voices none of the intellectual relativism that had made *What You Will* such a formidable reply to *Cynthia's Revels*. Reading *Satiromastix* as the sole answer to Jonson consequently makes the Poets' War seem more conservative than it was. The main difference between Marston's and Dekker's attitudes toward Jonson is that the former criticizes his bad poetic program and the latter taxes him for not living up to his own high standards. Marston derides Jonson's ideals; Dekker revives them to define his failure. Personal satire thus plays a greater role in Dekker's drama. The irony of this situation, Davies suggests, is that any infighting (even to validate an ideal standard) risks endangering poetry: "To kill it quite in earnest, and in *Jest*." An early modern meaning of "quality" was "profession," and parodying any particular poet's "quality"—in Davies's pun on the now ordinary sense of the word—might trigger vilification of the entire craft.

Yet even though Dekker is obsessed with Jonson's idiosyncrasies, his response is carefully calibrated. *Satiromastix* negotiates the terms under which he is willing to accept Jonson's conception of poetic authority. To this end, he rewrites *Poetaster*, shifting its focus from the power of the poet and monarch to the constraints subjects must place on their sovereign jurisdiction. The conflict between *Poetaster* and *Satiromastix* cannot serve as a synecdoche for the Poets' War, but it remains one of its most acrimoniously contested engagements.

Poetaster was followed by *Satiromastix* within the last six months of 1601.[4] Suspecting that Dekker and Marston were planning to parody him, Jonson completed his play "in fifteen weeks" ("After the Second Sounding," line 14) as a preemptive strike. Dekker could not have finished his rejoinder until he had seen *Poetaster*, because he revives four of its main characters—Horace, Demetrius, Crispinus, and Tucca. So much of his play lampoons *Poetaster* that he relied on his audiences at Paul's and the Globe having already seen the then unpublished drama at Blackfriars. Indeed, Edward Pudsey, one such theatergoer, kept a commonplace book juxtaposing quotations from several Poets' War plays, including *Poetaster* and *Satiromastix*.[5] The same audience combined visits to the Globe, Paul's, and Blackfriars—the upscale Bankside playhouses—to judge plays that judged each other. Unlike the theaters in the northern sub-

Satiro--mastix.

OR

The vntrussing of the Humorous Poet.

As it hath bin presented publikely,
by the Right Honorable, the Lord Chamberlaine his Seruants; and priuately, by the
Children of Paules.

By *Thomas Dekker.*

Non recito cuiquam nisi Amicis idq̃; coactus.

LONDON,
Printed for *Edward White*, and are to bee
solde at his shop, neere the little North docre of Paules
Church, at the signe of the Gun. 1602.

TITLE PAGE OF *Satiromastix.*
Reprinted by permission of the Folger Shakespeare Library

urbs, these had an upper-class constituency that exerted a unifying influence on their separate repertoires.[6] It was to win over this audience that the Poets' War was waged.

I

Poetaster is Jonson's most comprehensive defense in drama of his humanist ideals. Set in Augustan Rome, the golden age of Latin literature, the play is based on two central distinctions: the differentiation of Virgilian and Ovidian norms and the demarcation of poets from poetasters. On a general level, *Poetaster* divides poetry into the opposed philosophies of rationalism and romanticism, epitomized by Virgil and Ovid, who constitute what we would now call "Apollonian" and "Dionysian" principles. Jonson's opinion of their value is firm but nuanced: he rewards Virgil with imperial patronage and banishes Ovid, albeit with regret. Horace/Jonson in Virgil's circle and Crispinus/Marston and Demetrius/Dekker in Ovid's recapitulate this division on a topical level, but with one major difference. Even though Ovid is misled by romanticism, he is not (unlike his debased associates) a hack or "poetaster."

Jonson invented comical satire to abolish romantic culture, and he re-creates the dichotomy between Plautus and Aristophanes in *Every Man Out* in the contrast between Ovid and Virgil. For Jonson, Virgilian poetry induced a painful but necessary state of self-consciousness that curbed Ovidian erotic fantasies. Jonson's Roman history is shaped by the poets' contrary fates, which enact their conflicting poetics. Ovid is exiled from the court on "pain of death" for corrupting Augustus's daughter Julia (4.6.52–59), while Virgil, honored by the emperor and elevated on a dais above him, recites the tale of Aeneas's *"guilty . . . match"* with Dido (5.2.66).[7] This episode, from the fourth book of the *Aeneid*, provides a corrective for Ovid's flawed romanticism. "Here," Virgil notes of his characters, *"first began their bane"* (5.2.68).

Ovid is a writer of eloquence and wit who values "sacred *poesy*" as the "spirit of arts" and "soul of science" (1.2.231–32) and contests his father's claim that law is superior. Lawyers, he answers, are "jaded wits . . . for common hire"; poets, moved by the "raptures of a happy Muse," are "Borne on the wings of her immortal thought" (1.2.241–44). But in rebelling against law, Ovid celebrates the appetitive as the sacred, in Epicurean poetry according to which the gods are projections of desire. In the masquerade he organizes, he and Julia impersonate Jupiter and Juno presiding over a "banquet of the gods" attended by courtiers, gallants, citizens, and poets (including Crispinus and Demetrius) who imitate members of the pantheon. The scene opens with Ovid's proclamation, read by Gallus, that to guarantee their pleasure, "It shall be lawful for every lover, / To break loving oaths, / To change their lovers, and make love to others" (4.5.29–31). Ovid then, following his own command, joins Mars and Mercury (Tucca and Hedon) in attempting to seduce Venus (Chloe), the wife of Vulcan (the jeweler Albius). Just as they begin, however, Caesar enters, breaks up the orgy, and rebukes them for blasphemy:

> Are you, that first the *deities* inspir'd . . .
> The first abusers of their useful light;
> Prophaning thus their dignities, in their forms:
> And making them like you, but counterfeits?
> O, who shall follow virtue, and embrace her,
> When her false bosom is found nought but air? . . .
> When you that teach, and should eternize her,
> Live, as she were no law unto your lives:
> Nor liv'd her self, but with your idle breaths?
>
> (4.6.34–47)

In deifying desire, Ovid's masquerade (his art of self-apotheosis) subverts the moral law upon which poetry and the state are based.[8] It is particularly harmful because it undermines public and private morality by striking at the royal household. How can Ovid be pardoned, the emperor asks, when he lives "As if there were no virtue, but in shade / Of strong imagination, merely enforc'd?" (4.6.68–69). In parting from Julia, he incorrigibly reaffirms his sacred madness beneath her chamber window:

> I am mad with love.
> There is no spirit, under heaven, that works
> With such illusion: yet such witchcraft kill me,
> Ere a sound mind, without it, save my life.
> Here, on my knees, I worship the blest place
> That held my goddess. . . .
> "The truest wisdom silly men can have
> Is dotage on the follies of their flesh."
>
> (4.9.99–109)

Jonson opposes the mock religion of desire that claims to transcend moral law, which was as much a part of the cultural milieu of late Elizabethan London as it was of Augustan Rome. But what was specifically Ovidian in his own culture? Helgerson believes that Jonson means to censure the amateur court poets of the 1590s.[9] But they were not central to his main concern, which was to confront rival playwrights. Indeed, Ovid's balcony-scene parting from Julia reevaluates the plangent rhetoric of its predecessors in *Romeo and Juliet* and *Antonio and Mellida*.

Virgil, Ovid's opposite, is a "rectified spirit" of "sovereign worth" (5.1.100, 116). Asper and Criticus's status had been enhanced by Elizabeth and Cynthia, but Augustus fuses his identity with Virgil's: "to CAESAR, VIRGIL / . . . shall be made / A second Surname, and to VIRGIL, CAESAR" (5.2.3–5). This is possible because Virgil's thought reveals an "*analytic* sum / Of all the . . . arts" in poetry "so ramm'd with life, / That it shall gather strength . . . with being, / And live hereafter, more admir'd, than now" (5.1.134–38). The strength of his work is its comprehensive moral vision:

> That, which he hath writ,
> Is with such judgement, labour'd and distill'd
> Through all the needful uses of our lives,
> That could a man remember but his lines,
> He should not touch at any serious point,
> But he might breathe his spirit out of him.
> (5.1.118–23)

Only this profound and universal poetry can forge what Stanley Fish calls a "community of the same."[10] Within this primary contrast between Ovidian and Virgilian perspectives Jonson inserts a semi-biographical fiction to vindicate himself and his work. But why did he choose to represent himself as Horace, a peripheral member of the court more indebted to Maecenas than Caesar, rather than as Virgil? Why would he take only a supporting role in the play's literary hierarchy? In subordinating Horace to Virgil, he had followed the satirist's own opinion. But more important, he had probably concluded that the prominence of his self-portrait as Criticus had been a tactical mistake and that by not representing himself as Virgil he could insist, with less personal risk, on the disputed concept of poetic sovereignty.

II

Horace, the ancient writer whom Jonson emulated most and whose life served as a pattern for his own in *Poetaster*, was an ego-ideal, a painstaking and meticulous poet-scholar-critic known for urbane moderation.[11] He served as a literary talisman through which Jonson attempted to stabilize his own passionate temper, while acting as though this stability had already been achieved. Horace's verse genres—satire, epistle, ode, and epode—and his plain style were fundamental to Jonson's poetics. His *Ars Poetica*, which Jonson translated twice and on which he wrote a commentary, now lost, was a foundation for academic humanism. On a more personal level, Jonson found in Horace's life a pattern that paralleled his own. The son of a freedman, Horace overcame his lower-class origin to become familiar with the intellectual, social, and political elite of his age, even though he was attacked. Jonson writes that he chose

> AUGUSTUS CAESAR'S times,
> When wit and arts were at their height in *Rome*,
> To show that VIRGIL, HORACE, and the rest
> Of those great master-spirits did not want
> Detractors, then, or practisers against them. . . .
> ("APOLOGETICAL DIALOGUE," LL. 101–5)

In Horace's *Satires* Jonson found an autobiographical account, rich in literary theory, through which he could discuss his own dilemma. He paid special attention to four Satires (1.4, 1.9, 1.10, and 2.1), which he altered to reflect his quarrel with Marston and Dekker.[12] Horace was especially relevant to comical satire because of the debt he expressed in Satire 1.4 to Eupolis, Cratinus, and Aristophanes, the "true poets" and "good men to whom Old Comedy belongs" (lines 1–2). Jonson had this association in mind when, in apologizing for *Poetaster*, he again evoked as his precedent "the old *comedy* . . . of ARISTOPHANES" (lines 186–90).

More particularly, Horace had been criticized when, in reviving the spirit of Old Comedy preserved in the work of Lucilius, he censured the latter's obscure vocabulary. "You need terseness," Horace warns, so "that the thought may run on, and not become entangled in the verbiage" (1.10.9–10). But his detractors called him wrong and malicious for having said so. Similarly, Jonson's Horace exposes Crispinus's strange locutions and anticipates being travestied, but in a play. Jonson consequently substitutes Crispinus for Lucilius and pairs him with Demetrius as poetasters who plot his disgrace. In the process, Crispinus is conflated with the boor from whom Horace flees on the Via Sacra in *Poetaster*'s adaptation (3.1) of Satire 1.9. His slander even drives Horace to consult Trebatius (following Satire 2.1) in Jonson's second long verse translation (printed only in 3.5 of the Folio).

When Tucca vows to have Horace whipped "for his *satires* and his humours," Crispinus, speaking for himself and Demetrius, volunteers: "We'll undertake him, Captain" (4.3.119). The poetasters have Ovid's passion, but his love becomes their hatred. And their punishment by Caesar's literary tribunal replicates Ovid's banishment, just as Horace's exoneration repeats Virgil's success. Jonson had already codified his attitude toward the poetasters, who illustrate faults of art and nature. Marston flew too high and Dekker too low; thus, Crispinus is too stylized and Demetrius technically incompetent. In *Poetaster*, however, Jonson's attack is so personal (when compared with *Every Man Out* and *Cynthia's Revels*) that he felt justified in falsely implying that it was his first.

When Jonson told Drummond that he "wrote his *Poetaster* on" Marston, he was referring to Rufus Laberius Crispinus, who reflects Marston's appearance, personal life, interests, and career. "Rufus" or "red" describes the color of Marston's hair (3.1.27). The same word denotes his fiery nature; his "ample velvet" breeches show the "stains of a hot disposition" (3.1.68–70). The rest of his name conflates those of two comic butts mocked by Horace. Laberius is a writer of sordid mimes (Satire 1.10.5–6) and Crispinus (1.1.120, 1.3.139, 1.4.13–16, 2.7.45) a rival who challenges Horace to see who can write faster. Crispinus also has Marston's short legs and tattered yet fashionable clothes. Although he wears a stylishly embroidered hat with ash-colored feather, his "satin sleeve" has begun "to fret at the rug" (3.1.67–68). His father, "a man of worship" (3.4.160–61), is deceased, and he is at odds with his mother, obviously over the related questions of his inheritance and his prodigality. Marston's father, a Coventry landowner and lawyer also named John, died in 1599, leaving the poet's inheritance contested and deferred. Crispinus is excessively proud of being a "gentleman" and keeps up appearances by pawning his wardrobe. He deals with moneylenders and is in arrears to his milliner and tailor while being prosecuted for debt by his apothecary for the purchase of sweetmeats. As for the arts, he plays the viol (4.3.54–55) and prides himself on his knowledge of architecture (3.1.30–35) and ability to write poetry, dance, and sing.

Crispinus envies Horace, a superior poet with access to society's political and literary elite. At first he fawns on him and promises to help him secure Maecenas's favor by ridiculing Virgil. He is a reveler in the worst sense of the word. Yet to Horace he describes himself very differently. "We are a scholar, I assure thee" (3.1.20), he lies when they first meet. "Nay," he continues, "we are new turn'd *Poet* too, which is more; and a *Satirist*, which is more than that: I write just in thy vein . . . I am for your *odes* or your *sermons* [i.e., epistles]," adding, "we are a pretty *stoic* too" (3.1.23–28). "To the proportion of your beard," Horace wryly responds, contrasting Crispinus's account of himself with the fiery red hair on his chin. Jonson knew that Marston invoked stoic concepts in *The Scourge*, *Histriomastix*, and *Antonio and Mellida*. But he also knew that Marston had more recently expressed doubts about their viability in *Antonio's Revenge*.

Jonson's biography of Marston in *Poetaster* begins with his inspiration through adulterous Ovidian love and ends with his slander of Jonson. "I do make verses, when I come in such a street as this," Crispinus informs the incredulous Horace, as he evokes an eroticized mythology from the urban setting they traverse:

> O your city-ladies, you shall ha' 'hem sit in every shop like the *Muses*— offering you the *castalian* dews, and the *thespian* liquors, to as many as have but the sweet grace and audacity to—sip of their lips. Did you never hear any of my verses?
>
> (3.1.38–43)

Marston is often classified as a satirist who shares a generational, philosophical, and literary bond with Jonson. His dramatic forays into the romantic sublime, such as *Antonio and Mellida*, are dismissed as burlesques. Yet his comedies after *Histriomastix* espouse a romantic norm in opposition to comical satire. Indeed, Marston's romanticism began with his first publication, *The Metamorphosis of Pygmalion's Image and Certain Satires* (1598), which combines an Ovidian mythological narrative with a collection of formal verse satires drawn from the work of Juvenal, Horace, and Martial. In it he assumes by turns the self-contradictory personae of sexual libertine and snarling satirist. *Pygmalion's Image*, based on the tenth book of the *Metamorphoses*, repeats Ovid's famous account of how Pygmalion sculpts a statue that is brought to life by his desire. But while Marston's model, Shakespeare's *Venus and Adonis*, explores the tension between erotic fantasy and tragic reality, *Pygmalion's Image* celebrates the triumph of narcissistic libido. Having fallen in love with his own workmanship (line 14), Pygmalion prays to Venus, and she inspires the statue with life. Only later did Marston insist that his eroticism was satiric.[13]

Awed by the beauty of Chloe (a rich jeweler's wife), Crispinus confesses in *Poetaster*: "lady, 'tis love and beauty make *Poets*: and since you like *Poets* so well, your love and beauties shall make me a *Poet*" (2.2.75–77). To complete his metamorphosis, he rushes off to beg a "garland" and obtain a "Poet's gown" from a pawn shop (2.2.224–25). Yet the only poem he ventures to sing—on love's blindness (4.3.67–78)—turns out to have been plagiarized from Horace (4.3.95–96). Documenting his own change of voice from *Pygmalion's Image* to *Certain Satires*, Marston writes in the latter: "I, that even now lisp'd like an Amorist, / Am turn'd into a . . . Satirist" (2.1–2). Crispinus then duplicates Marston's career as a love poet turned satirist who first solicits Jonson's friendship and then attacks him. He must have offended Apollo, or else "this heavy scourge / Could ne'er have lighted on me" (3.1.135–36), Horace observes, naming Marston's next volume of poems.

When Crispinus is finally indicted for slandering Horace, a single piece of evidence is adduced—a poem in Marston's accusatory style, featuring echoes of *The Scourge* and *Antonio's Revenge*. "Yes, it is mine," Crispinus acknowledges, before Tibullus reads what amounts to a signed confession:

> *Ramp up, my* genius; *be not retrograde:*
> *But boldly nominate a spade, a spade.*
> *What, shall thy lubrical and glibbery* Muse
> *Live, as she were defunct, like punk in stews? . . .*
> *Alas! That were no modern consequence,*
> *To have cothurnal buskins frighted hence.*
> *No; teach thy* incubus *to poetize;*
> *And throw abroad thy spurious snotteries,*
> *Upon that puffed-up lump of barmy froth, . . .*
> *Or clumsy chilblain'd judgement, that with oath*
> *Magnificates his merit; and bespawls*
> *The conscious time, with humorous foam, and brawls,*
> *As if his organons of sense would crack*
> *The sinews of my patience. Break his back,*
> *O Poets* all, *and some: For now we list*
> *Of strenuous venge-ance to clutch the fist.*
>
> Subscri. CRIS. (5.3.275–93)

With words lifted from Marston's mannered vocabulary, Crispinus summons his muse to throw "*spurious snotteries*" at Horace, the man of judgment, who "*magnificates his merit*" in an "*oath*" ("*By God, 'tis good*") as he censures the world through comical satire. In the high style of *Antonio's Revenge*—a barbaric, hateful rattle of obscure words—he summons his literary allies to break Horace's back. For Jonson, this passage epitomized Marston's poetry as a lewd tirade in the vein of his latest revenge tragedy. "Here be words," Caesar muses over Crispinus's poem, "able to bastinado a man's ears" (5.3.389–90). Several months later, in *2 Return from Parnassus*, Marston would be similarly described as "a Ruffian in his style" who "Cuts, thrusts, and foins at whomsoever he meets." But, unlike Jonson, its anonymous author would evince a measure of admiration for the way Marston managed a "pen-knife gallantly" on his "paper steed," as he wielded a "battering ram of terms" to assault "the walls of the old fusty world."[14] Indeed, Marston's tortured diction and syntax assure his place beside Chapman and Donne as a founder of the metaphysical style. His exaggerated poetic vocabulary marked a transition from one style of writing to another. His main problem was that he lacked Donne's muscular thought and control. Marston's two stylistic weaknesses, John Peter notes, "lie in his tendency on the one hand to write bombast, wordy and windy, and on the other to write gnomic brachylogies as obscure as those of Greville."[15]

Demetrius Fannius, in turn, is Jonson's representation of Dekker, who subsequently used the character as the basis for his self-portrait in *Satiromastix*. The actual Horace's Demetrius was a backbiter musician whom he calls a "monkey" in the *Satires* (1.10.79–80, 90–91); Fannius was a hack who disdained him (1.4.21–22 and 1.10.78–80). Both, Jonson implies, resemble Dekker. In terms of physical appearance, Demetrius Fannius has short arms—"half-arms" (3.4.318)—that make him resemble a puppet. And because, like Crispinus's, his clothes are tattered—"his doublet's a little decayed" (3.4.320)—Tucca promises to put the "poor, egregious, nitty [i.e., louse-eaten] rascal" in "fresh rags" (3.4.341, 344). His main vice is that he has "one of the most overflowing rank wits" and "will slander any man that breathes" (3.4.338–39). Years later, Jonson told Drummond that Dekker was a "rogue" (1:133).

Demetrius is a prolific poet, "overflowing" in his rankness, but ironically, he is still only a "poor journeyman" (5.3.182). Dekker remained impoverished throughout his long career, and in both 1598 and 1599 he had been imprisoned for debt—on the latter occasion at the insistence of the Chamberlain's Men. Like the apprentices he praised in *The Shoemakers' Holiday*, he had not yet become a master of his poetic craft. Indeed, Jonson links Dekker to the citizen's workshop to emphasize his lack of inspiration. As a "parcel-poet" and "dresser of plays" (3.4.322), he represents theater at its worst. In early modern English, the word "parcel" meant "part" when used as an adjective; Dekker is not fully a poet but only a piece of one, a "poetaster" who is pronounced "Parcel-guilty" at his arraignment (5.3.419). But the word has other resonances as well. A "parcel" was a small sum of money; a "parcel-poet" wrote only for gain. It could also mean a short passage in a literary work. Having collaborated too much, Dekker remained incomplete. Jonson knew that he was a "parcel-poet" from his own experience. They had co-written *Page of Plymouth* and had been part of a team that had scripted *Robert II, or The Scot's Tragedy*, for Henslowe.[16]

Although Dekker writes copiously, Jonson argues, his work is substandard, even unmetrical, more laughable than dangerous. He is a fool who cries out "Excellent" (3.4.227) in response to the child actors' selection of overwritten parcels of public and private drama. And like Crispinus, he is convicted on the basis of a slanderous lyric that reveals his moral and technical transgressions:

Our Muse *is in mind for th'untrussing a* poet,
I slip by his name; for most men do know it:
A critic, *that all the world bescumbers*
With satirical *humours, and* lyrical *numbers:* . . .
And for the most part, himself doth advance
With much self-love, and more arrogance. . . .
And (but that I would not be thought a prater)
I could tell you, he were a translator.
I know the authors from whence he has stole,
And could trace him too, but that I understand 'hem not full and whole. . . .
The best note I can give you to know him by,
Is, that he keeps gallants *company;*
Whom I would wish, in time should him fear,
Lest after they buy repentance too dear.

Subscri. DEME. FAN. (5.3.302–20)

Dekker's main argument is that Jonson is a translator who steals others' work because he lacks originality. Marston had initiated this line of criticism when he mocked Chrisoganus as a "translating scholar." In *Cynthia's Revels*, Dekker's surrogate vows to spread the rumor that "all" Jonson "does is dictated from other men." That Jonson was never able to defend himself successfully against this charge is evident in its reformulation by Dryden: "He was not only a professed Imitator of *Horace*, but a learned Plagiary of all the others," and if "*Horace, Lucan, Petronius Arbiter, Seneca*, and *Juvenal* had their own, . . . there are few serious thoughts which are new in him."[17] But in *Poetaster*, the argument of Demetrius's poem collapses—both conceptually and metrically—when he admits that he cannot read the texts he accuses his rival of plagiarizing. Jonson's interest in Latin literature paralleled Horace's interest in Greek; he viewed the project of translation as being at the heart of his own excellence. Since the ideal poet was necessarily a scholar, his work entailed translation. As George Parfitt explains, "other men may say just what Jonson believes, and if they do he is willing to let them say it for him."[18] Jonson underscored his reliance on classical authority in the play's first quarto by annotating his classical translations in its margins.

Jonson's reconstruction of the cultural and literary milieu of Augustan Rome attested by analogy to his legitimacy. "And, for his true use of translating men," Virgil explains in exoneration, "It still hath been a work of as much palm / In clearest judgments, as t' invent, or make" (5.3.365–67). Under cross-examination, Demetrius finally admits that he hates Horace only because "he kept better company . . . and that better men lov'd him than lov'd me: and that his writings thriv'd better than mine, and were better liked, and graced" (5.3.450–53). Before Crispinus and Demetrius swear not to bother Horace, the latter is fitted with a fool's cap and coat, and the former is purged when Horace receives permission from Caesar to feed him pills that cause him to vomit (in a scene borrowed from Lucian's *Lexiphanes*) those pieces of his vocabulary that Davies described as being "too raw" for wit to digest.[19] In the Folio version (5.3.464–530), Crispinus disgorges fourteen words and phrases that can still be located in Marston's prior work: "barmy froth," "chilblained," "clumsy," "clutched," "conscious," "damp," "glibbery," "incubus," "magnificate," "puffy," "quaking custards," "snarling gusts," "snotteries," and "spurious."[20] This purge is, however, only the beginning of a cure, and Virgil, "in place of a strict sentence," prescribes a "strict and wholesome diet" of the best Greek and Latin poets who eschew "wild, outlandish terms" (5.3.560–61, 536, 549). Informing Crispinus that bombast is a moral failing, Virgil cautions him to "bear your self more humbly; not to swell / Or breathe your insolent, and idle spite, / On him, whose laughter, can your worst affright" (5.3.563–65). The poetasters then swear an oath to either abstain from criticizing Horace or be committed to a "hospital of Fools" (5.3.609), and with this judgment the court is dissolved.

Jonson's last comical satire marks a new departure in that it does not defend drama. On the contrary, it condemns theater for being a corrosive influence. Wearied by attacks on himself and his program, Jonson concluded that the only useful function served by drama was to imagine a small enlightened community whose values paradoxically precluded theatricality. His two earlier surrogates had been men of the theater: Asper is a poet-player and Criticus a royal masque-maker. But in each of his comical satires Jonson had increasingly narrowed his chosen audience from some members of the public theater to the private theater to a coterie at the center of state power. He had in this regard become like Horace, who in his epistle to Augustus (*Epistles* 2.1) praises those "who prefer to put themselves in a reader's hands, rather than brook the disdain of a scornful spectator" (lines 214–15). Rejecting the commercial theater of his time that lauded Plautus, a playwright "eager to drop a coin in his pocket" (line 175), and an audience ready to "call in the middle of a play for a bear or for boxers" (lines 185–86), Horace preserved his integrity through patronage. He told Augustus that he hoped to contribute to the work Virgil had begun if he could discover in himself "power equal to my longing" (line 257). There is, however, a sense of defeat in Jonson's intimation that his fantasies of poetic authority could only be enacted in a idealized past of his own creation. Maecenas, the generic type of the aristocratic patron, emerges as the poet's sole benefactor.[21]

III

Satiromastix contains such a thorough caricature of Jonson that it continues to shape all biographical accounts of his early career. Makeup and costuming evidently helped to reinforce its effectiveness. A stage direction at the beginning of act 2, scene 2, for instance, informs us that Horace enters in "his true attire"—that is, the clothing that Jonson actually wore. Dekker's criticism encompasses his appearance, personality, and activities as a bricklayer, scholar, actor, patronage poet, and playwright. This skewering of Jonson's personal excesses shows a journalistic comic realism more richly detailed than Marston's; in the Elizabethan period, only Thomas Nashe's assault on Gabriel Harvey compares to it as a travesty of a contemporary writer. Dekker's Jonson comes to life with his large, pock-marked, swarthy, and menacing face, set over broad shoulders and a lean frame covered in shabby black clothing. A surly and malicious hypocrite, he pretends to be sociable for either vanity or profit. Assiduous, like a plodding bricklayer, Horace is a Catholic ex-felon, saved from the gallows by his recital of the neck-verse; a murderer; and a coward who lacks psychological balance and integrity. He feels secure only when dominating others and swears to hang himself if someone writes "Plays and Rhymes" better (5.2.292). At dinners in taverns he forces his work on others; his poems fly around the table like hailstones. He steals jests and indulges in self-praise or railing. His professional activities mock Horace's grand aspirations in *Poetaster*; Sir Quintilian Shorthose commissions him to write an epithalamion and Sir Vaughan asks him to dispraise baldness.

Dekker's Jonson indiscriminately attacks courtiers, magistrates, lawyers, gallants, citizens and their wives, players, and other poets. He is also a liar who denies the personal nature of his criticisms. Those who annoy him—whether friends or enemies, patrons or detractors—can expect to be parodied under pseudonyms in cryptic epigrams and plays.[22] He swears that his work avoids personal application, even in the most egregious cases. His "dastard wit will strike at men / In corners, and in riddles fold the vices / Of [his] best friends" (1.2.219–21). If his satire is general, Dekker asks, how is it possible for 80 percent of his audience, four fifths of the 500 spectators at Blackfriars, to identify his comic butts?

> I wonder then, that of five hundred: four
> Should all point with their fingers in one instant
> At one and the same man?
>
> (1.2.242–44)

Horace swears that he will not traduce Crispinus, Demetrius, and Tucca and then does so, until threatened. Dekker outdoes Marston in portraying Jonson's animosity toward actors. Tucca torments him for having murdered Gabriel Spencer: "Art not famous enough yet, . . . for killing a Player, but thou must eat men alive? thy friends? . . . wildman, thy Patrons?" (4.2.61–63). Jonson was a celebrity, a well-known, controversial poet whose presence at the theater when his works were performed inspired excitement, admiration, and ridicule. In Dekker's representation he appears "on the stage, when [his] Play is ended, . . . to exchange courtesies and compliments with Gallants in the Lords' rooms, to make all the house rise up . . . and to cry . . . 'that's he, that's he'" (5.2.303–7).

Much of *Satiromastix* reinstates charges that Marston had already made and Jonson had denied. Yet unlike Marston, Dekker believes that if Jonson were to prove himself worthy, he would be entitled to be revered as a true poet. In order to forestall that possibility, he hammers away at Jonson's inconsistencies. At stake was the basic issue of the moral responsibility of the satirist. If Jonson claimed for himself the crowning glory of satiric humanism, Cyrus Hoy explains, Dekker was eager to ask:

> How disinterested in fact was his exposure of folly and vice? How much secret pleasure did he take in railing against what he insisted were general types of offenders but which often seemed to bear a striking resemblance to particular persons? Could he who so arrogantly judged others bear the light of judgment on his own behavior?[23]

This debate arose because late Elizabethans distinguished between the proper and improper use of satire. Not everyone was willing to accept this distinction, but the rhetoric of the Poets' War becomes unintelligible without it. Dekker uses it to construct his chief indictment of Jonson:

> Should I but bid thy *Muse stand to the Bar*,
> Thy self against her wouldst give evidence:
> For flat rebellion 'gainst the Sacred laws,
> Of divine Poesy: herein most she missed,
> *Thy pride and scorn made her turn Satirist,*
> *And not her love to virtue* (as thou Preachest).
> (5.2.212–17)

Jonson argued that satire was necessary to confront a refractory world. But what Dekker grants him philosophically—the concept of poetic laureateship—he denies him existentially. "Under control of my dread Sovereign," Crispinus informs Horace, "We are thy Judges; thou that didst *Arraign* / Art now prepar'd for condemnation" (5.2.209–11). Dekker charges Jonson with having slandered his rivals in defiance of reason, the faculty that guarantees poetic authority. Thus, at the play's climax, King William Rufus includes Horace among the imposters who only usurp that power:

> If a clear merit stand upon his praise,
> Reach him a Poet's Crown (the honour'd Bays)
> But if he claim it, wanting right thereto,
> (As many bastard Sons of Poesy do)
> Race down his usurpation to the ground.
> *True Poets are with Art and Nature Crown'd.*
>
> (5.2.119–24)

After admitting that he does not even know who this fake Horace is, the king authorizes the dispassionate Crispinus, in whom he places complete confidence, to assess his merit:

> We make him thine *Crispinus*; wit and judgment
> Shine in thy numbers, and thy soul I know
> Will not go arm'd in passion 'gainst thy foe:
> Therefore be thou our self; whilst our self sit,
> But as spectator of this Scene of wit.
>
> (5.2.126–30)

This transfer of power from the monarch to the poet, the dream of humanist poetics, is completed when the king enjoins Crispinus to "Use thy Authority" (5.2.137). This command, identical to the one Caesar had given Virgil to judge Crispinus in *Poetaster* (5.3.398), reverses the latter's result. Crispinus arraigns Horace because his "Arrogance," "Self-love," "Detraction," and "Insolence" (5.2.220–22) disqualify him from possessing power, which he had wielded indiscriminately, "Careless what vein he pricks" (5.2.345). He believes, in Crispinus's words, that *"All Poets shall be Poet-Apes but you"* (5.2.339). Despite the plays' similar sense of politico-poetic authority, *Poetaster* is more concerned with identifying the poet and the king as homologues than *Satiromastix*, which specifies the limits of their power. Horace's punishment is doubled in the main plot, in which the tyrannical William Rufus is similarly compelled by his subjects to obey the law.

The scene of self-vindication in *Poetaster* is re-imagined by Dekker with a contrary result—Crispinus's purge is replaced by Horace's untrussing. At the play's conclusion, the "vile Monster-Poet" (5.2.170) and Bubo, his admirer, dressed as satyrs, are dragged onstage (by their horns) and chained to stakes, where they are baited by Tucca. Horace and Bubo thus pretend to be satyrs, only to be flayed of their disguises. Sir Vaughan, referring to Jonson's dual identity as bricklayer and scholar, asks Horace to explain why he and Bubo "go thus in Ovid's Mortar-Morphesis and strange fashions of apparel" (5.2.188–89). Apparently, the poet is more Ovidian than he had suspected. Assuming the role of a satirist or satyr, however, only leads to his being treated as a beast, as the Elizabethan entertainment industry triumphantly stages his baiting. Horace's attempts to defend himself are now rebuffed by Tucca and Crispinus, who explain that the man before them is not who he pretends to be but a thief, "a counterfeit Juggler, that steals the name of Horace" (5.2.244–45). It seems at first glance that when Dekker places Horace in Norman England he is being as moronic as Jonson supposed.[24] But this takes Dekker's irony at face value. He revels in the incongruity because he wants to alienate Jonson from the classical ideal he affirms. Horace is now tried for his crimes of slander and plagiarism on English soil. When the king asks, "How? counterfeit? does he usurp that name?" (5.2.246), Tucca brings out portraits of Jonson and Horace that he displays for the audience's edification conclusively to demonstrate their differences. The effect of this counterfeit presentment of two poets is to deconstruct Jonson's elaborate anagogical masquerade. Tucca accuses him of having stolen his identity from a dead Roman poet with whom he has little in common:

> look here, you staring Leviathan, here's the sweet visage of *Horace*; look perboiled-face, look; *Horace* had a trim long beard, and a reasonable good face for a Poet, . . . *Horace* did not screw and wriggle himself into great Men's familiarity, (impudently) as thou dost: nor wear the Badge of Gentlemen's company, as thou dost . . . : *Horace* lov'd Poets well, and gave Coxcombs to none but fools; but thou lov'st none, neither Wisemen nor fools, but thy self.
>
> (5.2.251–61)

Stripped of his hairy skin, the character who can only be thought of as Jonson is literally untrussed for pretending to be Horace. Under the scrutiny of King William, the poetasters agree that "stinging nettles" instead of bay leaves should "Crown his stinging wit" (5.2.224). Marston had used this motif at the conclusion of *Jack Drum*, where Planet fits Brabant/Jonson with a "Coronet of Cuckolds" and Sir Edward proposes to "solemnize" his "Coronation / With royal pomp." Dekker consequently bypasses Marston's more recent lenient treatment of Jonson in *What You Will*, reverting to his earlier roughness.

Branded an imposter, Horace/Jonson is released only after swearing an oath to reform his bad behavior (5.2.289–336), which includes a list of specific offenses: acting rudely at the theater; lavishing praise on his patrons while mocking them; complaining about the lack of appreciation for *Cynthia's Revels* at court; and passing out piles of his poetry during tavern meals. Indeed, many of Horace's transgressions stem from his capacity as a playwright, as Dekker insists on locating Jonson within the culture of the commercial theater from which he had distanced himself in *Poetaster*. Dekker's Jonson thus promises no longer to distract the audience by making "vile and bad faces" (5.2.300) at the players when they perform his dramas (in order to amuse gentlemen) or to exhibit himself at their conclusion for adulation.

IV

In *Poetaster* Jonson vilifies theater, and Dekker contextualizes this issue in two ways: personally, by referring to him as a failed actor; and theoretically, by reemphasizing the heuristic dynamic of theater he had rejected. Dekker is the sole source for the information that Jonson had begun his career in the theater as an actor and had taken the leading role of Hieronimo in *The Spanish Tragedy*. Tucca reminds Jonson that even though he had accused Dekker of being a "Journeyman Poet" in *Poetaster*,

> thou putst up a Supplication to be a poor Journeyman Player, and hadst been still so, but that thou couldst not set a good face upon't: thou hast forgot how thou amblest (in leather pilch) by a play-wagon, in the highway, and took'st mad Hieronimo's part, to get service among the Mimics.
>
> (4.1.128–32)

In *Cynthia's Revels*, Jonson had made fun of those who swore that "*the old Hieronimo* [i.e., *The Spanish Tragedy*] (as it was first acted) *was the only best and judiciously penned play of Europe*" (Induction, lines 209–11). Dekker implicates Jonson in a subsequent production of the play and explains that the poet's anger at the players began when he was incarcerated on suspicion of treason and slander for having written *The Isle of Dogs* for Pembroke's Men in 1597: "when the Stagerites banished thee into the Isle of Dogs, thou turn'dst Bandog . . . and ever since bitest" (4.1.132–33). He is like the vicious dogs baited at Paris Garden, where he had acted the part of Zulziman, the one time he played "the part of an honest man" (4.1.123–25).[25]

But Jonson also had a more recent connection to *The Spanish Tragedy* that might have prompted Dekker's parody. On 25 September 1601, Jonson, who had finished his third and final comical satire, returned to writing for the public theater, having abandoned the attitude of antagonism he had nurtured for the last two years. He gave up fighting to change the shape of Renaissance drama when he received the first of two payments from Henslowe for writing additions to *The Spanish Tragedy*, a play he had mocked as outdated in *Cynthia's Revels*. His exclusive association with the "little eyases" of Blackfriars came to an end with comical satire itself in *Poetaster*. Two years later, he collaborated with another, unnamed poet on *Sejanus* for the Chamberlain's Men. *Satiromastix* was staged by the autumn of 1601, and it is possible that Dekker responded to Jonson's work on *The Spanish Tragedy* by reminding him that he had more than a passing acquaintance with Kyd's popular revenge tragedy and the common theater for which it was written. Although Jonson acted superior to players, there was a time, Captain Tucca recalls, when:

> I ha' seen thy shoulders lapped in a Player's old cast Cloak, like a Sly knave as thou art: and when thou ranst mad for the death of Horatio: thou borrowedst a gown of *Roscius* the Stager (that honest Nicodemus) and sentst it home lousy.
>
> (1.2.354–57)

Edward Alleyn, as E. K. Chambers points out, was referred to as Roscius (the great Roman actor) by his contemporaries.[26] And it was to the Alleyn-Henslowe partnership that Jonson went, for cash, in the aftermath of his efforts at comical satire. Marston was certainly amused by Jonson's return to *The Spanish Tragedy* in 1601, and sometime between 25 September and 29 October (between Henslowe's payment to Jonson and the registry of *Antonio and Mellida* for publication) he added to his revised comedy a parody of one of the new episodes—the exchange between Hieronimo and the painter Bazardo on the limits of visual representation.[27]

But Dekker retained his faith in the humanist theory of drama that Jonson had surrendered. And in his main plot he displays a moralized Ovidian bias, the conviction that constant human desire is the most significant factor in social intercourse and that, when society is threatened by corrupt state power, playing can mediate social reconciliation. Dekker's coordinated plots demonstrate how the monarch and poet can on occasion exceed their legitimate power and how, when this occurs, their subjects must check these abuses through drama. Although Horace labors to execute increasingly trivial commissions, he is unaware that the king has become a tyrant and that a masque has been organized by ordinary individuals to reform him.

The play's crisis thus occurs when King William Rufus, asserting *droit du seigneur*, demands the favors of Caelestine, the bride of his loyal subject Sir Walter Terrill, on the couple's wedding night. Terrill is outraged at the king's suggestion but refuses to abrogate his oath of fealty. His oath, he says, is "law within a man" (5.1.41). Terrill and Caelestine then decide that they can remain loyal to their sovereign and true to each other only if she commits suicide and he presents her dead body to the king. In *Poetaster*, Caesar is shocked by Ovid's "banquet of the gods," but in *Satiromastix*, the monarch plans his own repast and selects Caelestine, against her will, as his bill of fare. Expecting her arrival, as he watches "the service of a Banquet" set before him, the king imaginatively transforms the scene into an affirmation of his divinity:

> Why so, even thus the Mercury of Heaven
> Ushers th'ambrosiate banquet of the Gods,
> When a long train of Angels in a rank
> Serve the first course, and bow their Crystal knees
> Before the Silver table, where Jove's page
> Sweet Ganymede fills Nectar. When the Gods
> Drink healths to Kings, they pledge them; none but Kings
> Dare pledge the Gods; none but Gods drink to Kings.
>
> (5.2.1–8)

Caelestine is prepared to die in order to escape the king's power, but this becomes unnecessary when her father Sir Quintilian (without either her or Terrill's knowledge) substitutes a sleeping potion for poison. Then the father and bridegroom present her body to the waiting king (obeying his command) in a "Masque of Death" that shames him into repenting. Approaching the king with what he believes to be Caelestine's corpse, Terrill, now a tragedian, denounces the monarch to whom he remains completely loyal as he apprises him of the limits of sovereign power:

> Now King I enter, now the Scene is mine,
> My tongue is tipped with poison; know who speaks,
> And look into my thoughts; I blush not King,
> To call thee Tyrant: death hath set my face,
> And made my blood bold.
>
> (5.2.61–65)

Dekker's audience would have known that the historical Sir Walter Tirel is suspected of having assassinated King William II (William Rufus, the son of William the Conqueror) in the New Forest on 2 August 1100, and he called on this subversive association to give an edge to his drama.[28] The tragic possibilities of the plot are averted and the play ends with an act of comic reconciliation because theater—a medium without the benefit of a poet's script— is created to negotiate the rights of subject and sovereign.

It is only through the intercession of drama that the king is forced to acknowledge error and remorse: "mine own guilt / Speaks more within me than thy tongue contains; / Thy sorrow is my shame" (5.2.84–86). The power of theatrical expression to give voice to moral outrage keeps the play from ending in regicide. In this sense, Sir Quintilian's "Masque of Death" deftly fulfills the dream of academic humanism. Through it the players prove Hamlet's theory that

> . . . guilty creatures sitting at a play
> Have by the very cunning of the scene
> Been struck so to the soul that presently
> They have proclaim'd their malefactions.
> (2.2.589–92)

But while "The Murder of Gonzago" in *Hamlet* prompts the guilty King Claudius to plot a second murder, the "Masque of Death" induces a moral catharsis in its royal spectator. Unlike comical satire, Dekker's play stages sovereignty primarily to correct it. Jonson had claimed that Dekker was hired by the players to parody him; he did so by redeeming drama while demeaning Jonson. Confronting the tyrannical king and untrussing the humourous poet are analogous acts of resistance, even though Dekker handles the king with more restraint than he treats Horace/Jonson. Dekker's opposition to the crown never reaches rebellion. Indeed, this would have been particularly unwise in the months following the execution of the earl of Essex. The king is left in office, but the poet is not. Dekker's political model depends on the concept of a loyal opposition that uses drama effectively as a political instrument to preserve liberty. Where Jonson glorifies the poet, narrating his great work without the mediation of actors to an appreciative monarch in *Poetaster*, Dekker insists on the power of actors—even without written scripts—to specify the conditions of obedience. He asserts the right of a loyal subject not to be molested by either the monarch or the poet, and he uses the genre of romantic comedy that Jonson had rejected to justify this argument.

Both Dekker, who impeached Jonson's "Quality" in *Satiromastix*, and Shakespeare, who berayed his "credit" in *Troilus and Cressida*, wrote their plays for the Chamberlain's Men at the end of 1601 with the intention of attacking Jonson's self-proclaimed poetic preeminence. But this connection between *Satiromastix* and *Troilus and Cressida* should not obscure a crucial difference between the authors' philosophical attitudes toward academic humanism. Only by contrasting their divergent responses can we begin to understand how radical Shakespeare's defiance of comical satire actually was and why he felt compelled to write his most severe criticism of Jonson in the wake of *Poetaster* and *Satiromastix*. For *Satiromastix* was a weak response to Jonson that lost its battle by conceding too much to the project of humanist poetics that Shakespeare rejected in *Troilus*.

In *Satiromastix*, Dekker accepted Jonson's intellectual premise that great poets were ideally suited to serve as moral educators, that they embodied an ideal form of ethical authority. He was prepared to admit, with Jonson, the impossibility of any man's being a good poet without first being a good man. His only objection was that his rival did not live up to the ideal he espoused and therefore had no right to assume moral and literary authority over his contemporaries. Shakespeare, on the other hand, offered a thoroughgoing critique of Jonson's humanist ideology, severing the link between moral judgment and creativity. The epistemological skepticism of the literary subplot of *Troilus and Cressida* deliberately dismantled the intellectual scaffolding upon which Jonson had constructed his humanist project. While Dekker left Jonson's literary program intact, Shakespeare demolished the standards they both supported.

Dekker drew back from the implications of a complete rejection of poetic authority, even though he was too honest about his own limitations to claim it for himself. But had he not granted so much to Jonson's intellectual premises that he undermined his own defense of theater? Shakespeare might have thought so when he wrote *Troilus and Cressida* and added the "little eyases" passage to *Hamlet* to register his anxiety at Jonson's success.

"There was for a while no money bid for argument, unless the poet and the player went to cuffs in the question."

—Hamlet

9 BEN JONSON AND THE "LITTLE EYASES"
Theatrical Politics in *Hamlet*

SHAKESPEARE'S ACKNOWLEDGMENT of the heated commercial competition among the Bankside theaters during the Poets' War is more explicit in the "little eyases" passage (2.2.337–62) of the First Folio *Hamlet* (1623) than anywhere else in his work. Although his plays teem with metatheatrical allusions, they offer few references to contemporary theater. In the "little eyases" passage, however, the focus abruptly shifts from text to context, from drama to theater, and from Elsinore to London when Rosencrantz reveals that the reputation of the "tragedians of the city," who have just arrived at court, has been undercut by a company of child actors who have railed against them on the stage. Twentieth-century theater historians generally agreed that Rosencrantz's statement, "there has been much to do on both sides," refers to *Poetaster* and *Satiromastix*. E. K. Chambers accordingly concludes that the Children of the Chapel's performance of "Jonson's *Poetaster*, containing raillery of the common stages, which stimulated a reply in Dekker's *Satiromastix* . . . together with their growing popularity, sufficiently explains the reference." And Harold Jenkins summarized contemporary critical thought in 1982 by observing that the "little eyases" reference is "universally recognized as an account of the boy actors who from Michaelmas 1600 were established at Blackfriars, where, according to Jonson's own dates, they acted his *Cynthia's Revels* before the end of the year and *Poetaster* in 1601, both of them gibing at the plays and playwrights of the public playhouses."[1]

Oddly, this hypothesis has been so enthusiastically endorsed as self-evident that little effort has been expended either to supplement it or to explain its implications. This neglect by consent has encouraged, ironically, a new skepticism about the theory's historical presuppositions, so that one recent critic goes so far as to dismiss it as a "myth" perpetuated by scholars intent on imagining a story of "cutthroat rivalry in the playhouse world" based on a misreading of "clusters of allusions" that "imply fights among dramatists, not companies."[2]

But before rejecting the dominant assumption that the passage refers to *Poetaster* and *Satiromastix*, it is important to remember that Rosencrantz's commentary is uniquely attuned to the climax of the Poets' War and cogently describes a "controversy" (2.2.354) that might justifiably be termed a "War of the Theaters." Insofar as Shakespeare refers to it as a "throwing about of brains" (2.2.358–59)—a wit-combat, if ever there was one—between "both sides" (2.2.352–53)—two commercial theaters, one private, one public—it is necessary to consider its personal *and* institutional dimensions. Still, the textual problems involved in reading Shakespeare's passage are daunting. Since my interpretation depends on the connection between the Folio version of 1623 and its quarto variants of 1603 and 1604/5, I include annotated reproductions of all three, which I will cite, when necessary, in their early modern spelling.[3]

I

Shakespeare usually avoids topicality in the narrow sense of the word, but it is impossible to understand the "little eyases" passage—silently following Theobald's modernization of the Folio's "little Yases"—without discussing its theatrical context and textual transmission.[4] In this brief dialogue the play's background is its foreground, and without a knowledge of Elizabethan theatrical history, readers can only be baffled. Yet in view of the superabundance of commentary lavished on *Hamlet*, surprisingly little attention has been devoted to examining this passage. Analysis must begin with the recognition that Shakespeare postulates a double analogy linking "the tragedians of the city" (2.2.328) with the Chamberlain's Men and the "aery of children, little eyases" (2.2.339), with the Children of the Chapel. So closely is the identity of "the tragedians" fused with that of the Chamberlain's Men that their defeat is imagined in terms of the children bearing off the symbol of the Globe as a trophy of their victory.[5] According to George Steevens, the Globe's emblem combined a representation of Hercules lifting the world with the motto "*Totus mundus agit histrionem.*"[6] Thus, when Hamlet asks, "Do the boys carry it away?" and Rosencrantz responds, "Ay, that they do, my lord—*Hercules* and his load too" (2.2.361–62), their exchange serves to identify the traveling company of actors at Elsinore with the late Elizabethan actors who impersonate them. A similar identification obtains when they are called "the best actors in the world" (2.2.396). This is, after all, a play fraught with such intense self-reflexivity that when Hamlet tells the ghost he will remember him "whiles memory holds a seat / In this distracted globe" (1.5.96–97), it is hard not to hear, "as long as the theater has a gallery audience."

Rosencrantz's allusion likewise assimilates the "aery of children, little eyases"—a nest of young hawks—with the Children of the Chapel. When Shakespeare added this passage to *Hamlet* in 1601 (the year after the play premiered), the Globe had just been provisionally allied with Paul's in producing *Satiromastix*. This collaboration explains why he mentions only *one* "aery" that molests the tragedians. The allusion to the Chapel children even particularizes their location. Whereas to get to Paul's theater, spectators descended below ground level to a cloister fourteen feet lower than the cathedral floor, the Blackfriars buildings were on an embankment and the theater itself was reached by ascending a "great pair of winding stairs" to what had been the Parliament Chamber of the Upper Frater. Shakespeare's reference to it as a hawk's nest perched on the Bankside particularized it as the source of predatory attacks. Several years later Thomas Middleton recalled this allusion in *Father Hubburd's Tale* (1604) when he advised a theatergoer, "if his humour so serve him, to call in at Blackfriars, where he should see a nest of boys able to ravish a man."[7]

What must have made the assault from Blackfriars even more wounding was the fact that in 1596 James Burbage had bought and refurbished that theater for the Chamberlain's Men until community protest vetoed the plan, causing his sons Richard and Cuthbert to rent it out in 1600 for use by the company—the Children of the Chapel—that became their fiercest opponent.[8] When in 1601 Shakespeare wrote the "little eyases" passage into his drama, the Chamberlain's Men was the only company of common players under direct attack from a private theater, and the Children of the Chapel was the only private acting company currently producing plays attacking the "common stages" (2.2.342). Jonson is the only dramatist known to have written for Blackfriars between 1600 and 1601, and Shakespeare directed the passage at this readily identifiable adversary.

What then does Shakespeare mean when he states that "there was for a while no money bid for argument, unless the poet and the player went to cuffs in the question"? How did Jonson "wrong" the "children" by making them "exclaim against their own succession"? (2.2.350–51). The answer to

FI (1623), PAGES 262–63

Page 262

TLN 1360

Ham. Why did you laugh,when I said, Man delights
not me?
Rosin. To thinke, my Lord,if you delight not in Man,
what Lenton entertainment the Players shall receiue
from you: wee coated them on the way, and hither are
they comming to offer you Seruice.
Ham. He that playes the King shall be welcome; his
Maiesty shall haue Tribute of mee: the aduenturous
Knight shal vse his Foyle and Target: the Louer shall

TLN 1369

not sigh *gratis*, the humorous man shall end his part in
peace: the Clowne shall make those laugh whose lungs
are tickled a'th' sere: and the Lady shall say her minde

TLN 1372

freely; or the blanke Verse shall halt for't: what Players
are they?
Rosin. Euen those you were wont to take delight in
the Tragedians of the City.
Ham. How chances it they trauaile? their resi-
dence both in reputation and profit was better both
wayes.
Rosin. I thinke their Inhibition comes by the meanes
of the late Innouation?
Ham. Doe they hold the same estimation they did
when I was in the City? Are they so follow'd?
Rosin. No indeed, they are not.

TLN 1384

Ham. How comes it? doe they grow rusty?
Rosin. Nay, their indeauour keepes in the wonted
pace; But there is Sir an ayrie of Children, little
Yases, that crye out on the top of question; and
are most tyrannically clap't for't: these are now the
fashi-

"the Clowne . . ."
(cut from Q2;
present in Q1)

Page 263

fashion, and so be-ratled the common Stages (so they
call them) that many wearing Rapiers, are affraide of
Goose-quils, and dare scarse come thither.
Ham. What are they Children? Who maintains 'em?
How are they escoted? Will they pursue the Quality no
longer then they can sing? Will they not say afterwards
if they should grow themselues to common Players (as
it is like most if their meanes are not better) their Writers do them wrong, to make them exclaim against their
owne Succession.
Rosin. Faith there ha's bene much to do on both sides:
and the Nation holds it no sinne, to tarre them to Con-
trouersie. There was for a while, no mony bid for argument, vnlesse the Poet and the Player went to Cuffes in
the Question.
Ham. Is't possible?
Guild. Oh there ha's beene much throwing about of
Braines.
Ham. Do the Boyes carry it away?

TLN 1408

Rosin. I that they do my Lord, *Hercules* & his load too.
Ham. It is not strange: for mine Vockle is King of
Denmarke, and those that would make mowes at him
while my Father liued; giue twenty, forty, an hundred
Ducates a peece, for his picture in Little. There is something in this more then Naturall, if Philosophie could
finde it out.

TLN 1415

Flourish for the Players.

the "little Yases"
passage (cut from
Q2; adapted in Q1)

"his picture in Little"
(an analogy with the
boy actors rendered
meaningless through
cuts in Q1 and Q2)

Reprinted by permission of the Folger Shakespeare Library

QI (1603), SIGS. E2ᵛ–E3ʳ

SIG. E2ᵛ

> *Ham.* Why did you laugh then,
> When I faid, Man did not content mee?
> *Gil.* My Lord, we laughed, when you faid, Man did not
> content you.
> What entertainement the Players ſhall haue,
> We

SIG. E3ʳ

> We boorded them a the way : they are comming to you.
> *Ham.* Players, what Players be they?
> *Roff.* My Lord, the Tragedians of the Citty,
> Thoſe that you tooke delight to ſee ſo often. (ſlie?
> *Ham.* How comes it that they trauell? Do they grow re-
> *Gil.* No my Lord, their reputation holds as it was wont.
> *Ham.* How then?
> *Gil.* Yſaith my Lord, noueltie carries it away,
> For the principall publike audience that
> Came to them, are turned to priuate playes,
> And to the humour of children.
> *Ham.* I doe not greatly wonder of it,
> For thoſe that would make mops and moes
> At my vncle, when my father liued,
> Now giue a hundred, two hundred pounds
> For his picture : but they ſhall be welcome,
> He that playes the King ſhall haue tribute of me,
> The ventrous Knight ſhall vſe his foyle and target,
> The louer ſhall ſigh gratis,
> The clowne ſhall make them laugh (for't,
> That are tickled in the lungs, or the blanke verſe ſhall halt
> And the Lady ſhall haue leaue to ſpeake her minde freely.

simplification of "ayrie of Children" (present in FI: TLN 1386) →

deletion of "the humorous man . . ." (present in FI: TLN 1369–1370) →

adaptation of the "little Yases" passage (present in FI: TLN 1384–1408), with transposition of FI's phrasing "the Boyes carry it away" (TLN 1407)

"his picture" (a remnant of FI's phrase "his picture in Little")

Q2 (1604), SIGS. F2ʳ⁻ᵛ

SIG. F2ʳ

> *Ham.* Why did yee laugh then, when I ſayd man delights not me.
> *Roſ.* To thinke my Lord if you delight not in man, what Lenton
> entertainment the players ſhall receaue from you, we coted them
> on the way, and hether are they comming to offer you ſeruice.
> *Ham.* He that playes the King ſhal be welcome, his Maieſtie ſhal
> haue tribute on me, the aduenterous Knight ſhall vſe his foyle and
> target, the Louer ſhall not ſigh gratis, the humour Man ſhall end
> his part in peace, and the Lady ſhall ſay her minde freely : or the
> black verſe ſhall hault for't. What players are they?
> *Roſ.* Euen thoſe you were wont to take ſuch delight in, the Trage-
> dians of the Citty.

deletion of "the Clowne . . ." (present in FI: TLN 1370–1371) ←

SIG. F2ᵛ

> *Ham.* How chances it they trauaile : their reſidence both in repu-
> tation, and profit was better both wayes.
> *Roſ.* I thinke their inhibition, comes by the meanes of the late
> innouaſion.
> *Ham.* Doe they hold the ſame eſtimation they did when I was in
> the Citty ; are they ſo followed.
> *Roſ.* No indeede are they not.
> *Ham.* It is not very ſtrange, for my Vncle is King of Denmarke, and
> thoſe that would make mouths at him while my father liued, giue
> twenty, fortie, fifty, a hundred duckets a peece, for his Picture
> in little, s'bloud there is ſomthing in this more then naturall, if
> Philoſophie could find it out. *A Floriſh.*

"his Picture in little" (part of an analogy between the king and the "little Yases" present in FI) —

deletion of the "little Yases" (present in FI: TLN 1384–1408) ←

Reprinted by permission of the Henry E. Huntington Library and Art Gallery these questions is identical: in *Poetaster* he used the child actors to ridicule the acting profession generally and to parody, under aliases, individual members of the Chamberlain's Men. When he forced the children to travesty the "common players" (2.2.349), he compelled them to endanger their own futures in slandering their elders' quality. Jonson's last comical satire is a fully articulated expression of what Jonas Barish has termed the "antitheatrical prejudice." Thus, when Shakespeare wrote that "for a while" the "nation" was transfixed by the spectacle of "the poet" and "the player" punching each other verbally—going "to cuffs in the question"—he must have viewed *Poetaster* as Jonson's hardest blow. For it was the most impressive statement in the English Renaissance of the poet's superiority to the player and of the script's priority to its enactment.

One symptom of the competitive dynamic of early modern culture was an impulse to establish hierarchies within the arts that ordered their significance and utility. In Renaissance Italy, in works such as Baldesar Castiglione's *The Courtier*, this obsession with artistic rank developed into its own genre, the *paragone* or debate on the relative value of the arts (such as whether or not painting was superior to sculpture or music to literature) that involved questions of professional status. But in England at the end of the sixteenth century this disputation entailed a unique rivalry between artistic collaborators. Without poets, players would be forced back into minstrelsy and crude improvisation; without players, poets were denied the power and prestige of dramatic spectacle. Like Chaucer's Miller and Reeve, however, Shakespeare's Poet and Player are locked in an occupational rivalry excited by the anxieties their interdependence aroused. During the Elizabethan period, poet-scholars such as Jonson often complained of being exploited by either poet-players, against whom they competed as artisans, or the actors' "politicians" (business managers), to whom they sold their scripts. Playwrights voiced outrage at the economic injustice of a theatrical system that rewarded famous players far more than prominent poets. The most notorious example of this resentment is also our first record of Shakespeare's success in London: the dying poet-scholar Robert Greene's denunciation of "those Puppets . . . that spake from our mouths," the ungrateful players whose number included an arrogant *Johannes fac totum* who both acted and wrote: "an upstart Crow, beautified with our feathers," who was "in his own conceit the only Shake-scene in a country." "Let those Apes imitate your past excellence," Greene implores Marlowe, Nashe, and Peele, urging them to boycott the players and "never more acquaint them with your admired inventions."[9] This professional *agon* of the poet and the player with which Shakespeare's career began reached its climax in 1601 on the stages of Blackfriars, the Globe, and Paul's.

II

At the opening of *Poetaster*, both poets and players are denounced as unproductive and immoral by the paranoid tribune Asinius Lupus and Ovid Senior, who insist that the latter's son should continue to study law and stop writing poetry for the stage. "These players," Lupus warns, "are an idle generation, and do much harm in a state, corrupt young gentry very much" (1.2.36–38), and Ovid Senior endorses Tucca's opinion that Homer, the archetypal poet, was only "a poor, blind, rhyming rascal, that liv'd obscurely up and down in booths and tap houses" (1.2.84–86). But while Jonson's Augustan Rome has extraordinary poets such as Virgil and Horace whose presence belies this denigration, the players deserve their bad reputation. There are no exemplary actors in Jonson's ancient Rome nor, by analogy, in his Renaissance London. Not only does he vindicate the idealized poet Horace against his detractors, the magistrate Lupus and the actor Aesop, but he also thoroughly discredits Aesop, who is sentenced to be whipped for slandering Jonson's alter ego. Through a punitive fiction designed to establish their difference, the poet's triumph is sealed with the player's debasement. Paralleling the general division in *Poetaster* between Horace and Ovid as types of legitimate and illegitimate poetry, moreover, the actors, who furnish Ovid's banquet with props and for whom he has begun to write, are tainted by this association. Horace, who does not compose for the stage, finds fulfillment as a poet at the court of Augustus; Ovid, the passionate poet who works on the tragedy of *Medea* and stages a sacrilegious masquerade, is sent into exile; and Aesop, who slanders poets, is taken away to be lashed.

If modern readers come to the "little eyases" passage with any preconception about its meaning, it invariably stems from Harbage's untenable premise of a rigid dichotomy between the public and private theaters. Harbage, of course, viewed these two kinds of theaters as rival institutions with corporate identities that expressed competing social ideologies. "The traditions of the two," he writes, "are as distinct as the size of their actors. The wandering minstrel and Corpus Christi actor standing in the far vista of the one tradition are replaced by the courtly reveler and academic amateur in that of the other."[10] Yet one attractive quality of Harbage's formulation is that it defines the "War of the Theaters" as a cultural controversy of immense social significance, in contrast to the personal bickering that fascinated nineteenth-century scholars, such as Fleay and Penniman, from whom he derived his martial metaphor. Harbage's critics, however, have long recognized that his theory of the rival repertoires posits too stark an antithesis between theatrical institutions whose histories, as Robert Weimann aptly explains, consisted of generations of formal, thematic, and intellectual symbiosis. Indeed, Ann Jennalie Cook has emphasized how similar the audiences of both kinds of theater seem to have been.[11] The distinction between "public" and "private" theater was a legal fiction. Nevertheless, the private theaters had five distinguishing characteristics that set them apart from their public counterparts: they were small indoor, rather than large outdoor, venues; they charged relatively more for admission; their performers were exclusively boys, not men; their repertoires featured more satire and music; and they steered away from history plays. Otherwise, both kinds of theater offered variety. The repertoires of the great hall and the amphitheater experienced such intense mutual influence during the sixteenth century that it is impossible to distinguish between their ideological perspectives. The best coterie productions, Lyly's erudite comedies written for Blackfriars and Paul's over a decade earlier, were readily assimilated by Shakespeare. Conversely, when the private companies surfaced again, they drew their best poets from the common stages. Marston, characteristically favoring Shakespeare's generic choices, wrote *Antonio's Revenge* and *What You Will* for Paul's from 1600 to 1601 as variations on *Hamlet* and *Twelfth Night* at the Globe. But this mimetic symbiosis did not prevent poets who wrote for the children (such as Marston in *Histriomastix* and Jonson in *Poetaster*) from taking advantage of the prejudice that private theater was inherently superior. When, for instance, Rosencrantz explains that the children are "most tyrannically clapp'd for't" (2.2.340–41)—that is, most vehemently applauded for goading the adults—he adds:

These are now the fashion, and so berattle the common stages—so they call them—that many wearing rapiers are afraid of goose-quills and dare scarce come thither.

(2.2.341–44)

The tone of the phrase "common stages" is so derogatory—echoing Jonson's identical use of it in *Cynthia's Revels* (Induction, line 182, and 4.3.118–19)—that Rosencrantz qualifies it with a disclaimer. Indeed, Jonson had used the phrase in the first of these two instances, as I indicate in chapter 6, to ridicule Marston's dependence on Shakespeare. Although the adjective "common" could mean "universal," here it means "base," much as Hamlet uses it to describe Gertrude's reaction to the King's recent death (1.2.74). But what Harbage fails to account for and Shakespeare's "little eyases" passage conceals is that in 1601 the Globe and Paul's had formed a tentative alliance against Jonson at Blackfriars.

How could Harbage have construed the stage-quarrel between *Poetaster* and *Satiromastix* as illustrating the essential difference between the private and public theaters when the former, produced by the Children of the Chapel, was answered in the latter by *both* the Chamberlain's Men and the Children of Paul's? More important, how was it possible for a private theater to align itself with a public theater to attack a second private theater? Harbage never confronts this fundamental contradiction because he never establishes a concrete historical context for Shakespeare's reference to the "little eyases." For him, the War of the Theaters (epitomized by the attack on the public repertoire in Beaumont and Fletcher's *Knight of the Burning Pestle*) was coterminous with the English Renaissance itself. His historical dichotomy is too inflexible to account for Jonson's charge in *Poetaster* that a conspiracy was being plotted against him by company politicians from the Globe and Paul's. The alliance that Jonson suspected materialized in synchronized productions of *Satiromastix* (as its title page advertises) at both theaters. But because *Hamlet* focuses on the rivalry between Blackfriars and the Globe, Harbage wrongly assumes that the "little eyases" passage confirms his historical paradigm. When read in terms of its full theatrical context, however, it captures a more complex historical moment.

In act 3, scene 4 of *Poetaster*, Jonson depicts the formation of an alliance between representatives of Paul's and the Chamberlain's Men to make "a huge deal of money" (line 327) by ridiculing him as a character on their stages. The two politicians who forge this union are Captain Pantilius Tucca (probably a caricature of Ralph Hanham, linked by Jonson to the procurement of child actors) and Histrio (a likely proxy for Augustine Phillips, who served as a business manager for the Chamberlain's Men in 1601). Tucca represents not only the general interests of the private theaters but, more particularly, the revival at Paul's. Jonson found a precedent for his satire of Hanham as Tucca in Guilpin's *Skialetheia*, which also parodied Jonson as Chrisoganus.[12] Dekker confirms that the character is a stand-in for an individual associated with Paul's. "*I wonder what language* Tucca *would have spoke, if honest* Captain Hanham *had been born without a tongue?*" he bluntly asks in the first quarto of *Satiromastix*, after having raised his own "*ghost of* Tucca" (an imitation of an imitation) to haunt "*Paul's Churchyard*" ("To the World," lines 32–34, 46). Jonson parodies Hanham as an erstwhile soldier, con man, and theatrical impresario who has at his disposal a pair of child actors (the Pyrgi) whom he auditions—with recitations of excerpts from public and private plays—for Histrio. That he is affiliated with Paul's is underscored by his promise to reward his new poet Crispinus/Marston with "a quarter share" (3.4.109). Jonson's Tucca signals one of the most distinctive features of the revival at Paul's: for the first time the company was run by a business syndicate rather than the master of the choristers—as an organization modeled, Chambers explains, "on the principle adopted by the ordinary playing companies."[13]

According to Jonson, the politicians of both public and private theaters knew that parodying him could provide a source of ready cash. We'll "hang upon him like so many horse-leeches," Tucca boasts, "the players and all" (4.3.127–28). Jonson consequently begins his account of this sordid conspiracy by explaining, through a satiric *roman à clef*, how Marston became affiliated with Paul's. Tucca/Hanham and Crispinus/Marston became colleagues, he indicates, after the former saved the latter from arrest for debt. Jonson might have remembered, exaggerated, or invented this incident, and he featured it to embarrass Marston about his financial difficulties in 1601, depicting him as a bankrupt spendthrift who insists on his gentility. Although Marston, a gentleman by birth, had in 1599 inherited half of his wealthy father's "plate and household stuff," he did not receive a settlement until six years later. Soon after *Poetaster* premiered, he was evicted (on 14 October 1601) for more than a month from the rooms in the Middle Temple that he had occupied with his father, for nonpayment of dues.[14]

After Tucca, who calls him both "my *Genius*" (3.4.375) and "my POET-ASTER" (3.4.293), saves Crispinus, he introduces him to Histrio and all unite to slander a great poet for profit. But first, the private impresario beckons the public actor to discuss business while showering him with rude epithets such as "*Stiff* toe," "shifter," "stalker," "two-penny tear-mouth," and "two-penny rascal" (3.4.123–204). Asked about his current project, Histrio explains that his company has just "hir'd" Demetrius "to abuse HORACE, and bring him in, in a play" (3.4.321–23). Demetrius will be able to "do it impudently enough," Tucca concurs, because "he has one of the most overflowing rank wits" and "will slander any man that breathes" (3.4.336–39).

Excited by the plan, Tucca urges Histrio to permit Crispinus to collaborate on it, and Histrio agrees, even though he admits that he does not know him (3.4.158) (Marston had never written for the Chamberlain's Men). The intended collaboration between the Globe and Paul's is then formalized by an act of economic exchange. Tucca promises to "make a gathering" or "purse" for Histrio's underling Demetrius, to "put the poor slave in fresh rags" (3.4.343–44), and Histrio gives Crispinus money "in earnest" (3.4.166) of his services. Their technical vocabulary is contractual. Tucca tells Demetrius that a share of the theater's daily receipts will be designated as his profit, while Histrio gives Crispinus a down payment for a script. Crispinus "pens high, lofty, in a new stalking strain," Tucca informs Histrio, alluding to Marston's bombast; "he was born to fill thy mouth" (3.4.161–63). In an effusive mood, Tucca even volunteers to become the patron of Histrio's company. If for some reason they should come to "lack service," he suggests, "you shall play in my name, rascals, but you shall buy your own cloth [furnished for the players' livery], and I'll have two shares for my countenance" (3.4.355–57).

Another strong indication that the Chamberlain's Men are parodied by Histrio's troupe is found in Jonson's discussion of their repertoire, which cites their theater's name and its locale in relation to his own. "I would . . . see a play; if I knew when there were a good bawdy one," Tucca complains to Histrio, "but they say, you have nothing but *humours, revels,* and *satires,* that gird, and fart at the time" (3.4.188–91). "No, I assure you, Captain, not we," Histrio objects, distinguishing the Globe from Blackfriars. "They are on the other side of *Tiber:* we have as much ribaldry in our plays, as can be. . . . All the sinners in the suburbs come and applaud our action daily" (3.4.193–96). But Tucca still warns the public players against parodying him in their own topically charged plays:

I hear, you'll bring me o' the stage there; you'll play me, they say: I shall be presented by a sort of copper-lac'd scoundrels of you. Life of PLUTO, and you stage me, stinkard, your mansions shall sweat for't, your taber- nacles, varlets, your *Globes,* and your *Triumphs.*

(3.4.197–201)

When Histrio informs Tucca that *his* plays are sexually explicit, not the "*hu- mours, revels,* and *satires*" acted on the other side of the Tiber, Jonson at a stroke differentiates Blackfriars and the Globe in terms of their repertoires and locations. The Tiber in this context is the Thames, on the north side of which Blackfriars was situated, while on the south bank, in "the suburbs" of Southwark, noted for its brothels, stood the Globe, the name of which (dis- guised only by a plural) Jonson slips into his dialogue. One would have to go to Blackfriars, not the Globe, Histrio implies, to see comical satires, such as *Cynthia's Revels* or *Poetaster,* that purged humours.

With the exception of his own work at Blackfriars, then, Jonson saw little difference between the agendas of the public and private theaters, personified by Histrio and Tucca. Although he insisted on the superiority of his drama, he did not base his conception of himself as a poet—a role grounded in clas- sical and Renaissance literary theory—on affiliation with a particular venue. Indeed, although he wrote *Poetaster* for Blackfriars, he now conceived of him- self as wholly removed from the degraded subculture of the entertainment in- dustry manipulated by his adversaries. Jonson's two prior comical satires had been optimistic about the ability of drama to transform experience. In *Poet- aster,* however, the player's mimesis is denigrated in favor of the poet's direct address, as Jonson's theater undoes itself.[15]

The antitheatrical prejudice of *Poetaster* is further personalized in Jonson's parodies of seven members of the Chamberlain's Men under the pseudonyms Histrio, Aesop, Poluphagus, Oenobarbus, Friskin, Mango, and, finally, Seven-Shares and a Half. Of these, two—Histrio and Aesop—were impersonated by Chapel children, the second in a nonspeaking role.[16] Four are mentioned only once (in the passage cited below), when all but Seven-Shares and a Half (referred to at the end of the scene) and Histrio, to whom Tucca speaks, are discussed as potential guests at the business supper Histrio is coaxed into lavishing on Tucca so that they can discuss a common interest—leasing child actors needed for the female roles in their productions.

> TUCCA   . . . let's have good cheer tomorrow night at supper, stalker, and then we'll talk . . . and do not bring your eating player with you there; I cannot away with him: He will eat a leg of mutton, while I am in my porridge, the lean POLUPHA-GUS . . . Nor the villainous-out-of-tune fiddler OENOBAR-BUS, bring not him. . . . Do not bring your Father AESOP, your politician; unless you can ram up his mouth with cloves: the slave smells ranker than some sixteen dunghills, and is seventeen times more rotten: Marry, you may bring FRISKIN, my *zany*: He's a good skipping swaggerer; and your fat fool there, my MANGO, bring him too: but let him not beg rapiers, nor scarves, in his over-familiar playing face, nor roar out his barren bold jests, with a tormenting laughter, between drunk and dry. Do you hear, Rascal?
>
> (3.4.276–304)

In 1601, the Chamberlain's Men seems to have included the following nine sharers: William Shakespeare, Richard Burbage, John Heminges, Augustine Phillips, Henry Condell, William Sly, Richard Cowley, Thomas Pope, and Robert Armin.[17] Which of them, then, were mocked by Jonson in Tucca's invitation? The actors he cites are more difficult to identify than the poets, whose work still bears inspection; since we know very little about the personal idiosyncrasies of Shakespeare's fellows, analysis of them remains more tentative. But by refining the speculations of T. W. Baldwin, H. D. Gray, Percy Simpson, and Gerald Bentley (among whom there is considerable agreement), we can arrive at a set of identifications.[18]

"Seven-shares and a half" (3.4.354) refers to Richard Burbage, whose two and a half shares of ownership in the Globe and one share of the Chamberlain's Men are exaggerated to emphasize his considerable cut of their profits.

Called Father Aesop in the First Quarto, the company's principal politician appears to be a parody of John Heminges. The word "politician" has the same specialized meaning in *Poetaster* that it had in *Histriomastix*: it designates an actor who engages in transactions with outside persons or authorities on behalf of the company. From 1596 to 1630 Heminges was the leading politician of the Chamberlain-King's Men. Bentley notes that he "was always the sharer who received payment for plays performed before the court by the company."[19] "This and his prominence in the negotiations of the company and the law-suits arising out of them," writes Chambers, "suggest that he acted as their business manager."[20] Two of the players, Histrio and Oenobarbus (Aenobarbus or "bronze-bearded" in the Latin of F1), are said to be musicians. Histrio, then, is probably Augustine Phillips, who was both a company musician (like the fiddler Oenobarbus) and a politician (like Aesop). Tucca chides him that, "We must have you turn fiddler again, get a bass viol at your back" (3.4.133–34). When Phillips died in 1605, he left his bass viol to "Samuel Gilburne, [his] late apprentice," who replaced him in the company. Phillips, who was also to leave his "fellow" Shakespeare "a thirty shilling piece in gold," was a prosperous sharer.[21] Furthermore, Histrio's association with Aesop in *Poetaster* as a person engaged in the company's official business is confirmed by the fact that in 1601 Phillips had "political" duties for the company as its official representative in the *Richard II* affair, several months before Jonson wrote *Poetaster*.[22] Another sharer known to have been a musician is Richard Cowley, who might be the bronze-bearded "out-of-tune fiddler" Oenobarbus. Chambers notes that Cowley had taken a musical role in the second part of *The Seven Deadly Sins* (around 1590), before joining the company at its inception.[23] Two fools, Friskin and Mango, the first fast and the second fat, come last in Tucca's list. Friskin (Frisker in F1), whose name signifies a person of brisk and lively spirit, "a skipping swaggerer," might be Armin, the wise fool of *As You Like It* and *Twelfth Night*; Jonson mocks him as a "zany"—a fool's fool. Mango would then be Thomas Pope, the fat comedian, who, if he had acted the roles of Carlo Buffone and Sir Toby Belch, would last have roared out "barren bold jests . . . between drunk and dry" in *Twelfth Night*. A year earlier, Samuel Rowlands in *The Letting of Humour's Blood in the Head Vein* had asked why "*Pope* the Clown" spoke in such a "boorish" manner when he would "counterfeit the Clowns upon the Stage." A line of low humour, according to the poet John Taylor, ran from Scoggin through Tarlton and Kemp to Pope.[24] Although the name "Mango," meaning "slave-dealer," links him to the outspoken buffoon of New Comedy, it was also Elizabethan slang for "pimp." The devouring Poluphagus is then possibly Henry Condell. There is insufficient evidence for an indisputable identification, but since Condell was very thin when he later played "the lean gentleman" Surly in *The Alchemist*, he could be "lean Poluphagus."[25] Shakespeare and Sly are hence conspicuous by their absence, being the only two players who, as Jonson implies in his apology for *Poetaster*, "might have sat still, unquestion'd," when he "tax'd" only "some" sharers. In *Histriomastix*, Marston singled out the player-poet-politician Munday for special opprobrium. But in *Poetaster*, Jonson exempts the poet-player Shakespeare while excoriating the company's politicians, Heminges and Phillips—the only two sharers whom he physically represents on the Blackfriars stage.

Jonson does not treat the seven players he mentions in the same manner; he modulates Tucca's tone between what the Elizabethan rhetorician George Puttenham would call the "merry scoff" and "dry mock." Armin and Pope, the company's clowns, are called tolerable dinner companions capable of "good cheer." Of the three unfit for society—Heminges, Condell, and Cowley—only Heminges is berated, in a primitive scatalogical assault, as being seventeen times more rotten than the sixteen dunghills that smell better than him. Shakespeare's reference to Jonson as a jakes in *Troilus and Cressida* was an appropriate form of revenge for attacking the players, and it is lauded by Burbage and Kemp in *2 Return from Parnassus* for this reason. Yet of all the players, it is only Heminges and Phillips with whom Jonson goes to cuffs in *Poetaster*. Both are informers who fear the subversiveness of poets and invent accusations against them that they report to the same paranoid magistrate. "From base motives of commercialism, envy, and ignorance," writes David Bevington, "the common players" are depicted by Jonson "in cynical league with an oppressive governmental bureaucracy to enforce conformity."[26]

What makes Histrio/Phillips and Aesop/Heminges vile is that, as the company's politicians, they betray poets by becoming government spies who accuse Ovid and Horace of treason. Histrio informs the magistrate Asinius Lupus (the asinine wolf) that Ovid and the courtiers have "directed a letter to me, and my fellow-sharers," asking to borrow several royal stage properties, including "a scepter and a crown, for JOVE" (4.4.11–12). This is "rebellion," fumes Lupus, who hastens to reveal Ovid's "conspiracy" to Caesar. In a parallel episode, Aesop convinces the same magistrate to accuse Horace of treason for having composed a "dangerous, seditious libel" (5.3.47) against the emperor. The evidence that Lupus adduces is an emblem by Horace of a vulture and a wolf feeding on the body of an ass, with the inscription: "*Thus, oft, the base and ravenous multitude / Survive, to share the spoils of fortitude*" (5.3.79–80). "Is not here an Eagle? And is not that Eagle meant by CAESAR?" he demands of Horace, pointing to the emblem's vulture. After being corrected by Horace, the magistrate seizes on two other details. "A Wolf? good. That's I;

I am the wolf. My name's LUPUS, I am meant by the wolf," he continues, adding, "An Ass? Good still: That's I too. I am the ass." "If you will needs take it," Horace concludes, "I cannot with modesty give it from you" (5.3.99–100). When Lupus is asked who informed him that the emblem was seditious, he explains that a "player" who is "a sycophant-like slave and a politician" gave him "the first light of it" (5.3.107–10), at which point Aesop/Heminges is called before Caesar, who, without hearing him speak, commands him to be whipped. The threat posed by the title of Marston's *Histriomastix* is realized in *Poetaster*.

These false accusations of treason against Ovid and Horace by Histrio/Phillips and Aesop/Heminges illustrate Jonson's concern that the politicians of the Chamberlain's Men were allied with the most regressive segment of the Elizabethan legal system in persecuting poets. Still, it remains uncertain whether this episode was meant to reflect on the company's unwitting involvement in the Essex conspiracy. In modern treatments of English Renaissance theater, the common players are often celebrated as dangerous subversives whose Protean shape-shifting challenged the fixed hierarchies of an authoritarian state. But to Jonson their agents were censors seeking to suppress free thought. They were the enemies of true poetry who sponsored a blend of depraved and trivial drama. They were, moreover, "usurers or brokers" (3.4.309), members of a profession involved in a network of criminal activity and sexual deviance that included child abuse and prostitution (3.4.309–13). Each of these stereotypical vices, regularly attributed to professional actors in the last quarter of the sixteenth century, is chronicled by Jonson to substantiate his argument that poets are superior to players. One of his most provocative accusations in this vein is his aspersion that players are pederasts. When Histrio asks to borrow two child actors from Tucca, he is at first rebuffed with the admonition that he will only make "ingles" of them. Since the adult actors need boys to supply the parts of women in their plays, Histrio negotiates with Tucca to rent the Pyrgi, two children Tucca manages. Having seen one "do a little of a lady," Histrio inquires, "What will you ask for 'hem a week, Captain?" which prompts a taunt that the player will only force the boys into child prostitution: "No, you mangonizing slave, I will not part from 'hem: you'll sell 'hem for engles" (3.4.273–76). A "mango," explains Thomas Cooper's *Thesaurus Linguae Romanae et Britannicae* (1587) is "a bawd that painteth and pampereth up boys, women, or servants to make them seem the trimmer, thereby to sell them the dearer." Although "engle" (or "ingle") might mean "friend," in this context it meant "catamite." Jonson does not object to boys being dressed like women (in such gender-bending roles as Rosalind in *As You Like It* or Viola in *Twelfth Night*) but to their sexual abuse by the players, who have a reputation for being able "to help to a piece of flesh" (3.4.310). This is the same threat that Ovid Senior foresees even for poets when he worries aloud: "What? shall I have my son a stager now? an engle for players?" (1.2.15–16)

It is impossible to know how seriously to take Jonson's aspersion that children were exploited by the Elizabethan entertainment industry. They were often purchased from their parents or guardians and either rented by impresarios or apprenticed to actors. Philip Henslowe, for example, writes in his diary how he "bought my boy James Bristow of William Augusten [a player] the 18 of December 1597" for eight pounds.[27] Henslowe then rented Bristow to the Admiral's Men for three shillings a week. Jonson implies that a similar deal is being worked out between Tucca and Histrio with more sinister implications. Theatrical entrepreneurs, in Jonson's opinion, would sell anything for profit, especially sex, which was one of the foundations of their appeal. The sex play at the Globe could be found both onstage and off, he suggests, since it was one of the "common retreats for punks decay'd i' their practice" (3.4.312). Jonson played down this criticism when he apologized for what he saw as *Poetaster*'s mild jest at the expense of a few of the players, but Shakespeare apparently did not believe him.

III

Still, the terms of Shakespeare's analogy between "the tragedians of the city" humiliated by the "little eyases" and the Chamberlain's Men attacked by the Children of the Chapel were exaggerated for effect and even, to an extent, untrue. This is certainly the case with Rosencrantz's assertion that the players' credit has been so thoroughly damaged by the child actors who "cry out on the top of question" and have so "berattled the common stages" that they have lost their elite audience of gentlemen "wearing rapiers" and been forced to travel. *Hamlet* was acted at the Globe, and the Chamberlain's Men were never shouldered out of London by the Children of the Chapel. Although they occasionally toured and performed in such venues as the Inns of Court, aristocratic and royal houses, and town halls, the most traveling the Chamberlain's Men had to do to perform *Hamlet* in 1601 was across the Globe from the tiring-house in London to Elsinore onstage.[28] It is possible that *Hamlet* was acted not only in London but also at Cambridge, Oxford, and "elsewhere," as the title page of the First Quarto states. Yet the threat of endless travel (or "travaile" as Q2 and F1 suggestively spell it) was only a primordial nightmare in 1601.[29] During the Renaissance the first permanent theaters since antiquity were built in Europe. "For the first time in more than a thousand years," Stephen Orgel observes, theater "was real in the way that 'real estate' is real; it was a location, a building, a possession."[30] Anxiety about the loss of this sense of place is registered in *Hamlet*, just as anxiety about the children's success is revealed in Histrio's scheme for caricaturing Jonson: "O, it will get us a huge deal of money . . . and we have need on't; for this winter has made us all poorer than so many starv'd snakes: Nobody comes at us; not a gentleman" (3.4.327–30). The Chapel Children had already scored a reputation for satire with the gentlemen by the winter of 1600/01, and the business agents at Paul's and the Globe knew that lampooning Jonson was a way of cashing in on the competitive game of self-evaluation he had invented. *Satiromastix* and *Troilus and Cressida* were the results. In *Hamlet*, a play of unanswerable questions, the word "question" is Shakespeare's technical term for "theme" or "subject matter to be debated." He uses it in this specialized sense when discussing how a clown should not vainly improvise when "some necessary question of the play be then to be consider'd" (3.2.42–43). It is questionless, however, that his depiction of the harassed Chamberlain's Men as homeless tragedians contradicts Jonson's characterization of them as predators. Acting is, Hamlet vouches (in an argument echoed in Sonnet 111), a profession individuals might choose only if "their means are no better" (2.2.349–50). Rather than staging the player's triumph over the poet, then, Shakespeare—with either disarming candor or false modesty—acknowledges the stigma attached to his social identity.

Shakespeare's distress, however, seems more the result of a perception that the children had prevailed in the exchange among Jonson's *Poetaster*, Dekker's *Satiromastix*, and his own *Troilus and Cressida* than a wholesale condemnation of the Poets' War. The success of the Chapel Children who "carry it away" did not reduce the Chamberlain's Men to traveling players; Harbage might even have been right in arguing that the children were incapable of ruining the adults financially.[31] The company's return to the road was an anxious joke rather than a current event. "There would have been no Elizabethan drama, if players had remained strollers," writes M. C. Bradbrook, who argues that James Burbage's construction of the Theater in Shoreditch in 1576 was "the most significant date in the history of English drama."[32] The children, forced to rebel against their elders, threatened (if audiences took them seriously) to undo this progress by returning public theater to the site of its primitive wanderings. Professional actors, with skill and some luck, repeated the theater's evolution in their own careers, beginning with touring troupes in the provinces before joining major companies in the city. Although "the world once went hard with me, when I was fain to carry my playing Fardle a footback," the wealthy player had recalled almost a decade earlier to the poor poet-scholar Roberto in *Greene's Groatsworth of Wit*, "my very share in playing apparel will not be sold for two hundred pounds."[33] Suspecting that success has spoiled Histrio, Tucca warns him that he still might "march in a tawny coat, with one sleeve, to Goose-fair," and "travel, with thy pumps full of gravel, . . . after a blind jade and a hamper: and stalk upon boards, and barrel heads, to an old cracked trumpet" (3.4.134–35, 168–70). Residence in the city was certainly better, "both in reputation and profit" (2.2.330).

So how literally can the "little eyases" passage be taken? Scholars have tended to vacillate on this issue, duplicating the text's own ambiguities. The notes in the New Arden edition of *Hamlet*, for instance, warn readers to "resist" mistaking "the tragedians of the city" for the Chamberlain's Men, but identify the "aery of children" who drive them out of town as "a clear topical reference to the Children of the Chapel."[34] Yet how could seventeenth-century London choristers ruin the reputations of fictitious Danish actors? In order to make sense of Shakespeare's fiction, we must identify "the tragedians"—even if only partially and on a provisional basis, for the length of this passage— with the Chamberlain's Men who impersonate them. Both the players in *Hamlet* and the "aery" that attacks them are composites of fact and fiction. We are invited to accept the players at face value as well as to see them as the actors who play them, to elide imagination and reality, drama and theater. Shakespeare's interplay between character and actor was a unique feature of the play's original production. The first audience of *Hamlet* was coaxed to acknowledge that "the tragedians" were and were not the Chamberlain's Men who counterfeited them in an imaginary Denmark on a real London stage. "In performance," writes Kenneth Rowe, "the actor becomes typically a split personality, one part becomes the character he is playing, the other remains the actor in detached technical control."[35] Shakespeare's audience was invited to share the divided consciousness of actors who were simultaneously inside and outside of their roles.

A phrase in this scene that has given critics considerable trouble is Rosencrantz's observation that the adult players' "inhibition comes by the means of the late innovation" (2.2.332–33). Since "innovation" in *1 Henry IV* (5.1.78) is used by Shakespeare to signify a "political revolution," and since "inhibition" was the legal word for the closing of a theater, John Dover Wilson sees in this phrase a covert allusion to the Essex conspiracy and claims that there must have been an original text referring to the inhibition of the Chamberlain's Men as punishment for producing *Richard II* in support of the earl's "innovation." Only later, he argues, did Shakespeare change this passage to refer to the War of the Theaters.[36] But this hypothesis is a red herring: although investigated, the company was never inhibited. The passage's political terminology is, however, directly relevant to another rebellion: the "innovation" or revolt of the Children of the Chapel, who, in attacking the "common play- ers" and "common stages," had been made to rebel against an established theatrical order, represented by the Chamberlain's Men. The children were revolutionary in another sense as well. No child acting companies had sched- uled regular performances in London for almost a decade when Paul's re- sumed production at the end of 1599, followed by Blackfriars a year later. This is precisely the meaning of the passage printed in the first, short quar- to of *Hamlet*, which bears comparison with its cognates in the Second Quar- to and First Folio:

> HAM How comes it that they travell? Do they grow restie?
> GIL   No my Lord, their reputation holds as it was wont.
> HAM How then?
> GIL   Yfaith my Lord, noveltie carries it away,
>   For the principall publike audience that
>   Came to them, are turned to private playes,
>   And to the humour of children.
>
> (SIG. E3ʳ)

Asked by Hamlet in Q1 how the players fare, Guilderstone (Guildenstern's lit- erary mutant) replies by using the word "noveltie," instead of F1's "fashion" (TLN 1389), rendering "these are now the fashion" as "noveltie carries it away." The revival of child acting at Paul's and Blackfriars had encouraged an important segment of the Globe's audience to be fascinated with a novelty: the return of the choristers as actors after their disappearance for almost a decade. In the First Folio text, Shakespeare uses the word "Innovation" (TLN 1380), with its undercurrent of rebellion, to suggest that the children have (like Claudius) carried out a *coup d'état* against their elders. The irony of this "Innovation" (or civil war) is that it is unwittingly waged against their benev- olent professional progenitors by heirs forced to renounce their patrimony (as small as it might be) by attacking their "quality." But is the text of the First Quarto as specific—citing Jonson at Blackfriars as the source of competition for "the tragedians"—as the Folio's "little eyases" passage? Was it composed during a prior period in which the adult actors' "reputation" still held "as it was wont," as Q1 would have it, just as the "principall publike" audience was beginning to be attracted to the "noveltie" of renewed "private playes"? There is, I believe, sufficient textual evidence to indicate that this was not the case. On the contrary, it seems likely that the discussion of the "little Yases" in the Folio of 1623 (F1) was added to *Hamlet* at the end of 1601, only to be paraphrased by a recorder-adaptor in the First Quarto of 1603 (Q1). In summarizing his attitude toward the conflict, Shakespeare would again couple, in the same scene, the matter of Troy (evoked by the player's recitation) with a literary commentary on the Poets' War. But part of the exchange between Hamlet and his former friends was then excised, perhaps at publication, from the more reliable Second Quarto of 1604/5 (Q2). Like the Prologue "armed, but not in confidence," of *Troilus and Cressida*, which also only appears in the Folio yet dates back to the same year, 1601, through its explicit reference to *Poetaster*, the "little eyases" passage retains Shakespeare's early response to Jonson, even though it was printed twenty-two years after it was first staged.

Despite a revolution in Shakespeare bibliography won by the Revisionists who have given us two good versions of *King Lear* and *Hamlet*, the consensus is still that Q1 *Hamlet*, in line with A. W. Pollard's original distinction, is nonauthoritative. Instead it is a "bad" quarto, so altered by an intermediary's influence that it does not consistently preserve Shakespeare's work. Pollard's distinction, corroborated by W. W. Greg, will remain one of the greatest achievements of the New Bibliography even if it only clarifies our understanding of Q1's adaptation. The corruption of Q1, extreme in the last two acts, is especially evident when compared to the longer, less distorted edition that replaced it with a title page boasting, "Newly imprinted and enlarged to almost as much again as it was, according to the true and perfect Copy." Still, Q1's partisans, such as Steven Urkowitz, continue to believe that it preserves Shakespeare's early draft.[37] No one can deny that Q1 is fascinating as a distinctly inferior contemporary version of what we find in Q2 and F1. Yet it is hard to imagine that anyone could attribute to Shakespeare responsibility for a transcription of the play that renders its most famous line as "To be, or not to be, I there's the point" (sig. D4ᵛ). Only Mark Twain tops this in *Huckleberry Finn* with the duke's actorly improvisation: "To be or not to be; that is the bare bodkin." Q1's poetry in the difficult soliloquies consistently descends to this low standard. F1 and Q2 (the opening of which was set from a copy of Q1) are slightly different from each other. Both editions are flawed by compositors' errors that leave insoluable cruxes. Furthermore, F1 lacks Hamlet's final soliloquy on Fortinbras, and the "little eyases" passage is missing from Q2. Nevertheless, the rhetoric and logic of Q1 are often so badly corrupted that it does not satisfactorily represent "Shakespeare."

My position, in line with Greg, H. D. Gray, G. I. Duthie, Jenkins, and Kathleen Irace, along with all major modern editors of the play, is that a text similar to the one behind F1 was memorially reproduced in Q1. After a rigorous testing in recent Revisionist scholarship, the theory that the First Quarto of *Hamlet* is a memorial reconstruction, probably concocted by the actor who played Marcellus (and perhaps doubled as Voltemand, Lucianus, and the Prologue to "The Mouse Trap") is more compelling than ever. It was this anonymous actor who, perhaps with the help of others, but without the benefit of a script, re-created the *Hamlet* of 1601 from memory but diluted and distorted its complex language and ideas before running out of steam in the brief fifth act. Irace's statistical analysis of the text of Q1 has yielded the most convincing evidence yet for understanding its status as an often engaging, at times useful, but ultimately ridiculous fake.[38] Holding this view, however, does not mean having to accept that the text behind the first printed *Hamlet* was either produced for touring or published by "pirates."[39] Though Q1 appears to have been adapted for production, whether it was ever put to dramatic use is an open question. But its transpositions and adaptations point to something other than a compositor's eyeskip, since they change the order of scenes and their internal development, transform characterization, and drastically simplify and distort Shakespeare's brilliant language.[40] And while many of these transpositions can be and have been defended on theatrical grounds as independent revisions, possibly intended for the stage, Q1's inept handling of complex ideas and phrasing in F1 is often impossible to justify. Its commentary on theatrical rivalry between "publike" and "private playes" is therefore more likely to be an adaptation of a Shakespearean original, better preserved in F1, than a transcription of a prior version of the play, written before *Poetaster* and *Satiromastix* were staged. This means, of course, that the First Quarto is based on a manuscript containing material written at the end of 1601.

The theory that Q1 is a "recorded" text, shaped by oral transmission, is strengthened by the fact that its metatheatrical commentary, which appears in prose in Q2 and F1, is transcribed as strangely irregular poetry. Someone who was remembering dialogue might have had a difficult time deciding whether Shakespeare's eloquent rhetoric was in prose or verse; a compositor, with the text open before him, would be less likely to make that error.

A comparison of the phrasing of the First Quarto and the First Folio indicates that "Marcellus" misremembered the "little eyases" passage the Folio preserves. Q1's phrase, "noveltie carries it away" (sig. E3^r), as we have previously seen, substitutes "noveltie" for F1's "fashion." But in doing so, it adds this cognate to F1's statement that the boys "carry it away," creating a semantic pastiche. The recorder-adaptor of Q1 consequently reiterates and transposes phrasing from the more concrete "little eyases" dialogue as he paraphrases and condenses its contents from memory in seven lines. In the process, however, an arresting image in F1—of the boys carrying off the Globe—became a dead metaphor.

This same process of adaptation occurs in Q1's description of how "the principall publike audience" has "turned to private playes, / And to the humour of children" (sig. E3ʳ). Like F1, Q1 uses a key Jonsonian concept—"humour"—in its discussion of the threat from the "private" theater to specify Jonson at Blackfriars as the instigator of the attack on the Chamberlain's Men by the "little Yases." In doing so, it again transposes and conflates phrases found in F1. It drops one character (between the lover and the clown) in F1's roll call, deleting the clause "the humorous man shall end his part in peace" (TLN 1369–1370), only to combine its Jonsonian catchword with the ending of F1's phrase "ayrie of Children" to produce "the humour of Children." When it was written, this new phrase would have meant "Jonsonian comedy at Blackfriars." Comical satire was marked by its therapeutic impulse to purge the "humorous man" who would "end his part in peace." In all likelihood Shakespeare was alluding to the fact that the Chamberlain's Men had acted *Every Man Out* when he included this character type and plot paradigm in *Hamlet*. Even though Jonson published the play in an unusually proprietary manner, the company retained title to its new comic formula, which served as a reminder of their varied repertoire and perhaps, paradoxically, of their literary sophistication as well. That the word "humour" referred to Jonson is hard to miss. The alternative title of Dekker's *Satiromastix* (which was probably its original theatrical title) was *The Untrussing of the Humorous Poet*, and Jonson, in his response, has both Crispinus/Marston and Demetrius/Dekker employ the word contemptuously in their attacks on him as a poet hostile to the Globe and Paul's. Demetrius's poem puns on the word "world" to mean Globe when he grouses that Jonson is "*A* critic *that all the world bescumbers* / *With* satirical *humours*" (5.3.304–5), just as Crispinus plays the word "bespawl" off the name of Paul's theater when he complains that Jonson "*bespawls* / *The conscious time, with humorous foam*" (5.3.287–88).

One of the features of Q1 that initially makes it appear to predate F1's version is its assertion that the tragedians have not yet lost their reputation. When asked if their status has slipped, Guilderstone denies it: "No my Lord, their reputation holds as it was wont." Does Q1, then, render an account of the company's success before the "little eyases" had become threatening? This seems unlikely given that Guilderstone states in the same passage that the "principall publike audience that / Came to them, are turned to private playes" and "the humour of children." Surely the loss of the Globe's most important theatergoers and the company's need to travel would entail a loss of reputation! It is tempting to try to make bad drama good by discovering a witty paradox in this, to assume, for instance, that Q1 means that although the audience is captivated by the novelty of the Chapel Children, they still revere the Chamberlain's Men.

But this reading does not come to terms with the passage's inconsistency. Q1, which is both less daring about stating anything negative about the adult actors' credit and more incoherent than F1, has it both ways. The Chamberlain's Men are allowed to keep their reputation, even as they are driven out of town by their rivals! Again, this variation between F1 and Q1 can be explained as the latter's corruption of the former's Ur-text. In F1, from Hamlet's query, "what Players are they?" to the "Flourish" for their entrance, the prince asks thirteen questions. Among these, he inquires if the tragedians "hold the same estimation they did," if they are "so follow'd," only to be answered, "No indeed, they are not." When he then asks if they "grow rusty," he is again informed, "Nay, their indeavour keepes in the wonted pace" (TLN 1385–1386). The statement that their "indeavour" (or ability) remains intact although their "estimation" (or reputation) has waned is a complex thought butchered in Q1. The best thing about the "bad" quarto is that it assists in understanding F1's densely allusive "little eyases" passage by furnishing a reduced, although inconsistent, paraphrase, even as it corroborates the backdating of the Folio's commentary to 1601.

Further evidence that the "little eyases" passage was written at the turn of the seventeenth century is found in Q2's truncated version of this discussion. The surrounding dialogue in Q2 is almost identical with that found in F1, except for some transpositions of phrasing (the kind of local errors a compositor would make), printing accidentals, the omission of an oath in the latter, and, most important, two cuts of different lengths. One is Hamlet's brief reference to the "Clowne"; the other, which is considerably longer, covers a twenty-five-line stretch of dialogue between Rosencrantz's confirmation that the tragedians are no longer held in the same estimation, "No indeed, they are not" (TLN 1383), and Hamlet's philosophical deduction that this "is not strange" (TLN 1409) in a world perverted by regicide, fratricide, and incest. In Q2, these two lines, slightly varied, are set in sequence in what appears to be the result of an excision.

> ROS   No indeede are they not.
> HAM   It is not very strange, for my Uncle is King of Denmarke, and
>   those that would make mouths at him while my father lived,
>   give twenty, fortie, fifty, a hundred duckets a peece, for his
>   Picture in little. . . .
>
> (SIG. F2ᵛ)

One of Jenkins's major contributions was to sense the logical inconsistency in Q2's comparison between the fall of the tragedians and Claudius's rise.[41]

Whereas the texts of both Q1 and F1 liken the children's rise to the usurper's, Q2's cut—excising the account of the children's triumph—forces readers to jump from the adults' failure to Claudius's success without a middle step in the argument. It is more plausible that this middle stage in the analysis—the charge that the children had caused the adults' distress—was cut from Q2 than that it was added to Q1 and F1. Q2 also tellingly includes a vestige of the joke found in F1 about people now paying more ("twenty, fortie, fifty, a hundred duckets a peece") for less (Claudius's "Picture in little"). In the theater, the Folio text implies by analogy, audiences that attend Blackfriars pay more for admission, only to get less—miniature actors. But since all reference to the child actors is left out of Q2, other than the oblique hint of "the late innovation" that has caused the tragedians' "inhibition," its phrase "Picture in little" loses its point. Readers of the so-called "good" quarto might easily miss the now obscure witticism that depends on its topical allusion to the size of the boy players. Consequently, the "little eyases" passage must either have already been cut from the script from which the Second Quarto was printed or else deleted from its publication in 1604/5. By that time, not only was the allusion to the War of the Theaters out of date, but the Children of the Chapel had gained royal patronage, becoming, under Queen Anna, the Children of Her Majesty's Chapel. It might have been imprudent not to have omitted it after 1603, whether in performance or print, along with Hamlet's long argument, at the beginning of the same conversation with his school friends, that Denmark (Anna's native land) was "a prison" (2.2.239–69). Yet if this is true, how could the same censor of Q2 have missed Hamlet's slur on Danish drinking habits (1.4.17–38), cut from F1, when Marston's reference to "a Dane-like barbarous Sot" was excised from the 1616 edition of *Jack Drum's Entertainment?*[42]

According to Hamlet, the Children of the Chapel's victory (like all victories in the play) was also a loss, since it depended on their being forced to "exclaim against their own succession" in *Poetaster*, to disinherit themselves in favor of the poet who dictated what Q1 calls "the humour of children." The most serious threat the children posed was their potential to alienate the audience they shared with the Globe, driving away their highest-paying customers—the principal public audience, those "wearing rapiers." The children would do so, it was feared, by travestying the adult companies, repertoire, and audience so completely that its elite members would be ashamed and even afraid to patronize "the common stages" for fear of becoming laughingstocks. "A Gentleman, or an honest Citizen, shall not Sit in your penny-bench theaters," Tucca complains in *Satiromastix*, "but . . . his humour must run upo'th Stage: you'll ha' *Every Gentleman in's humour*, and *Every Gentleman out on's humour*" (4.2.52–57).

That poets wielding "goose-quills" should anatagonize gentlemen "wearing rapiers" not only implies that pens are mightier than swords but also brands the poets who employ them in this manner as fools. They are silly geese whose instrument of choice is what Shakespeare in *Twelfth Night* calls "a goose-pen" (3.2.50). At the beginning of Shakespeare's career, Robert Greene had referred to him as an "upstart crow," an ambitious player who had disguised himself in a poet's "borrowed feathers." Shakespeare (whose coat of arms now bore a falcon supporting a spear) invoked the same ornithological metaphor to characterize the child actors as hawks and their poets as geese, hardly able to worry an audience of rapiered gallants. What he seems to have been genuinely concerned about was the defection of the highest-paying customers at the Globe, the sector of the audience that was being aggressively courted by the private theaters. The First Quarto calls them "the principall publike audience" not necessarily because they were in the majority (although it is possible that at some performances they were), but because their attendance was a benchmark for financial and artistic success of a particular kind. The loss of these theatergoers would certainly have touched the Globe's credit, in both senses of the word.

Jonson wrote *Poetaster* as both a defense of poetry and a self-vindication that ridiculed the acting profession generally and mocked several members of the Chamberlain's Men under aliases. "Now, for the Players, it is true, I tax'd 'hem," he conceded, "And yet, but some; and those so sparingly, / As all the rest might have sat still, unquestion'd, / Had they but had the wit, or conscience, / To think well of themselves. But, impotent they / Thought each man's vice belong'd to their whole tribe" ("Apologetical Dialogue," lines 141–46). Those he had not ridiculed (like Shakespeare), he suggests, were angry merely because they suspected themselves to be guilty of the same vices as the sharers he had parodied. Here, however, contrary to his usual practice of disavowing personal satire, Jonson admits that he criticized particular actors in order to exonerate himself of the charge that he attacked them indiscriminately as a class. The poet who has Horace swear his practice is to "spare men's persons, and but tax their crimes" (3.5.134) now admits what he had previously denied in order to minimize Shakespeare's grounds for taking offense. Shakespeare could have sat by unmoved, Jonson insists, had he not mistaken the specific parodies in *Poetaster* for a wholesale condemnation of his profession. But Jonson's denial that he was making satiric generalizations in *Poetaster* is strategic rather than truthful. His mockery of individual sharers in the Chamberlain's Men adds a scandalous topicality to his general critique of the players.

Shakespeare is not impartial in his assessment of this rivalry between the poet and the player, but his response is a complex blend of empathy and accusation.

For instance, he entirely exempts the children from blame, which he places on their poets, managers, and audience. The word "tar" (or "tarre") refers to the act of provoking dogs to violence, so when he writes that "the Nation holds it no sinne, to tarre them [both sides] to Controversie" (TLN 1400–1401), Shakespeare implicitly compares the Poets' War to a blood sport between animals incited to attack each other. "Pride alone / Must tarre the mastiffs on, as 'twere a bone" (1.3.389–90), he had written in his recent black comedy on the Trojan War. Although never at the Globe, blood sports involving mastiffs, such as bull-baiting and bear-baiting, were, up until the eighteenth century, sometimes staged in the same London amphitheaters that featured plays. Shakespeare imagines the poets and players prodded to fight each other by an audience eager to view their contention. But if Shakespeare is prepared to blame London audiences for the current controversy, his censure shades into partisan theatrical politics when he sympathizes with the child actors compelled to victimize themselves by performing plays that attack their own quality. Hamlet's warning that these same children would perceive the "wrong" that "their writers" had done them if they themselves became "common players" is prophetic. Nathaniel Field and John Underwood, who appeared in *Cynthia's Revels*, and William Ostler, who acted in *Poetaster*, later joined the King's Men.[43]

The victimization of the Children of the Chapel could only benefit their managers and poets, so when Hamlet asks, "Who maintains 'em? How are they escoted?" what appears to be an innocent question might well have prompted original audience members to consider how these same children were being treated at Blackfriars. Such scrutiny might in turn have brought to mind the recent scandal involving the kidnapping of children by the Blackfriars syndicate, which had impressed choristers into their service without regard to parental consent. This was exactly what had happened when Henry Clifton, a gentleman from Norfolk, complained to the Court of Star Chamber that on 13 December 1600 James Robinson (an agent acting for the Children of the Chapel under the commission granted to Nathaniel Giles) had violently seized his son Thomas on his way to school. When Clifton attempted to retrieve his son, the syndicate defied him, claiming their right to impress even a nobleman's scion into the Queen's service. It was only through the intercession of Sir John Fortescue, Chancellor of the Exchequer and member of the Privy Council, that Thomas was returned the next day.[44] If Jonson in *Poetaster* was willing to accuse the Chamberlain's Men of abusing its young charges, Shakespeare had only to allude to the Blackfriars syndicate to return the aspersion of impropriety. The Children of the Chapel were not only impressed into service but victimized a second time in being forced to "cry out" against their own future prospects until their voices cracked with age.

Despite his sympathy for the child actors, however, Shakespeare stigmatizes Blackfriars for being a threat to the Globe's justified reputation, equating the audience being lured by the Children of the Chapel away from the Chamberlain's Men with the citizens of Denmark who now favor Claudius, the malevolent usurper, and forget their legitimate dead king. Hamlet observes that it is not "strange" in an unnatural world that depraved spectators would so value the children. Like Gertrude, they see no difference in the substitution. On the contrary, the success of bad art in Denmark and England is secured by these unnatural spectators who are incapable of judging the quality of what they see—unable to distinguish between two companies as different as the deposed king Hamlet and the imposter Claudius, or the sun god "Hyperion" and (appropriately) a "satyr" (1.2.140).

IV

Part of the difficulty of reading the "little eyases" passage from *Hamlet* in terms of its theatrical context stems from the likelihood that its discussion of theatrical politics was added to the tragedy almost a year after its premiere. That is, *Hamlet* seems to have been written in the wake of *Histriomastix* and *Every Man Out*, but the interpolation followed *Cynthia's Revels* and *Poetaster*. The *Hamlet* of 1600 was composed after Marston had begun to use the Children of Paul's to ridicule the adult actors, player-poets, player-politicians, and popular repertoire in *Histriomastix*. The arrival of the actors at Elsinore might then have been devised to counter Marston's re-creation of the "rude mechanicals" of *A Midsummer Night's Dream* as Sir Oliver Owlet's Men in *Histriomastix*. Marston had, after all, used Shakespeare's metatheatrical interlude to argue that the professional actors of his day were just as bad as these fictitious amateurs.[45] *Hamlet* was originally written in a bid to hold on to the elite audience that was being enticed away from the Globe. Perhaps because Shakespeare perceived the connection between *Histriomastix* and *Poetaster* in 1601, he added the "little eyases" allusion to a work that was from its inception a general defense of the players. Shakespeare was able to graft his rebuttal onto his preexisting fiction because the terms of the quarrel had remained the same when the Children of the Chapel replaced the Children of Paul's as the adult actors' principal detractor. Dekker chose the literary title *Satiromastix* as a response to Jonson, who had become the new "Histriomastix" (or "Player-Whipper") after Marston had subdued his parody of the public theater and Paul's began collaborating with the Chamberlain's Men against Jonson. The neologism echoes Marston's charge in *Histriomastix* that Chrisoganus/Jonson pretended to "carry just *Ramnusia's* whip / To lash the patient" (3:257–58).

Dekker thereby not only recalled Marston's denigration of Jonson but also retaliated for the projected whipping of Aesop in *Poetaster*. *Histriomastix* and *Satiromastix* thus define the trajectory of Paul's participation in the Poets' War as its boys turned from an attack on the public theater to parody Jonson's affiliation with Blackfriars.

By 1601, the more general preoccupation of *Hamlet* with acting and role-playing was focused on an urgent topical concern. Although it is often treated as a detachable digression and cut from modern performances, the "little eyases" passage is key to understanding the play's historical context, since it localizes the debate on professionalism that the rest of the text treats in a more abstract manner. Its relevance to the play as a whole can be visualized in terms of three concentric circles of increasing generality that constitute a defense of the Chamberlain's Men against Jonson's attack on them in *Poetaster*; the generic representation of professional actors; and the play's philosophical concern with questions of "acting" and "action."

One of the central contributions of modern *Hamlet* criticism is its understanding of the play's unique emphasis on the theatrical nature of human experience. Through the work of Anne Barton, Charles Forker, Maynard Mack, William Ringler, Alvin Kernan, James Calderwood, Robert Weimann, and a legion of others, it is clear that the question of "acting" is more emphatic in this play than anywhere else in the canon and that the drama derives much of its philosophical power from exploration of this central theme,[46] especially from a meditation on the fundamental ambiguity of "acting," with its antithetical connotations of "performing" and "pretending," "being" and "seeming." "Every major personage in the tragedy is a player," writes Maynard Mack, ". . . and every major episode a play." The effect of this heightened metadrama, as S. L. Bethell first noticed, is to elicit a "multi-conscious" response from an audience made to feel the simultaneity of the real world and the play-world and to see them as equally valid tropes for experience.[47] "The actors," Rosalie Colie observes, offer "a living metaphor, a desire within the play to illustrate what the abstracted theme is."[48]

In attempting to account for the dominance of the theatrical metaphor in *Hamlet*, critics have generally assumed that Shakespeare intended to justify his own profession and, by extension, to defend the public theater from "attacks upon the stage that were continuous through most of the last quarter of the sixteenth century."[49] What has not been sufficiently appreciated is that between 1599 and 1601 two of the most trenchant indictments of the public stage did not come from Puritans or city authorities but from *within* the theater itself. In fact, *Histriomastix* and *Poetaster* repeat the litany of antitheatrical arguments tendered by the civic authorities, left-wing Protestant extremists, and disaffected intellectuals who evoked the English common law, Plato, and Scripture to criticize dramatic performances. It was no accident that *Histriomastix* would live on as the title of William Prynne's famous treatise of 1633; Marston's play would thus serve as a precursor to the successful movement to close the London theaters in 1642. In his comedy, Marston had shown how unsatisfactory Chrisoganus/Jonson's tenure with Sir Oliver Owlet's Men had been, and in *Poetaster*, Jonson returned the insult by revealing how sordid Crispinus/Marston's involvement with Histrio's Men currently was. Whatever other cultural polemics *Hamlet* might have responded to, the "goose-quills" wielded first by Marston at Paul's in 1599 and then by Jonson at Blackfriars in 1601 against the "common players" were impossible to ignore. But Shakespeare defended the common stages not by emphasizing the didactic power of poetry to transform its audience or the status of its performers, but by insisting that theatricality was the fundamental condition of human experience.

During the English Renaissance it was the usual practice for polemical tracts either to deride the theater as a source of moral corruption, as Stephen Gosson does in *The School of Abuse*, or to defend it as a powerful means of inculcating virtue. Sidney's *Apology for Poetry* and Heywood's *Apology for Actors* are linked by the proposition that drama is a subset of "poetry" that deploys a wide range of fictional constructs to move an audience to moral action. What is different about *Hamlet* is that it questions this defense when the actors at Elsinore are used to challenge Jonson's cathartic theory of drama. Hamlet's thesis that "the purpose of playing . . . is to hold as 'twere the mirror up to nature: to show virtue her feature, scorn her own image, and the very age and body of the time his form and pressure" (3.2.20–24) seems to support Jonson's claim in *Every Man Out* that art should tender an "*Imitatio vitae, Speculum consuetudinis, Imago veritatis*," designed to faciliate "the correction of manners" through an image of "the time's deformity / Anatomiz'd in every nerve and sinew." Yet in Hamlet's formulation of theatrical mimesis there is a significant shift in emphasis: it is the players, not their scripts, who mirror life by reflecting the form and pressure of the time. Thus, if *Hamlet* serves "to hold the mirror up to nature," Kernan keenly observes, it does not reflect "some certain truth, some clear moral which can be taken home by the audience," but "a condition of life like the theater itself, ambiguous, changing, transient."[50]

Shakespeare, contrary to Jonson's position in *Every Man Out* and *Cynthia's Revels*, is skeptical about drama's moral instrumentality. "The Mouse Trap" does "catch the conscience of the King" (2.2.605) and "tent him to the quick" (2.2.597) to the extent that Claudius recognizes the performance as a topically charged dramatization of his offense. But when he then examines his conscience in the chapel, he refuses to be morally transformed by what he has seen because it would require restitution of crown and queen. Not only does the mirroring of his murder of King Hamlet have no lasting moral effect but it also incites Claudius to repeat the action, to kill Hamlet, the play's patron, presenter, and co-author. Hamlet himself anticipates this failure when he acknowledges that "for me to put him to his purgation would perhaps plunge him into more choler" (3.2.305–7). The cathartic theory of drama fails because its audience is intractable. Shakespeare questions the humanist apology for theater when he could have annexed it as a defense; instead, he uses the player's craft as a conceptual framework for exploring the deepest problems that individuals face in their efforts to know and need to act.

With *Every Man Out*, Jonson initiated a trend of including explicit literary theory in drama, and in *Hamlet* Shakespeare directs his doubts about cathartic mimesis to the same segment of his audience that Jonson had tried to wrest from him. Hamlet's concept of an ideal audience of "judicious" spectators (3.2.26) appeals to the same elite group—Q1's "principall publike audience"—who were now frequenting Paul's and Blackfriars as well as the Globe. Like Jonson, Hamlet divides theatergoers into two classes when he categories the First Player's speech as being from a play too good to be popular—"caviary to the general" (2.2.437)—but applauded by those of superior judgment. Like Jonson, he believes that the "censure" of the "judicious" must "o'erweigh a whole theatre of others" (3.2.26–28), especially "the groundlings, who for the most part are capable of nothing but inexplicable dumb shows and noise" (3.2.10–12). Jonson would continue to make this distinction to the end of his career. What is novel, however, is to find Shakespeare so closely attuned to the interests of this "principall" audience that Hamlet emphasizes the need to control the clown's unscripted improvisations. That *Hamlet* hit its mark is indicated by the reaction of Gabriel Harvey, the pedantic Cambridge don who praised it for being among Shakespeare's works that can "please the wiser sort."[51]

It was chiefly for this elite audience whose allegiance was being tested in the stage-quarrel that *Hamlet* was written. Hamlet, both a prince and a student at Wittenberg, is a hero designed to appeal to the "gentlemen" and "gallants," but in a manner that both complements and opposes Jonson's approach. The play tenders a supportive relationship between its aristocratic university-trained hero and the "common Players." In reference to these same actors, the hero formulates an absolute equipoise between thought and action that he himself is never able to achieve. Jonson expected his judicious spectator to envision the possibility of psychological transformation; Shakespeare required his to realize a sense of estrangement. Watching *Hamlet*, audience members were asked to imagine themselves as incurable and to use one controlling humour—melancholy—as a psychological perspective through which to view experience.

Hamlet is a powerful representation of the anxious circumspection that pervaded late Elizabethan culture. Jonson tried to address this same uneasy spirit by sublimating it in the creation of a new and more positive self. Asper, the presenter who becomes an actor playing the part of Macilente, the envious humourist in *Every Man Out*, is an interesting foil and even prototype for Hamlet. Both characters take on a second role consisting of a "humorous" or "antic disposition"; both deliver soliloquies on their alienation; and both contrast their troubled perceptions of experience with the patient equanimity of Stoicism. But while Macilente is "the humorous man" who ends "his part in peace," Hamlet, who suffers an incurable melancholy, discovers only that "the rest is silence" (5.2.358).

There is good reason to believe that Shakespeare's defense of the players was already part of the *Hamlet* of 1600, and that he went back to the play and added an allusion to the "little eyases" to record his recent experience with *Poetaster*. Before "The Murder of Gonzago" is performed, Hamlet instructs the First Player to add to its script "a speech of some dozen or sixteen lines," which he "would set down" (2.2.541–42). His purpose is to turn "The Murder of Gonzago" into "The Mouse Trap," a play that will come to be understood, as Hamlet wittily suggests, "tropically" (3.2.237–38) or "trapically," as Q1 spells it (sig. F4ʳ). Shakespeare, like his hero, inserted topical material into an extant script. In doing so, however, he followed Jonson's example even more closely than he followed Hamlet's, adding theater criticism to a play that had already been staged. He imitated the technique Jonson had employed to parody Munday in *The Case Is Altered* and Marston and Dekker in *Every Man Out*. Part of the wit of the "little eyases" passage, then, is in its use of a Jonsonian literary form—the interpolated critical dialogue—to respond to his criticism. Shakespeare's metatheatrical commentary, hovering between fact and fiction, includes a general account of the origin, development, and conclusion of the War of the Theaters: how it started when the children began to "berattle the common stages," then continued as a "throwing about of brains" with "much to do on both sides," only to end with "the boys [carrying] it away." To have seen events in this light, Shakespeare must have viewed *Satiromastix* as having failed to defend adequately the player's status against the poet's assault. In other words, the boys won because Dekker's play at the Globe was a weak theoretical response to the dichotomy between poet and player that Jonson had postulated in *Poetaster*. This weakness is especially evident if *Satiromastix* is compared to Marston's prior, more intellectually rigorous attack on Jonson's

poetics in *What You Will*. Dekker was content to show the positive effect of
theater as a social influence, even on the king. He ridiculed Jonson for being
so hostile to players that he had killed one of them and mocked him for being
not only an arrogant poet but also a failed actor. But his assent to the cathartic theory of theater and Jonson's conception of poetic authority was at odds
with Marston and Shakespeare's skepticism.

Yet it is also probable that Shakespeare, in his interpolated admission in
Hamlet that Blackfriars had bested the Globe, included *Troilus and Cressida*
along with *Satiromastix* in this assessment. But whether Shakespeare was
merely being self-effacing about his own participation in the Poets' War or his
response to Jonson was generally perceived as being as ineffective as he suggests is difficult to determine, because not everyone agreed that the Chapel
children had beaten the Chamberlain's Men in their game of brain-tossing.
One who dared to dissent from this opinion was the irrepressible Kemp in *2
Return from Parnassus*, who boasts to his crony Burbage that, despite the verbal aggression of *Poetaster*, their "fellow Shakespeare" has not only "put them
all down" (poet and poetaster alike) but in the process has given Jonson "a
purge that made him beray his credit."

An Armed Epilogue

Troilus and Cressida and the Impact of
the Poets' War

WHEN ROSENCRANTZ informed Hamlet late in 1601 that the reputation of the Chamberlain's Men had been sullied by the Children of
the Chapel at Blackfriars, the Poets' War had ended. Rivalries among
poets and players would continue, of course, but in new and different configurations. By that time, Jonson's *Poetaster*, his most outrageous comical satire—with caricatures of Marston, Dekker, and several of the Chamberlain's Men—had been produced, and Dekker's *Satiromastix* had answered him
at Paul's and the Globe with more impudence than insight. During this interval between the premiere of *Poetaster* and the "little eyases" passage in *Hamlet*,
the Chamberlain's Men acted *Troilus and Cressida* to defend their reputation.
So we now come full circle and return to Shakespeare's purge of Jonson, with
which this study began.

What made *Troilus and Cressida* particularly amusing for its sophisticated
audience was its parodic re-creation of the stage-quarrel between Jonson and
Marston as part of the Trojan War, not in the heroic rivalry of Achilles and
Hector but in the scurrilous contention of the supposed comrades-in-arms
Ajax and Thersites. During the final phase of the Poets' War, Shakespeare, in
a remarkable dialectical maneuver affirming his erudition, took Jonson pris-
oner on his own ground. Jonson had used Rome's Golden Age to contextualize Elizabethan theater, but Shakespeare evoked an even earlier classical precedent, the Greek Bronze Age, for his own version of theatrical politics. The
conflicting models of the classical world in *Poetaster* and *Troilus* reflect rival

etiologies of Elizabethan drama. Yet whatever victory Shakespeare might have achieved in the eyes of his educated auditors was Pyrrhic. For *Troilus*'s nihilism corroded both the romantic and the satiric norms of the Poets' War, and through it Shakespeare repudiated festive comedy even as he demolished comical satire.

Animating Jonson's humanist project from 1599 to 1601 was his conviction that his moral and literary judgment, tempered by classical scholarship, could transform Elizabethan culture. Satire was part of the arsenal of a new philosophical idealism. His neoclassical program enabled him to form a new conception of poetic authority that lent credence to his theatrical intervention. No matter how withering comical satire had been or how much it dwelt on the difference between the real and the ideal, it was always explicitly authoritarian, based on the assumption of a fixed moral order by which psychological excesses could be measured and eliminated. But if Jonson was not at first aware of the risk he was taking, by the time he wrote *Poetaster* he had no illusions about the derision his project would encounter.

Jonson had in effect already abandoned his hope of regenerating commercial theater when he sent out the metal-jacketed Prologue of *Poetaster* to fend off his attackers:

> If any muse, why I salute the stage,
> An armed *Prologue*; know, 'tis a dangerous age:
> Wherein, who writes, had need present his *Scenes*
> Forty-fold proof against the conjuring means
> Of base detractors and illiterate apes,
> That fill up rooms in fair and formal shapes.
> 'Gainst these, have we put on this forc'd defense:
> Whereof the *allegory* and hid sense
> Is, that a well-erected confidence
> Can fright their pride, and laugh their folly hence.
>   (PROLOGUE, LL. 5–14)

What had begun in *Every Man Out* as an offensive foray against his competitors had hardened into the defensive posture with which his spokesman held the stage against the assault of Envy. The militant Prologue was on guard particularly against "that common spawn of ignorance, / Our fry of writers"—Marston and Dekker—who continued to "beslime" Jonson's "fame" (lines 18–19). If Jonson should "once more, / Swear that his play were good"—as he had done in *Cynthia's Revels*, only to be parodied for doing so in *What You Will*—his audience should not take it as "arrogance" but as the self-affirmation of an author who observes an Aristotelian mean between the extremes of "full-blown vanity" and "base dejection" (lines 21–22). Jonson had always maintained that he occupied this middle ground and that what his enemies maliciously misinterpreted as self-love was the constant firmness of one who knew the strength of his own muse. Between 1599 and 1601, his assault on Elizabethan culture had been transformed into a contentious debate over the very issue he had always assumed as a guiding principle—that it was possible for poets to know themselves and accurately assess their own value.

By the end of 1601 the continuous onslaught on Jonson's reputation was beginning to take its toll. Although he apparently remained committed to the same literary ideals, the commercial theater no longer seemed to be the right venue for effecting meaningful change. On the contrary, it trapped him in a series of increasingly brutal and unproductive attacks on his character and work. He presented a bold façade in *Poetaster*, but his message was quite different from his first two comical satires. He was now convinced that only nondramatic poetry, especially the epic, could satisfactorily represent the highest form of artistic expression. Because of the contentious culture in which it was mired, commercial theater could at best serve a secondary function in clarifying this literary distinction, pointing beyond itself to something greater. In Jonson's imperial Rome and in his Elizabethan London, poet-scholars were better off reading their verses directly to their patrons, free of the players' corrupting mediation. Jonson identified himself with Horace, but in *Poetaster* it is Virgil's recitation of the *Aeneid* at the court of Augustus that constitutes the apex of literary performance and indicates the extent of Jonson's disaffection with contemporary commercial theater.

The principal cause of Jonson's ongoing debate with Shakespeare was the incompatibility of his own univocal vision of human perfectibility and confident self-assertion with the radical irony at the heart of his rival's poetics. Thus, within months of *Poetaster*'s premiere, Shakespeare's Prologue to *Troilus* would similarly enter in armor to dramatize their differences. Displaying none of his predecessor's self-assurance, this new theatrical emissary was meant to challenge Jonson's spokesman by refusing to vouch for the merit of either Shakespeare or the Chamberlain's Men:

> and hither am I come,
> A prologue arm'd, but not in confidence
> Of author's pen or actor's voice, but suited
> In like conditions as our argument,
> To tell you, fair beholders, that our play

> Leaps o'er the vaunt and firstlings of those broils,
> Beginning in the middle; starting thence away
> To what may be digested in a play.
> Like or find fault, do as your pleasures are,
> Now good or bad, 'tis but the chance of war.
>
> (PROLOGUE, LL. 22–31)

Shakespeare's uncommitted spokesman, like the play he could not defend, was a figure of subversive relativity operating in a world where theatrical success, like war, was a matter of chance. Furthermore, by introducing an account of the Trojan War, the stuff of classical myth, relating in Latinate diction how "The princes orgillous, their high blood chaf'd, / Have to the port of Athens sent their ships" (Prologue, lines 2–3), Shakespeare presented a startlingly new version of himself. Although he had begun his reaction to comical satire in *As You Like It* by tentatively aligning himself with nature, here, in *Troilus*, he changed course and assumed the countervailing standard of art. Always more agile than his stereotypical literary persona, which, like George Romney's imaginary portrait of "The Infant Shakespeare," would forever define him as Nature's child, he invaded Jonson's domain in the final engagement of the Poets' War. He would mimic Jonsonian neoclassicism—invoking Horace's famous literary dictum in *The Art of Poetry* that an epic should begin *in medias res*—to empty his drama of authority. He would cast his play in epic terms, but only to strip it of meaning.

Through his prologue to *Troilus and Cressida* Shakespeare denies Jonson's conceptual distinction between epic and drama before undermining the rational *telos* of the *Aeneid* with the *Iliad*'s problematic contradictions of heroic individualism. Although he based his play primarily on Chaucer's *Troilus and Criseyde*, after reading Chapman's partial translation of the *Iliad* (published in 1598), Shakespeare invented a sardonic version of the classical past to counter Jonson's antiseptic pseudohistory. His selection of the Trojan War was particularly apt since the *Aeneid*'s political history was predicated on the *Iliad*'s conflict. Shakespeare was in effect exploring the same classical material Jonson had re-created in *Poetaster*, but at a more primal, one might say "authoritative," phase of its development. Just as Jonson had initially sought to demonstrate his superiority over Shakespeare by supplanting New Comedy with Old in *Every Man Out*, Shakespeare replaced Roman with Greek epic to gain the advantage of priority in *Troilus and Cressida*, questioning his rival's identity while constructing a new genealogical myth of the origin of Western civilization. During the Middle Ages and the Renaissance the issue of whether the Trojan War could be justified was left unresolved, and Shakespeare's familiarity with the medieval denigration of the legend in such works as William Caxton's *Recuyell of the Historyes of Troye* (1475) predispc•ed him to view both Greek and Trojan warriors with monumental mockery. His armed Prologue steps forward with an epic voice emptied of conviction.

Troilus and Cressida imitates comical satire in exposing the delusion of romantic love: Ovid's isolation from Julia is recapitulated in Troilus's separation from Cressida, just as Cressida's betrayal of Troilus is prefigured in Fallace's deception of Delirio. But Shakespeare's play undermines the delusion of honor shared by epic and comical satire. The reputation of Achilles depends solely on the legend of his having killed Hector, which the Myrmidons actually did, after sundown, when their adversary was unarmed. Hector's honor is also as corrupt as the "putrefied core" (5.8.1) he discovers sealed up within the armor for which he murders. The aggressive public world in which Aeneas himself appears—unable to recognize the "great" Agamemnon who stands before him—is as flawed as its libidinous private counterpart. The war is based on a personal quarrel with heavy public consequences. The pursuit of renown is, however, at its most ridiculous in the figure of Ajax, whose envy of Achilles and confidence in his own merit make him an easy target for the derision of both the Greek generals and Thersites. It was to this episode that Shakespeare added a touch of caricature and a pastiche of Jonsonian literary motifs and techniques in order to "purge" Jonson's "credit."

Although Dekker conceived of the term "Poetomachia" (by 11 November 1601) to refer to his wrangling with Jonson, nowhere before the dueling Prologues of *Poetaster* and *Troilus and Cressida* was this martial metaphor represented visually. Marston had written of "*Scoff's* artillery" in *What You Will*, but he had never staged a battle. Indeed, the principal metaphors for the Poets' War were medical and juridical—a purge and an arraignment. That is why Dekker's description might have been influenced by the Globe's production of *Troilus and Cressida*. That Marston appreciated the philosophical import of Shakespeare's diffident Prologue is evident from his imitation of it at the conclusion of the first quarto of *Antonio and Mellida* (1602). For in this revised printed version of his play (registered on 24 October 1601), he has Andrugio apologize in words lifted from *Troilus and Cressida*:

> *Gentlemen, though I remain an armed Epilogue, I stand not as a peremptory challenger of desert, either for him that composed the Comedy, or for us that acted it: but a most submissive suppliant for both. What imperfection you have seen in us, leave with us, and we'll amend it; what hath pleased you, take with you, and cherish it.*

(1:63)

Marston's *"armed Epilogue"* launches a rear-guard assault on Jonson's "armed Prologue," but it does so by adopting the same submissive strategy Shakespeare's "prologue arm'd" had employed. He refuses to defend the work of either *"him that composed the Comedy, or . . . us that acted it,"* echoing what Shakespeare had called "author's pen or actor's voice." Marston concludes with Shakespeare, against Jonson, that evaluating a work's merit was the audience's prerogative, not the author's.

Shakespeare and Jonson's collision on the stages of the Globe and Blackfriars between 1599 and 1601, which culminated in their paired Prologues, had two far-reaching consequences. First, it originated the legend of their witcombats. All subsequent contrasts between them, conceived in terms of either private or professional contention, from the early seventeenth century to the present, originate with this controversy. Second, and more important, it shaped the formal and conceptual dynamics of Shakespeare's comedies from *As You Like It* through *Twelfth Night* to *Troilus and Cressida*, as each of these plays responded to the philosophical issues Jonson posed in *Every Man Out*, *Cynthia's Revels*, and *Poetaster*.

At one time or another *Troilus* has been made to fit all the generic categories Shakespeare employed. But one of the earliest commentaries, which must be given considerable weight, is the epistle from the "never writer, to the ever reader" added to the second "state" of the 1609 First Quarto, which describes *Troilus and Cressida* as *"a comedy," "the birth"* of a *"brain, that never undertook anything comical vainly."*[1] This play, the anonymous writer concludes, deserves as much praise *"as the best Comedy in* Terence *or* Plautus." It was from the start, however, sufficiently strange, sophisticated, and arcane to ensure that it was a theatrical failure. Nonetheless, when the same writer states that it was *"never staled with the stage, never clapperclawed with the palms of the vulgar,"* this does not necessarily mean that it was never produced at the Globe, only that it was not enthusiastically received.[2]

Campbell first drew attention to this theatrical interface in *Comicall Satyre and Shakespeare's* Troilus and Cressida, and subsequent critics have, for the most part, repeated his portrait of Shakespeare as an assimilator of Jonsonian satire. "Shakespeare composed *Troilus and Cressida* during the years when the vogue of comical satire was at its height," he writes. "In constructing the play according to the fully developed principles of the new form, he but furnished another instance of his habit of following the dramatic fashion."[3] But Campbell was so intent on seeing Shakespeare as a passive assimilator of influence, attempting "to try his hand at a type of play which Jonson and Marston were then writing," that he never suspects that he might have had ideas about satire in his own right or felt uncomfortable with Jonsonian comedy. For if a swelling satiric undercurrent began to inundate romantic sentiment in Shakespeare's comic sequence, *As You Like It, Twelfth Night,* and *Troilus and Cressida,* his work also became more rigorously anti-Jonsonian. In each phase of the Poets' War Shakespeare gave ground to Jonsonian satire, but without embracing its attendant optimism. Shakespeare in *Troilus and Cressida* identifies failure as an essential condition of experience, and his play presents what Graham Bradshaw, evoking Nietzsche, refers to as a "genealogy of ideals" that undermines all attempts at self-vindication.[4] Nothing could be further from the affirmative authoritarian spirit of comical satire.

Nineteenth- and twentieth-century critics have examined the private and public realms of Shakespearean biography to discover what prompted him to write *Troilus and Cressida,* a radical departure from his usual practice. Some Romantic critics explained the play as expressing Shakespeare's despairing attitude toward events in his personal life, while moderns have often considered it a distraught response to Essex's aborted coup in February 1601.[5] Whatever other approaches readers find viable, the central thrust of the play's topicality is theatrically oriented. Although both domains overlapped, its specific referentiality is focused more explicitly on the politics of late Elizabethan theater than on the theater of national politics.

Jonson's theatrical assault on late Elizabethan culture had originated in a contentiously debated question: was it possible for writers to know themselves and accurately estimate their own cultural value? As both Jonson and his detractors realized, his new program demanded its audience's assent to his judgment as a condition of its own probity. Shakespeare and Marston, however, blasted his ideas. In *Troilus and Cressida,* people are held to be incapable of unmediated self-knowledge, since we depend on others to tell us who we are and only know ourselves through their reflections. Jonson's "confidence" in his own merit is as ridiculous as Ajax's self-love. Chaucer used the story of Troilus and Cressida to emphasize the ceaseless mutability of external experience, in a version that ends with Troilus's disembodied laughter echoing from beyond a world of change and decay. Shakespeare hews closely to Chaucer's narrative to dramatize the same theme: the failure of idealized expectation. But what differentiates his Renaissance version of the story from Chaucer's medieval rendition is a new skepticism, which he advances to check Jonson's manipulative idealism. The antecedents of Shakespeare's self-scrutiny can be found in Erasmus's *Praise of Folly* and Montaigne's *Essays.* Through his dissection of the notion of value, literary criticism began within late Elizabethan drama to interrogate the process of self-reflection.

Who, then, won the Poets' War? As we look back over the span of four centuries, Shakespeare's victory seems confirmed by his subsequent influence on

Western culture. In opposing Jonson he proposed a modernist poetics that voices the most eloquent expression of the human condition. But during the period that the Poets' War rattled the London stages this conclusion was not obvious. Rosencrantz would have us believe that, after "much to do on both sides," *Satiromastix* and *Troilus and Cressida* had failed to answer *Poetaster* adequately and that Jonson's company of children had managed to "carry it away." This failure seems also to be implicitly signaled by the "never writer," who claims *Troilus* was never "*staled with the stage*," even though it was registered with the Stationers as having been performed by Shakespeare's company. Yet its short production made an impact on some spectators. Jonson appears to have felt its sting when, in apologizing for *Poetaster*, he alludes to the unexpectedly harsh tone of Shakespeare's glance at him as Ajax in *Troilus and Cressida*. The university student who penned *2 Return from Parnassus* knew exactly what that involved. Nevertheless, unlike Rosencrantz, who concedes that the children have triumphed in the exchange, "Kemp" exults in Shakespeare's success in putting down his competitor. Taken together, these conflicting eyewitness accounts indicate that, after two years of combat, no clear winner had emerged and the question of authorial self-reflection the Poets' War raised had not been, nor could ever be, definitively answered. It would instead, from that time forward, be remembered in the legend of Shakespeare and Jonson as mighty opposites upon whose antagonism our conception of literature depends.

CHRONOLOGICAL APPENDIX

PHASE ONE

1. Jonson's *Every Man Out of His Humour* (autumn 1599), performed by the Chamberlain's Men at the Globe

The Jonson First Folio states that this play, entered in the Stationers' Register on 8 April 1600, was first staged "in the year 1599." Because he parodies the Chorus of *Henry V* at the beginning of his play ("After the Second Sounding," lines 281–86) and at 4.8.176–81, Jonson must have written *Every Man Out* after April 1599, the *terminus ad quem* of Shakespeare's history. In that month Essex confidently began his doomed invasion of Ireland, an event that Shakespeare's Chorus of act 5 (lines 24–35) could still mention with heroic expectation in a passage among those faulted by Jonson for violating the unity of place.

There are indications that *Every Man Out* was written not only after April but also nearer to year's end. Its staging at that time is made probable by two references to its place of production, the Globe theater, which, according to Chambers, was erected in autumn 1599.[1] Herford and Simpson, who cite Jonson's mention of "this fair-filled Globe" (revised Epilogue, line 24) and his recollection of the recent period "when the house was a building" (Prologue, line 329), reach the same conclusion: *Every Man Out* was acted early in the Globe's first season (9:185–86).

Once it was staged, however, Jonson added his parodies of Orange and Clove to the script, sometime after the production of *Histriomastix* and before Dekker imitated two elements of it in *Patient Grissil*, completed by 29 December 1599.

(See chapter 3, note 12.) Jonson further expanded his manuscript for publication in the First Quarto of 1600.

2. Marston's *Histriomastix* (autumn–winter 1599), performed by the Children of Paul's at the cathedral theater

Although it was not published until 1610, since Jonson mentions *Histriomastix* and parodies its language in *Every Man Out*, acted late in 1599, it was probably written in that year. This is argued by Small, Herford and Simpson, and Caputi.[2] An alternative dating, however, is suggested by Philip Finkelpearl, who thinks that the play was written for the Christmas Revels of the Middle Temple at the end of 1598. This view has had a remarkable impact on scholarship and has been repeated, without further examination, in introductions to the plays of Marston, critical assessments of his work, and histories of Elizabethan theater.[3] A close examination of the theatrical context in which *Histriomastix* was produced and to which it contributes nevertheless confirms that the play could not possibly have been completed before the final months of 1599.

The central factor we have to consider in dating *Histriomastix* is its undisputed relation to *Every Man Out*. All the critics I have cited so far have generally assumed that *Histriomastix* must have been written before *Every Man Out*, since it is an object of satire in the latter work. Herford and Simpson, for instance, declare that *Every Man Out* establishes the *terminus ad quem* for *Histriomastix*. Finkelpearl seems untroubled by the fact that Jonson's improvised allusion to *Histriomastix* would in his view have been written about a year after Marston's play was initially produced. But this lapse of time between the purported production of *Histriomastix* in December 1598 and Jonson's satire in late 1599 exhibits one of the weaknesses of his chronology. Jonson would have replied sooner, especially since he had been personally alluded to in the play as Chrisoganus, Marston's pompous yet sage philosopher-poet. As I indicate in chapter 3, the pattern of Marston's consecutive rivalries with Hall and Jonson, from 1598–1599, confirms this later dating.

If we accept 1599 rather than 1598 as the first possible year of its composition, we can also conclude, on independent grounds, that it was produced after August of that year. Small in particular underscores the significance of a short anxious joke in *Histriomastix*: "The Spaniards are come" (3:291). He observes that this line was calculated to reawaken fears of a Spanish invasion in August 1599 that sent shock waves through London. According to Stow's *Annals*, Spanish naval preparations at that time prompted the alarmed citizens of London to equip sixteen ships with six thousand soldiers and to assemble thousands of horsemen and footmen to defend the city, which had chains drawn across its streets and candles set "at every man's door, there to burn all night . . . upon pain of death."[4] A state of anxious waiting persisted from 8 until about 23 August, when the crisis passed. Small is not correct in assuming that he was able, through this contextual reference, "to determine the very month in which the play was produced—August,

1599."[5] At best we can surmise, following Fleay's position, that Marston was opening a recently closed wound when, shortly after the crisis had ended and "the fear had passed away," he mischievously evoked memories of that troubled period.[6]

3. Shakespeare's *As You Like It* (between January and 25 March 1600), performed by the Chamberlain's Men at the Globe

It is far-fetched to assume, based mainly on Jaques' allusion to the Globe theater's motto (2.7.139–40), that *As You Like It* was staged in 1599. A more convincing dating is made possible by the fact that Shakespeare designed the role of Touchstone with Robert Armin in mind, since the name elides his two professional affiliations as goldsmith and fool. If we can discover when Armin joined the company, we can date *As You Like It*, which, by all accounts, showcased his talents. But historians have found it difficult to discover exactly when during the 1599–1600 season he replaced William Kemp as a principal comedian and sharer. It now seems likely to have been in the first quarter of 1600. We know that Armin had made the transition by 4 August of that year, because *Tarlton's Jests*, the second part of which was registered on that day, states that "at this hour . . . at the Globe on the Bankside, men may see him."[7] This citation appeared during the same month that the script of *As You Like It* was both registered and blocked by the stationers. But how long before August did Armin first play Touchstone?

The common assumption that Armin joined the Chamberlain's Men in 1599 now appears to be false. He was then at the Curtain, perhaps with Lord Derby's Men. Evelyn Joseph Mattern provides credible evidence that Armin was still associated with a different troupe at the Curtain at least until the Christmas holidays of that year. In his Dedication, dated 28 December 1599, to *Quips Upon Questions* (1600), Armin indicates that he has not yet joined the Lord Chamberlain's Servants when he writes:

If I scape Monday, which is ominous to me, I shall think myself happy: and though Friday be for this year Childermas [i.e., though two unlucky days coincide], yet it is no such day of danger to me; then on Tuesday [Christmas or New Year's Day?] I take my Journey (to wait on the right honorable good Lord my Master whom I serve) to Hackney.

Childermas Day (December 28) fell on a Friday in 1599. Thus, since the earl of Oxford, who had strong ties with his son-in-law, the earl of Derby, had a house at King's Hold in Hackney, near the Curtain, and since both aristocrats wrote comedies and were interested in sponsoring theatrical productions, Armin was still probably serving one of these lords at this time. In either case, Mattern argues, Armin's phrase "my Master" could not apply to Lord Hunsdon, the Lord Chamberlain, who lived at Blackfriars and whose men performed before the Queen at Richmond, about fifteen miles across London from Hackney, on the day after Christmas.[8]

As You Like It was consequently produced after Armin joined the company in 1600, at around the time, from 11 February to 11 March, when Kemp, in *Nine Days' Wonder*, described himself as having danced his way "out of the world." Early in 1600, Armin was still being published under the pen name Snuff, Clonnico de Curtanio (Clown of the Curtain Theater), in *Quips Upon Questions* and *Fool Upon Fool*, while the Chamberlain's Men were performing at the new Globe. Armin probably joined them sometime before 25 March, the final day on which Marston could have initially written *Antonio and Mellida* (see note 30), which shows familiarity with Shakespeare's comedy. Marston's Rossaline, with her witty sexual innuendo, has a Shakespearean pedigree, and her suitor Alberto's lament that he will address his passions to nature, "For woods, trees, sea, or rocky Apennine / Is not so ruthless as my Rossaline" (1:53–54), replicates Orlando's doggerel (3.2.88–112).

4. Marston's *Jack Drum's Entertainment* (after 25 March but before 8 September 1600), performed by the Children of Paul's at the cathedral theater

Entered in the Stationers' Register on 8 September 1600, this play is dated in the late spring or early summer of the same year by Caputi, who closely follows Small's arguments.[9] Caputi notes that the references to the "peace with Spain" (3:182) and the Irish troubles in the phrases "I'll to Ireland" (3:207) and "he will waste more substance than Ireland soldiers" (3:186) could not have been written before the current English involvement beginning in 1599. Furthermore, two other topical references indicate that the play was written in the subsequent year. The drama alludes to the fact that it is "women's year" (3:186) or leap year, which occurred in 1600, and it also mentions "Kemp's Morris" (3:182), his famous dance from London to Norwich that took place from 11 February to 11 March of that year. Caputi could be right in suggesting that Sir Edward Fortune's line, "'Tis Whitsuntide and we must frolic it" (3:182), might "have referred to a holiday outside the play as well as one within it."[10] Since Whitsun was the Christian equivalent of May Day, *Jack Drum*, in which Marston refers to himself as "the new poet *Mellidus*" (3:221), could have premiered around that time, but certainly after 25 March 1600, the last possible date for the initial composition of *Antonio and Mellida*.

Phase Two

5. Jonson's *Cynthia's Revels* (between 29 September and 31 December 1600), performed by the Children of the Chapel at Blackfriars

Its title page in Jonson's First Folio states that *Cynthia's Revels* was acted at Blackfriars by the Children of Queen Elizabeth's Chapel in 1600. Herford and Simpson, following Chambers, are even more exact in stating that it must have been acted soon after this group became incorporated in the third quarter of the year. "We learn from a contract made on 2 September with Richard Burbage for the use of this theatre that Henry Evans 'intended then presently,' i.e. at once, 'to erect or set up a company of boys' " (9:188). Jonson staged *Cynthia's Revels* sometime between 29 September, when the lease became effective, and the end of 1600.

One vexing problem concerning *Cynthia's Revels* is whether it was presented at court. Herford and Simpson (9:188) first denied that it was produced there on Twelfth Night, 6 January 1601, and then, misled by Chambers, Percy Simpson incorrectly corrected himself:

> I am sorry to say that the Oxford *Jonson* is responsible for the statement that there is "no evidence" that the piece was ever performed at Court (vol. I, p. 393). . . . The Children of the Chapel acted the play, and their choir-master Nathaniel Gyles took them to Court with it on 6 January 1601: the warrant quoted in *The Elizabethan Stage*, vol. iv. p. 166, says: "Nathaniel Gylles mr of the children of the Chapple, for a showe wth musicke and speciall songes p'pared for the purpose" was paid £5 for it. The description fits *Cynthia's Revels* with the four lyrics in the second scene of act I, the third scene of act IV, the sixth scene of act V, and the Court masques in the seventh and ninth scenes of act V. F.G. Fleay first made this identification, Sir E. K. Chambers accepts it, and I now feel no doubt about the reference.[11]

Yet it seems likely that neither *Cynthia's Revels* nor *Twelfth Night* (see number 6 below) was seen at court during the Christmas holidays of 1601. Because both the Children of the Chapel and the Chamberlain's Men performed before the Queen on 6 January 1601, it would seem possible that Jonson and Shakespeare somehow contended with each other on this occasion. Leslie Hotson, however, proves that the children produced not a full play but a musical program on 6 January, since they were scheduled to "come before the Queen at Dinner with a Carol"—before the midday meal—whereas plays were scheduled for performance after supper. At a time when the standard court fee for a play was ten pounds, they received half that sum for singing. The only other time they are noted as having appeared at Whitehall is 22 February, when, for ten pounds, they presented a "play" at night. If *Cynthia's Revels* were performed at this later date, Jonson took the occasion to reprimand (through his allegory of the doomed Actaeon) the earl of Essex's sympathizers shortly before his execution.[12]

But neither the Quarto nor the Folio title page of *Cynthia's Revels* indicates that it was performed at court. Furthermore, beneath its statement that the play was acted privately at Blackfriars is an epigraph from Juvenal's *Satires*, which rebukes patrons for not affording poets the support that only actors are willing to provide:

> *Quod non dant Proceres, dabit Histrio.*
> *Haud tamen invideas vati, quem pulpita pascunt.*[13]

"What nobles will not give, a player will," Juvenal remarks. "Yet envy not the poet whom the stage maintains." In place of a statement of royal performance, Jonson complains that patrons will not help poets, who are forced to rely on the the-ater—in this case the private theater—as their sole venue. Marston seems to be tormenting Jonson with this rejection in *What You Will* by staging Lampatho Doria's frustrated attempt to offer a play called *Temperance* at court. "What sot elects that subject for the Court?" the Duke asks, dismissing the idea as absurd (3:290). In *Satiromastix* Horace/Jonson is coaxed not to complain when his plays are "misliked at court" (5.2.325), and this might suggest that *Cynthia's Revels* had to have been performed before the Queen for this comment to make sense. Still, bad publicity from Blackfriars might have preempted a court appearance: the play could have been misliked by some at court without being staged there.

6. Shakespeare's *Twelfth Night, or What You Will* (between 6 January and 25 September 1601), performed by the Chamberlain's Men at the Globe

After working on *Hamlet* in 1600, Shakespeare moved on to *Twelfth Night* in 1601, paced by Marston's *Antonio's Revenge* and *What You Will*. Chambers notes that *Twelfth Night* is not earlier than 1600, "since the snatches of song" in 2.3 seem to be derived from Robert Jones's *First Book of Songs and Airs*, published in that year.[14] It seems likely, moreover, that it was produced before *What You Will* in 1601, since, as Finkelpearl points out, Marston's "parasitic" comedy has "many su-perficial resemblances to *Twelfth Night*."[15]

In *The First Night of* Twelfth Night, Leslie Hotson argues that *Twelfth Night* premiered on Twelfth Night, 6 January 1601, but this date is now accepted only as one of its inspirations. Hotson points out that the Chamberlain's Men acted at court on that date, and that Virginio Orsino, Duke of Bracciano, was a participant in the Queen's Twelfth Night festivities. Hotson consequently reads the play as a political allegory addressing this specific occasion. But Elizabeth Donno soundly rejects this assumption, because "the portrayal of a lovesick Orsino would be an af-front both to the queen and to her noble visitor" and "the time available for Shake-speare to write the play and for the actors to rehearse it was far too short—only some ten days." News of the duke's intended visit was received on 26 December.[16] We cannot be certain what the Chamberlain's Men presented on that occasion, but since Duke Orsino wrote home describing the play that they acted at Whitehall on Twelfth Night as "*una commedia mescolata, con musiche e balli*" (a mingled come-dy, with music and dances), *Twelfth Night*, which has music but no dances, would be ruled out. When Lord Hunsdon, the Lord Chamberlain, specifically noted his intention to ask his players to choose a work for the occasion, he stipulated only that it should be of a subject to please the Queen, "best furnished with rich ap-parel" and having "great variety and change of Music and dances."[17] On this count alone a safer guess concerning what (if any) Shakespeare play was selected would be *Much Ado About Nothing*, which not only includes music and dances but also was already available. It is possible, however, that the conjunction between Twelfth

Night and the name Orsino resonated in Shakespeare's memory and found its way into the comedy he was then writing. This would mean, as Lothian and Craik argue, that 6 January 1601 must serve as the *terminus a quo* of its composition.[18] *Twelfth Night* appears to have been staged at the Globe during the first half of 1601 (shortly before Marston completed *What You Will*), long before John Manningham saw it revived at the Inns of Court in February 1602.

Stanley Wells and Gary Taylor have argued that "Feste's avoidance of the phrase 'out of my element' because the word element 'is overworn'" indicates "that *Twelfth Night* post-dates Dekker's *Satiromastix* . . . which three times pokes fun at the expression 'out of [one's] element' (1.2.134–6; 1.2.186–8; 5.2.324–7)."[19] But Dekker's target, like Shakespeare's, is *Cynthia's Revels*, and it is more plausible to assume that he is repeating Feste's joke than to believe, in effect, that *Twelfth Night* and *What You Will* were produced at the conclusion of the third phase of the Poets' War, after *Poetaster* and *Satiromastix*. What is more, Tom Cain convincingly emphasizes the cluster of verbal echoes from *Twelfth Night* in *Poetaster*, which adds further support to the notion that Shakespeare's comedy preceded Jonson's.[20] Since Jonson was first paid by Henslowe on 25 September for additions to *The Spanish Tragedy*, the Poets' War was ending by that date. Nevertheless, building on Riggs's theory that Shakespeare purged Jonson in *Twelfth Night*—in response to *Poetaster*—Cain conjectures that the *Parnassus* author is actually "referring to the Middle Temple performance of *Twelfth Night* in February 1602," viewed by John Manningham. But there is, on the contrary, strong evidence that *2 Return from Parnassus* had already alluded to Shakespeare's purge of Jonson at St. John's College during the Christmas Revels of 1601 (see number 13 below). By December 1601, in his "Apologetical Dialogue," Jonson had already complained of the "purge" when he expressed regret that "some better natures by the rest so drawn" had "run in that vile line" (lines 150–52). While Cain appreciates *Twelfth Night*'s anti-Jonsonian bias, he should have accepted the thesis he rejects, that *Twelfth Night* was Jonson's "pre-medication" by Shakespeare.[21]

7. Marston's *What You Will* (between 6 January and 25 September 1601), his last play for the Children of Paul's, performed at the cathedral theater

That *What You Will* is calculated to answer *Cynthia's Revels* should be obvious to readers who consider the homologies in character, plot, and language outlined in chapter 6. Marston restructured Jonson's comic plot, repeated his phrasing, contradicted his ideas, and reinterpreted Criticus as the ridiculous Lampatho Doria. For this reason *What You Will* could not have been written before September 1600, the first possible date for *Cynthia's Revels*, and since it shows no familiarity with *Poetaster*, it must have been completed before Jonson arraigned Marston as Crispinus in that play, which was probably staged by 25 September 1601 (see number 8 below).

What You Will was also produced after *Twelfth Night, or What You Will*, the subtitle of which it lifts along with other details of plot and characterization. If the use of the name Orsino in Shakespeare's play is a remembrance of the nobleman who visited with Elizabeth on 6 January 1601, then Marston's imitation of *Twelfth Night* was also composed after that date. What is more, if Marston had known of the frontal assault against him in *Poetaster*, he would surely have answered it instead of concentrating his satire on the less vitriolic *Cynthia's Revels*. *What You Will*, which combines passages from *Twelfth Night* and *Hamlet*, was evidently composed after these two popular plays. On 11 March 1601, the Privy Council directed the Lord Mayor to suppress plays at Paul's during Lent, so the play had to have been staged either before or after this period. Small, without much convincing evidence, assumes that it was written in April or May of that year.[22]

PHASE THREE

8. Jonson's *Poetaster* (between late spring and 25 September 1601), performed by the Children of the Chapel at Blackfriars

Jonson would have finished *Poetaster* before beginning to write additions to *The Spanish Tragedy* for Henslowe, for the first of which he was paid on 25 September. The First Quarto's title page states that *Poetaster* was acted "sundry times privately" at Blackfriars by the Children of Her Majesty's Chapel, and the Folio gives the year as 1601. Herford and Simpson surmise that "this must have been early in the year, for the performance is proved to have taken place in the spring by the admission of the player Histrio in Act II, scene IV, lines 328–9, 'this winter ha's made us all poorer, then so many starv'd snakes.'" (9:189). But Chambers, approaching the problem from another angle, observes that the first performance of *Poetaster* "must have come very near that of *Satiromastix*, for Horace knows that Demetrius has been hired to write a play on him." He therefore concludes that its production "may reasonably be placed in late spring or early autumn of the same year."[23] This dating is supported by Hoy's discovery that *Satiromastix* was written after 14 August 1601 (see below). That *Poetaster* was finished before 24 October is indicated by the First Quarto of Marston's *Antonio and Mellida*, which, registered with the Stationers on that day, ends with an "*armed Epilogue*" answering the "armed *Prologue*" that opens *Poetaster* (as indicated in my dating of *Troilus and Cressida* below).

9. Dekker's *Satiromastix* (after *Poetaster* was acted, but before 24 October 1601), performed by the Chamberlain's Men at the Globe and the Children of Paul's at the cathedral theater

Chambers notes that Dekker could not have finished *Satiromastix* before he had seen *Poetaster*, "to many details of which it retorts."[24] Yet Hoy was able further to narrow the focus by observing that "the reference in *Satiromastix*, V.ii.243, to 'the *Whipping a' th' Satyre*' suggests that the play was not completed at least until after 14 August 1601 when the verse satire of that name was entered in the Stationers' Register."[25] Dekker's play was produced, then, after *Poetaster*, which it imitates (staged by 25 September), before being registered for publication on 11 November 1601. If I am right in assuming, below, that the *"armed Epilogue"* in the First Quarto of *Antonio and Mellida* alludes to *Troilus and Cressida*, which was written to rectify the conceptual weakness of *Satiromastix*, Dekker's comedy as well as Shakespeare's would have been staged by 24 October 1601, the day on which Marston's altered play was registered.

10. Shakespeare's *Troilus and Cressida* (after *Poetaster*, which it echoes, had been acted, but before 24 October 1601), performed by the Chamberlain's Men at the Globe

A very late but certain *terminus ad quem* for *Troilus and Cressida* is determined by the play's entry in the Stationers' Register on 7 February 1603 as "the book of *Troilus and Cressida* . . . acted by my Lord Chamberlain's Men." Robert Kimbrough has unsuccessfully attempted to move this terminus slightly forward into 1602 by calling attention to possible imitations of *Troilus and Cressida* in *The Family of Love* by Middleton. But two major problems weaken his analysis. First, the parallel passages he cites might be of too general a nature to establish indebtedness; and, second, the date of *The Family of Love* has never been sufficiently ascertained. Kimbrough cites R. H. Barker in *Thomas Middleton* as having determined that *The Family of Love* "can scarcely be dated much later than 1602," even though it was registered on 12 October 1607. Yet Barker places a question mark after the year in his Chronological Appendix, where he tentatively concludes that "an early date, say 1602–3, seems indicated."[26] Harbage and Schoenbaum, in the *Annals of English Drama*, place *The Family of Love* in the year 1602, but they also hedge on this by adding the stipulation "c. 1602–1607."[27]

Stronger internal evidence for establishing the earliest possible date for *Troilus and Cressida* is found in its direct references to *Cynthia's Revels* and *Poetaster*. Shakespeare's "prologue arm'd, but not in confidence," is a clear response to the "armed *Prologue*" of *Poetaster*, who maintains "a well erected confidence." That Shakespeare's prologue was composed at the same time as the remainder of the play is supported by the parody of Mercury's description of Criticus in *Cynthia's Revels* (2.3.123–45), Alexander's description of Ajax (1.2.19–30), and the assemblage of verbal "echoes of Jonsonian devices" in the body of the play, analyzed by Abbie Findlay Potts in "*Cynthia's Revels, Poetaster*, and *Troilus and Cressida*." Potts concludes that in *Troilus and Cressida*, "Shakespeare carefully studied *Cynthia's Revels*, 1600, and the *Poetaster*, 1601," even though she overlooks the strongest evidence of all: its answer to Jonson's prologue.[28] Shakespeare's strategic rejoinders and casual borrowings from Jonson therefore indicate that *Troilus and Cressida* was not written before late spring 1601—the earliest date at which *Poetaster* can have been produced. Evidence suggesting that it was staged before the end of the year is found in the First Quarto of *Antonio and Mellida* and *2 Return from Parnassus*.

The prologue to *Troilus and Cressida* was imitated in the epilogue of *Antonio and Mellida* by 24 October 1601, at which time Marston's play, with several significant revisions, was registered for publication. At the conclusion of the First Quarto of *Antonio and Mellida*, entered in the Stationers' Register on 24 October 1601, an "Epilogus" apologizes for the play with the following echo-laden words: "*Gentlemen, though I remain an armed Epilogue, I stand not as a peremptory challenger of desert, either for him that composed the Comedy, or for us that acted it: but as a most submissive suppliant for both*" (1:63). This epilogue could not have been part of *Antonio and Mellida* in 1600, because it bears the indelible mark of two plays written in 1601—*Poetaster* and *Troilus and Cressida*.

In contrast to Jonson's "armed *Prologue*," the embodiment of confidence at the opening of *Poetaster*, Marston's "*armed Epilogue*" in *Antonio and Mellida* imitates Shakespeare's "prologue arm'd, but not in confidence / Of author's pen or actor's voice" (lines 23–24). We can be certain that the epilogue of *Antonio and Mellida* is a later addition because *Poetaster* (5.3.391–565) includes an elaborate series of linguistic parodies of its sequel, *Antonio's Revenge*.[29] Through his epilogue to *Antonio and Mellida*, Marston for the first time replied in print (and even perhaps on the stage) to Jonson's criticism of him in *Poetaster*, by imitating *Troilus and Cressida*. That Marston tinkered with *Antonio and Mellida* in 1601, after it had been already produced, to requite Jonson for current injuries is evident as well in another interpolated parody aimed at Jonson's refurbishment of *The Spanish Tragedy*, which Henslowe paid for on 25 September of the same year. Jonson's Hieronimo forces Bazardo to admit that he cannot "paint a doleful cry" (3.12a.122), while Marston's fool Balurdo asks another painter to limn him a belch: "paint me 'uh,' " he insists, "or nothing" (1:53).[30] Marston dismisses Jonsonian pathos, in the aftermath of the Poets' War, with a burp.

By the end of 1601, Shakespeare's parody of Jonson as Ajax in *Troilus and Cressida* had become the basis of Jonson's complaint in his apology for *Poetaster* that Shakespeare had "run in that vile line" and the boast by Kemp to Burbage in *2 Return from Parnassus* that their "fellow *Shakespeare*" had given Jonson "a purge that made him beray his credit" (see numbers 12 and 13 below). Ajax/Jonson's self-love and his torment by Thersites/Marston's railing, perfectly suited to gall him, constitute a powerful critique of Shakespeare's two contemporaries engaged in the Poets' War. I assume that Shakespeare inflected this satire with references to Jonson and Marston before he added the "little eyases" passage to *Hamlet*, where he provided an epilogue to the quarrel.

11. Jonson's "Apologetical Dialogue" added to *Poetaster* for only one performance (after *Satiromastix* and *Troilus*, but before 21 December 1601), when it was probably staged with Jonson himself at Blackfriars

Since the "*armed Epilogue*" of the revised *Antonio and Mellida* refers to the prologues of *Poetaster* and *Troilus and Cressida*, Jonson's and Shakespeare's comedies had to have been written before Marston's was registered on 24 October 1601. (See number 10 above.) By the end of the same year Jonson apologized for *Poetaster*. We know this because he tells us in his First Folio version of *Poetaster* that the

"Apologetical Dialogue" was originally to have appeared in the First Quarto, but had been suppressed "*by Authority*" and cut. Since he also states that it "*was only once spoken upon the stage*" (4:317), this performance took place before the quarto was registered on 21 December 1601. At that time, then, *Poetaster, Satiromastix,* and *Troilus and Cressida* had all been staged, and the anonymous author of *2 Return from Parnassus* was about to make his famous joke about Shakespeare's purge of Jonson. The dramatic context for this performance (probably with Jonson as the "Author") can then be precisely defined: the "Apologetical Dialogue" answers criticism of *Poetaster* in *Satiromastix* and *Troilus and Cressida* (in which one of a "better" nature ran "in that vile line").

12. Shakespeare's addition of the "little eyases" discussion (including 2.2.337–62, cut from Q2) to *Hamlet* (soon after *Poetaster, Satiromastix,* and *Troilus* had been staged in 1601), acted by the Chamberlain's Men at the Globe

This is Shakespeare's final commentary on what he here views as a War of the Theaters. It is an afterthought equivalent to Jonson's "Apologetical Dialogue," an overview of the just-concluded struggle. Since Shakespeare's passage alludes to the competing performances of *Poetaster* and *Satiromastix* in 1601, it was certainly written after *The Whipping of the Satyr,* referred to in the latter (see number 9 above), was registered on 14 August and before the end of the year, by which time the stage-quarrel was over.

But when was *Hamlet* first produced at the Globe? It probably premiered in 1600, after which it was followed by Marston's staging of *Antonio's Revenge* at Paul's to capitalize on Shakespeare's revival of revenge tragedy.[31] Marston's reference to himself as "the new poet *Mellidus*" in *Jack Drum*—while "Kemp's Morris" (from 11 February to 11 March 1600) was still news—situates *Antonio and Mellida*'s first performance early in the year.[32] *Antonio's Revenge,* the most thoroughly travestied play in *Poetaster,* was consequently staged after 11 March 1600 (when *Antonio and Mellida* was new) but before 25 September 1601 (by which time Jonson had attacked it at Blackfriars). During this period, Marston saw *Hamlet* at the Globe and was evidently so impressed with it that he darkened the plot and characters of his continuation of *Antonio and Mellida* (which already echoed *Romeo and Juliet*) to conform to its more ominous tone. In the Induction to *Antonio and Mellida,* for example, Marston suggests that Feliche will have a bigger role in the second part, but when *Antonio's Revenge* opens the character has just been executed.

The echoes of *Hamlet* in *Antonio's Revenge,* according to Marston's recent Cambridge editors, are "precisely the kind we should expect if Marston had seen Shakespeare's play, perhaps more than once, but not yet been able to read it," in contrast to "the more exact recollections of *Hamlet* in *The Malcontent* (1603)."[33] (The problem with this date for Marston's play, however, is that unless he picked up his "more exact recollections" from the corrupt First Quarto of 1603, *The Malcontent* had to have been staged the following year, when a more reliable printed version of Shakespeare's tragedy became available.)

W. Reavley Gair conceives of the productions of *Hamlet* at the Globe and *Antonio's Revenge* at Paul's as part of their collusion: "The two theaters may have agreed to co-operate on a play of a similar kind, written, however, from the different viewpoints of boy and adult actor, to form a united challenge to their common rival, the Children of the Chapel."[34] But the brilliant work of Donald McGinn, David Frost, and Harold Jenkins, who have copiously annotated the pattern of minor verbal echoes of *Hamlet* in *Antonio's Revenge*, strongly suggests Marston's indebtedness to Shakespeare.[35] We have come to understand (a) that Marston's drama often imitates Shakespeare's; (b) that *Antonio's Revenge*, an example of this ongoing process, combines verbal echoes not only of *Hamlet* but also of *Titus Andronicus* and *Richard III*; (c) that Marston continued to acknowledge *Hamlet* in *The Malcontent*; and (d) that his dependence on Shakespeare caused Jonson, in *Cynthia's Revels*, to accuse him of deriving his "best grace from common stages."

If I am right in arguing that between 1600 and 1601 Marston wrote, in sequence, *Antonio and Mellida*, *Jack Drum's Entertainment*, *Antonio's Revenge*, and *What You Will*, then both *Hamlet* and *Twelfth Night* were first staged before *What You Will*. The "little eyases" passage thus criticizes *Poetaster*, a play which, in turn, satirizes *Antonio's Revenge*, which imitates *Hamlet*. This dual position of *Hamlet* explains why it can be imitated by *Satiromastix*, as Fredson Bowers suggests, even though the "little eyases" passage must have included Dekker's play in its consideration of the "throwing about of brains" (2.2.358–59) between the Globe and Blackfriars.[36]

13. Production of the anonymous *2 Return from Parnassus* (Christmas Revels, 1601) by students at St. John's College, Cambridge

Leishman, in considering the date of *2 Return from Parnassus*, writes that "the statement on the first page of the Halliwell-Phillipps MS. that the play was 'acted in Sᵗ Johns College in Cambridge Anᵒ 1601' is confirmed both by the astronomical dialogue between Sir Raderick and Immerito (see note on line 1065) and by the fact that the latest contemporary allusions are all to events of 1601," especially to *Poetaster* and *Satiromastix*.[37] This must consequently have been a play written by a scholar at Cambridge for the Christmas Revels of that year. In late December 1601, the author knew of the final stage of the Poetomachia, how Horace/Jonson medicated Crispinus/Marston in *Poetaster* and Shakespeare shortly thereafter "purged" Jonson in *Troilus and Cressida*. By this time, Jonson had already, in his apology for *Poetaster*, lamented having been treated harshly by Shakespeare, and Shakespeare had summed up the stage-quarrel from his own perspective in the "little eyases" passage of *Hamlet*. Leishman makes only one exception to his dating: the play's prose prologue was probably added for a second performance in 1602/3.

Notes

PASSAGES FROM Shakespeare's plays, unless otherwise specified, are quoted from *The Riverside Shakespeare*, ed. G. Blakemore Evans, 2nd ed. (Boston: Houghton Mifflin, 1997). I have lightly modernized spelling and some punctuation for all non-Shakespearean early modern texts. Quotations from Jonson's writings, including the "Conversations with Drummond," are derived from *Ben Jonson*, eds. C. H. Herford and Percy Simpson, 11 vols. (Oxford: Clarendon, 1925–1952). Quotations from Marston's dramas are from *The Plays of John Marston*, ed. H. Harvey Wood, 3 vols. (London: Oliver and Boyd, 1934–1939). Since this edition does not assign line numbers, references are by volume and page. His nondramatic poetry is quoted from *The Poems of John Marston*, ed. Arnold Davenport (Liverpool: Liverpool University Press, 1961). Passages from Dekker's plays are from *The Dramatic Works of Thomas Dekker*, ed. Fredson Bowers, 4 vols. (Cambridge: Cambridge University Press, 1953–1961). All citations from these works will hereafter be referenced in the text.

Introduction: The Elizabethan Dramatists as Literary Critics

1. Richard Helgerson, *Self-Crowned Laureates: Spenser, Jonson, Milton and the Literary System* (Berkeley: University of California Press, 1983), 144.

2. Thomas M. Greene, "Ben Jonson and the Centered Self," *Studies in English Literature* 10 (1970): 325–48; and Jonathan Dollimore, *Radical Tragedy: Religion, Ideology, and Power in the Drama of Shakespeare and His Contemporaries* (Chicago: University of Chicago Press, 1984), 249.

3. What is most remarkable about Small's study, *The Stage-Quarrel Between Ben Jonson and the So-Called Poetasters* (1899; reprint, New York: AMS Press, 1966), is that, despite its mistakes and limitations, it explores the topicality of the Poets' War with unprecedented success. In this regard, Small shaped a master narrative that has been accepted by twentieth-century theater historians from E. K. Chambers to Anne Barton with little reservation. The scope of his achievement, however, is diminished by his failure to conceptualize the issues of literary theory beneath the controversy's topical veneer. According to Small, the "stage-quarrel" between Jonson on the one hand and Marston, Dekker, and Shakespeare on the other was an escalating war of wits that began when Marston attempted to praise Jonson as a character called Chrisoganus in *Histriomastix* but enraged him instead, prompting Jonson to mock his vocabulary in *Every Man Out of His Humour*. This led to a series of plays in which these two playwrights traded caricatures: (*Jack Drum's Entertainment, Cynthia's Revels, What You Will*, and *Poetaster*), before Dekker and Shakespeare offered parodies of Jonson in *Satiromastix* and *Troilus and Cressida*. Based on Small's model, I have extrapolated the following sequence:

	JONSON	MARSTON	DEKKER
Histriomastix	Chrisoganus		
Every Man Out		Clove	Orange
Jack Drum's Entertainment	Brabant Senior		
Cynthia's Revels	Criticus	Hedon	Anaides
What You Will	Lampatho Doria	Quadratus	
Poetaster	Horace	Crispinus	Demetrius
Satiromastix	Horace	Crispinus	Demetrius
Troilus and Cressida	Ajax	Thersites	

4. The argument of this book has been particularly influenced by David Bevington's survey of the Poetomachia in *Tudor Drama and Politics: A Critical Approach to Topical Meaning* (Cambridge: Harvard University Press, 1968); Oscar James Campbell's *Comicall Satyre and Shakespeare's* Troilus and Cressida (San Marino: The Huntington Library, 1970); W. David Kay's *Ben Jonson, Horace, and the Poetomachia* (Ph.D. diss., Princeton University, 1968) and "The Shaping of Ben Jonson's Career: A Reexamination of Facts and Problems," *Modern Philology* 67 (1970): 224–37; Cyrus Hoy's *Introductions, Notes, and Commentaries to Texts in* The Dramatic Works of Thomas Dekker, 4 vols. (Cambridge: Cambridge University Press, 1980); E. A. J. Honigmann's *Shakespeare's Impact on His Contemporaries* (Totowa, N.J.: Barnes and Noble, 1982); and Helgerson's *Self-Crowned Laureates*.

5. Bevington, *Tudor Drama and Politics*, 279.

6. Frederick Fleay, *A Chronicle History of the London Stage: 1559–1642* (London: Reeves and Turner, 1890), 119.

7. See Josiah H. Penniman, *The War of the Theatres* (Boston: Ginn, 1897); and Small, *The Stage-Quarrel Between Ben Jonson and the So-Called Poetasters*.

8. Sydney Musgrove, *Shakespeare and Jonson* (Auckland: Pilgrim Press, 1957), 7; and John J. Enck, "The Peace of the the the Poetomachia," *PMLA* 77 (1962): 386.

Gabriele Bernhard Jackson, *Vision and Judgment in Ben Jonson's Drama* (New Haven: Yale University Press, 1984), 29*n*, treats such analysis as irrelevant. "The question of the identification of Crispinus and Demetrius as Marston and Dekker and of Horace as Jonson along with all the subsidiary identifications which may or may not be valid," she writes, "are omitted as irrelevant to the subject under discussion." As a sop, she refers readers to Penniman and Small.

Enck's formalism is rooted in the early twentieth-century concentration on the so-called intrinsic qualities of literature instead of its "extraneous" context. This overreaction to the excesses of nineteenth-century biographical speculation surfaces in the work of Oscar James Campbell, "The Dramatic Construction of *Poetaster*," *Huntington Library Bulletin* 9 (1936): 37–62; and Ernest William Talbert, "The Purpose and Technique of Jonson's *Poetaster*," *Studies in Philology* 42 (1945): 225–52. Any study of the Poets' War must consider: (1) the relation of literature to the personal and cultural conditions that produce it; (2) the intertextual patterns of imitation and parody that fuse separate works, causing their mutual dependence on each other for completion; and (3) the process of revision that yields variant texts irreducible to a single archetype.

9. Frederick Fleay in *A Chronicle History of the Life and Work of William Shakespeare* (London: John C. Nimmo, 1886) refers to this controversy as the "war of the theaters" (42) and as the "stage quarrel" (138); in *A Biographical Chronicle of the English Drama, 1559–1642*, 2 vols. (London: Reeves and Turner, 1891), 2:69, he uses a compromise formation and writes of the "three years' stage war between Jonson and Marston." By the time Penniman wrote *The War of the Theatres* (1897), this phrase had become common parlance. There is nothing inherently misleading about Small's reference to the "Poetomachia" as a "stage-quarrel"— once we recognize that this term is a conflation based on Jonson's confession to Drummond in 1619 that he had "quarrels with Marston" resulting from Marston's having "represented him in the stage."

10. Alfred Harbage in *Shakespeare and the Rival Traditions* (New York: Macmillan, 1952) tends to stereotype the audience of the private theaters as aristocratic degenerates, a gang of skeptical libertines. The adults' audience was, in this view, healthy, optimistic, and sincere, and the children's following was perverse, negative, and duplicitous. The popular theater was as well-adjusted as its democratic constituency and the private theater as twisted as the privileged class that patronized it. Current scholarship has revised this assessment by showing that members of the Inns of Court, who are often associated with the private theaters, demonstrated a wider range of tastes. Gray's Inn, for instance, sponsored Francis Bacon's masque for Queen Elizabeth and encouraged the philosophical tradition he advocated.

Harbage's social history of the theater has been challenged by Ann Jennalie Cook in *The Privileged Playgoers of Shakespeare's London, 1576–1642* (Princeton: Princeton University Press, 1981). The question that Cook asks goes to the heart of his theory—who was attending theatrical performances in London on weekdays at two o'clock in the afternoon? Much of Shakespeare's audience must have come from a leisure class. Cook concludes that "the privileged represented the most consistent patrons of the drama, no matter where or when it was performed." The majority of gentlemen and would-be gentlemen thus "made it possible for them to dominate the audience of the huge public theatres as well as the small private playhouses" (273 and 272). But Martin Butler, *Theatre and Crisis, 1632–1642* (Cambridge: Cambridge University Press, 1984), in Appendix II, "Shakespeare's Unprivileged Playgoers 1576–1642," counters Cook's argument by pointing to the extensive evidence indicating that the public theaters had a mixed audience. The privileged were in attendance, but to assume that only this class (along with a small group of cutpurses and prostitutes) frequented the public theaters is wrong. It was against this mixed audience that the private theaters could offer, for a higher fee, to exclude some of the underclass. In doing so they created the aura of being elite. The higher tariff they imposed on their customers eliminated just enough of the "garlic-breathed stinkards" to be trumpeted for its snob appeal, even though the difference between the two audiences would have been more quantitative than qualitative in this respect. This de facto exclusion of the unprivileged was used as a premise to praise and bond (indeed to create) its "fashionable" audience.

The distinction between the outdoor and indoor theaters as "public" and "private" was based on a legal fiction used to allow the children to perform within London. Playhouses erected for the purpose of staging public performances were banished to the suburbs, and in 1599 the Chamberlain's Men exchanged one suburb for another, moving from the Theater and Curtain, in Shoreditch, half a mile outside the Bishopsgate entrance, northeast of the city, to the Globe in Southwark, centrally across the Thames. The theatrical entrepreneurs who backed the revived child acting companies at Paul's and Blackfriars circumvented the law by maintaining that their performances were actually "private" dress rehearsals for later presentations at court, although they charged a fee for admission that was at least double that of their competitors in the suburbs. This difference—a point of pride—could also be strategically enlisted, when necessary, to stigmatize the adult companies.

11. Gregory Bateson, *Steps to an Ecology of Mind* (New York: Ballantine, 1972), 182.

12. See the Chronological Appendix for the analysis behind my dating of the Poets' War plays.

13. Herbert Berry, *Shakespeare's Playhouses* (New York: AMS Press, 1987), 121, states that "we have no reviews of the thousands of productions that passed on the stages of Shakespeare's playhouses," and concludes that "this silence about how plays were played and received is one of the most important ways in which our understanding of drama in Elizabethan, Jacobean, and Caroline times is sadly inferior to our understanding of drama in later times." But we have yet fully to examine the variety of Elizabethan criticism.

14. George Chapman, *All Fools*, ed. Frank Manley (Lincoln: University of Nebraska Press, 1968), lines 13–19.

15. Helgerson, *Self-Crowned Laureates*, 150; and Stephen Orgel, "What is a Text?" in *Staging the Renaissance: Reinterpretations of Elizabethan and Jacobean Drama*, eds. David Scott Kastan and Peter Stallybrass (New York: Routledge, 1991), 84, 87.

16. See Jeffrey Masten, "Playwrighting: Authorship and Collaboration," in *A New History of Early English Drama*, eds. John D. Cox and David Scott Kastan (New York: Columbia University Press, 1997), 357–82, and Leah S. Marcus, *Puzzling Shakespeare: Local Reading and Its Discontents* (Berkeley: University of California Press, 1988), 39, in which she writes of Shakespeare's theatrical career as occurring during a period "before the drama had been institutionalized as a branch of 'authored literature.' "

17. Harold Ogden White, *Plagiarism and Imitation During the English Renaissance: A Study in Critical Distinctions* (Cambridge: Harvard University Press, 1935), 201.

18. Joseph Loewenstein, "Plays Agonistic and Competitive: The Textual Approach to Elsinore," *Renaissance Drama* 19 (1988): 80.

19. Andrew Gurr, *Playgoing in Shakespeare's London* (Cambridge: Cambridge University Press, 1987), 113.

20. The estimate is proposed by Andrew Gurr, *The Shakespearean Stage 1574–1642*, 3rd ed. (Cambridge: Cambridge University Press, 1992), 213.

21. See Robert Weimann, *Shakespeare and the Popular Tradition in the Theater* (Baltimore: Johns Hopkins University Press, 1978); Annabel Patterson, *Shakespeare and the Popular Voice* (Oxford: Basil Blackwell, 1989); and Michael Bristol, *Carnival and Theater: Plebeian Culture and the Structure of Authority in Renaissance England* (London: Methuen, 1985).

22. Q1 *Hamlet* (sig. E3^r), quoted from *Shakespeare's Plays in Quarto*, eds. Michael J. B. Allen and Kenneth Muir (Berkeley: University of California Press, 1981).

23. Steven Mullaney, *The Place of the Stage: License, Play, and Power in Renaissance England* (Chicago: University of Chicago Press, 1988), 52, 54.

24. Robert C. Evans, *Ben Jonson and the Poetics of Patronage* (Lewisburg, Penn.: Bucknell University Press, 1989), 9–10.

25. Franco Moretti, *Signs Taken for Wonders* (London: Verso, 1983; rev. 1988), 42.

26. Robert Weimann, *Authority and Representation in Early Modern Discourse* (Baltimore: Johns Hopkins University Press, 1996), 67, 1.

27. See Phyllis Rackin, *Stages of History: Shakespeare's English Chronicles* (Ithaca: Cornell University Press, 1990).

1. Shakespeare's Purge of Jonson: The Theatrical Context of *Troilus and Cressida*

1. Thomas Fuller, *The History of the Worthies of England* (London: Printed by J. G. W. L. and W. C., 1662), 126.

2. William Gifford, introduction to *The Works of Jonson*, 2 vols. (London: G. and W. Nichol, etc., 1816), 1:lxv–lxvi.

3. I. A. Shapiro, "The 'Mermaid Club,' " *Modern Language Review* 45 (1950): 6–17. See also S. Schoenbaum, "Gifford and the Mermaid Club," in *Shakespeare's Lives* (Oxford: Clarendon, 1970), 294–96. Shapiro admits that Shakespeare might have known the Mermaid Tavern and its owner William Johnson, as Leslie Hotson indicates in "Shakespeare and Mine Host of the Mermaid" in *Shakespeare's Sonnets Dated and Other Essays* (London: R. Hart-Davis, 1949), 76–88, but proves that Gifford manufactured a Shakespearean myth through a loose conflation of evidence and imagination. Gifford relied on two pieces of evidence. The first is Thomas Coryate's letter from Ajmere, India (1615), to "the High Seneschal of the right Worshipful Fraternity of Sirenaical Gentlemen, that meet the first Friday of every Month, at the sign of the Mermaid," which sends regards to Ben Jonson and Inigo Jones, among others, but does not mention Shakespeare. Gifford's second source is a verse letter to Ben Jonson, sometimes attributed to Francis Beaumont, that recalls: "What things have we seen, / Done at the Mermaid! heard words that have been / So nimble, and so full of subtle flame." Even though it is true that Jonson can be linked to a series of meetings at various taverns like the Mermaid and later the Apollo from 1613 onward, Shapiro concludes, there is "a total lack of evidence" for attendance by Shakespeare, who was probably back in Stratford at this time, or by Ralegh, who was imprisoned.

4. Schoenbaum, *Shakespeare's Lives*, 95, and "Shakespeare and Jonson: Fact and Myth," *The Elizabethan Theatre II*, ed. David Galloway (New York: Macmillan, 1970), 5. Gary Taylor, *Reinventing Shakespeare* (Oxford: Oxford University Press, 1989), 3–4. M. C. Bradbrook, *Shakespeare: The Poet in His World* (New York: Columbia University Press, 1978), 148–49, writes that Jonson's "exchanges with Shakespeare must remain part of the legend only." Anne Barton, *Ben Jonson, Dramatist* (Cambridge: Cambridge University Press, 1984), 89, gives a more tentative response, however, when she admits that Shakespeare might have purged Jonson, but concludes that if "he was at last impelled, uncharacteristically, to give Jonson a taste of his own medicine, the rebuke cannot now be traced. It must, in any case, have constituted a small part of what clearly became a concentrated and angry attack on the author of *Poetaster*."

5. Anonymous, *2 Return from Parnassus*, lines 1769–73, in *The Three Parnassus Plays (1598–1601)*, ed. J. B. Leishman (London: Ivor Nicholson & Watson, 1949), 337.

6. Leishman, *The Three Parnassus Plays*, 370, presents this argument in his appendix on "The Purge." The position was tentatively advanced by Josiah H. Penniman in *The War of the Theatres* (Boston: Ginn, 1897), 149, who writes that *Satiromastix* "was by Shakespeare's company at Shakespeare's theatre, and therein may have consisted the giving of the 'purge' to Jonson by Shakespeare." Leishman's reiteration gave the theory wide credence and is usually reproduced without further substantiation by those who credit it, such as Bradbrook, *Shakespeare: The Poet in*

His World, 136, and Sydney Musgrove, *Shakespeare and Jonson* (Auckland: Pilgrim Press, 1957), 7, who agrees that "It is likely enough that student gossip, inaccurate as ever, has got so confused among the fogs of the literary backstairs that it attributed to Shakespeare some work in which he had no share." Even though Robert Kimbrough, *Shakespeare's* Troilus and Cressida *and Its Setting* (Cambridge: Harvard University Press, 1964), 20, writes that "it is obvious that Shakespeare was having fun at Jonson's expense" (in *Troilus and Cressida*), he believes that the reference in *2 Return from Parnassus* is "clearly" to *Satiromastix*. Schoenbaum, "Shakespeare and Jonson: Fact and Myth," 5, echoes that it was "Dekker, not Shakespeare, [who] administered a purge to Jonson in *Satiromastix*; perhaps, as it is suggested by J. B. Leishman . . . the anonymous university playwright thought of the Globe and the Chamberlain's Men as Shakespeare's theatre and Shakespeare's company: guilt by association. Perhaps he was simply confused. . . ." But Musgrove, Kimbrough, and Schoenbaum paraphrase the Penniman-Leishman hypothesis without weighing the evidence. Furthermore, Schoenbaum's remark that Jonson was literally purged in *Satiromastix* is not true. Horace/Jonson is threatened with a purge, but none is given. Among adherents to Leishman's position, only Marjorie L. Reyburn, "New Facts and Theories about the Parnassus Plays," *PMLA* 74 (1959): 325–35, attempts further to substantiate his thesis. Reyburn, 325, desires "by means of previously unused internal evidence to establish beyond any possibility of doubt J. B. Leishman's well-reasoned, but inconclusive identification." Her strategy is to show that the student author of *2 Return from Parnassus* is familiar with *Satiromastix*, which therefore must be alluded to in the former's crucial description of Shakespeare's purging of Jonson. But her evidence does not exclude the possibility that the author of *2 Return from Parnassus* also knew of Shakespeare's involvement in the quarrel. The student author's acquaintance with contemporary drama is, as Leishman notes, up to date and far ranging.

7. Everard Guilpin, *Skialetheia, or A Shadow of Truth, in Certain Epigrams and Satires*, ed. D. Allen Carroll (Chapel Hill: University of North Carolina Press, 1974), 47–48. Both Carroll (118) and George L. Geckle, *John Marston's Drama: Themes, Images, Sources* (Rutherford, N.J.: Fairleigh Dickinson University Press, 1980), 34 and 48n, list classical precedents for the name that is here applied to Jonson.

8. As E. K. Chambers points out in *William Shakespeare: A Study of Facts and Problems*, 2 vols. (Oxford: Clarendon, 1930), 2:23–24, the grant of this coat of arms was made in 1596, and such devices usually bore "the Invention or Conceit of the Bearer," so that the "word" was probably of Shakespeare's own devising. Musgrove, *Shakespeare and Jonson*, describes this allusion to Shakespeare as "a friendly pulling of the genteel leg, clear enough to those in the know but sufficiently concealed behind the technical details of the coat itself which bears no resemblance to Shakespeare's, not to be a public mockery" (4).

9. Anne Barton, "Shakespeare and Jonson," in *Shakespeare, Man of the Theater: Proceedings of the Second Congress of the International Shakespeare Association, 1981*, eds. Kenneth Muir, Jay Halio, and D. J. Palmer (Newark: University of Delaware

Press, 1983), 161. Barton, 160, also identifies another point of rivalry in noting how Jonson "allows one of his characters [Fungoso] to describe another as 'a kinsman to Justice Silence,' in full consciousness of the very different comic kingdom that reference will conjure up" (5.2.22).

10. This revision is mentioned in passing by Schoenbaum, "Shakespeare and Jonson: Fact and Myth," who suggests that perhaps "Shakespeare heeded his friend's advice and deleted—not an absurdity, surely—but a penetrating paradox" (4). See also J. Dover Wilson, "Ben Jonson and *Julius Caesar*," *Shakespeare Survey* 2 (1949): 36–43. For a vindication of the witty paradox of Shakespeare's imputed original line, see G. A. Starr, "Caesar's Just Cause," *Shakespeare Quarterly* 17 (1966): 77–79.

11. Morse Allen, *The Satire of John Marston* (Columbus, Ohio: F. J. Heer, 1920), 36.

12. For a list of these words and their sources, see chapter 8, note 20.

13. Stephen Greenblatt, *Shakespearean Negotiations* (Berkeley: University of California Press, 1988), 4.

14. The contention that the character Ajax functions as the purge mentioned in *2 Return from Parnassus* has a long history, during which the case has never been adequately presented. In *A Chronicle History of the Life and Work of William Shakespeare* (London: John C. Nimmo, 1886), 36, Frederick Fleay claims that Ajax is Jonson and Dekker is Thersites. Later he adds the groundless assumption that Chapman is Achilles and Shakespeare, Hector (221). However, in *A Biographical Chronicle of the English Drama, 1559–1642*, 2 vols. (London: Reeves and Turner, 1891), 1:366, he again speculates that Ajax is Jonson, but now declares that Thersites is Marston, not Dekker. Then in the second volume of this study, published in the same year, he once more changes his mind. Thersites is still Marston (as in the first part), but now Ajax is Dekker and Achilles has become Jonson (2:189). Another early commentator on this problem, who might have had some influence on Fleay, was Robert Cartwright, *Shakespeare and Jonson: Dramatic Versus Wit-Combats* (London: J. R. Smith, 1862), who first compared the Prologues of *Troilus and Cressida* and *Poetaster* (12) and speculated that Thersites provided a character study of Jonson (13).

Roscoe Addison Small, *The Stage-Quarrel Between ben Jonson and the So-Called Poetasters* (1899; reprint, New York: AMS Press, 1966), 170, subsequently picked up the identification of Ajax with Jonson, writing that it "is certain that, as Fleay has suggested, the description applies exactly to Jonson" and that "the character of Ajax is at least in part a personal hit at Jonson." C. H. Herford and Percy Simpson in *Ben Jonson*, 11 vols. (Oxford: Clarendon, 1925–1952), 1:28, and William Elton, "Shakespeare's Portrait of Ajax in *Troilus and Cressida*," *PMLA* 63 (1948): 744–48, argue this very point. E. K. Chambers at first rejected the identification in *The Elizabethan Stage*, 4 vols. (Oxford: Clarendon, 1923), 4:40, where he repeats Penniman's theory. He also conjectures with uncharacteristic abandon that if Penniman is incorrect, Shakespeare might have "acted Horace/Jonson in *Satiro-*

mastix." In *William Shakespeare*, 1:72, he again states that the purge was "probably" *Satiromastix*, but acknowledges in an overview of *Henry V, The Merry Wives of Windsor, As You Like It*, and *Troilus and Cressida* that "there may be glances at Jonson in all of these." Here he admits that the purge has "often been taken to be the description of Ajax in *Troilus and Cressida*, 1.2.19, which seems unnecessarily elaborate for its place, refers to 'humours,' and has not much relation to the character of Ajax as depicted in the play" and concludes that all, "except *Troilus and Cressida*, are too early in date, since the writer of *3 Parnassus* clearly regarded the 'purge' as an answer to the 'pill.' " More recently, E.A.J. Honigmann, *Shakespeare's Impact on His Contemporaries* (Totowa, N.J.: Barnes and Noble, 1982), 103, supports the theory that Shakespeare purged Jonson in *Troilus and Cressida* in his brief treatment of "The War of the Theatres," and Park Honan, *Shakespeare: A Life* (Oxford: Oxford University Press, 1998), 278, concurs that the poet "jokingly included a few of Jonson's traits as Ajax of *Troilus and Cressida*."

15. Elton, "Shakespeare's Portrait of Ajax in *Troilus and Cressida*," 745.

16. *The Works of Thomas Nashe*, ed. Ronald B. McKerrow, 5 vols. (London: Sidgwick and Jackson, 1910), 3:38 and 3:11. In *Have with You to Saffron-Walden*, Nashe writes of Harvey, "with his gown cast off, untrussing, and ready to beray himself." He had previously discussed "Monsier Ajaxes of excremental conceits and stinking kennel-raked up invention."

17. Clifford Leech, "The Incredibility of Jonsonian Comedy," in *A Celebration of Ben Jonson*, eds. William Blissett, Julian Patrick, and R. W. Van Fossen (Toronto: University of Toronto Press, 1973), 5.

18. For a general treatment of this topic, see Mary Claire Randolph, "The Medical Concept in English Renaissance Satire," *Studies in Philology* 38 (1941): 125–57. A specific application to Jonson is outlined in John Thatcher French, "Ben Jonson: His Aesthetic of Relief," *Texas Studies in Literature and Language* 10 (1968): 161–75. Discussing the cultural background for this practice, Gail Kern Paster, "Purgation as the Allure of Mastery: Early Modern Medicine and the Technology of the Self," in *Material London, ca. 1600*, ed. Lena Cowen Orlin (Philadelphia: University of Pennsylvania Press, 2000), 198, observes that "the extent to which internal medicine in the early modern period relied on the use of purgatives is almost astonishing."

19. John Weever, Preface to *The Whipping of the Satyr*, in *The Whipper Pamphlets*, ed. Arnold Davenport (Liverpool: Liverpool University Press, 1951), 6–7.

20. Edward C. Baldwin, "Ben Jonson's Indebtedness to the Greek Character Sketch," *Modern Language Notes* 16 (1901): 194, writes that Jonson recognized the kinship between drama and the character sketch because of "the analytic and expository quality of his mind, which led him to be interested more in the type than in the individual, and more in the exhibition than in the development of character." And John J. Enck, "The Peace of the Poetomachia," *PMLA* 77 (1962): 389, explains that by "appropriating another classical model for English Jonson consolidated his formulae for portraiture."

21. J. Dover Wilson, "Ben Jonson and *Julius Caesar*," 36, writes that although it expresses a "commonplace of the age," nevertheless, "the wording of the eulogy on Crites is so similar to that of Antony's on Brutus, that an echo can hardly be questioned." Wilson further adds that Drayton combined both Shakespeare's and Jonson's wording in praising Mortimer in the 1603 edition of *The Baron's War*:

> He was a man, then boldly dare to say,
> In whose rich soul the virtues well did suit,
> In whom, so mixed, the elements all lay
> That none to one could sovereignty impute,
> As all did govern, yet all did obey,
> He of a temper was so absolute
> As that it seemed, when Nature him began,
> She meant to show all that might be in man.

Here, Wilson concludes, lines 4 and 5 derive from Jonson's "without emulation of precedency," while "so mixed, the elements," a formulation that Jonson does not use, recalls Shakespeare's phrasing. These lines are not in Drayton's original *Mortimeriados* (1596), so he added them sometime between its original and revised publication. Drayton represents a contemporary reader, who, like Shakespeare in *Troilus and Cressida*, associated the praise of Criticus in *Cynthia's Revels* with that bestowed on Brutus in *Julius Caesar*.

22. Chambers, *William Shakespeare*, 1:72; Kenneth Muir, ed., *Troilus and Cressida*, (Oxford: Clarendon, 1982), 6. Enck, "The Peace of the Poetomachia," 391, admits that it is outlined "gratuitously, for the scene itself and his later traits."

23. This parody contains echoes of what would become *The Underwood* XXV ("An Ode to James, earl of Desmond, writ in Queen Elizabeth's time, since lost, and recovered"). Lines 8–13 of the "Ode" read: "*Cynthius*, I apply / My bolder numbers to thy golden *Lyre*: / O, then inspire / Thy Priest in this strange rapture; heat my brain / With *Delphic* fire: / That I may sing my thoughts, in some unvulgar strain." Cyrus Hoy, *Introductions, Notes, and Commentaries to Texts in* The Dramatic Works of Thomas Dekker, 4. vols. (Cambridge: Cambridge University Press, 1980), 1:62, points out that Jonson's holograph manuscript of the "Ode," preserved in the library of Christ Church, Oxford (lines 1–23 of which are reproduced in Herford and Simpson's *Ben Jonson* [8:178]), is even closer to the version Dekker had seen in manuscript.

24. Mary Edmond, "Pembroke's Men," *The Review of English Studies* 25 (1974): 129–36, shows that Jonson joined the Tylers and Bricklayers' Company in June 1595 and made payments of his accumulated fees in June and October 1596, April 1599, July 1601, November 1602, and May 1611. Affiliation with this guild, which had its advantages, is reflected in his concept of writing as a form of manual labor. Jonson translated Horace's *Art of Poetry*, and in *Discoveries* he maintains its estimation that "things wrote with labour . . . will last" (8:638) and cau-

tions that a novice's writing should be encouraged, "no matter how slow the style be at first, so it be labour'd and accurate" (8:615). He also informed Drummond that he first wrote his poetry out in prose, a technique that Camden had taught him (1:143), which certainly would have extended the time necessary for its production. "If there was any fault in his language," John Dryden writes of Jonson in *An Essay of Dramatic Poesy* (1668), " 'twas, that he weaved it too closely and laboriously." See *John Dryden*, ed. Keith Walker (Oxford: Oxford University Press, 1987), 112.

25. Quoted from John Davies's *Wit's Bedlam* (London, 1617), sigs. K2^{r-v}.

26. John Davies of Hereford, "Paper's Complaint," lines 29–46, in *The Scourge of Folly* (London, 1611?), 231. Davies's coupling of Jonson and Shakespeare in this and the succeeding passage imitates *2 Return from Parnassus* in evoking not only the purge but also the scene in which Ingenioso and Judicio analyze a list of contemporary writers that links Jonson and Shakespeare (lines 292–304), in Leishman's edition of *The Three Parnassus Plays*, 242–43. Both passages commend the style but censure the content of *Venus and Adonis*.

27. "Paper's Complaint," lines 141–48, and his tribute to Shakespeare are from Davies, *The Scourge of Folly*, 234 and 76–77. See also Davies's comments on *Poetaster* and *Satiromastix* in *Wit's Pilgrimage* (1610?), quoted in the epigraph to chapter 8.

28. "On Shakespeare," lines 9–10, in *John Milton, The Complete Poems and Major Prose*, ed. Merritt Hughes (Indianapolis: Bobbs-Merrill, 1957).

29. Quoted from S. Schoenbaum, *William Shakespeare: A Documentary Life* (New York: Oxford University Press, 1975), 206. The metaphoric elephant that Shakespeare evokes was recalled much later, as Herford and Simpson point out (*Ben Jonson* 1:186), in Jasper Mayne's tribute "To the Memory of Ben Jonson" in *Jonson Virbius* (1638): "Scorn then their censures, who gav't out, *thy Wit* / As long upon a *Comoedie* did sit / As *Elephants* bring forth."

30. "Confidence" was a key attribute of Jonson's spokesmen, and although Shakespeare reacts to the Prologue of *Poetaster*, he probably knew of other examples of this formula in *Every Man Out* ("After the Second Sounding," line 222), *Cynthia's Revels* (3.2.13–15), and *Poetaster* (5.3.60).

31. Alfred Harbage, *Shakespeare and the Rival Traditions* (New York: Macmillan, 1952), 116 and 118.

32. For an account of this incident, see C. H. Herford and Percy Simpson's *Ben Jonson*, 11 vols. (Oxford: Clarendon, 1925–1952), 1:18–19. A letter from Philip Henslowe to Edward Alleyn on 26 September 1598 notes with obvious derision that "I have lost one of my company . . . slain . . . by the hands of Benjamin Jonson bricklayer," in *Henslowe's Diary*, eds. R. A. Foakes and R. T. Rickert (Cambridge: Cambridge University Press, 1961), 286. Spencer, who had been imprisoned with Jonson during the *Isle of Dogs* fiasco, had previously killed one Feeke in an altercation on 3 December 1596.

33. Honigmann, *Shakespeare's Impact on His Contemporaries*, 103.

34. Dekker's later work with Jonson on the coronation speeches for James I is cited by Chambers, *The Elizabethan Stage*, 3:290. In his published version of *The Magnificent Entertainment: Given to King James* (1604), Dekker again mocks Jonson's pedantry. See *Ben Jonson: The Critical Heritage, 1599–1798*, ed. D. H. Craig (London: Routledge, 1990), 91–92. Marston dedicated the first quarto of *The Malcontent* (1604) to "*Beniamino Ionsonio, Poetae Elegantissimo Gravissimo, Amico Suo Candido et Cordato*" (1:138). They would, however, become estranged soon after as a result of the suppression of *Eastward Ho*.

2. Jonson on Shakespeare: Criticism as Self-Creation

1. G. K. Hunter, "English Folly and Italian Vice: The Moral Landscape of John Marston," in *Jacobean Theatre*, eds. John Russell Brown and Bernard Harris (New York: Capricorn, 1967), 85.

2. Anne Barton, *Ben Jonson, Dramatist* (Cambridge: Cambridge University Press, 1984), x. Percy Allen, *Shakespeare, Jonson, and Wilkins as Borrowers* (London: Cecil Palmer, 1928), 45, had earlier noted that "Jonson's first attempts at drama probably found him, temporarily, under Shakespeare's influence among the Romantics. . . . Romanticism, however, could not hold Jonson for long. Eager acquisition and absorption of classical learning, working upon an intensely satiric and rationalistic temperament—together, no doubt, with a tinge of native jealousy—drew him swiftly, and permanently, away from Shakespeare and his fellow romantics."

3. Harold Bloom, *The Anxiety of Influence, A Theory of Poetry* (New York: Oxford University Press, 1973), 13.

4. W. David Kay, "The Shaping of Ben Jonson's Career: A Reexamination of Facts and Problems," *Modern Philology* 68 (1970): 231. See also his discussion of *Every Man Out* in *Ben Jonson: A Literary Life* (New York: St. Martin's, 1995), 43–62.

5. John Gordon Sweeney III, *Jonson and the Psychology of the Public Theater: To Coin the Spirit, Spend the Soul* (Princeton: Princeton University Press, 1985), 18, 34. Sweeney writes that through comical satire Jonson "asks us to participate in significant theater, theater that promises self-knowledge and realizes the instructive potential of fiction" (9).

6. Oscar James Campbell, *Comicall Satyre and Shakespeare's* Troilus and Cressida (San Marino: The Huntington Library, 1970), 54–81.

7. See *Ben Jonson*, eds. C. H. Herford and Percy Simpson, 11 vols. (Oxford: Clarendon, 1925–1952), 3:410–11, for the difficulty of dating the third quarto, and 3:599–600, 602–3, and 9:185–86 for his alternative endings.

8. Barton, *Ben Jonson, Dramatist*, 44.

9. Elizabeth Woodbridge, *Studies in Jonson's Comedies* (1898; reprint, New York: Gordian Press, 1966), 29.

10. Robert Ornstein, "Shakespearian and Jonsonian Comedy," *Shakespeare Survey* 22 (1969): 43.

11. Quoted from the introduction to *Every Man in His Humor*, ed. Gabriele Bernhard Jackson (New Haven: Yale University Press, 1969), 2.

12. Barton, *Ben Jonson, Dramatist*, 47.

13. These concluding purges assume a mechanical regularity after Saviolina, a lady of the court, is tricked into accepting the country boor Sogliardo as a true gentleman and is consequently derided "out of her humour" (5.2.130). Shift, who had passed himself off as a fearless highwayman, is then forced by Puntarvolo to admit that he only pretended to be brave to "get my self a name, and be counted a tall man" (5.3.66–67). This confession, in turn, destroys Sogliardo's naive confidence in him. "Here," observes Macilente, "were a couple unexpectedly dishumour'd" (5.3.76). Macilente subsequently poisons Puntarvolo's dog, curing him of his excessive natural affection, and gleefully notes: "Puntarvolo and his dog are both out of humour" (5.3.77–78). Then, when Carlo Buffone mocks Puntarvolo, the distraught knight turns on him, seals his mouth with wax, and demands, "Now, are you out of your humour, sir?" (5.6.86). Fungoso, the parasitical man of mode who imitates the conspicuous self-display of Fastidious Brisk, is the next character to be purged, and after being threatened with arrest for debt, he bluntly renounces his obsession in familiar language: "Nay, I am out of those humours now" (5.9.45). Macilente then arranges for the doting husband Delirio to view his wife Fallace's infidelity with Brisk, a sight that opens his eyes to the absurdity of his fawning solicitude and exposes the passion of his wife and her lover. This crescendo of climaxes ends with a political epiphany, as Macilente, who has masterminded many of the play's satiric "devices," unexpectedly enters the presence of Queen Elizabeth and is himself purged of envy.

14. For a general explication of this phenomenon, see Ernest B. Gilman's *The Curious Perspective: Literary and Pictorial Wit in the Seventeenth Century* (New Haven: Yale University Press, 1978).

15. Stephen Orgel, "Making Greatness Familiar," in *Pageantry in the Shakespearean Theater*, ed. David M. Bergeron (Athens: University of Georgia Press, 1985), 23. David Scott Kastan, "Proud Majesty Made a Subject: Shakespeare and the Spectacle of Rule," *Shakespeare Quarterly* 37 (1986): 460.

16. John J. Enck, "The Peace of the Poetomachia," *PMLA* 77 (1962): 388.

17. Walter Cohen, *Drama of a Nation: Public Theater in Renaissance England and Spain* (Ithaca: Cornell University Press, 1985), 282.

18. L. C. Knights, "Ben Jonson: Public Attitudes and Social Poetry," in *A Celebration of Ben Jonson*, eds. William Blissett, Julian Patrick, and R. W. Van Fossen (Toronto: University of Toronto Press, 1973), 171.

19. Quoted from Russ McDonald, *Shakespeare & Jonson/Jonson & Shakespeare* (Lincoln: University of Nebraska Press, 1988), 1.

20. Jonson repeatedly uses the veiled plural when discussing specific problems with Shakespeare's work. His apology for *Poetaster* similarly laments Shakespeare's composition of *Troilus and Cressida* by stating that he is sorry that, among the

players, "Some better natures" were "drawn / To run in that vile line" (lines 150–52).

21. Barton, *Ben Jonson, Dramatist*, 160, and *The Diary of John Manningham of the Middle Temple 1602–1603*, ed. Robert Parker Sorlien (Hanover, N.H.: The University of New England Press, 1976), 48.

22. John J. Enck, *Jonson and the Comic Truth* (Madison: University of Wisconsin Press, 1966), 224–25.

23. Sir Philip Sidney, *An Apology for Poetry*, ed. Forrest G. Robinson (Indianapolis: Bobbs-Merrill, 1970), 44. Bernard Weinberg, *A History of Literary Criticism in the Italian Renaissance*, 2 vols. (Chicago: University of Chicago Press, 1961), 2:737. Henry L. Snuggs, "The Source of Jonson's Definition of Comedy," *Modern Language Notes* 65 (1950): 543–44, traces Jonson's passage to the fourth book of Minturno's *De Poeta* (Venice, 1559), 280–81, devoted to comedy, where in a marginal gloss on page 280 the question "*Quid sit Comoedia?*" is answered:

> . . . *quid ipso Comoedia sit, quem ego instituo poetam, is facilè perspexerit, sive Ciceronem secuti definiamus illam esse imitationem vitae, speculum consuetudinis, imaginem veritatis . . . non gravem, sed certè iucundam, atque ridiculam, et quidem ad correctionem vitae accommodatam.*

Snuggs admits that Jonson could have seen this definition, attributed to Cicero by Donatus, in a variety of sources. "It appears in nearly all, if not all, sixteenth-century editions of Terence," he continues; "it must have been in the Terence which Jonson presumably read at Westminster School. The definition, moreover, is often quoted by Renaissance writers." But, he concludes, "Jonson not only took the Ciceronian definition but also translated literally part of Minturno's context and paraphrased another part. He lifted the marginal gloss without translation." Matthew Steggle, "Jonson's *Every Man Out* and Commentators on Terence," *Notes and Queries* 242 (1997): 525–26, similarly links the names Cordatus and Asper to prominent interpreters of the Latin playwright.

24. See George Parfitt, "Jonson and Classicism" in *Ben Jonson: Public Poet and Private Man* (London: J. M. Dent, 1976), 104–23, and "The Nature of Translation in Ben Jonson's Poetry," *Studies in English Literature* 13 (1973): 344–59.

25. Cohen, *Drama of a Nation*, 300. Cohen emphasizes the reactionary side of the neoclassical revival when he writes that "Jonson senses that the direction of history runs counter to his hopes, that any dynamism would only be degenerative, he can only hope for no more than a static future" (294). Don E. Wayne counters this in *Penshurst: The Semiotics of Place and the Poetics of History* (Madison: University of Wisconsin Press, 1984), 146–50.

26. Sidney, *An Apology for Poetry*, 37.

27. Cordatus provides a history of ancient comic innovation:

"No, I assure you, Signior. If those laws you speak of had been delivered us ab initio and in their present virtue and perfection, there had been some reason of obeying their powers: but . . . that which we call Comoedia was at first nothing but a simple and continued Song, sung by one . . . person, till SUSARIO invented a second, after him EPICHARMUS a third; PHORMUS, and CHIONIDES devised to have four Actors, with a Prologue and Chorus; to which CRATINUS (long after) added a fifth, and sixth; EUPOLIS more, ARISTOPHANES more than they: every man in the dignity of his spirit and judgement supplied something. And (though that in him this kind of Poem appeared absolute and fully perfected) yet how is the face of it chang'd since, in MENANDER, PHILEMON, CECILIUS, PLAUTUS, and the rest; who have utterly excluded the Chorus, altered the property of the persons, their names, and natures, and augmented it with all liberty, according to the elegancy and disposition of those times wherein they wrote? I see not then, but we should enjoy the same license, or free power, to illustrate and heighten our invention as they did; and not be tied to those strict and regular forms, which the niceness of a few (who are nothing but form) would thrust upon us" ("AFTER THE SECOND SOUNDING," LL. 247–70).

28. Renu Juneja, "The Unclassical Design of Jonson's Comedy," *Renaissance and Reformation* 4 (1980): 76. Nevertheless, Helen Ostovich, " 'So Sudden and Strange a Cure': A Rudimentary Masque in *Every Man Out of His Humour*," *English Literary Renaissance* 22 (1992): 322–24, sees the possible influence of Old Comedy on Jonson, especially through the appearance of the Queen of Heaven at the end of Aristophanes' *Birds*.

29. Sidney, *An Apology for Poetry*, 45. Hanna Scolnicov, *Experiments in Stage Satire: An Analysis of Ben Jonson's* Every Man Out of His Humour, Cynthia's Revels, *and* Poetaster (Frankfurt: Peter Lang, 1987), 19–27, makes the case for Jonson's primarily using the phrase "*Vetus Comoedia*" to refer to Athenian comedy of the fifth century B.C., known to us basically through the work of Aristophanes. She also maintains (correcting Herford's annotation) that Jonson identifies *The Devil is an Ass* as a work of "*Comoedia Vetus*" in order to emphasize how it overgoes the morality tradition, as he ridicules "the devil's prowess in comparison with human enormities" (22–23).

30. Frank Kermode, *The Genesis of Secrecy: On the Interpretation of Narrative* (Cambridge: Harvard University Press, 1979), 162.

31. See James Shapiro, *Rival Playwrights: Marlowe, Jonson, Shakespeare* (New York: Columbia University Press, 1991), 150–70, who focuses on Jonson's antithetical attitudes toward Shakespeare at the openings of his own and his rival's first folios.

32. See "Appendix II: The Dates of Composition" in Gabriele Bernhard Jackson's edition of *Every Man in His Humor*, 221–39.

33. Francis Beaumont, "To my dear friend, Mr. Benjamin Jonson, upon his FOX," lines 12–13, in *Volpone* (London, 1607), sig. A2^r.

34. Jackson, ed., *Every Man in His Humor*, 221–22.

35. McDonald, *Shakespeare & Jonson*, 31.

36. T. J. B. Spencer, "Ben Jonson on his beloved, The Author Mr. William Shakespeare," *The Elizabethan Theater IV*, ed. G. R. Hibbard (Hamden, Conn.: Archon, 1974), 23.

37. *The Yale Edition of the Works of Samuel Johnson*, ed. Allen T. Hazen et al., 16 vols. (New Haven: Yale University Press, 1958–), 7:69. The wonderful paradox of Ben Jonson's attitude allowed him to praise Shakespeare's comedy as unmatched in his rival's folio and yet condemn it as facile, commercial, and intellectually indefensible in his own.

38. Anonymous, *Gesta Grayorum, or The History of the High and Mighty Prince, Henry, Prince of Purpoole* (London, 1688), 22.

39. Francis Meres, *Palladis Tamia, Wit's Treasury, Being the Second Part of Wit's Commonwealth* (London, 1598), 283.

40. Ibid., 282. A translation of Fitzgeffrey's tribute, "Ad Beniaminum Ionsonium," in *Affaniae: sive Epigrammatum Libri Tres* (Oxford: 1601) is reprinted in *Ben Jonson: The Critical Heritage, 1599–1798*, ed. D. H. Craig (London: Routledge, 1990), 85–86.

41. Ornstein, "Shakespearian and Jonsonian Comedy," 43.

42. E. Pearlman, "Ben Jonson: An Anatomy," *English Literary Renaissance* 9 (1979): 364–93.

43. Translated from *Aeli Donati quod Fertur Commentum Terenti*, ed. Paul Wessner, 3 vols. (Stuttgart: B. G. Teubner, 1962), 1:16–17.

44. Eugene M. Waith traces the background of the request for applause to Roman comedy in " 'Give Me Your Hands': Reflections on the Author's Agents in Comedy," in *The Author in His Work: Essays on a Problem in Criticism*, eds. Louis Martz and Aubrey Williams (New Haven: Yale University Press, 1978), 197–211.

45. Anonymous, *Lingua* (London, 1607), sig. H2^v.

46. Craig, ed., *Ben Jonson: The Critical Heritage*, 361–62.

47. Cohen, *Drama of a Nation*, 285. Both the public and the private theaters had long-standing traditions of topical satire in which contemporary individuals and events were lampooned directly through impersonation and obliquely through allusion. The private companies neither invented nor monopolized its use. All that can be said is that they generally took greater risks more often.

3. Representing Jonson: *Histriomastix* and the Origin of the Poets' War

1. Philip Finkelpearl, "John Marston's *Histrio-Mastix* as an Inns of Court Play: A Hypothesis," *The Huntington Library Quarterly* 29 (1966): 228, writes that "even with a prodigious amount of 'doubling' it is difficult to see how a company much

smaller than twenty-five could produce the play." "At several places in the action more than twenty actors are required on stage," he objects, estimating that Paul's had only eleven principal actors. He concedes, however, that "Act II, Sc. i of Marston's *Antonio's Revenge* requires seventeen." Tom Cain, in his edition of *Poetaster* (Manchester: Manchester University Press, 1995), 40, conjectures that "the size of the Blackfriars company in 1601 was at least twenty (the number on stage in IV.vi)." At the 1995 meeting of the Shakespeare Association of America, in Alan Somerset's seminar ("As it hath been publikely acted"), however, Roslyn L. Knutson proposed that *Histriomastix* was unactable in its printed state. In an essay entitled "The Devil in the Details: *Histriomastix* and the Number of Players in Paul's Boys, 1599–1603," she determined that the first quarto text required "fourteen players who would do no doubling at all," which is not problematic, but that when smaller roles were factored in it needed "forty-five players to manage at least eighty-nine roles" (6). It is consequently possible that the first quarto of *Histriomastix* (1610) retains portions of the script of the old morality play Marston had doctored before it was abridged for performance at Paul's.

2. Richard Simpson, *The School of Shakespeare*, 2 vols. (New York: J. W. Bouton, 1878), 2:4–8, was the first post-Renaissance critic to recognize that the anonymously printed *Histriomastix* (first issued in 1610) was by Marston. But he missed the mark in viewing Chrisoganus as an authorial self-portrait that inadvertently includes some of Jonson's characteristics. Frederick Fleay, in *A Biographical Chronicle of the English Drama, 1559–1642*, 2 vols. (London: Reeves and Turner, 1891), 2:71, correctly identified Chrisoganus with Jonson, but his assumption that Chrisoganus is wholly complimentary generated a kind of *pseudodoxia epidemica*. Josiah H. Penniman, *The War of the Theatres* (Boston: Ginn, 1897), 33, accepted Fleay at his word, and from that point onward the matter seemed settled. Roscoe Addison Small, *The Stage Quarrel Between Ben Jonson and the So-Called Poetasters* (1899; reprint, New York: AMS Press, 1966), 89, thus writes that "Chrisoganus is evidently intended as a compliment to Jonson," depicting "his ideal literary man." E. K. Chambers, *The Elizabethan Stage*, 4 vols. (Oxford: Clarendon, 1923), 1:381*n*, canonized Small's guess that Jonson might have "taken offense at Marston's portrait of him, intended to be complimentary." C. H. Herford and Percy Simpson in *Ben Jonson*, 11 vols. (Oxford: Clarendon, 1925–1952) (1:25) concur that Marston attempted to fashion "the scholastic pedant Chrisoganus into the likeness of the great contemporary chastizer of Ignorance. The portrait was certainly meant to be flattering." Anne Barton, *Ben Jonson, Dramatist* (Cambridge: Cambridge University Press, 1984), 59, agrees that Chrisoganus "is evidently intended as a compliment to Jonson."

3. Alvin Kernan, "John Marston's Play *Histriomastix*," *Modern Language Quarterly* 19 (1958), 137–38, and chapter 4, "The Satirist in the Theater," in *The Cankered Muse* (New Haven: Yale University Press, 1959), 143–49. Also see David Bevington's incisive description of Chrisoganus in *Tudor Drama and Politics: A Critical Approach to Topical Meaning* (Cambridge: Harvard University Press, 1968), 280–81.

4. David Riggs, *Ben Jonson: A Life* (Cambridge: Harvard University Press, 1989), 79.

5. George L. Geckle, *John Marston's Drama: Themes, Images, Sources* (Rutherford, N.J.: Fairleigh Dickinson University Press, 1980), 47.

6. Everard Guilpin, *Skialetheia, or A Shadow of Truth, in Certain Epigrams and Satires*, ed. D. Allen Carroll (Chapel Hill: University of North Carolina Press, 1974), 47–48.

7. See Mikhail Bakhtin, *Rabelais and His World*, trans. Helene Iswolsky (Bloomington: Indiana University Press, 1984), 303–67.

8. Jonson read *Skialetheia* and borrowed from it, taking the name "Captain Tucca," used in *Poetaster*, from its "Satire Preludium," lines 25–34. In his dedication in the first quarto of *Satiromastix*, Dekker identifies "Tucca" as a parody of a contemporary—probably Ralph Hanham ("To the World," lines 29–35).

9. John Aubrey states that Jonson had not always been plagued by his complexion and that he "was (or rather had been) of a clear and fair skin," only to add that he "had one eye lower than t'other, and bigger, like Clun the Player: perhaps he begot Clun." See Aubrey's *Brief Lives*, ed. Oliver Lawson Dick (London: Secker and Warburg, 1949), 178.

10. Guilpin, *Skialetheia*, 8. After the death of his father, Guilpin's mother Thomasin married William Guarsi, Marston's uncle, on 29 June 1592. There are numerous links between the Guilpins and the Marstons from this date that are summarized by R. E. Brettle in "Everard Guilpin and John Marston (1574–1634)," *The Review of English Studies* 16 (1965): 396–99, and by D. Allen Carroll in his introductory chapter on "Everard Guilpin: Literary Life and Relations," in his edition of *Skialetheia*, 5–12. Verbal and conceptual affinities found in *Skialetheia*, *Certain Satires*, and *The Scourge* are also documented in Carroll's notes.

11. The full sequence of Marston's attack on Hall (and Guilpin's connection with it) from 1598 to 1599 is as follows:

1. Hall censures a group of contemporary poets, not including Marston or Guilpin, in *Virgidemiae* (1597);
2. Marston criticizes Hall throughout *Certain Satires* (1598), but especially in "Reactio," a poem that mocks Hall's literary opinions;
3. Guilpin, in *Skialetheia* (1598), states that although some praise Hall— "The double volum'd Satyr"— for "his Rods in piss" [the English equivalent of the Latin word *virgidemiae*], "Yet other-some, who would his credit crack / Have clapp'd Reactio's Action on his back" (6.93–96);
4. Marston informs readers (*The Scourge*, "Satyra Nova," lines 46–49) that Hall caused an epigram characterizing him as a dog who needed castrating "to be pasted to the latter page" of every copy of Marston's Ovidian narrative *Pygmalion's Image* (bound up with *Certain Satires*) that "came to the stationers of Cambridge";

5. Marston responds to this provocation in "Satyra Nova," a poem addressed to Guilpin, which he adds to the 1599 edition of *The Scourge*, published before the bishops' ban in June of that year. Guilpin had attended Emmanuel College, Cambridge, with Joseph Hall, and has therefore been suspected of supplying Marston with background for his parody.

12. I accept as most probable the theory that *Histriomastix* was undertaken by Marston for the revival of the Children of Paul's by November 1599. The date of winter 1598, proposed by Finkelpearl, "*Histrio-Mastix* as an Inns of Court Play," 223–34, is, I believe, untenable. Jonson also probably designed "Orange" and "Clove," who mentions *Histriomastix*, as roles to be acted at the Globe, since before the quarto of *Every Man Out* was printed in 1600 Dekker had already imitated Jonson's description of Clove in the stationer's shop (3.1.29–33) and had repeated one of his Marstonisms—the strange word "synderesis" (3.4.22)—in *Patient Grissil* (2.1.19–23 and 2.1.59), completed by 29 December 1599. The quarto was registered on 28 March 1600, shortly before *Every Man Out* was entered on 8 April. Jonson used the same procedure in his almost contemporaneous parody of Anthony Munday as Antonio Balladino, which he inserted into the performance script of *The Case Is Altered* (1.2) long before it was published. William Elton, however, in *Shakespeare's* Troilus and Cressida *and the Inns of Court Revels* (Brookfield, Vt.: Ashgate, 2000), continues to see the influence of the law school environment that Finkelpearl suggested.

13. Richard Helgerson, *Self-Crowned Laureates: Spenser, Jonson, Milton and the Literary System* (Berkeley: University of California Press, 1983), 102, and Riggs, *Ben Jonson*, 67–68.

14. John Weever, *Faunus and Melliflora, or The Original of Our English Satires* (London, 1600), sig. F3ʳ.

15. After pleading benefit of clergy (having proven that he could read Latin), Jonson was punished for manslaughter resulting from his duel on 22 September 1598 by being branded on the thumb with "the Tyburn T" and by forfeiting his possessions. The indictment against Jonson was first printed in *The Athenaeum*, 6 March 1886: 337–38.

16. S. Schoenbaum, "The Precarious Balance of John Marston," *PMLA* 67 (1952): 1069–78.

17. This quotation appears in Munday's dedication of *Gerileon of England, The Second Part* (1592), which excuses his delay in translating the work. Quoted from Celeste Turner, *Anthony Mundy: An Elizabethan Man of Letters* (Berkeley: University of California Press, 1928), 92.

18. Ibid., 59. My analysis has been guided by Turner's comments on *Histriomastix* in her chapter on "Antonio Balladino," 121–31. Turner updated some of her findings in "Young Anthony Mundy Again," *Studies in Philology* 56 (1959): 150–68. See also Mark Eccles's discussion of "Anthony Mundy" in *Studies in En-*

glish Renaissance Drama, eds. J. W. Bennett, Oscar Cargill, and Vernon Hall, Jr. (New York: New York University Press, 1959), 95–105.

19. Quoted by Anthony Caputi in *John Marston, Satirist* (Ithaca: Cornell University Press, 1961), 83.

20. Riggs, *Ben Jonson*, 79. A similar explanation is offered by George E. Rowe, *Distinguishing Jonson: Imitation, Rivalry, and the Direction of a Dramatic Career* (Lincoln: University of Nebraska Press, 1988), 20, who states that during the Renaissance "the intensity of competition" between corivals "increases the more closely they are linked (hence, for example, Jonson's focus on Marston in the War of the Theaters)." Rowe cites Girard's statement in *Violence and the Sacred* (Baltimore: Johns Hopkins University Press, 1977), 49, that "Order, peace, and fecundity depend on cultural distinctions: it is not these distinctions but the loss of them that gives birth to fierce rivalries."

21. Francis Meres, *Palladis Tamia, Wit's Treasury, Being the Second Part of Wit's Commonwealth* (London, 1598), 277.

22. Arnold Stein, "The Second English Satirist," *Modern Language Review* 38 (1943): 274.

23. This appears as an annotation in *Certain Satires* (5.15).

24. Arnold Davenport is quoted from his introduction to *The Poems of John Marston* (Liverpool: Liverpool University Press, 1961), 17.

25. Hallett Smith in *Elizabethan Poetry* (Ann Arbor: University of Michigan Press, 1968), 242, writes that "Marston does not have, like Hall, a set of values based upon academic life, upon ancient simplicity and decency, and upon a moral earnestness which wished to correct the faults visible in a changing society."

26. Diogenes Laertius, *Lives of Eminent Philosophers*, trans. R. D. Hicks (Cambridge: Harvard University Press, 1958), 2:43.

27. Jonathan Dollimore, *Radical Tragedy: Religion, Ideology, and Power in the Drama of Shakespeare and His Contemporaries* (Chicago: University of Chicago Press, 1984), 167.

28. For an analysis of the connection between this theological concept, usually spelled "synteresis," and the Christian mystical tradition, based on the Neo-Platonic notion of a divine spark, see Caputi, *John Marston, Satirist*, 59–60.

4. Shakespeare in Love: The Containment of Comical Satire in *As You Like It*

1. For their relative dating, see the Chronological Appendix.

2. *Ben Jonson: The Critical Heritage, 1599–1798*, ed. D. H. Craig (London: Routledge, 1990), 92.

3. See Edward W. Tayler's *Nature and Art in Renaissance Literature* (New York: Columbia University Press, 1964) and Frank Kermode's introductions to *English Pastoral Poetry: From the Beginnings to Marvell* (New York: Norton & Co., 1972) and *The Tempest* (London: Methuen, 1954). More recently, Derek Attridge ex-

4. SHAKESPEARE IN LOVE 297

plores the problems involved in this dialectic in "Puttenham's Perplexity: Nature, Art, and the Supplement in Renaissance Poetic Theory," *Literary Theory/Renaissance Texts*, eds. Patricia Parker and David Quint (Baltimore: Johns Hopkins University Press, 1986), 257–79.

4. Harry Levin, *Playboys and Killjoys: An Essay on the Theory and Practice of Comedy* (New York: Oxford University Press, 1982), 12, contrasts these terms.

5. From its initial publication in 1590 to 1642, *Rosalind* went through a remarkable ten editions.

6. Consider how closely Shakespeare follows Lodge. Both *Rosalind* and *As You Like It* have double plots: the first involves a usurper, Torismond (Shakespeare's Duke Frederick), who sends the rightful king, Gerismond (Duke Senior), into exile in the forest of Ardennes (Arden); the second concerns the conflict between two brothers, the unnaturally cruel Saladyne (Oliver) and his innocent younger sibling Rosader (Orlando), whom he deprives of his inheritance. The plots are brought together when Rosalind, the daughter of the exiled ruler, and her friend Alinda (Celia), daughter of the usurper, watch Rosader (Orlando) win a match with a professional wrestler during which Rosalind also "falls" for him. Following his victory, threatened by his older brother, he escapes into the forest with Adam, a faithful old servant. Nevertheless, the lovers' reunion is assured when Torismond (Duke Frederick) forces Rosalind to leave court and his own daughter Alinda (Celia) willingly accompanies her into the same forest in search of her exiled father. To disguise their identities, the latter then adopts the name Aliena and the former, to shield them from assault, cross-dresses, calling herself Ganymede.

When they enter the forest, Aliena and Ganymede encounter an aged shepherd, Corydon (Corin), and his friend, the young Montanus (Silvius), who is in love with a disdainful mistress, Phebe. The women purchase the farm on which the old shepherd works and, by the end of the play, Rosalind discovers love, as does Alinda (Celia); unites the pastoral Petrarchan lovers; and presents herself to her father. The integration of the two main plots continues when the disguised Rosalind again meets Rosader (Orlando), who has fallen in love with her and hangs poems in her honor on the surrounding trees. Taken in by her disguise, he agrees to practice courting Ganymede as a surrogate Rosalind and she uses this opportunity to question and criticize love. The first movement toward closure occurs when Saladyne (Oliver), who seeks his brother in Ardennes (Arden), is reconciled with him, becomes morally transformed, and is engaged to Aliena. Ganymede, who has become the love object of Phebe, then promises to satisfy all the discontented lovers at her next appearance. Returning dressed in female attire, she joins the beguiled Phebe to Montanus (Silvius) and satisfies her own lover. The marriage of the two brothers is then coordinated with the political restoration of her father Gerismond (Duke Senior).

7. Oscar James Campbell, "Jaques," *The Huntington Library Bulletin* 8 (1935): 94.

8. Peter G. Phialas, *Shakespeare's Romantic Comedies: The Development of Their Form and Meaning* (Chapel Hill: University of North Carolina Press, 1966), 232.

9. David Bevington, "Shakespeare vs Jonson on Satire," *Shakespeare 1971, Proceedings of the World Shakespeare Congress,* eds. Clifford Leech and J.M.R. Margeson (Toronto: University of Toronto Press, 1972), 121.

10. Campbell, "Jaques," 91.

11. Russ McDonald, *Shakespeare & Jonson/Jonson & Shakespeare* (Lincoln: University of Nebraska Press, 1988), 8, 78.

12. *Sir John Harington's A New Discourse of a Stale Subject, called The Metamorphosis of Ajax,* ed. Elizabeth Story Donno (New York: Columbia University Press, 1962), 82. Donno notes on the same page that the first name of this same person, sometimes called James Wingfield, is also recorded in official documents of the period as "Jaques" or "Jakes."

13. Helen Gardner, "*As You Like It,*" in *More Talking of Shakespeare,* ed. John Garrett (London: Longmans, 1959), 31.

14. Quoted from *Ben Jonson,* eds. C. H. Herford and Percy Simpson, 11 vols. (Oxford: Clarendon, 1925–1952), 1:28*n*.

15. Arthur Gray, *How Shakespeare 'Purged' Jonson: A Problem Solved* (Cambridge: W. Heffer & Sons, 1928), 20. Gray assumes that *As You Like It* contains Shakespeare's purge of Jonson mentioned in *2 Return from Parnassus,* even though it was said to have been administered the following year, after *Poetaster.*

16. Campbell, "Jaques," 101, stresses the character's connection to Jonson but blunders in arguing that Feliche, the satirist of *Antonio and Mellida,* Marston's second play, also serves as a precedent for Jaques, through whom "Shakespeare deprecates the savage manner of Marston and Jonson." But Shakespeare could only have had *Every Man Out* in mind, since *Antonio and Mellida* followed *As You Like It.* Marston's Rossaline, who makes witty sexual innuendos in that play, is an imitation of Shakespeare's character. See the Chronological Appendix (number 3).

17. Robert N. Watson, *Ben Jonson's Parodic Strategy: Literary Imperialism in the Comedies* (Cambridge: Harvard University Press, 1987), 1–2. See also Terrance Dunford, "Consumption of the World: Reading, Eating, and Imitation in *Every Man Out of His Humour,*" *English Literary Renaissance* 2 (1984): 131–47.

18. C. L. Barber, *Shakespeare's Festive Comedy: A Study of Dramatic Form and its Relation to Social Custom* (Princeton: Princeton University Press, 1959), 223–39.

19. Sir Philip Sidney, *An Apology for Poetry,* ed. Forrest G. Robinson (Indianapolis: Bobbs-Merrill, 1970), 77. In *The Pilgrimage to Parnassus* (1598/99), Dromio enters, drawing "*a clown in with a rope,*" and explains that "clowns have been thrust into plays by head and shoulders, ever since Kemp could make a scurvy face" (lines 665–67), in *The Three Parnassus Plays, 1598–1601,* ed. J. B. Leishman (London: Ivor Nicholson & Watson, 1949).

20. For background on Charles Chester, the model for Carlo Buffone, see Charles Nicholl, *A Cup of News: The Life of Thomas Nashe* (London: Routledge and Kegan Paul, 1984), 103–6.

21. See S. Schoenbaum, *William Shakespeare: A Documentary Life* (New York:

Oxford University Press, 1975), 166–73. Jonson dedicated the folio version of *Every Man In* to his former tutor and friend in 1616.

22. What might have been equally galling was that Sogliardo is a rich country clown whose brother Sordido, like several of Shakespeare's Stratford neighbors, illegally kept corn off the market during a time of famine. For this they were cited in a Privy Council letter of 22 August 1597 as being "more like to wolves or cormorants than to natural men." Quoted by E. K. Chambers, *William Shakespeare: A Study of Facts and Problems*, 2 vols. (Oxford: Clarendon, 1930), 2:100. Park Honan, *Shakespeare: A Life* (Oxford: Oxford University Press, 1998), 240–42, mentions the "Note of Corn and Malt," drawn up by Adrian Quiney on 4 February 1598, which lists Shakespeare's household as possessing considerable holdings (eighty bushels) during this period of continuing shortages and social unrest at Stratford.

23. Jonson would render his own account of Ovid's exile in *Poetaster*, when he shifted the terms of his opposition to Shakespeare from a Greek to a Roman context, as he moved from an Aristophanic to an Horatian perspective.

24. Sidney, *An Apology for Poetry*, 33, 21.

25. For the actors' testimony, see the suit of "John Witter v. John Heminges and Henry Condell" in Charles William Wallace, "Shakespeare and His London Associates," *University of Nebraska Studies* 10 (1910): 54. Honan, *Shakespeare: A Life*, 268, cites a reference to the Globe's construction in the inquisition into the assets of Sir Thomas Brend, on whose land the theater was erected. Platter's diary is quoted from S. Schoenbaum, *William Shakespeare: A Compact Documentary Life* (New York: Oxford University Press, 1980), 209.

26. Bernard Beckerman, *Shakespeare at the Globe* (New York: Columbia University Press, 1962), x.

27. William Kemp, *Nine Days' Wonder (1600)*, ed. G. B. Harrison (London: John Lane, The Bodley Head, 1923), 3.

28. Gerald Eades Bentley, *The Profession of Player in Shakespeare's Time* (Princeton: Princeton University Press, 1984), 43.

29. Kemp's emancipation left him free for further travel. To the ballad-mongers who composed rhymes of his exploits he boasts that "I William Kemp," who had almost been "rent in sunder with your unreasonable rhymes, am shortly God willing to set forward as merrily as I may" (*Nine Days' Wonder* 29). David Wiles, *Shakespeare's Clown: Actor and Text in the Elizabethan Playhouse* (Cambridge: Cambridge University Press, 1987), 36–39, speculates about Kemp's trips to Italy and Germany, before returning to England to join Worcester's Men.

30. See the Chronological Appendix (number 3).

31. Armin's association with the goldsmiths' guild and their emblem in his role as Touchstone is pointed out by Hotson in *Shakespeare's Motley* (London: Rupert Hart-Davis, 1952), 115. Jane Belfield, "Robert Armin, 'Citizen and Goldsmith of London,' " *Notes and Queries* 27 (1980): 158–59, indicates that Armin was an apprentice to the goldsmith John Louyson in 1581. He belatedly became free of the company in January 1604 and on 15 July 1608 took James Jones as an apprentice.

Most scholars who have considered the question agree that the parts of Touchstone and Feste were written with Armin in mind. Discussions of his career, aside from Hotson's sometimes misleading *Shakespeare's Motley*, include: T. W. Baldwin, "Shakespeare's Jester," *Modern Language Notes* 39 (1924): 447–55; Austin K. Gray, "Robert Armine, the Foole," *PMLA* 42 (1927): 673–85; and Charles Felver, "Robert Armin, Shakespeare's Fool: A Biographical Essay," *Research Studies 5, Kent University Bulletin* 49 (1961).

A general appraisal of the fool's social function is found in: Barbara Swain, *Fools and Folly During the Middle Ages and the Renaissance* (New York: Columbia University Press, 1932); Enid Welsford, *The Fool: His Social and Literary History* (London: Faber and Faber, 1935); Robert Goldsmith, *Wise Fools in Shakespeare* (East Lansing: Michigan State University Press, 1955); Walter Kaiser, *Praisers of Folly: Erasmus, Rabelais, Shakespeare* (Cambridge: Harvard University Press, 1963); and William Willeford, *The Fool and His Scepter: A Study in Clowns and Jesters and Their Audience* (Evanston: Northwestern University Press, 1969).

32. *The Collected Works of Robert Armin*, ed. J. P. Feather, 2 vols. (New York: Johnson Reprint Company, 1972), 2:sigs. D^{r-v}. Charles Felver, "Robert Armin: Shakespeare's Source for Touchstone," *Shakespeare Quarterly* 7 (1956): 135–37, corrects Hotson's assumption that Armin referred to himself as "Tutch" to imitate Shakespeare's character.

33. John Davies, line 30 of "*To honest-gamesome* Robin Armin" in *The Scourge of Folly* (London: 1611?), 229.

34. The only viable treatment of this autobiographical reference is by William M. Jones in "William Shakespeare as William in *As You Like It*," *Shakespeare Quarterly* 2 (1960): 228–31. Jones stresses the detachable quality of the episode and conjectures that "the boy from Stratford" had "been in London long enough to joke about his own clownish origins" (229). He also believes that Shakespeare designed the role for himself and uses it to satirize "the pedantic learning that Jonson sometime boasted" (231).

35. John Ward is quoted from S. Schoenbaum, *Shakespeare's Lives* (Oxford: Clarendon, 1970), 297.

36. Jones, "William Shakespeare as William," 231.

37. Wiles, *Shakespeare's Clown*, 146.

38. Phyllis Rackin, *Stages of History: Shakespeare's English Chronicles* (Ithaca: Cornell University Press, 1990), 244. Another good example is the schoolboy William Page in *The Merry Wives of Windsor* (4.1), who struggles through a lesson in Latin grammar.

39. Gardner, "*As You Like It*," 17.

40. Stuart Daley, "Where Are the Woods in *As You Like It*?" *Shakespeare Quarterly* 34 (1983): 175. See also Mark Eccles, "The Shakespeares and the Ardens," in *Shakespeare in Warwickshire* (Madison: University of Wisconsin Press, 1961), 3–23.

41. Both quotations are from Schoenbaum, *William Shakespeare: A Documen-*

tary Life, 149. Unfortunately, all that the old narrator's selective memory could recall of this performance was seeing another old man.

42. Bentley, *The Profession of Player in Shakespeare's Time*, 228.

43. William Camden, *Remains of a Greater Work* (London, 1605), 40: "Man, earthly, or red."

44. T. W. Baldwin, *William Shakespeare's Small Latine and Lesse Greeke*, 2 vols. (Urbana: University of Illinois Press, 1944), 1:116–20, grounds Touchstone's learned fooling in the rhetorical strategies of Aristotle, Cicero, and Quintilian. Agnes Latham notes the reference to Lyly's *Euphues* (5.1.43–44) in her edition of *As You Like It* (London: Methuen, 1975).

45. E. K. Chambers, *Shakespeare: A Survey* (New York: Hill and Wang, 1958), 158, and Edwin Greenlaw, "Shakespeare's Pastorals," *Studies in Philology* 13 (1916): 131. Publication of pastoral literature first written in the 1580s and 1590s prolonged its influence. The period's finest collection of pastoral verse, *England's Helicon*, was printed in 1600, the same year *As You Like It* premiered. Two years earlier a translation of Montemayor's *Diana* (the original of which inspired Sidney) and Marlowe's *Hero and Leander* (both alluded to by Shakespeare) were issued.

46. Quoted from *Spenser's Poetical Works*, eds. J. C. Smith and E. De Selincourt (Oxford: Clarendon, 1970).

47. Murray Levith, *What's in Shakespeare's Names* (Hamden, Conn.: Archon, 1978), 89, and S. A. Tannenbaum, "The Names in *As You Like It*," *The Shakespeare Association Bulletin* 15 (1940): 255–56.

48. *The Vision of William Concerning Piers the Plowman*, ed. Walter W. Skeat, 2 vols. (1886; reprint, Oxford: Oxford University Press, 1969), 1: B, Passus XV, 148, and C, Passus VI, 22–25.

49. *The Canterbury Tales* (Fragment VII, lines 703 and 930) in *The Works of Geoffrey Chaucer*, ed. F. N. Robinson (Boston: Houghton Mifflin, 1957).

50. Donn Ervin Taylor, " 'Try in Time in Despite of a Fall': Time and Occasion in *As You Like It*," *Texas Studies in Literature and Language* 24 (1982): 129.

51. Francis Meres, *Palladis Tamia, Wit's Treasury, Being the Second Part of Wit's Commonwealth* (London, 1598), 281–82.

52. Henry Willobie, *Willobie His Avisa*, ed. G. B. Harrison (New York: Barnes and Noble, 1966), 115–17.

53. Ibid., 121. Shakespeare is cited as the author of *The Rape of Lucrece* in the opening poem (19). Park Honan, *Shakespeare: A Life*, 359, notes that Willobie's elder brother "married Eleanor Bampfield, whose sister in the same month married Thomas Russell," the overseer of Shakespeare's will. He also mentions "a semi-erotic" verse by H.M. of the Middle Temple ("The Strange Fortune of Alerane, or My Lady's Toy") that pairs references to *Willobie His Avisa* and *The Rape of Lucrece*.

54. Meres, *Palladis Tamia*, 281.

55. Anonymous, *The Return from Parnassus*, lines 1032–1033, 1200–1203, and *2 Return from Parnassus*, line 302, in *The Three Parnassus Plays (1598–1601)*, ed. J. B. Leishman (London: Ivor Nicholson & Watson, 1949).

56. *The Diary of John Manningham of the Middle Temple 1602–1603*, ed. Robert Parker Sorlien (Hanover, N.H.: The University Press of New England, 1976), 75.

57. Rosalie L. Colie, *Shakespeare's Living Art* (Princeton: Princeton University Press, 1974), 284.

58. See E. A. J. Honigmann, *Shakespeare's Impact on His Contemporaries* (Totowa, N.J.: Barnes and Noble, 1982), 109–20, and Harry Levin, "Two Magian Comedies: *The Tempest* and *The Alchemist*," in *Shakespeare and the Revolution of the Times* (New York: Oxford University Press, 1976), 219, 231. An example of this later engagement occurs, as Honigmann points out, when Polixenes describes "streak'd gillyvors" as being created through grafting, "an art which . . . shares with great creating Nature," and in doing so proves that "art itself is Nature" (4.4.82–97). Annoyed by this witty suggestion that art and nature are indistinguishable, Jonson regrets in "To the Reader" of *The Alchemist* that he ever used these terms to clarify his difference from Shakespeare:

> But how out of purpose, and place, do I name Art? when the Professors are grown so obstinate contemners of it, and presumers on their own Naturals, as they are deriders of all diligence that way, and, by simple mocking at the terms, when they understand not the things, think to get off wittily with their Ignorance. Nay, they are esteem'd the more learned, and sufficient for this, by the Many, through their excellent vice of judgment. (5:291)

The plural screens a singular indictment. Shakespeare was a "professor" (or practioner) of "Art" who preferred his copious imagination. Jonson rebukes him for overestimating his wit, depending on his "natural" ability (his instinct or folly), and even gaining a reputation for being "learned" in his "Ignorance" for subverting the distinction between art and nature. Thomas Cartelli further explores Jonson's reaction to Shakespeare's late pastoral comedy in "*Bartholomew Fair* as Urban Arcadia: Jonson Responds to Shakespeare," *Renaissance Drama* 14 (1983): 151–72.

59. Quoted from Chambers, *William Shakespeare: A Study of Facts and Problems*, 2:224.

60. *An Essay of Dramatic Poesy* in *The Works of John Dryden*, ed. Keith Walker (Oxford: Oxford University Press, 1987), 110.

61. "Upon Master William Shakespeare, the Deceased Author and His Poems," in *Poems Written by William Shakespeare, Gentleman* (London, 1640), lines 1 and 10.

62. John Freehafer, "Leonard Digges, Ben Jonson, and the Beginning of Shakespeare Idolatry," *Shakespeare Quarterly* 21 (1970): 75.

5. Marston's Festive Comedy: Punishing Jonson in *Jack Drum's Entertainment*

1. See chapter 6, note 1, for speculation about Paul's repertoire and the Chronological Appendix for the dating of *Jack Drum's Entertainment*.

2. That pastoral comedy was realizing a new popularity at the time is indicated by Paul's production in the same year of *The Maid's Metamorphosis*, a recycled mythological drama inspired by Lyly. William Percy even submitted a parcel of "Pastorals and Comedies" (dating from 1601 to 1603) for their consideration. See E. K. Chambers, *The Elizabethan Stage*, 4 vols. (Oxford: Clarendon, 1923), 2:21, and W. Reavley Gair, *The Children of Paul's: The Story of a Theatre Company* (Cambridge: Cambridge University Press, 1982), 128.

3. See chapter 3, note 12.

4. On Marston's awareness of the danger of inflated diction, see Elizabeth M. Yearling, " 'Mount Tufty Tamberlaine': Marston and Linguistic Excess," *Studies in English Literature* 20 (1980): 257–69.

5. This point was was first made by Richard Simpson in *The School of Shakespeare*, 2 vols. (New York: J. W. Bouton, 1878), 2:5.

6. Jonson repeated this procedure years later when he added a caricature of Inigo Jones as In-And-In Medlay to *A Tale of a Tub* (1633).

7. Oscar James Campbell, *Comicall Satyre and* Troilus and Cressida (San Marino: The Huntington Library, 1970), 161 and 163. Simpson in *The School of Shakespeare*, 2:129, identifies Brabant Senior with Jonson, but Roscoe Addison Small in *The Stage-Quarrel Between Ben Jonson and the So-Called Poetasters* (1899; reprint, New York: AMS Press, 1966), 96–100, presented evidence that made the claim feasible. Chambers, *The Elizabethan Stage*, 4:21, agrees that "there is little doubt that the critical Brabant Senior is Jonson." "*Jack Drum's Entertainment*," explains Morse Allen in *The Satire of John Marston* (Columbus, Ohio: F. J. Heer, 1920), 40, represents "a distinct attack upon a dramatic practice of Jonson's, with incidental references to certain of his personal characteristics." Anne Barton, in *Ben Jonson, Dramatist* (Cambridge: Cambridge University Press, 1984), 61, similarly views Brabant as "a cunningly angled attack on the author of *Every Man Out*."

8. George R. Price, *Thomas Dekker* (New York: Twayne, 1969), 23, 25. As Price notes elsewhere, however, Henslowe paid Dekker for altering *Phaeton* in December 1600 for a performance at court (171).

9. K. Gustav Cross, "The Authorship of *Lust's Dominion*," *Studies in Philology* 55 (1958): 39–61, and Cyrus Hoy, introduction to *Lust's Dominion*, in *Introductions, Notes, and Commentaries to Texts in* The Dramatic Works of Thomas Dekker, 4 vols. (Cambridge: Cambridge University Press, 1980), 4:56–72.

10. Chambers, *The Elizabethan Stage*, 4:21.

11. This is particularly true now that Middleton's part in the composition of *Blurt, Master Constable*, around 1601–2, is disputed. The play is now usually attributed to Dekker, who might have had a collaborator. Dekker continued to write for Paul's after Marston left and composed *Westward Ho* and *Northward Ho* for them with John Webster in 1604 and 1605.

12. See the Chronology of Authentic Works in Price's *Thomas Dekker*, 171–72.

13. Chambers, *The Elizabethan Stage*, 2:19.

14. A study of the poet's own domestic arrangements following his marriage to

Anne Lewis on 14 November 1594 is found in Mark Eccles, "Jonson's Marriage," *The Review of English Studies* 47 (1936): 257–72.

15. Chambers, *The Elizabethan Stage*, 4:21.

16. Philip Finkelpearl, *John Marston of the Middle Temple* (Cambridge: Harvard University Press, 1969), 127–29, details the network of correspondences linking Sir Edward Fortune with Sir William Cornwallis, whose estate in Highgate is recalled as the site of Marston's play. Both Jonson and Marston's cousin Everard Guilpin had personal relations with Cornwallis, and since criticism of the former is confined entirely to scenes in which Brabant Senior and Ned Planet appear, it is possible that Marston was suggesting their difference. Planet's "method of satire is contrasted with Brabant Senior's," Campbell, *Comicall Satyre*, 165, writes, "to show that there is a right and a wrong way to satirize." His surname suggests the constancy of the celestial orbs, and his nickname is the same that Marston used for his cousin in *The Scourge*. Satire X, written "TO HIS VERY FRIEND, MASTER E. G.," is addressed to "Ned" (lines 27, 45, and 77), "good Ned" (lines 31 and 57), and "Ned" that "gentle lad" (line 9). Guilpin had, of course, called Jonson "Chrisoganus" in *Skialetheia*.

17. Campbell, *Comicall Satyre*, 155, 165.

18. Anthony Caputi, *John Marston, Satirist* (Ithaca: Cornell University Press, 1961), 121.

19. Reginald Foakes, "John Marston's Fantastical Plays: *Antonio and Mellida* and *Antonio's Revenge*," *Philological Quarterly* 41 (1962): 236.

20. Madeleine Doran, *Endeavors of Art: A Study of Form in Elizabethan Drama* (Madison: University of Wisconsin Press, 1954), 21.

21. Richard Levin, *New Readings vs. Old Plays: Recent Trends in the Reinterpretation of Renaissance Drama* (Chicago: University of Chicago Press, 1979), 128. Levin engaged Foakes on this point in "The Proof of the Parody," *Essays in Criticism* 24 (1974): 312–17, by denying that parody was predominant in the playwright's conception and that his clumsiness and bad writing were deliberate. T. F. Wharton in "Old Marston or New Marston: The *Antonio* Plays," in the same journal (25[1975]: 357–69), agreed that these dramas were not dominated by parody.

22. G. K. Hunter, introduction to his edition of *Antonio and Mellida* (Lincoln: University of Nebraska Press, 1965), xvi and xvii.

23. Ibid., xx, xxi, and Gair, *The Children of Paul's*, 143–44. Hunter's view is shared by Ejner J. Jensen, "The Style of the Boy Actors," *Comparative Drama* 2 (1968): 100–14, and Maurice Charney, "The Children's Plays in Performance," *Research Opportunities in Renaissance Drama* 18 (1975): 19–24. In *Shakespeare: The Dark Comedies to the Last Plays* (Charlottesville: University of Virginia, 1971), 39n, Foakes acknowledges that he too has "been partly persuaded by Hunter."

24. T. F. Wharton, *The Critical Fall and Rise of John Marston* (Columbia, S.C.: Camden House, 1994), 83.

25. Campbell, *Comicall Satyre*, 155, did, however, suspect that Marston lost control of *Jack Drum*, which ended up containing more than just satire, since he calls it a "hodge-podge of underdeveloped romantic, comic, and satiric motifs"

and states that "Marston stuffed his play with every sort of stage entertainment that he thought would appeal to his audience." Finkelpearl in *John Marston of the Middle Temple*, 133, similarly admits that "the plot sounds like a 1590's romantic comedy," since Pasquil and Katherine "are deeply in love and given to unending expressions of their passion," but he is convinced that Marston was ultimately "satirizing their lovemaking as hyperbolic and cloying."

26. François Laroque, *Shakespeare's Festive World: Elizabethan Seasonal Entertainment and the Profession of the Stage* (Cambridge: Cambridge University Press, 1993), 136.

27. See A. C. Hamilton's discussion of this episode in "Sidney's *Arcadia* as Prose Fiction," in *Sidney in Retrospect*, ed. Arthur F. Kinney (Amherst: University of Massachusetts Press, 1988), 145–50. The main plots of both *Antonio and Mellida* and *Jack Drum's Entertainment* are based on episodes in the *Arcadia*. In *Antonio and Mellida*, the hero appareled himself as an Amazon warrior in order to secretly approach Mellida despite her father Piero's prohibition, duplicating Pyrocles's transvestite disguise in courting Philoclea against Basilius's command in the *Arcadia*. The *Arcadia* also provided the source for the jealous love plot concerning Camelia's involvement with Planet and Brabant Junior in its account of Helen of Corinth, Amphialus, and Philoxenus. I disagree with Michael C. Andrews, "*Jack Drum's Entertainment* as Burlesque," *Renaissance Quarterly* 24 (1971): 226–31, that Marston parodies these imitations of *Arcadia*.

28. Sir Philip Sidney, *Arcadia*, ed. Maurice Evans (Harmondsworth: Penguin, 1997), 91.

6. The War of the Private Theaters: *Cynthia's Revels* or *What You Will*

1. It was only in the first year of its operation—from 1600 to 1601—that Jonson used his affiliation with Blackfriars to attack Marston and Dekker at Paul's, and they used Paul's stage to blast him.

All that we know about Paul's repertoire from 1599 to 1601 is that it included five plays by Marston (*Histriomastix, Antonio and Mellida, Jack Drum's Entertainment, Antonio's Revenge,* and *What You Will*); at least one, *Satiromastix,* and probably more by Dekker; and two anonymous comedies, *The Maid's Metamorphosis* and *The Wisdom of Doctor Dodipoll,* in 1600. A version of *The Spanish Moor's Tragedy,* a collaboration by Dekker and Marston, might also have been featured, and *Blurt, Master Constable* was probably written soon after. For speculation that works by William Stanley and William Percy were produced, see W. Reavley Gair, *The Children of Paul's: The Story of a Theatre Company* (Cambridge: Cambridge University Press, 1982), 116–18, 53. For the same period, all that is left of the Children of the Chapel's repertoire is *Cynthia's Revels* and *Poetaster.* Chapman's three comedies from about 1602, *The Gentleman Usher, May-Day,* and *Sir Giles Goosecap,* probably filled the gap left by Jonson's diminished production from 1602 to 1605.

Later the two private repertoires were almost indistinguishable. In 1605, for instance, Edward Kirkham brought Marston's *Parasitaster, or The Fawn,* with him from Blackfriars to Paul's when he switched companies. See E. K. Chambers, *The Elizabethan Stage,* 4 vols. (Oxford: Clarendon, 1923), 2:51. At one time or another between 1600 and 1606, Jonson, Marston, and Dekker wrote for both companies. The pattern of competition between these private venues changed when Marston stopped sparring with Jonson, left Paul's, and collaborated with him and Chapman on *Eastward Ho* (1605) at Blackfriars.

2. Quoted from Gair, *The Children of Paul's,* 118. Paul's in 1575 became the first private commercial playhouse in London; Blackfriars opened a year later. During its first period of operation, from 1575 to 1590/91, Lyly dominated the repertoire, and during its second period, from 1599 to around 1606–1608 (according to Gair, 172–75), Marston and then Middleton. Performances appear to have been held on Sunday and Monday, between four and six o'clock, possibly in Haydon's house, a structure built in the 1570s in the northwest corner of the Chapter House precinct (55). That Paul's theater remained dormant thereafter was guaranteed by a yearly payment of twenty pounds promised by Philip Rossiter of the Children of Her Majesty's Chapel to Pearce (173). When the Children were displaced at Blackfriars by the King's Men, the new syndicate of seven "housekeepers" who now held the lease assumed half of this bribe.

3. The relevant facts are found in Chambers, *The Elizabethan Stage,* 2:41–42; Irwin Smith, *Shakespeare's Blackfriars Playhouse; Its History and Its Design* (New York: New York University Press, 1964); Michael Shapiro, *Children of the Revels: Boy Companies of Shakespeare's Time and Their Plays* (New York: Columbia University Press, 1977); and Andrew Gurr, *The Shakespearean Stage, 1574–1642,* 3rd ed. (Cambridge: Cambridge University Press, 1992), 49–55.

4. Andrew Gurr, *Playgoing in Shakespeare's London* (Cambridge: Cambridge University Press, 1987), 163.

5. Thomas Dekker, *The Gull's Hornbook,* ed. R. B. McKerrow (New York: AMS Press, 1971), 38. See also Gair's chapter, "The Decay of St. Paul's," in *The Children of Paul's,* 13–43.

6. Anthony Caputi, *John Marston, Satirist* (Ithaca: Cornell University Press, 1961), 159, and W. David Kay, *Ben Jonson, Horace, and the Poetomachia* (Ph.D. diss., Princeton University, 1968), 207–51, refer to this episode as a "burlesque" of Jonson's play.

7. See Arnold Davenport's introduction to *The Poems of John Marston* (Liverpool: Liverpool University Press, 1961), 15–16.

8. Anne Barton, *Ben Jonson, Dramatist* (Cambridge: Cambridge University Press, 1984), 79.

9. This diagram is indebted to C. R. Baskervill's chart in *English Elements in Jonson's Early Comedy* (Austin: University of Texas Press, 1911), 257. Jonson, however, confuses his own elaborate pattern at 5.11.104–6 by identifying the four unmasked female courtiers as Philautia, Gelaia (Moria's daughter), Phantaste, and Moria (in place of Argurion).

10. John Weever, *The Whipping of the Satyr*, lines 259–62, in *The Whipper Pamphlets*, ed. Arnold Davenport (Liverpool: Liverpool University Press, 1951).

11. In reaction to Jonson's three couplings of Marston with Dekker as Clove and Orange in *Every Man Out*, Hedon and Anaides in *Cynthia's Revels*, and Crispinus and Demetrius in *Poetaster*, Marston pairs Jonson with Simplicius Faber (Simple Maker) in *What You Will* and Dekker links him with Asinius Bubo (Stupid Owl) in *Satiromastix*. E. A. J. Honigmann, *John Weever: A Biography of a Literary Associate of Shakespeare and Jonson* (Manchester: Manchester University Press, 1987), 42–51, identifies both characters with Weever. But in *The Whipping of the Satyr* Weever condemned Jonson as the "Humourist" shortly before *Satiromastix* was staged and would not have been depicted as his servile follower.

12. Barton, *Ben Jonson, Dramatist*, 74.

13. Caputi, *John Marston, Satirist*, 157, writes that the "importance" of the Induction to *What You Will* for an understanding "of Marston's work in satirical comedy cannot be overstressed" as "an overgrowth of the poetomachia." But he never appreciates the depth of Marston and Jonson's philosophical conflict because he believes their main difference was only "structural."

14. Richard Hardin analyzes the nuances of this name in "Marston's Kinsayder: The Dog's Voice," *Notes and Queries* 227 (1982): 134–35. Hardin observes that in the satire to Guilpin added to the second edition of *The Scourge* (1599), Marston quotes John Hall's epigram (which had been pasted into some copies of *Pygmalion's Image*), which states that Marston was not in reality a dog-catcher but a "*dog . . . best cured by cutting and kinsing*" (10.51). In the margin next to Hall's epigram he comments, "Mark the witty allusion to my name."

15. I have here amended Wood's meaningless "*Chirall*" to "*Chival*" or "horse." Quadratus is appropriately paraphrasing Comedy's rebuke of Envy in the Induction to *Mucedorus* (London, 1598): "Mars shall himself breathe down / A peerless crown upon brave envy's head, / And raise his chival with a lasting fame" (lines 27–29). Marston had played on the same line from *Richard III*—"*A man, a man, a kingdom for a man*"—both at the opening and as a refrain for his "Cynic Satire" (7.1) in *The Scourge of Villainy*.

16. *The Battle of Alcazar* (2.3.101) in *The Works of George Peele*, ed. A. H. Bullen, 2 vols. (Boston: Houghton Mifflin, 1888). Pistol's mangling of Peele is pointed out by A. R. Humphreys in his note on 2.4.175 in the New Arden edition of *The Second Part of King Henry IV* (London: Methuen, 1966).

17. Quoted from the Coverdale Bible (Cologne?, 1535). Dryden uses the term in the same way in *Absalom and Achitophel* (1681), in which the latter attempts to prove "the King himself a Jebusite" (line 213), in *John Dryden*, ed. Keith Walker (Oxford: Oxford University Press, 1987).

18. Alfred Harbage, *Shakespeare and the Rival Traditions* (New York: Macmillan, 1952), 109, and David Riggs, *Ben Jonson: A Life* (Cambridge: Harvard University Press, 1989), 74, consider Marston's reply as being based primarily on class prejudice. Jonson, they claim, designated himself a true poet in order to gain ac-

cess to an upper-class audience of courtiers and gentlemen from which he was alienated by low birth, poverty, and his unrewarding profession. He criticized the gentry to justify a new meritocracy of which he offered himself as a prime example. Marston then chastised him to defend the privileged class Jonson attacked. This interpretation alone reduces their complex poetics to a crude class bias.

19. The extensive literature on this topic includes Rosalie L. Colie's *Pseudodoxia Epidemica* (Princeton: Princeton University Press, 1966); David Willbern, "Shakespeare's Nothing," in *Representing Shakespeare: New Psychoanalytic Essays*, eds. Murray Schwartz and Coppélia Kahn (Baltimore: Johns Hopkins University Press, 1980), 244–63; and Edward W. Tayler, "*King Lear* and Negation," *English Literary Renaissance* (20) 1990: 17–39.

20. In quoting this passage, I have emended "not rules of Art" to "your rules of Art" in order to remedy a misprint preserved in Wood's edition.

21. Samuel Daniel later used a similar tactic against Jonson when the latter criticized the lack of erudition in his masque-making. See W. David Kay, *Ben Jonson: A Literary Life* (New York: St. Martin's Press, 1995), 79–80.

22. George Puttenham, *The Art of English Poesie*, eds. Gladys Doidge Willcock and Alice Walker (Cambridge: Cambridge University Press, 1936), 18.

23. Marston's poetics thus exemplifies what David Summers in *The Judgment of Sense: Renaissance Naturalism and the Rise of Aesthetics* (Cambridge: Cambridge University Press, 1987), 2, calls "the development of art based on point of view at the dawn of the modern period" in which "the beautiful itself is conformity to human sense before it is evidence of transcendental value."

7. Shakespeare at the Fountain of Self-Love: *Twelfth Night* at the Center of the Poets' War

1. David Riggs, *Ben Jonson: A Life* (Cambridge: Harvard University Press, 1989), 84.

2. Riggs's truncated chronology of the Poets' War follows Ralph W. Berringer's influential article, "Jonson's *Cynthia's Revels* and the War of the Theatres," *Philological Quarterly* 22 (1943): 1–22. Because Berringer incorrectly believes that Chrisoganus is complimentary in *Histriomastix* and that Brabant Senior does not ridicule Jonson in *Jack Drum*, he concludes that Marston "detonated the 'War of the Theatres' in *What You Will* by parodying passages of *Every Man Out of His Humour* and *Cynthia's Revels* and caricaturing Jonson in the satiric scholar Lampatho Doria" (20).

3. See the Chronological Appendix.

4. J. M. Lothian and T. W. Craik, in their introduction to *Twelfth Night* (New York: Methuen, 1975), mention Turner's "attractive theory" that "*What You Will* may have been Shakespeare's working title . . . before Marston preempted it in the Spring of 1601 and one which required modification before the play was made public" (xxxiii). Yet Robert Fleissner in "Shakespeare's Carte Blanche—Appropri-

ated by Marston," *English Studies* 56 (1975): 390–92, forcefully counters this mistake. Now that Fleay's conjecture that Malvolio was based on Malevole in *The Malcontent* has been dismissed as a chronological impossibility and Shakespeare's influence on Marston has been better understood, Fleissner explains, "the old notion that Shakespeare was responding to *What You Will* in composing *Twelfth Night* is no longer taken seriously by scholars" (391). Shakespeare follows the lead of *Cynthia's Revels, or the Fountain of Self-Love* in calling his own play *Twelfth Night, or What You Will.* Each juxtaposes an occasion of revelry with a reference to its psychological undercurrent.

5. Philip Finkelpearl, *John Marston of the Middle Temple* (Cambridge: Harvard University Press, 1969), 176, and David Farley-Hills, *Jacobean Drama: A Critical Survey of the Professional Drama, 1600–25* (New York: St. Martin's, 1988), 44.

6. George L. Geckle, *John Marston's Drama: Themes, Images, Sources* (Rutherford, N. J.: Fairleigh Dickinson University Press, 1980), 93–94.

7. P. A. Daniels first identified this source in a note to *The Works of John Marston*, ed. A. H. Bullen, 3 vols. (London: John C. Nimmo, 1887), 1:lxviii. See also Anthony Caputi, *John Marston, Satirist* (Ithaca: Cornell University Press, 1961), 160–67. The Tersandro-Oranta-Luigi story is imitated in the Albano-Celia-Jacomo triangle.

8. John Hollander, "*Twelfth Night* and the Morality of Indulgence," *Sewanee Review* 67 (1959): 220–38. Andrew Gurr concludes even more specifically in *Playgoing in Shakespeare's London* (Cambridge: Cambridge University Press, 1987), 267n, that "*Twelfth Night* was written after *Every Man Out* and partly as a reply to the idea of dramaturgy expressed in that play."

9. Harold Jenkins, "Shakespeare's *Twelfth Night*," in *Shakespeare: The Comedies; A Collection of Critical Essays*, ed. Kenneth Muir (Englewood Cliffs, N. J.: Prentice Hall, 1965), 72.

10. David Bevington, "Shakespeare vs Jonson on Satire," *Shakespeare 1971, Proceedings of the World Shakespeare Congress*, eds. Clifford Leech and J.M.R. Margeson (Toronto: University of Toronto Press, 1972), 120. He corroborates C. H. Herford's opinion in his preface to *Ben Jonson*, ed. Brinsley Nicholson, 3 vols. (London: T. F. Unwin, 1893), 1:xliii. See Hollander, "*Twelfth Night* and the Morality of Indulgence," 220.

11. Judith Kegan Gardiner, " 'A Wither'd Daffodil': Narcissism in *Cynthia's Revels*," in *Craftsmanship in Context: The Development of Ben Jonson's Poetry* (The Hague: Mouton, 1975), 40.

12. *The Yale Edition of the Works of Samuel Johnson*, eds. Allen T. Hazen et al., 16 vols. (New Haven: Yale University Press, 1958–), 7:326.

13. *The Diary of John Manningham of the Middle Temple 1602–1603*, ed. Robert Parker Sorlien (Hanover, N. H.: The University Press of New England, 1976), 133.

14. Nancy S. Leonard, "Shakespeare and Jonson Again: The Comic Forms," *Renaissance Drama* 10 (1979): 46.

15. *The Ethics of Aristotle: The Nicomachean Ethics*, trans. J.A.K. Thomson (London: Penguin, 1976), 300–301.

16. Cristina Malcolmson, " 'What You Will': Social Mobility and Gender in *Twelfth Night*," in *The Matter of Difference: Materialist Feminist Criticism of Shakespeare*, ed. Valerie Wayne (Ithaca: Cornell University Press, 1991), 29–57.

17. Ibid., 39.

18. "Of Apolonius and Silla" in *Barnabe Riche, His Farewell to Military Profession*, ed. Donald Beecher (Ottawa: Dovehouse Editions, 1992), 180.

19. Although the *OED* lists Crooke as having first used the word "Caesarean" in 1615, it is possible that Shakespeare had this similar coinage in mind a few years earlier. Cesario is certainly in this sense, like Macduff, "not of woman born."

20. See Paul Mueschke and Jeannette Fleisher, "Jonsonian Elements in the Comic Underplot of *Twelfth Night*," *PMLA* 48 (1933): 722–40.

21. Oscar James Campbell, *Comicall Satyre and Shakespeare's* Troilus and Cressida (San Marino: The Huntington Library, 1970), 185.

22. A. W. Schlegel, *A Course of Lectures on Dramatic Literature, 1809–11*, trans. John Black (London, 1846), quoted from *Twelfth Night*, ed. John F. Andrews (London: Dent, 1991), 207.

23. Caputi, *John Marston, Satirist*, 136.

24. Finkelpearl, *John Marston of the Middle Temple*, 176–77.

25. Riggs, *Ben Jonson*, 75.

26. Nevertheless, the note on line 1 of *The Riverside Shakespeare* emphatically states that "the bird of loudest lay / On the sole Arabian tree" is "clearly not the phoenix."

8. "Impeaching Your Own Quality": Constructions of Poetic Authority in *Poetaster* and *Satiromastix*

1. John Davies, *Wit's Pilgrimage* (London, 1605), sig. P3^r. The phrase "Imps of Phoebus" refers primarily to poets (the offspring of Apollo) attacking their own profession, not to the child actors rebuking the adults as W. Reavley Gair suggests in *The Children of Paul's: The Story of a Theatre Company* (Cambridge: Cambridge University Press, 1982), 137. Davies again calls poets "Phoebus' Imps" in "Paper's Complaint" (line 147, quoted in chapter 1, on page 44).

2. Even though Dekker speaks of the Poetomachia only in reference to *Poetaster* and *Satiromastix*, his play resonates with motifs from all three of Jonson's comical satires and Marston's commentaries on them.

3. In his introduction to the play, Fredson Bowers writes that since it was registered as "A book called the untrussing of the humorous poets" (ending with a mistaken plural) and since *Satiromastix* was printed only on the title page, the latter was its "literary title" and the former "the theatrical" (*The Dramatic Works of Thomas Dekker*, 4 vols. [Cambridge: Cambridge University Press, 1953–1961], 1:301).

4. See the Chronological Appendix for details.

5. Cyrus Hoy points this out in *Introductions, Notes, and Commentaries to Texts*

in The Dramatic Works of Thomas Dekker, 4 vols. (Cambridge: Cambridge University Press, 1980), 1:197.

6. Andrew Gurr, *Playgoing in Shakespeare's London* (Cambridge: Cambridge University Press, 1987), 72–79.

7. Ovid was banished to Tomis in A.D. 8, the same year that Julia, Augustus's granddaughter (not daughter, as Jonson has it) was sent into exile, and this has led to a suspicion that the two events were linked.

8. See Gaius Suetonius Tranquillus, *The Twelve Caesars*, trans. Robert Graves (Hammondsworth: Penguin, 1954), 93. From reading Suetonius's *The Twelve Caesars*, Jonson knew that it was not Ovid but Augustus who had commissioned a "Banquet of the Gods." "Augustus' private banquet, known as 'The Feast of the Divine Twelve,' . . . caused a scandal," Suetonius writes. "The guests came dressed as gods and goddesses, Augustus himself representing Apollo."

9. Richard Helgerson, *Self-Crowned Laureates: Spenser, Jonson, Milton and the Literary System* (Berkeley: University of California Press, 1983), 111–14.

10. See Stanley Fish, "Authors-Readers: Jonson's Community of the Same," *Representations* 7 (1984): 26–58.

11. W. David Kay's *Ben Jonson, Horace, and the Poetomachia* (Ph.D. diss., Princeton University, 1968) is the most thorough study of Jonson's use of Horace as a persona in *Poetaster*. Eugene M. Waith's "The Poet's Morals in Jonson's *Poetaster*," *Modern Language Quarterly* 12 (1951): 13–19, presents an incisive reading of Horace's superiority to Ovid.

12. Horace's poems are cited from *Satires, Epistles, and Ars Poetica*, ed. and trans. H. R. Fairclough (Cambridge: Harvard University Press, 1926).

13. Critics have been polarized in their readings of *Pygmalion's Image*, uncertain as to whether or not its ironies negate or reinforce Marston's libertine stance. K. Gustav Cross, "Marston's *Metamorphosis of Pygmalion's Image*: A Mock-Epyllion," *Études Anglaises* 13 (1960): 331–36, and Anthony Caputi, *John Marston, Satirist* (Ithaca: Cornell University Press, 1961), 14–22, agree that the poem burlesques its romantic narrative. But Arnold Davenport, "The Quarrel of the Satirists," *Modern Language Review* 37 (1942): 123–30, and Philip Finkelpearl, *John Marston of the Middle Temple* (Cambridge: Harvard University Press, 1969), 94–104, are more persuasive in their argument that even though Marston's poem contains ironic elements, its final effect is to sanction desire. It is for this reason, they conclude, that the poem conforms to rather than parodies an Ovidian norm.

14. Anonymous, *2 Return from Parnassus*, in *The Three Parnassus Plays (1598–1601)*, ed. J. B. Leishman (London: Ivor Nicholson & Watson, 1949), 279–84.

15. John Peter, "John Marston's Plays," *Scrutiny* 17 (1950): 141–42.

16. E. K. Chambers, *The Elizabethan Stage*, 4 vols. (Oxford: Clarendon, 1923), 3:303.

17. Quoted from *An Essay of Dramatic Poesy* in *John Dryden*, ed. Keith Walker (Oxford: Oxford University Press, 1987), 83–84.

18. George Parfitt, *Ben Jonson: Public Poet and Private Man* (London: J. M. Dent, 1976), 24.

19. See *Lexiphanes*, in *Lucian*, trans. A. M. Harmon, 8 vols. (Cambridge: Harvard University Press, 1936), 5:319. Lycinus convinces Lexiphanes to allow Sopolis the physician to purge him of his habit of "distorting his language, making these preposterous combinations, and taking himself very seriously in the matter, as if it were a great thing for him to use an alien idiom." After being purged, Lexiphanes is instructed to read the "best poets" (323).

20. While not all of Crispinus's vomit can be traced to Marston, these specimens, here listed alphabetically, are culled from his dramatic and nondramatic work, with half found in *Antonio's Revenge*.

1. barmy froth (line 492): *The Scourge* ("In Lectores," line 8, 6.2) and *Jack Drum* (3:182).
2. chilblained (line 485): *Jack Drum* (3:199) and *Antonio's Revenge* (1:69).
3. clumsy (line 519): *Jack Drum* (3:199) and *Antonio's Revenge* (1:69).
4. clutched (line 519): *Antonio's Revenge* (1:23, 1:85).
5. conscious (line 506): *The Scourge* (8.95), *What You Will* (2:240), and *Antonio's Revenge* (1:78).
6. damp (line 506): *Antonio's Revenge* (1:78) (plural).
7. glibbery (line 475): *Antonio and Mellida* (1:16, 1:21, 1:45) and *Jack Drum* (3:185).
8. incubus (line 468): *Antonio's Revenge* (1:73).
9. magnificate (line 280): *Certain Satires* (2.66) and *The Scourge* (3.192; "Proemium in Librum Secundum," line 3).
10. puffy (line 494): *Pygmalion's Image* ("Author in Praise," line 23), *Certain Satires* (2.139), and *The Scourge* ("In Lectores," line 42; 4.55).
11. quaking custard (line 525): *The Scourge* (2.4) (custards quake).
12. snarling gusts (line 525): *Antonio's Revenge* (1:69).
13. snotteries (line 483): *The Scourge* (2.71) (singular).
14. spurious (line 483): *The Scourge* (2.35).

For a detailed analysis of Jonson's parodies of Marston's language, see Tom Cain's excellent notes, especially for this scene, in his edition of *Poetaster* (Manchester: Manchester University Press, 1995).

21. Anne Barton, *Ben Jonson, Dramatist* (Cambridge: Cambridge University Press, 1984), 90, recognizes how with *Poetaster* Jonson had arrived "at an impasse" in "the evolution of his own comic style."

22. For a detailed treatment of Dekker's strategy for warning potential patrons about his rival's failings, see Robert C. Evans, *Jonson and the Contexts of His Time* (Lewisburg, Penn.: Bucknell University Press, 1994), 22–35.

23. Hoy, *Introductions, Notes, and Commentaries*, 1:194–95.

24. Roscoe Addison Small, *The Stage-Quarrel Between Ben Jonson and the So-*

Called Poetasters (1899; reprint, New York: AMS Press, 1966), 121–22, and Barton, *Ben Jonson, Dramatist*, 87–88, assume that Dekker was working on the overplot concerning William Rufus and Sir Walter Terrill when, in haste, he added the Horace material to react to Jonson, although this material destroyed the putative unity of his work. Evans in *Jonson and the Contexts of His Time*, however, defends the intellectual coherence of Dekker's play (22–35).

25. For conjecture on the poet's early acting career, see Fredson Bowers, "Ben Jonson the Actor," *Studies in Philology* 34 (1934): 392–406. Bowers suggests that Jonson first became an actor with Pembroke's Men in 1595/96, for whom he played Hieronimo on tour, and that he continued with the company when it came to London in February 1597, at which time he acted the unknown part of Zulziman at the Swan in Paris Garden.

26. Chambers, *The Elizabethan Stage*, 2:297.

27. For details of the parody, see the Chronological Appendix, number 10.

28. See Edward A. Freeman, *The Reign of William Rufus and the Accession of Henry the First*, 2 vols. (Oxford: Clarendon, 1882), 2:325–35.

9. Ben Jonson and the "Little Eyases": Theatrical Politics in *Hamlet*

1. E. K. Chambers, *The Elizabethan Stage*, 4 vols. (Oxford: Clarendon, 1923), 2:43, and *Hamlet*, ed. Harold Jenkins (London: Methuen, 1982), 1–2. This scholarly consensus, however, has been complicated by the problem of whether the "little eyases" passage also alludes to the Children of Paul's.

2. Roslyn L. Knutson, "Falconer to the Little Eyases: A New Date and Commercial Agenda for the 'Little Eyases' Passage in *Hamlet*," *Shakespeare Quarterly* 46 (1995): 4. Knutson follows Grace Ioppolo, *Revising Shakespeare* (Cambridge: Harvard University Press, 1991), 145, in claiming that the "humour of children" passage in Q1 *Hamlet* was added to Shakespeare's early work. But she differs from Ioppolo in doubting that Shakespeare wrote the "little eyases" passage (30*n*) and insisting that it was composed between 1606 and 1608 to scold the Children of Blackfriars for producing political satire "that put the entire playhouse industry at risk" (31).

More to the point, Joseph Loewenstein's "Plays Agonistic and Competitive: The Textual Approach to Elsinore," *Renaissance Drama* 19 (1988): 63–96, provides a useful typology of the ways modern critics have contextualized the passage as a reaction to the War of the Theaters, which he views as involving "important authorial and historical emergencies" (64). He indicates in this marvelously suggestive essay how the genre of revenge tragedy came to prominence in the third phase of the Poets' War. I agree with his hypothesis that *Hamlet* "went into production without any allusion to the War of the Theaters" (66). Like Loewenstein, I appreciate Paul Werstine's open-ended questioning of the origins of Q2 and F1 in "The Textual Mystery of *Hamlet*," *Shakespeare Quarterly* 39 (1988): 1–26, and I consequently present no general theory of their genesis and status in relation to each other. But I am nevertheless convinced that the argument that the "little eyases" discussion was deleted from the copy behind the Second Quarto is stronger than Loewenstein's suggestion that it was subsequently added to produce what later became the Folio text (86–87n).

3. My three excerpts begin with Hamlet's question, "Why do you laugh?" and end with the players' entrance. Quotations from the *Hamlet* quartos of 1603 and 1604 are cited, in the text, by page signatures. For the First Folio of 1623 I have used the system of through line numbers devised by Charlton Hinman for his edition of *The First Folio of Shakespeare* (New York: Norton, 1968).

4. Lewis Theobald first submitted "eyases"—"Young Nestings, Creatures just out of the Egg"—as a substitute for "Yases" in *The Works of Shakespeare*, 7 vols. (London, 1733), 7:275n.

5. Steven Mullaney, in *The Place of the Stage: License, Play, and Power in Renaissance England* (Chicago: University of Chicago Press, 1988), stresses how the public theaters were situated in the liberties of the suburbs north and south of London. But these theaters were still associated with the prestigious capital. Dekker, for instance, in *The Bellman of London* (1608), writes of itinerant players who "forsake the stately and our more than Roman City Stages, to travel upon the hard hoof from village to village for cheese and buttermilk" (*Thomas Dekker, The Non-Dramatic Works*, ed. Alexander Grossart, 5 vols. [New York: Russell & Russell, 1963], 3:81). Shakespeare thus dignifies the players by referring to them as the "tragedians of the city," while Jonson speaks of how "all the sinners" of "the suburbs" attend their performances.

6. See *The Plays of William Shakespeare . . With . . Notes by Samuel Johnson and George Steevens*, 10 vols. (London, 1778), 10:256n, and Richard Dutton's convincing support of Steevens's position in "*Hamlet, An Apology for Actors*, and the Sign of the Globe," *Shakespeare Survey* 41 (1988): 35–43.

7. See Andrew Gurr, *The Shakespearean Stage 1574–1642*, 3rd ed. (Cambridge: Cambridge University Press, 1992), 156–59. Charles William Wallace, *The Children of the Chapel at Blackfriars 1597–1603* (Lincoln: University of Nebraska Press, 1908), 21, observes that "the buildings of the Blackfriars precinct were situated on the high embankment north of the Thames and east of the old Fleet ditch—now New Bridge street . . . opening on a short, narrow, irregular passage-way, still called 'Playhouse Yard.'" The full contract of sale by Sir William More to James Burbage specifying the nature of the property is printed in C. C. Stopes, *Burbage and Shakespeare's Stage* (London: Alexander Moring, 1913), 170–74. For the underground location of Paul's, see W. Reavley Gair, *The Children of Paul's: The Story of a Theatre Company* (Cambridge: Cambridge University Press, 1982), 50. *Father Hubburd's Tale* is quoted by Chambers, *The Elizabethan Stage*, 2:50.

8. Irwin Smith, *Shakespeare's Blackfriars Playhouse; Its History and Its Design* (New York: New York University Press, 1964), 175–79.

9. Robert Greene, *Greene's Groatsworth of Wit, Bought with a Million of Repentance (1592)*, ed. D. Allen Carroll (Binghamton, N.Y.: Medieval & Renaissance Texts & Studies, 1994), 84–85.

10. Alfred Harbage, *Shakespeare and the Rival Traditions* (New York: Macmillan, 1952), 29.

11. See the Introduction, note 10, for an overview of London theater audiences.

12. Based on plausible inference, Captain Tucca has been identified with Ralph Hanham by Tom Cain, who builds a composite portrait in his edition of *Poetaster* (Manchester: Manchester University Press, 1995), 48–50. Cain assumes that the "captayne Haname," who twice pawned linen to Henslowe in 1593, is the same "Captain Rafe Hamon" who desired "one of the companies that now go into Ireland" in August 1601. Obviously a well-known figure of the time in theatrical circles, he was first parodied by Guilpin under the name Tucca in "Satire Preludium," lines 25–34, of *Skialetheia*. Tucca and Hanham are both defined by the overlapping domains of pawnbroking, theater, and the military.

13. Chambers, *The Elizabethan Stage*, 1:379.

14. Arnold Davenport mentions Marston's expulsion in the introduction to *The Poems of John Marston* (Liverpool: Liverpool University Press, 1961), 1. He was reinstated on 27 November 1601. The terms of his father's will are discussed by David G. O'Neill, "The Commencement of Marston's Career as a Dramatist," *The Review of English Studies* 22 (1971): 444.

15. For a close exploration of the tensions in comical satire that led up to this break with theater, see Robert C. Jones, "The Satirist's Retirement in Jonson's 'Apologetical Dialogue,' " *ELH* 34 (1967): 447–67. Alan Sinfield also probes the contraditions in Jonson's program in his essay "*Poetaster*, the Author, and the Perils of Cultural Production," in *Material London, ca. 1600*, ed. Lena Cowen Orlin (Philadelphia: University of Pennsylvania Press, 2000), 75–89.

16. I disagree on this point with Tom Cain's recent edition of *Poetaster*, which makes Histrio, not Aesop, responsible for Lupus's slander of Horace, even though the character who will be whipped is called into the room as "Master Aesop" and directly addressed as such (5.3.114, 121). This same player Aesop was first specifically mocked by Tucca at 3.4.295–98 for his bad breath and body odor. Tucca tells Histrio that he should not invite him to their supper unless "you can ram up his mouth with cloves." Tucca tends to say that others smell bad, but his treatment of Aesop is special. When Aesop appears in the fifth act, Tucca continues this vein of humor by calling him a "stinkard" and asking him if he is treating his halitosis, "Come Aesop: hast a Bay leaf i' thy mouth?" (5.3.121–22). The grouped entrance for act 5, scene 3 names Histrio instead of Aesop, but this is a mistake, as Herford and Simpson's edition recognizes in citing William Gifford's emendation to his 1816 *Works of Ben Jonson*. Gifford added Aesop to the cast with his stage direction, "*Enter Aesop, followed by Crispinus and Demetrius*," after 5.3.117. Aesop's name suggests both the Roman tragedian Aesopus and the earlier Greek Aesop, the teller of fables, who, like the slandering actor, was involved in the interpretation of beast allegories.

17. E. K. Chambers, *William Shakespeare: A Study of Facts and Problems*, 2 vols. (Oxford: Clarendon, 1930), 1:79, cites the patent of 1603 for the renamed King's

Men, which lists eight of these sharers, plus Robert Fletcher, a protégé of James I, who appears to have held an honorific position in the company. Thomas Pope was the only sharer to leave the company by that time.

18. Roscoe Addison Small, *The Stage-Quarrel Between Ben Jonson and the So-Called Poetasters* (1899; reprint, New York: AMS Press, 1966), 58, was pessimistic about this matter and concluded that, "without doubt, these were easily recognizable by an Elizabethan audience; but their identity is no longer discoverable." The first scholar to find credible supporting evidence for identification, however, was T. W. Baldwin in his often unreliable study, *The Organization and Personnel of the Shakespearean Company* (New York: Russell and Russell, 1927), 232–34. He was followed by Henry David Gray, "The Chamberlain's Men and the *Poetaster*," *Modern Language Review* 42 (1947): 173–79, who independently agrees with Baldwin in four cases. I accept as possible only one of Gray's revisions of Baldwin, the equation of Frisker with Armin. Gray, however, blunders in seeing Aesop as Shakespeare, an error corrected by Percy Simpson in "A Modern Fable of Aesop," *Modern Language Review* 43 (1948): 403–5. (Simpson's article only restores the identity of Aesop as Heminges, which had been posited by Baldwin, without evaluating the other identifications, although he is impresssed by the high correlation of identifications independently made by Baldwin and Gray.) In only one case—on the question of the sharer represented as Poluphagus—do I differ with their hypotheses.

19. The definition of the cant term "politician" is found in *Ben Jonson*, eds. Herford and Simpson, 11 vols. (Oxford: Clarendon, 1925–52), 1:427. Percy Simpson, "A Modern Fable of Aesop," 405, quotes Middleton's *A Mad World, My Masters*: "which is your Politician amongst you? . . . he that works out Restraints, makes best legs at Court, and has a suit made of purpose, for the company's business." Gerald E. Bentley discusses Heminges as the business manager of the Chamberlain-King's Men in *The Profession of Player in Shakespeare's Time* (Princeton: Princeton University Press, 1984), 151–55. Demonstrating Heminges's unique service as the company's manager for approximately thirty-four years, Bentley writes: "On occasions he was joined by another sharer: twice by Thomas Pope, once by George Bryan, once by Richard Cowley, and once by Augustine Phillips, but generally his name appears alone. . . . About fifty such payments to Heminges for court performances are recorded, reaching a total of well over £3,000" (151).

20. Chambers, *The Elizabethan Stage*, 2:321.

21. Bentley, *The Profession of Player in Shakespeare's Time*, 19–20.

22. Chambers, *The Elizabethan Stage*, 2:205. Tom Cain's introduction to *Poetaster*, 40–44, considers the long-standing possibility that Jonson is here somehow commenting on the production of *Richard II*, sponsored by the Essex conspirators at the Globe on the afternoon before the earl's rebellion on 8 February 1601. The parallel is suggestive but does not significantly explain *Poetaster*'s core fiction. Further work needs to be done on the problem.

23. Chambers, *The Elizabethan Stage*, 2:312–13.

24. Samuel Rowlands, *The Letting of Humour's Blood in the Head Vein* (London, 1600), sig. D2ᵛ, Satire 4, lines 10–11. Rowlands and Taylor are cited by Baldwin, *The Organization and Personnel of the Shakespearean Company*, 231. Baldwin also notes that Pope left a collection of arms in his will, and that this might link him to Mango's begging of rapiers. David Wiles, *Shakespeare's Clown: Actor and Text in the Elizabethan Playhouse* (Cambridge: Cambridge University Press, 1987), 32, mentions that Pope and Kemp were among five itinerant "instrumentalists and tumblers" who had actually visited Elsinore in 1586 and, unlike Yorick, survived the experience.

25. Bentley, *The Profession of Player in Shakespeare's Time*, 293, includes a cast list from *The Alchemist*. It is, however, from the 1618/19 season.

26. David Bevington, *Tudor Drama and Politics: A Critical Approach to Topical Meaning* (Cambridge: Harvard University Press, 1968), 285.

27. Chambers, *The Elizabethan Stage*, 2:153.

28. The title page of the first quarto of *Hamlet* states that the play was performed at Cambridge and Oxford. This does not necessarily mean, however, that this butchered version of the play was presented there. Richard Dutton, "*Hamlet, An Apology for Actors*, and the Sign of the Globe," 37, conjectures that the force of the in-joke could "vary depending on whether the lines were delivered within the Globe itself ('We're still here, in spite of them') or elsewhere ('Look what we've been driven to')."

29. See Alan Somerset, "'How Chances It They Travel?' Provincial Touring, Playing Places, and the King's Men," *Shakespeare Survey* 47 (1994): 45–60.

30. Stephen Orgel, *The Illusion of Power: Political Theater in the English Renaissance* (1975; reprint, Berkeley: University of California Press, 1991), 2.

31. Harbage, *Shakespeare and the Rival Traditions*, 46–47. Nevertheless, David Farley-Hills, "How Often Did the Eyases Fly?" *Notes and Queries* 38 (1991): 461–66, speculates that the Children might have performed up to three times a week and were a more substantial threat than had been formerly imagined. Any friction between the Chamberlain's-King's Men and the child acting companies, however, was laid to rest when in 1608 they replaced the Children of the Chapel at Blackfriars and then paid to keep Paul's dormant. For a sense of the difficulty of assessing Elizabethan theatrical economics based mostly on capacity estimates, see Theodore B. Leinwand, *Theatre, Finance and Society in Early Modern England* (Cambridge: Cambridge University Press, 1999), 140–43.

32. M. C. Bradbrook, *The Rise of the Common Player: A Study of Actor and Society in Shakespeare's England* (Cambridge: Cambridge University Press, 1962), 17–18.

33. Greene, *Greene's Groatsworth*, 68.

34. *Hamlet*, ed. Harold Jenkins, notes on 2.2.327 and 2.2.337.

35. Kenneth Thorpe Rowe, *A Theater in Your Head* (New York: Minerva, 1960), 82.

36. See *Hamlet*, ed. John Dover Wilson (Cambridge: Cambridge University Press, 1934), 177. This odd assumption that the Chamberlain's Men suffered an

"inhibition" for their part in Essex's "late innovation" is one of the cobwebs of criticism surrounding the play. The Chamberlain's Men were not "inhibited" in 1601. In fact, they played before the Queen on 24 February, the night before the earl's execution. Talk of Essex's rebellion was certainly in the air when Shakespeare wrote this passage, and this might have influenced the language he employs. But the theme of "innovation" was a central topic of *Hamlet*, and the Essex argument, without corroborating evidence, savors of special pleading. Shakespeare explicitly discusses another "innovation," one that threatened his own theatrical sovereignty: the revitalization of the child acting companies.

37. A. W. Pollard presented his case in *Shakespeare Folios and Quartos* (London: Methuen, 1909). Albert Weiner's introduction to his edition of *Hamlet: The First Quarto* (Great Neck: Barron's Educational Series, 1979) rejects the theory of memorial reconstruction, as does Steven Urkowitz in " 'Well-sayd olde Mole': Burying Three *Hamlet*s in Modern Editions," in *Shakespeare Study Today*, ed. Georgianna Ziegler (New York: AMS Press, 1986), 37–70, and "Back to Basics: Thinking about the *Hamlet* First Quarto," in *The Hamlet First Published (Q1, 1603)*, ed. Thomas Clayton (Newark: University of Delaware Press, 1992), 257–91. The majority of scholars in this volume, however, dismiss Q1 as spurious.

38. Kathleen Irace's convincing statistical argument that Q1 is a memorial reconstruction was made possible by W. W. Greg, *The Merry Wives of Windsor, 1602* (Oxford: Clarendon, 1910), who proposed that the Q1 version of that play was a "bad" quarto, probably recalled by the actor who played the Host. Henry David Gray, "The First Quarto of *Hamlet*," *Modern Language Review* 10 (1915): 171–80, then applied this theory to Q1 *Hamlet* and determined that the play was also probably reconstructed by the actor who played Marcellus. G. I. Duthie, *The "Bad" Quarto of* Hamlet (Cambridge: Cambridge University Press, 1941), presented further confirmation that the play was memorially reconstructed, by emphasizing how Marcellus recalled his lines and those around them with greater consistency.

In a compelling restatement of the Marcellus Quarto theory, Irace, in "Origins and Agents of Q1 *Hamlet*," in *The Hamlet First Published*, ed. Clayton, 90–122, and *Reforming the Bad Quartos: Performance and Provenance of Six Shakespearean First Editions* (Newark: University of Delaware Press, 1994), confirms its plausibility by noting that despite the fact that Q1 *Hamlet* is just over half the length of F1, over 90% of the lines spoken and overheard by "Marcellus" in the First Quarto of *Hamlet* closely parallel those spoken and overheard by the same character in the Folio, while the average of highly correlated lines in Q1 and F1 is 33%. (Irace defines a high correlation as consisting of lines that share more than half of the same words.) Since "only the actor or actors playing Marcellus, Voltemand, the player Lucianus, and the player speaking the Prologue are likely reporters," based on a similar correlation, it is possible that "Marcellus" could "easily have doubled in all three smaller roles" (*Reforming the Bad Quartos* 118–19). What is more, the same phenomenon occurs in three other short quartos: the Host in *Merry Wives* and Exeter in *Henry V* have an 80%, and Clifford in *Richard Duke of York* a 90%, correlation with their folio lines.

Furthermore, Irace calls attention to the implications behind the gradual shortening of Q1 as it moves away from the first-act scenes involving Marcellus. "Remarkably, in these Marcellus scenes Q1 is only 9% shorter than the Folio—in contrast to omissions of 45% to 56% in the rest of the play, including non-Marcellus scenes in act 1" ("Origins" 98). This selective retention of material, Irace concludes, means that the scripts the reporter knew "had not been abridged prior to their reconstruction." The reporter, then, must have been acquainted with something close to the First Folio's dialogue, since if he or his accomplices "had known only an intermediate abridgment, we would expect their own roles should have been cut along with the rest of the play, making the correlation of their roles somewhat lower, closer to the average for each play as a whole" (*Reforming the Bad Quartos* 165). One of the consequences of this deduction is that it becomes ridiculous to assume that Q1 is an early version of Q2. It is impossible to believe that Shakespeare liked the lines he wrote for Marcellus and those around him so much that he kept both their quality and their length largely intact when revising and augmenting the play. It makes more sense to posit an actor selectively remembering the lines he spoke and overheard to a greater extent than the rest.

Stanley Wells and Gary Taylor, *William Shakespeare: A Textual Companion* (New York: Norton, 1987), 23–28, also emphasize how memorial reconstruction must be part of what Heminges and Condell in the First Folio call those "surreptitious copies, maimed, and deformed by the frauds and stealths of injurious impostors." A premium was placed on memory in Elizabethan culture, which is known for prodigious acts of recollection, such as Jonson's boast: "I can repeat whole books that I have read" (8:578). Thomas Heywood in *The Rape of Lucrece* (London, 1608) protests that "some of my plays have (unknown to me, and without any of my direction) accidentally come into the Printer's hands . . . so corrupt and mangled, (copied only by ear) that I have been as unable to know them, as ashamed to challenge them" (sig. A2ʳ). Shakespeare and the Chamberlain's Men had to have been so embarrassed by the "mangled" Q1 that they released Q2 *Hamlet* (1604/5) to supplant it—so that it would not undermine Shakespeare's reputation. Wells and Taylor consequently reject the authenticity of the first quartos of *The First Part of the Contention* (1594); *Richard Duke of York* (1595); *Romeo and Juliet* (1597); *Richard III* (1597); *Henry V* (1600); *Merry Wives* (1602); and *Hamlet* (1603). The theory that these texts are early Shakespeare works, they contend, is "fundamentally untenable," because: 1) it ignores evidence of "aural and memorial methods of transmission" in the period; 2) it stealthily isolates for discussion "individual passages in individual texts" without considering whole works or surveying similar texts; 3) the bad quartos differ substantially from genuine cases of authorial revision, where two legitimate versions exist; and 4) memorial reconstructions have a verbal texture that "soars and plummets," and thus cannot be assigned to any one period of Shakespeare's development. "The fluctuations in style and verbal confidence coincide," they conclude, "not with any discernible artistic motive, but with the presence or absence of certain characters played by certain actors" (27).

Laurie E. Maguire in *Shakespearean Suspect Texts: The "Bad Quartos" and Their Contexts* (Cambridge: Cambridge University Press, 1996), chastizes the New Bibliography for its rage for order, but she ends up agreeing with Greg and Gray that the first editions of *Merry Wives* (286) and *Hamlet* (256) were probably memorial reconstructions. Thus, despite taking a beating, Greg's indirect contribution to our understanding of the early texts of *Hamlet* remains profound. Reviewing only the linguistic features of Q1 *Hamlet* for clues to its provenance, Maguire questions the New Bibliography only to acknowledge its theoretical power. Claiming to be neither a New Bibliographer nor a Revisionist, she seeks to impugn as much of the evidence she can find for the memorial reconstruction theory of what she calls "suspect" texts. Nevertheless, she concludes that for texts such as Q1 *Hamlet* "memorial reconstruction" remains "an ingenious possibility and an attractive possibility," but not a "fact" (337–38). Greg—who modified, overdeveloped, and contradicted the theory himself—seems to have taken it that way all along. Of the forty-two "suspect" play texts that Maguire examines from Shakespeare's age, she feels that thirty-four are "not memorial" (334). But in accepting the premise that the best theoretical model for appraising the textual genesis of Q1 *Hamlet* is provided by the New Bibliography, she justifies Harold Jenkins's observation in his edition that the theory of memorial reconstruction remains "one of the achievements of twentieth-century textual scholarship" (19).

39. Scott McMillan, "Casting the *Hamlet* Quartos: The Limit of Eleven," in Clayton, ed., *The Hamlet First Published*, 179–94, argues that this version of the play was not reduced for travel, since it requires more, not fewer, actors to perform. Peter Blayney rehabilitates the reputations of the printers of the early quartos in "Shakespeare's Fight with What Pirates?" a paper presented at the Folger Shakespeare Library on 11 May 1987.

40. These issues, such as the different placement of the "To be or not to be" soliloquy and the changed characterization of Gertrude in her new scene with Horatio, are evident signs of adaptation.

41. In the longer note on 2.2.335–58 in his edition, Jenkins states that although "the Q2 text, comparing two changes in popular 'estimation,' may be read consecutively, . . . the omission leaves us to compare the players' loss with Claudius's gain. The real comparison between the two cases is in the fickleness of a public favour which readily transfers itself from the old established to the upstart; and the full text is required to bring this out" (472n).

42. This field of speculation is entertained by Jenkins in his introduction to *Hamlet*, 44–45, and longer note on 2.2.335–58. See James A. Kilby on "Marston's Drinking Danes" in *Notes and Queries* 10 (1963): 347. I disagree with Kathleen Irace ("Origins" 118–20) that "the War of the Theaters" passage, as she calls it, can be used as a satisfactory basis for distinguishing between Q2 as a manu-

script copy and F1 as a theatrical transcript, since the joke about those eager to possess Claudius's "Picture in little" in Q2 shows a trace in this phrase of the "little eyases" dialogue.

43. Smith, *Shakespeare's Blackfriars Playhouse*, 182.

44. See Wallace's chapter, "Star Chamber Proceedings against the Use of the Children of the Chapel as Actors," in *The Children of the Chapel*, 77–83.

45. See James P. Bednarz, "Marston's Subversion of Shakespeare and Jonson: *Histriomastix* and the War of the Theaters," in *Medieval and Renaissance Drama in England* 6 (1993): 103–28.

46. Among the many relevant treatments of this topic are: Maynard Mack, "The World of *Hamlet*," *The Yale Review* 41 (1952): 502–23; Anne Barton, *Shakespeare and the Idea of the Play* (London: Chatto & Windus, 1962); Charles R. Forker, "Shakespeare's Theatrical Symbolism and Its Function in *Hamlet*," *Shakespeare Quarterly* 14 (1963): 215–30; Harry Berger, "Theater, Drama, and the Second World: A Prologue to Shakespeare," *Comparative Drama* (1968): 3–20; Nigel Alexander, *Poison, Play, and Duel* (Lincoln: University of Nebraska Press, 1971); James Calderwood, *Shakespearean Metadrama* (Minneapolis: University of Minnesota Press, 1971) and *To Be and Not to Be: Negation and Metadrama in* Hamlet (New York: Columbia University Press, 1983); Robert Weimann, *Shakespeare and the Popular Tradition in the Theater* (Baltimore: Johns Hopkins University Press, 1978); Meredith Anne Skura, *Shakespeare the Actor and the Purposes of Playing* (Chicago: University of Chicago Press, 1993); and Louis Montrose, *The Purpose of Playing: Shakespeare and the Cultural Politics of the Elizabethan Theater* (Chicago: University of Chicago Press, 1996).

47. Mack, "The World of *Hamlet*," 502, notes that "the most pervasive of Shakespeare's image patterns in this play . . . is the pattern evolving around the three words, 'show,' 'act,' 'play.'" S. L. Bethell, *Shakespeare and the Popular Dramatic Tradition* (London: Staples Press, 1944), 30.

48. Rosalie L. Colie, *Shakespeare's Living Art* (Princeton: Princeton University Press, 1974), 219.

49. William Ringler, "Hamlet's Defense of the Players," in *Essays on Shakespeare and Elizabethan Drama in Honor of Hardin Craig*, ed. Richard Hosley (Columbia: University of Missouri Press, 1962), 201.

50. Alvin Kernan, *The Playwright as Magician: Shakespeare's Image of the Poet in the English Public Theater* (New Haven: Yale University Press, 1979), 106.

51. Gabriel Harvey's note is quoted from *The Riverside Shakespeare*, 1965.

An Armed Epilogue: *Troilus and Cressida* and the Impact of the Poets' War

1. For an analysis of the First Quarto's two states, see David Bevington's Arden Shakespeare edition of *Troilus and Cressida*, third series (Walton-on-Thames: Thomas Nelson, 1998), 1–4.

2. Quoted from *Shakespeare's Plays in Quarto*, eds. Michael J. B. Allen and Kenneth Muir (Berkeley: University of California, 1981), 705–6. Jarold W. Ramsey, "The Provenance of *Troilus and Cressida*," *Shakespeare Quarterly* 21 (1970): 223–39, makes a credible case for the play's creation as a regular part of the Globe's repertoire, instead of being commissioned for production at the Inns of Court.

3. Oscar James Campbell, *Comicall Satyre and Shakespeare's* Troilus and Cressida (San Marino: The Huntington Library, 1938), 185.

4. Graham Bradshaw, *Shakespeare's Scepticism* (Ithaca: Cornell University Press, 1987), 126.

5. For an overview of the range of Shakespeare's varied concerns in composing the play, see Bevington's introduction to *Troilus and Cressida*, 6–19.

Chronological Appendix

1. E. K. Chambers, *The Elizabethan Stage*, 4 vols. (Oxford: Clarendon, 1923), 2:415. Thomas Platter, quoted by Chambers, states that he saw *Julius Caesar* at the Globe on 21 September 1599.

2. Roscoe Addison Small, *The Stage-Quarrel Between Ben Jonson and the So-Called Poetasters* (1899; reprint, New York: AMS Press, 1966), 67–90; Herford and Simpson, eds., *Ben Jonson*, 11 vols. (Oxford: Clarendon, 1925–1952), 1:24–25; and Anthony Caputi, *John Marston, Satirist* (Ithaca: Cornell University Press, 1961), 251–59.

3. Philip Finkelpearl proposes this theory in "John Marston's *Histrio-Mastix* as an Inns of Court Play: A Hypothesis," *Huntington Library Quarterly* 29 (1966): 223–34, and repeats it, with an additional piece of evidence, in *John Marston of the Middle Temple* (Cambridge: Harvard University Press, 1969), 120n. It is accepted by W. Reavley Gair in his introduction to the Revels Plays edition of *Antonio's Revenge* (Baltimore: Johns Hopkins University Press, 1978), 7, and in *The Children of Paul's: The Story of a Theatre Company* (Cambridge: Cambridge University Press, 1982), 116–17.

4. Small, *The Stage-Quarrel*, 82–83.

5. Ibid., 82.

6. Frederick Fleay, *A Biographical Chronicle of the English Drama, 1599–1642*, 2 vols. (London: Reeves and Turner, 1891), 2:105–6.

7. Anonymous, *Tarlton's Jests* (London, 1613), sig. C2^r.

8. *As You Like It, A New Variorum Edition of Shakespeare*, ed. Richard Knowles with a survey of criticism by Evelyn Joseph Mattern (New York: Modern Language Association, 1977), 375.

9. Caputi, *John Marston, Satirist*, 259–60, and Small, *The Stage-Quarrel*, 93–95.

10. Caputi, *John Marston, Satirist*, 260.

11. Percy Simpson, "A Modern Fable of Aesop," *Modern Language Review* 43 (1948): 404. See Chambers, *The Elizabethan Stage*, 2:42 and 3:364.

12. Leslie Hotson, *The First Night of* Twelfth Night (New York: Macmillan,

1954), provides the fascinating array of primary documentation related to the festivities of 6 January 1601 at Whitehall. Chambers, *The Elizabethan Stage*, 4:166, lists the 22 February date on which the Children might have performed Jonson's play. In a clear reference to the earl's disgrace, Cupid tells Mercury that "The Huntress and Queen of these groves, DIANA," in order to quell "some black and envious slanders hourly breath'd against her, for her divine justice on Actaeon" (1.1.91–94), has decreed a revels. If this does not refer to the earl's secret return from Ireland in disgrace in June 1600, it might have been added to rebuke the disgruntled Essex faction shortly before his execution on 25 February.

13. See *Juvenal and Persius*, ed. G. G. Ramsay (Cambridge: Harvard University Press, 1979), Satire VII, lines 90 and 93.

14. E. K. Chambers, *William Shakespeare: A Study of Facts and Problems* (Oxford: Clarendon, 1930), 2:405.

15. Finkelpearl, *John Marston of the Middle Temple*, 176.

16. Quoted from Elizabeth Story Donno's introduction to *Twelfth Night*, rev. ed. (Cambridge: Cambridge University Press, 1998), 1–2.

17. Quoted from Hotson, *The First Night*, 299–300 and 15.

18. *Twelfth Night*, eds. J. W. Lothian and T. W. Craik (London: Methuen, 1975), xxxiv–xxxv.

19. Stanley Wells and Gary Taylor, *William Shakespeare: A Textual Companion* (New York: Norton, 1997), 123. Tom Cain in his edition of *Poetaster* (Manchester: Manchester University Press, 1995), 37, agrees that *Twelfth Night* satirized the Jonsonian word "element" before Dekker repeated the same joke in *Satiromastix*.

20. See the section on "*Twelfth Night* and *Poetaster*" in *Poetaster*, ed. Tom Cain, 36–38.

21. Ibid., 36.

22. Chambers, *The Elizabethan Stage*, 2:20, cites the ban. Small, *The Stage-Quarrel*, 107, uses Jacomo's statement, "The wanton spring lies dallying with the earth" (2:238), to suggest inconclusively that the play was acted at that time.

23. Chambers, *The Elizabethan Stage*, 3:366.

24. Ibid., 3:293.

25. Cyrus Hoy, *Introductions, Notes, and Commentaries to* The Dramatic Works of Thomas Dekker, 4 vols., (Cambridge: Cambridge University Press, 1980), 1:181.

26. Robert Kimbrough, Troilus and Cressida *and Its Setting* (Cambridge: Harvard University Press, 1964), 18–19, quotes R. H. Barker, *Thomas Middleton* (New York: Columbia University Press, 1958), 10. Barker's two slightly different estimations are found in *Thomas Middleton*, 10, 159.

27. Alfred Harbage, *Annals of English Drama*, revised by S. Schoenbaum (Philadelphia: University of Pennsylvania Press, 1964), 82.

28. Abbie Findlay Potts, "*Cynthia's Revels, Poetaster*, and *Troilus and Cressida*," *Shakespeare Quarterly* 5 (1954): 297.

29. See chapter 8, note 20, for specimens of *Antonio's Revenge* in Crispinus/Marston's vomit.

30. Jonson's addition to *The Spanish Tragedy* is quoted from *The Works of Thomas Kyd*, ed. Frederick Boas (Oxford: Clarendon, 1901).

31. I substantially agree with E. A. J. Honigmann's seminal essay "The Date of *Hamlet*," *Shakespeare Survey* 9 (1956): 24–34, that while the play could have been written in 1600, the "little eyases" passage could not have been composed before 1601.

32. K. Gustav Cross, "The Date of Marston's *Antonio and Mellida*," *Modern Language Notes* 72 (1957): 328–32, explains that when Marston has a painter enter with two pictures in act 5, scene 1, one inscribed "*Anno Domini* 1599" and the other "*Aetatis suae* 24" ("in his twenty-fourth year"), they indicate the year of the play's composition and its author's current age. This suggests that the comedy was first written between early October 1599 (since Marston was christened on the seventh of that month) and 25 March 1600 (marking the end of the Old Style year). A date toward the end of this range is warranted by the description of Marston as the *new* poet Mellidus in *Jack Drum*.

33. See the introduction to *Antonio's Revenge* in *The Selected Plays of John Marston*, eds. MacDonald P. Jackson and Michael Neill (Cambridge: Cambridge University Press, 1986), 96.

34. Introduction to W. Reavley Gair's edition of *Antonio's Revenge* (Manchester: Manchester University Press, 1978), 16.

35. See Donald McGinn, *Shakespeare's Influence on the Drama of His Age, Studied in* Hamlet (New Brunswick: Rutgers University Press, 1938); David L. Frost, *The School of Shakespeare: The Influence of Shakespeare on English Drama 1600–42* (Cambridge: Cambridge University Press, 1968); and *Hamlet*, ed. Harold Jenkins (London: Methuen, 1982), 7–13.

36. See Fredson Bowers, "The Pictures in *Hamlet* iii.iv: A Possible Contemporary Reference," *Shakespeare Quarterly* 3 (1952): 280–81.

37. *The Three Parnassus Plays (1598–1601)*, ed. J. B. Leishman (London: Ivor Nicholson & Watson, 1949), 24–26. *Poetaster*, ed. Tom Cain, *57n*, disregards Leishman's careful dating in suggesting that 2 *Return from Parnassus* might have premiered late in 1602.

INDEX

Malvolio, 175–77, 192–93; neo-classicism, 69–71; and pastoral, 160; with patrons, 87–89, 216; makes personal attacks, 111, 216, 249; plagiarist, 130, 163, 214, 219; advocates poetic authority, 51, 55, 62; purges festive comedy, 63, 76; as satirist, 217, 219; and self-love, 29, 183–85; self-presentation, 29, 34, 219; scholar and translator, 90–91, 214; attacks Shakespearean comedy, 57, 63–64, 66–68, 76–77; loves Shakespeare, 13; slights Shake-speare, 24–25, 26; called "slow," 41–45, 52; wit-combats with Shakespeare, 19–20

—works: *The Alchemist*, 63, 67, 129, 302n58; *Bartholomew Fair*, 67, 75, 129; *The Case Is Altered*, 57, 77; *Cynthia's Revels*, 35, 92, 141, 157–65, 168, 175, 180, 188–89, 193, 225, 232; and the court, 269; dating, 268–70; *The Devil is an Ass*, 291n29; epigrams on Marston, 49, 158; *Every Man In His Humour*, 56–60, 129, 147, Folio Prologue, 72–76; *Every Man Out of His Humour*, 55–71, 79–81, 105–107, 128, 289n13; dating, 265–66; "An Execration Upon Vulcan," 88; *The Isle of Dogs* (with Nashe), 7, 287n32; *The Magnetic Lady*, 72; "My Picture Left in Scotland," 85; "Ode to James, Earl of Desmond," 40, 286n23; *Page of Plymouth* (with Dekker), 213; *Poetaster*, 203–24, 225; Prologue, 45; "Apologetical Dialogue," 31; dating, 272, 274–75; parody of the Chamberlain's Men, 31; purge of Marston, 210–15; *Richard Crookback*, 76; *Robert II, or the Scot's Tragedy* (with Dekker and others), 213; *Sejanus*, 76; 221;

additions to *The Spanish Tragedy*, 76, 221; *The Staple of News*, 26; *A Tale of a Tub*, 303n6; "To the Memory of . . . Mr. William Shakespeare," 13; *Volpone*, 63

Kastan, David Scott, 65
Kay, W. David, 4, 56, 57, 311n11
Kemp, William, 21–22, 32, 35, 115–16, 121, 147, 267–68; leaves the Chamberlain's Men, 299n29
Kermode, Frank, 107
Kernan, Alvin, 84, 92, 253
Kilby, James A., 320n42
Kimbrough, Robert, 283n6
Kirkham, Edward, 156, 306n1
Knight of the Burning Pestle, The, 233
Knights. L. C., 66
Knutson, Roslyn L., 293n1, 313n2
Kyd, Thomas, *The Spanish Tragedy*, 15

Langland, William, 124
Language and identity, 28
Leech, Clifford, 33
Leinwand, Theodore B., 317n31
Leishman, J. B., 22, 31, 287n6
Leonard, Nancy, 181
Levin, Harry, 129–30
Levin, Richard, 145, 304n21
Lingua, 78
Lodge, Thomas, *Rosalind*, 107–108, 121, 124–28, 149, 297n6
Loewenstein, Joseph, 15, 313n9
Love's Martyr, 198–99
Lucian, *Lexiphanes*, 215, 312n19
Lucilius, 78
Lyly, John, 15, 232; *Endymion*, 123, 160

Machiavellian history, 18
Mack, Maynard, 252
Maecenas, 215
Maguire, Laurie E., 320n38
Maid's Metamorphosis, The, 303n2

Malcolmson, Cristina, 185

Manningham, John, 15, 68, 126, 181, 195, 197

Marcus, Leah, 14

Marlowe, Christopher, 15, 121, 230

Marston, John, 197; as Clove, 135–38; dancing, 197; and Dekker, 135–38; as Don Kinsayder, 166, 307*n*14; evicted from Middle Temple, 234; on fantasticness, 173–74; mixes genres, 134; as Hedon, 159–64, 172; beaten by Jonson, 100; caricatures Jonson, 21; writes love poetry, 158, 163–64, 211; as Mellidus, 138–39, 141; metaphysical style, 213; obscene, 157–58; parodic reading of, 144–46; and pastoral comedy, 146–50; at Paul's, 133–34; questions poetic authority, 103–104, 150; poetry and pleasure, 172; comments on "The Phoenix and Turtle," 199; romantic rhetoric, 146; as Rufus Laberius Crispinus, 28, 210–13, 246; sado-masochistic, 101; satires banned and burned, 99–100; satiric comedy, 178; self-contradictory, 92, 101–103, 211; and self-love, 160–61, 163; Shakespeare imitator, 156, 158, 177–78; varied styles, 161; as Theriomastix, 136; vomits odd vocabulary, 21, 28, 166, 203, 215, 312*n*20

—works: *Antonio and Mellida*, 140, 148, 150, 208, 211, 212; Epilogue, 261–62; dating, 324*n*32; *Antonio's Revenge*, 312*n*20; *Certain Satires*, 101, 137, 211; *Histriomastix*, 83–104, 239; dating, 266–67; *Jack Drum's Entertainment*, 134, 138–51, 178; dating, 268; poems in *Love's Martyr*, 199; *The Malcontent*, 51, 198, 288*n*34; *The Metamorphosis of Pygmalion's Image*, 158, 178, 211,

311*n*13; *Parasitaster, or The Fawn*, 306*n*1; *The Scourge of Villainy*, 91, 99, 101–103, 136, 165–66, 212; *What You Will*, 165–73, 198; dating, 271–72; and *Twelfth Night*, 171, 175–78, 181–82, 194–98

Martial, 75

Masten, Jeffrey, 14

Mattern, Evelyn Joseph, 116, 267

Mayne, Jasper, 287*n*29

McDonald, Russ, 67, 76, 108

McGinn, Donald, 276

McMillan, Scott, 320*n*39

Meres, Francis, *Palladis Tamia*, 15, 77, 99, 125

Mermaid Tavern, 19–20, 282*n*3

Meun, Jean de, 98

Middle Temple, 266, 271

Middleton, Thomas, 139, 303*n*11, 316*n*19; *Family of Love, The*, 273; *Father Hubbard's Tale*, 227

Milton, John, "On Shakespeare," 45

Minturno, Antonio Sebastiano, *De Poeta*, 68

Montaigne, Michel de, 263

Moretti, Franco, 17–18

Mucedorus, 166, 307*n*15

Mullaney, Steven, 16, 314*n*5

Munday, Anthony, 92, 117, 136; as Posthaste, 94–97

Muir, Kenneth, 38–39

Musgrove, Sydney, 283*n*6

Nashe, Thomas, 15, 44, 216, 230, 285*n*16

Neoclassicism, 69, 70–71

New Bibliography, the, 244, 320*n*38

New Comedy, 71, 78

Nietzsche, Friedrich, 102, 263

Oddi, Sforza, *I Morti Vivi*, 179, 182, 194–95

Old Comedy, 71, 78, 209, 291*n*29